EDUCATION AS CULTURAL IMPERIALISM

Martin Carnoy

*Stanford University and
Center for Economic Studies*

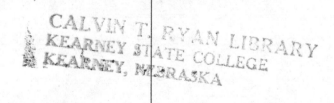
DAVID McKAY COMPANY, INC. | NEW YORK

To Judith

EDUCATION AS CULTURAL IMPERIALISM

Second Printing, October 1974

International Standard Book Number: 0-679-30251-4 (paper)
0-679-30246-8 (cloth)
Library of Congress Catalog Card Number: 73-93964
Manufactured in the United States of America
Designed by Angela Foote

*As Roman imperialism laid the foundation of
modern civilisation, and led the wild barbarians of
these islands {Britain} along the path of progress, so
in Africa today we are repaying the debt, and
bringing to the dark places of the earth—the abode of
barbarism and cruelty—the torch of culture and
progress, while ministering to the material needs of
our own civilisation . . . we hold these countries
because it is the genius of our race to colonise, to trade,
and to govern.*

—Lord Lugard

"The Dual Mandate in British Tropical Africa,"
1922

*. . . the public school system is a powerful
instrument for the perpetuation of the present social
order. . . . The child . . . is trained to submit to
authority, to do the will of others as a matter of
course, with the result that habits of mind are formed
which in adult life are all to the advantage of the
ruling class.*

—Harry Kelly

"The Modern School in Retrospect," 1925

ACKNOWLEDGMENTS

The ideas of many people caused me to write *Education as Cultural Imperialism*, but I owe a particular intellectual debt to Marcus Raskin, Ivan Illich, and Albert Memmi, all of whose writings provide the framework for my own analysis. A group of economists and educational historians in Cambridge, Massachusetts, including Sam Bowles, Herbert Gintis, Marvin Lazerson, and Michael Katz, also had a profound effect on my thinking, even though I may not agree with all their formulations.

At a different but as important level, I would like to thank my collaborators. They helped me wade through mountains of reading material and contributed on a day-to-day basis to the understanding of how education and society interacted in colonial India and in nineteenth-century Latin America. I have listed Marc Weiss and Isaura Belloni Schmidt as coauthors of the India and Latin America sections of the book, but this clearly understates their total contribution to the work. Yale Braunstein also provided valuable research assistance. I would also like to thank Jeannette Lynch for her skillful typing and retyping of the manuscript. Don Adams, Richard Sack, Roland Paulston, Philip Altbach, and Eqbal Ahmad read the draft manuscript and commented on it. I would like to thank them for taking the time to review a colleague's work and help him improve it.

The Spencer Foundation, through the Stanford School of Education innovative projects fund, provided support for research assistance. I appreciate it.

Finally, my greatest debt of gratitude is to my family—Judith, David, and Jonathan—who withstood my seemingly interminable writing and my overzealous commitment to the external gratification of publication.

CONTENTS

SCHOOLING AND SOCIETY

In most societies, formal schooling is an important institution for transmitting knowledge and culture from generation to generation, and for developing human traits that contribute to economic output, social stability, and the production of new knowledge. Part of the production of this knowledge is the view that the society has of the school system itself. For an institution to play an important role in society, it must be "legitimate": people who use it must believe that it serves their interests and needs.

Educators, school administrators, and teachers stress the enlightening function of the school; they claim that formal schooling is an important component of a lifelong process of education, teaching youth not only an understanding of important phenomena but also the process of learning itself. Employers see schooling as providing skills, preparing youth for economic functions in an increasingly complex

1

technological society, including socializing them to fit into new kinds of economic organizations. Parents and eventually pupils themselves regard schooling as a key to higher incomes and status, a step toward success in a competitive, success-oriented economy. For those who are poor, this last function is held to be particularly crucial, for social mobility may mean the difference between lifelong poverty and access to the consumption society.

At a national level, these perceived effects of schooling on the individual are extended to society as a whole. Because schooling is seen as an important component of lifelong education, many jump to the conclusion that the population of a nation is ignorant or uncivilized if it has undergone little schooling. Nations have come to believe that to be accepted as civilized, they must be educated; and to be educated, they must be schooled. The corollary of this proposition is that schooling is in itself a liberating (civilizing) force and that it is a necessary prerequisite for nations to participate with the developed countries in the world project of material advancement.

> Now the situation is different. Unlike the burden put on the developed countries when they were at similar stages of economic development, the present technology and available knowledge demand ever-increasing technical skills and education of the labor force. If a country is to advance economically and participate actively in international trade, it must educate its population.[1]

Thus, the concept of individual material and moral improvement combined with social mobility—all purportedly due to schooling—is generalized into *national* economic growth and improvement, into nations—through expenditures on schooling—increasing their income per capita, "civilizing" themselves, and raising their status among nations in a competitive, industrializing world.

The legitimization of schooling in this way is particularly important because it is a link between the economic and social structure and the minds of children—the future work force and political participants. We are currently presented with an explanation of schooling's function which implies that in unjust, inequitable, and economically stagnant societies, schooling has provided and continues to provide the means for individual and societal liberation.[2] The formal education system— according to this view—acts to offset social inequities and inefficiencies by being an objective selector of intelligent and rational individuals for the highest positions in the social, political, and economic hierarchy.

In this book, we argue that this explanation is misleading. Our thesis is that educators, social scientists, and historians have misinterpreted the role of Western schooling in the Third World and in industrialized countries themselves. We argue that far from acting as a liberator, Western formal education came to most countries as part of imperialist domination.[3] It was consistent with the goals of imperialism: the economic and political control of the people in one country by the dominant class in another. The imperial powers attempted, through schooling, to train the colonized for roles that suited the colonizer. Even within the dominant countries themselves, schooling did not offset social inequities. The educational system was no more just or equal than the economy and society itself—specifically, we argue, because schooling was organized to develop and maintain, in the imperial countries, an inherently inequitable and unjust organization of production and political power.

The support for these arguments is generally not derived from new data. It comes from the analysis and interpretation of readily available books and documents—sources certainly accessible to those who attempt to convince us that schooling has served the poor to succeed and the rich to become benevolent. Why were all these myths perpetuated? Why was this our knowledge of the schools? We believe that it is because knowledge itself is "colonized":[4] colonized knowledge perpetuates the hierarchical structure of society. As long as people thought that schooling did the things that the authorities claimed it did, it was hoped that they would not try to change the schools. Those who supported schooling as a means to mass mobility wanted either to perpetuate the myth to support the social structure unchanged in their own interest or, as "disinterested" academics, were themselves colonized sufficiently to accept the system's rules for limited self-criticism.

Toward a Theory of Schooling and Society

The "traditional" theory of schooling is based on the widely held view that Western education brings people out of their ignorance and underdevelopment into a condition of enlightenment and civilization. This idea probably had its origins among alchemists in the seventeenth century:

> The endeavor to put all men through successive stages of enlighten-ment is rooted deeply in alchemy, the Great Art of the waning Middle Ages. John Amos Comenius, a Moravian bishop, self-styled pansophist, and pedagogue, is rightly considered one of the founders of modern schools. He was among the first to propose seven or twelve grades of compulsory learning. In his *Magna Didactica*, he described schools as devices to "teach everybody everything" and outlined a blueprint for the assembly-line production of knowledge, which according to his method would make education cheaper and better and make growth into full humanity possible for all.[5]

Comenius also adopted the technical language of alchemy to describe the art of rearing children: base elements (unschooled children) were refined (schooled) into gold (schooled children) by leading distilled spirits through twelve stages of successive enlightenment. "Education became the search for an alchemic process that would bring forth a new type of man, who would fit into an environment created by scientific magic." [6]

With the advent of capitalist forms of production, this pedagogical concept of human transformation was gradually coopted into the theory of capital accumulation. Just as the human mind could be transformed from ignorance into intelligence, human labor could be transformed from unskilled to skilled, from having a feudal outlook to being rational and competitive, from being socially dangerous to being orderly.[7] By receiving schooling, people could improve their market "worth" from very little with no schooling to high earning capability with large amounts of schooling. Thus, the transformation of unskilled man into a valuable input for the capitalist production process became an important function of schooling in capitalist society.

Schools also functioned to transform societies from feudalism and traditionalism to capitalism. But once schooling had contributed to the demise of feudalism and other forms of social organization, it continued to reinforce capitalist forms. Like any social organization, capitalism produced institutions that supported capitalist structures. So schools functioned to control social change (to maintain order), to produce better labor inputs for more material output, and to transform individuals into competitive men and women who functioned well and believed in the capitalist system.

The rationale for doing this rather than meeting a broader purpose of schooling which would be "to create men who are capable of new things; not simply of repeating what others have done—men who are creative, inventive, and discoverers who have minds which can be critical, can verify, and not accept everything they are offered"[8] is that the proponents of capitalism as an end in itself believe that capitalist institutions already provide the most perfect form of individual and collective development. They believe that capitalism is a revolutionary and progressive force in world history. In this view, as we shall show in chapter 2, capitalism is antiimperalistic and liberates people from irrational and hostile human relations.[9] Schooling is therefore a liberating force by simply helping each generation to function in the established capitalist structures, and capitalist man is the ultimate form of the transformation process. The development of the individual is limited to a more perfect fit into capitalist values and norms. more rational, more competitive, more motivated by extrinsic rewards, more responsive to market forces and economic and social change within the capitalist framework.

If we believe that the primary function of society is to produce *more* material goods, capitalism may indeed be an efficient economic and social organization to achieve this objective, and schooling is a productive force for development as long as it produces more human capital to be used in the productive process. We can say that schooling contributes to individual and collective development when it contributes to individual and collective increases in material output. Yet even within such a narrow definition of development, capitalism may not be as efficient as other forms of economic and social organization. If productivity is higher when workers identify with the production process rather than feel alienated from it, capitalist hierarchies could have net lower *material* productivity than worker controlled production.

Also, capitalism defines a particular international relation *between* economies. While an international capitalist system may be efficient and profitable for the already industrialized capitalist countries (about 20 percent of the world's population), it has not been particularly efficient for the nonindustrialized economies.

Once we go beyond a concept of development that is limited to individual and aggregate increases in material output, the view that schooling contributes to development in capitalist societies becomes more difficult to defend.[10] The goals of development may also be to equalize the consumption and social status accruing to work, to provide a high degree of intergenerational mobility, both upward and downward, and to give people more control over the decision-making process. If formal schooling—the way it is structured in capitalist societies—does not contribute significantly to these goals, it is developmental only in the sense of contributing to increased aggregate production and consumption. When we consider that this increased production and consumption is concentrated in higher-income groups, the role of schooling in development becomes even more narrow.

What Does Schooling Do?

The empirical data which would allow us to assess schooling's contribution to "development" is only somewhat helpful. There is ample evidence that schooling increases the incomes of those who go to school,[11] and increases their ability to function in a "modern," complex society.[12] From the standpoint of material advancement, these are positive effects of schooling on *individual* material welfare. When the individual goes to school, he or she has access to a larger slice of the economic and social pie, *provided that everybody else has not gone to school along with him.* As one individual gets more schooling than another, he will have greater access to the physical resources of the economy, enabling him to raise individual income. Can this type of argument be extended to entire nations in a world economy? If everyone in a society gets more schooling, does that mean that everyone will produce and earn more? Some studies have shown that people in high-income countries have a higher observed average level of schooling.[13] From such data it is too easily concluded that increased schooling leads to increased per capita income.

Other studies purport to show that a more highly schooled society is likely to be a more politically democratic society.[14] Like the income-schooling studies, these analyses are based on international data. The analyses observe that countries with more schooling per capita are also more likely to have Western-style democracies, i.e., free elections and representative government. It is concluded that raising the average level of schooling in a society will create more democratic institutions. Such notions may be correct when more schooling per capita is accompanied by other, simultaneous occurrences, such as concurrent investment in physical capital and increasingly equitable distributions of wealth and income, but these factors do not follow from higher schooling expenditures. In recent years, the earlier rapid increases in schooling have not necessarily led to increased rates of growth, but rather to a replacement of less schooled labor by more highly schooled labor in the employed labor force and to an increase in average schooling among the *unemployed*. We observe that the number of jobs has not been growing as rapidly as the number of schooled people, so that the increase in the average level of schooling has not been fully utilized by the economy.

Let us ask the question a different way: does the economy really need massive investments in formal schooling to increase its national economic output per capita? Most work skills are probably not taught in school, but on the job. On-the-job training is considerably cheaper than schooling, and, in many kinds of skilled work, can be substituted for schooling. It was not long ago that U.S. business enterprises hired bright high school graduates or even dropouts to work them up from office boy to an executive position in the firm instead of bringing in college graduates who might be less willing to be trained in the specific ways of the firm.[15] Before World War II, engineers and lawyers in the United States were also often trained as apprentices.

However, as a high school education became more and more identified with lower levels of *social* competence—the lack of social attributes "required" for a business or professional career—businesses began to hire only college graduates and only college graduates could get access to the professions.

Zymelman argues that the relationship between formal education and productivity is not as important as between productivity and occupational structure; that is, an industry which has a higher percentage of skilled workers has a higher productivity even if its workers are not as highly schooled as in another industry.[16] Obviously, there is a trade-off between on-the-job training and schooling in the formation of certain *types* of skills, i.e., those that are directly applicable to production.[17] Therefore, on the basis of acquiring these skills alone, alternative forms of training may be much cheaper than formal schooling.

But it is naive to assume that schools are merely places to develop vocational skills. That is not the only, or even the primary, function of schools. Schools transfer culture and values and they channel children into various social roles. They help maintain social order. It is difficult to conceive of eliminating the school as an allocator of roles without drastic changes in the economic and social structure itself. The common school is the institution that developed within capitalist economic and social structures to prepare individuals for assuming various roles in those structures. Those who have the qualities most desirable by the economy and society—verbal ability, awareness of time, and the internalized responsiveness to extrinsic rather than intrinsic rewards—perform best in school. On the whole, schools reward those who are, in capitalist societies, most desirable from the standpoint of capitalistic economic, social, and political institutions. Those with qualities needed by capitalist economic structures are therefore in part identified by schools, while in the feudal system family origin was the sole source of future social position. When the economic structure changes to another relationship in production, such as in China and Cuba, schools serve a much more vocational function. The dichotomy between school and work is greatly reduced, and the *work place* rather than some institution *external* to the work place serves to select people for various roles. In capitalist societies, schooling is an important determinant of future social roles, even if schooling teaches little that is applicable to future work.

Yet, isn't mass education one way to equalize the distribution of income? Not necessarily. There is no evidence that mass education distributed largely on the basis of parents' education and income (the way it is now in most capitalist societies) equalizes the distribution of income and wealth. Increasing the average level of schooling in the population without altering the class distribution of schooling *maintains* the present income structure.[18] Because wealthy children get access to the higher levels of schooling while poor children get much less schooling, there is no reason to believe that giving everybody access to a school should make much difference in who gets what in the society. We find that in societies where per capita income is increasing rapidly, whether from the exploitation of natural resources, such as petroleum, or from the growth of manufacturing, there is a great deal of horizontal mobility (moving from rural to urban areas) and vertical mobility (father is a farmer, son is an urban unskilled worker), but the percentage of income captured by different income-class groups in the society remains about the same (or becomes more unequal) over time unless conscious efforts are made to redistribute wealth and income.[19]

If the society as a whole puts a high value on equalizing incomes, even an unchanged distribution would mean that the society could feel worse off. The United States is a case in point. The continued existence of poverty in the midst of plenty has had intangible as well as tangible costs for the population as a whole. Although income per capita and consumption per capita increased between 1960 and 1970, there is a distinct possibility that, on the average, Americans felt worse off in 1970 than in 1960. Expectations of distribution and the quality of life were not met.

Other psychological effects of schooling may also be important in determining the contribution of schooling to society: Individuals and society may feel better off as a result of having more schooling even if there is no increased income, nor increased ability to function in a more complex technological setting, nor increased political participation, nor improved income distribution. In a world where knowing how to read and write is a "good thing," a person's self-esteem may be higher simply from knowing these simple skills. Educators have stressed this aspect of schooling for many years. On the other hand, going to school can be painful—a direct negative effect of schooling on children which most educators seem to forget.

The pain of schooling can be a permanent effect that more than counteracts the increase in self-esteem from learning how to read and write, if, indeed, the child who spends time in school *does* learn to read or write. Many children in the world are brought into school only to fail. Does the negative impact of failure on the individual's self-esteem outweigh the positive effects of having attended school (literacy, higher income, etc.)? In the aggregate, is there a net negative effect of schooling associated with the "failures" that outweighs the positive effects associated with those who succeed? If, for example—as in Latin America—60 percent of those children who enter school do not finish the third grade, is their total welfare lowered by more than the increase in welfare of the 40 percent who go higher in school? What about those who are in the labor force who have no schooling and those who never enter school? Are they worse off because a relatively small percentage of the population attains secondary and university schooling? No studies exist which can answer these questions. We can only suppose that as a fraction of the society becomes educated, those who have little or no education find themselves farther and farther below the mean income and social status. They probably feel themselves progressively more marginal to the dynamic sectors of the society.

Besides its possible psychological benefits and costs, schooling (and all forms of education) involves "real" resource costs as well. Teachers are paid from public and private funds, and students above a certain age give up some economic opportunities by attending school. Families often must contribute for uniforms, books, transportation, and in many countries, fees. For schooling to be a worthwhile investment of time and funds for the student and family, the real and psychic (monetary and nonmonetary) benefits must be larger than the real and psychic costs they incur. For the society as a whole, the net benefits must be larger than aggregate cost, taking into account the effect of schooling on those who do not go or have not gone to school and those who have had very little schooling because they were confounded by the schooling process or because more schooling was not available to them. Studies of the relative benefits and costs of schooling have limited their measurements to the income gains achieved by those who get schooling and the monetary resource costs they and society incur in providing schooling. If, indeed, there is a large social psychic cost to those who do not get very far in school, the gains attributed to schooling have been greatly overestimated.

Illich argues that the net effect of schooling on society *is* negative. Children are demeaned by schooling, adults are cast into roles by the amount of schooling they have rather than their willingness or potential capability to perform tasks (since this capability is not allowed to develop), and the society becomes oriented toward formalized expertise: the more schooling one has, the more his or her opinion is worth, often regardless of the person's good sense, humaneness, or other factors which may be considerably more important than the skills learned in school. As a result, Illich claims, the technology of today's industrial societies has little to do with people's needs, but serves the needs of experts; technology and knowledge are mystified by experts through technical jargon. This keeps the mass of people from understanding relationships in the society and separates them from technology and its control.[20]

Illich's discussion is based on an important reality: schooling is distributed in significant measure on the basis of parents' and even grandparents' characteristics—wealth, income, schooling, and occupation. The myth of school objectivity in measuring school performance ignores a host of factors outside the school which, under present conditions, are instrumental in predicting school success: nutrition and health care in the home; parents' reinforcement in schoolwork, parents' expectations for the child, and the family's ability to afford to keep children in school rather than earning income. But even if children spent all their time away from their families and in school after the age of six, and there were no home influence after that age, we would find that schools in most countries and locales are geared to reinforce the cultural and verbal skills of those who have spent their first years with higher-income and higher-schooled parents.

Children who are verbal and acculturated to the authority structure of a classroom, especially the reward-punishment system, can immediately concentrate on learning the curriculum instead of trying to understand what is expected of them. Of course, on the average, such children come to school at age six better fed and find the curriculum easier than children from poorer families. In large part, the tests which screen the fast learners from the slow end up screening the children of the relatively well-off and educated from the children of the poor and unacculturated. Since poor children generally do badly in school, they are branded as "failures" early in life, destined for jobs which require little skill and originality, simply because they were unable to succeed at these school tests and exercises.[21] Worse, perhaps, is the self-concept of these dropouts. The society reinforces, through schooling and other institutions, the self-image of incompetence and ignorance for those who do not succeed in school. As a result, society invests more schooling (earning capability) and gives a higher self-image to those who already have high-status parents when they enter school, and invests little schooling and may reduce the self-image of those who have low-status and poor parents.

Large numbers of children, therefore, do not either get to lead or participate as adults in the growth of material consumption. In most countries, many children do not attend school at all, since the school selection process usually begins by not making school available to everyone. Others take a few years of schooling but this is not enough to bring them into the skilled labor force or even to get them unskilled jobs in the dynamic growth sectors of the economy. If schooling is very efficient in this model of development, it helps preserve stability in the system by indirectly acting to make this group believe that they have *no right* to the fruits of development because they are not sufficiently *prepared* to participate in the development process. This is Illich's point again: people without schooling in a society where schooling is revered come to believe that they are not *worthy* of participating as fully in the development process as those with schooling. Those who have attended school for a few years may have direct indicators that they deserve to be "failures." Not making it to higher grades is proof that they don't have what it takes to get a piece of the "good life."

The efficient schooling system in this type of growth-maximizing development model clearly does not concern itself operationally with equalizing economic opportunity, even though the rhetoric surrounding schooling may concentrate heavily on its equalization aspects. If schools are to help in maintaining this *concept* of development as well as increasing the efficiency of the economic system, they have to be good political role teachers. Schools must help convince or reinforce children in believing that the system is basically sound and the role they are allocated is the *proper* one for them to play. Through such "colonization," the society avoids having to redistribute the increases in national product and reduces the necessity for direct repression of the populace.

An Alternative Theory

Our analysis of present-day formal schooling may seem overcritical, particularly since most of us were brought up on the concept of schooling as an equalizer of opportunity and an agent of social mobility and change.[22] Actually, schooling in capitalist societies *does* serve as a means to higher status for a *small percentage* of the urban poor and an even smaller number of rural poor, and it also may contribute to dissent and original thinking, which may be important intellectual forces for societal change. Nevertheless, these are not the *primary purposes* or functional characteristics of school systems. They are by-products of schooling which occur as it attempts to achieve its main function of transmitting the social and economic structure from generation to generation through pupil selection, defining culture and rules, and teaching certain cognitive skills.

If we accept the empirical reality that increasing the average level of schooling in capitalist economies does not lead to a more equal distribution of wealth and income, and if we accept the view that present-day schooling does not lead to changes in the social structure, what theory of the relation of schooling to the economic and social structure helps us to understand the functions of formal education in capitalist societies? [23] In order to explain why increased schooling does not improve income distribution or why it has a relatively small effect on social mobility, we have to explain how schooling fits children into social and economic roles in the capitalist structure.

In this book, we argue that even though European or U.S. schooling brings people *out of* traditional hierarchy, it also brings them *into* a capitalist hierarchy. While this process has elements of *liberation,* it includes elements of *dependency* and *alienation.* More important, the school does not create the conditions in which the pupil can begin to liberate himself or herself. Rather, the degree of liberation allowed by the school is *controlled* by those who are the most influential in setting goals for the society. In most cases, the modern, capitalistic society was/is controlled by foreigners (different culture, history, social structure) either directly or indirectly, and/or by a class of people who represent very different interests, consumption patterns, and cultural identity, from the bulk of the population. So schooling brings people out of a hierarchy in which they may be servants rather than their own masters (slaves and serfs) but may also have an important degree of choice and control over day-to-day work activities (farmers and artisans) into a different hierarchy where their roles are determined on the bases of different criteria, but in which they are dependent on working and social conditions determined by others. Through that dependency, they lose personal choice and, therefore, a form of freedom.

The farmer's or artisan's son who gets some schooling and then goes to work in the factory has available to him goods that were not available on the farm or village: lots of people, movies, modern clothes, and the very small possibility of getting a high-paying job. But the son also gives up control over his own time and the social conditions that surround him. The farmer or artisan could choose whether he wanted to work or not on a certain day. Of course, if he did not work, he might not produce as much, but his job would still be waiting for him the next day. The factory worker must punch a clock. Unless organized with other workers into unions, if he does not want to work on a certain day, he may be fired and will not be able to eat. The son, thanks to his schooling and migration to the city, has increased his choice of some goods but has also become *dependent* on working and social conditions set by others and *out of his control*.[24]

Thus, we observe that schooling is an institution for change in non-Western, feudal societies, and from the standpoint of a Western observer or a non-Western native struggling to better his economic condition, change may be positive and may increase human welfare. But an important characteristic of this change is that schooling brings people from one hierarchy into another. Even those who do not go to school are affected by this transformation because they *lack* schooling. They fall into the category of those with no schooling, putting them near the bottom of the social structure.

The school system, because of the nature of the new hierarchy it represents, we argue, is not available to everyone in equal doses. This means that the quantity and the nature of the schooling process can be and is used to maintain the hierarchical roles of different groups in the society from one generation to the next. Once the transition from feudalism to capitalism is made, therefore, the school system becomes less an agent of change and more and more an agent of *maintaining* the social structure. In that structure, people may have even less to say about their lives and the amount of goods they receive than before, but even if they have more say, they are far from benefiting fully from the wealth of their society and are far from controlling its direction.

Schooling as Imperialism and Colonialism We hypothesize that the spread of schooling was carried out in the context of imperialism and colonialism—in the spread of mercantilism and capitalism—and it cannot in *its present form and purpose be separated from that context*. This is not to say that schooling was not affected by the cultures into which it was introduced; however, the effect was small relative to the principal relationships that schooling was designed to promote.

Thus, although schooling which originated in the metropole promoted change from one hierarchy to another—from the traditional hierarchy of the colonized culture to some form of the hierarchy of European mercantilism or capitalism—this change was carefully defined. The structure of schools, since it came from the metropole, was based in large part on the needs of metropole investors, traders, and culture. As we shall show in later chapters, Western schools were used to develop indigenous elites which served as intermediaries between metropole merchants and plantation labor; they were used to incorporate indigenous peoples into the production of goods necessary for metropole markets; they were used to help change social structures to fit in with European concepts of work and interpersonal relationships; and, within advanced capitalist economies such as the United States, schools were used to fit white workers and, later, disenfranchised minorities into economic and social roles defined by the dominant capitalist class.

Since schooling was brought to non-Europeans as part of empire, and to workers in the metropoles as a function of capitalists' needs, it was integrated into an effort to bring indigenous peoples into imperial/colonial structures. But was the spread of schooling harmful? After all, did not the European teacher and the school built on the European capitalist model transmit European values and norms and begin to transform traditional societies into "modern" ones, ready to industrialize and compete in world markets? In order to accept the interpretation of many Western writers that schooling in the colonial period—which in Asia and Africa lasted until after World War II—contributed to development, we have to accept that imperialism and colonialism were in the long run beneficial to colonized peoples. Even if we are not willing to go that far, we would have to believe that four centuries of colonizing and exploiting Africans, Asians, indigenous Latin Americans, and white European workers themselves was, if not justified, at least *attenuated* by bringing them Western schooling. We would have to be convinced that, despite the negative aspects of imperialism and colonialism, formal schooling enabled the blacks, yellows, browns, and poor whites of the world eventually to emerge from their backwardness and ignorance to join the modern world.

But it should be obvious that formal schooling serves some actual or desired economic and social structure. When Western writers ascribe to imperial school systems the seeds of revolution and independence "in spite" of colonial economic and political structures, they ignore this basic understanding of the school system. Although it is possible that people acquired revolutionary ideas in schools, this was far from the schools' purpose. It is much more convincing to argue that schools put some working class Europeans and some non-Westerners in positions of relative authority in the colonial structure.

A few of the Africans, Asians, and Latin Americans drew on deep-seated anti-European feelings in the *unschooled* population to lead procapitalist independence movements; an even smaller number, recognizing the intimate connection between capitalist economic institutions and the European domination of their culture, went further to lead anticapitalist independence movements. But the vast majority of the tiny proportion of highly educated non-Europeans in colonized countries chose to emulate Europeans and leave their own people behind. The success story of colonial schooling is the small number of Third World "independence" leaders who chose to break the economic and political ties by which industrial countries control them.

Therefore, old-style imperialism and colonialism have all but disappeared and the great empires of the last century are dismantled, but educational systems in the ex-colonies remain largely intact after independence. Curriculum, language, and, in some cases, even the nationality of the teachers themselves, are carried over from the colonial period. In many ways, the relationship between the ex-colony and the ex-colonizer is stronger economically and culturally than during the colonial administration. So the presence of metropole nationals is not even necessary to assure the imperialistic characteristic of the schools after the introductory period. All that *is* necessary is a dependency relation between the metropole and the region or country or class or group in question. Once that economic, political, and/or cultural dependency is established, the imperial nature of the schools is assured. Changes in the metropole economy and culture are transmitted to the dependent group through the schools and other institutions. In each situation, the nature of the transmission varies according to the strength and nature of the dependency relationship.

Analogously, white workers and people of color in the United States also acquired revolutionary ideas inside and especially outside schools. They organized anticapitalist movements such as labor brotherhoods and political parties, largely among the unschooled. Nevertheless, other leaders arose among the poor who cooperated with northern capitalists. As we shall show, schooling became one mechanism by which poor whites and blacks could be temporarily appeased through this group of coopted leaders while their position in the society remained essentially unchanged. Rather than building independence and self-reliance among the poor in America, schools are used to ensure, as much as possible and apparently with some success, that those in the worst economic positions do not rebel against the system which represses them and identifies with leaders who would work within the framework of action set by the dominant ruling class.

In this sense, the relationship between that ruling class, centered in northern U.S. capitalism, and the poor was part of the same imperialism which led to the westward expansion and the war against Spain, and was analogous to the colonial relations of Europe with Africa, Asia, and Latin America. The connection between black education in the South and British education of black Africans, for example, was so direct that after World War I an American educator was sent to Africa to report to the colonial office on the adoption of U.S. "colonial" education in the British colonies.

We argue, then, that the purpose of Western schooling as it was instituted around the world was to make people useful in the new hierarchy, not to help them develop societal relationships which carried them beyond that social structure to others. So schooling does not help people reach stages beyond this capitalist/foreign or other class-controlled hierarchy, but tries to fit people to the needs of that hierarchy whether it benefits them or not. We define this as the *colonizing* aspect of schooling. Transformation from traditional to capitalistic hierarchies occurs, at least in certain sectors,[25] but the *tools* of change are not taught in the schools. Schooling as a colonial institution attempts to make children fit certain molds, to shape them to perform predetermined roles and tasks based on their social class. Neither children nor adults are brought to understand their relationship to institutions and how they can change those institutions to suit their needs. The introduction of school itself constitutes a type of change, but once that introduction is carried out, people are brought to a certain level of social consciousness and no further.

In our theory, schools are *colonialistic* in that they attempt to impose economic and political relationships in the society *especially* on those children who gain least (or lose most) from those relationships. Schools demand the most passive response from those groups in society who are the most oppressed by the economic and political system, and allow the most active participation and learning from those who are least likely to want change. While this is logical in preserving the status quo, it is also a means of colonizing children to accept unsatisfactory roles. In its colonialistic characterization, schooling helps develop colonizer-colonized relationships between individuals and between groups in the society. It formalizes these relationships, giving them a logic that makes reasonable the unreasonable.

After emancipation in 1893, for example, the continued oppression of blacks in the United States could be rationalized by Booker T. Washington because blacks were not as educated as whites. He believed that blacks should not be regarded as equal by whites until they made themselves worthy of equality by becoming equally educated.

Paulo Freire regards the colonial situation as the culture of silence.[26] The colonial element in schooling is its attempt to silence, to rationalize the irrational, and to gain acceptance for structures which are oppressive. Such colonization does not require imperialism (the way we have defined it) since one class can colonize others, men can colonize women, whites can colonize blacks, and so forth, all *within* an imperial nation.[27] But imperialism requires colonization. A nation or a people will not *choose* to be economically exploited or culturally dominated. They must be colonized to accept that role. Once colonized, their identity rests with the metropole's institutions, but these institutions never accept them even as fully as the colonized of the metropole.[28]

Colonialism within nations can give rise to subnational movements that have nationalistic characteristics. Blacks, Mexican-Americans, Puerto Ricans, and native Americans are all involved in such

movements within the United States. They are obviously analogous to
national independence movements in their desire to overthrow colonial
subjugation. Women's liberation, in its pure form, stresses women's
nationalism: complete (including sexual) independence from men. The
liberation struggle is often as much psychological as political.
"Independence" from colonial rule, in the common definition, means
the right to elect or choose national leaders, or a reordering of political
control. In the more profound definition, such superficial political
choice represents the tip of the independence iceberg. Liberation from
colonial rule requires a redevelopment of humanness and self-esteem; a
redefinition of what it means to be independent. When people are
colonized, they are *dependent* and do not even know how to behave in a
liberated condition. Decolonization, or liberation, demands personal
and societal struggles which go far beyond lowering one flag and
raising another.

The Approach of the Study

It is impossible to *prove* that schooling contributes to individuals'
colonized condition or that schooling is part and parcel of European
imperialism. These propositions are based on an *interpretation* of
historical data. We present this interpretation in a series of case
studies, showing in each how the evidence favors our analysis rather
than others.

The case studies can be divided into three general categories. In the
first, we deal with schooling under direct colonization, British in India
and British and French in West Africa (chapter 3). Although the
African case cannot strictly be called direct colonialism until the 1870s
and '80s, we have grouped it together with the India case because
eventually West Africa was subject to the same type of European
(British) policies that were being used in India. In the second, we
present two examples of schooling's growth in European-settled Latin
American countries—economic dependencies of Spain and Portugal
until bourgeois revolutions tied them to England and the United
States. These are examples of politically independent countries whose
ruling class in the pre-1930 capitalist period chose to serve as

intermediaries between industrializing countries and raw material producing plantation worker-slaves. In the third, we treat internal colonialism in the United States and the new "development imperialism" which emerged from U.S. post-World War II hegemony. The section on the United States is divided into three parts: chapter 5 gives a short analysis of the major reforms in American education and its present-day problems; chapter 6 describes the history of education for blacks in the United States; and chapter 7 deals with the extension of U.S. internal colonization to the Third World, particularly after 1945.

The analyses of these various cases show a distinct and conclusive pattern: In the mercantile period of European imperialism (1500 to about 1780), formal schooling both at home and abroad was restricted almost entirely to children of the wealthy. It was consumed by an aristocracy whose children did not need it to maintain positions of power and wealth, and it was invested in by a merchant class to enable its children to become professionals and bureaucrats. Schooling for the poor—when it existed at all—was usually religious training for conversion or moral maintenance. But even in this period, formal schooling in some places helped the European to colonize the native. In Brazil, the Jesuits formed communities with schools to turn nomadic Indians into plantation labor; in Peru, another group of Jesuits helped Inca nobility become intermediaries between the Spanish Vice-royalty and the former Inca subjects: the schooled nobility were made responsible for assigning Indian labor to the Spanish mines and plantations and for collecting taxes. Similarly, in India, the British East India Company created Moslem colleges to elicit the cooperation of the Moslem elite. The colleges were then used to develop an elite loyal to European values and norms.

Aside from these important exceptions, however, formal schooling was not used to incorporate people into the economic structure until capitalism began to dominate the economy. As the capitalist organization of work created a need for a new kind of society in Europe (particularly England)—a society organized around factories, shifts, wage structures, and work organized by others—schooling served to preserve the moral fabric of this society and to socialize children into it. Thus, as feudal organization broke down in Europe and, later, Latin

America, an institution was needed to hold things together under new and disruptive conditions. Missionaries and the Catholic Church first provided schooling for the poor, and later were aided by the state.[29]

Both the United States and Latin America were settled by Europeans, and these Europeans formed a parallel and militarily dominant society alongside indigenous peoples. When political independence came, it was the European settlers who determined the new relationship to Europe. The pattern of school development paralleled that relationship. U.S. striving for autarchy rapidly created stresses in the traditional society which schooling helped solve (at least temporarily).

In Latin America, structural stresses came later because European settlers chose to continue dependency relations with Europe, especially a powerful Britain. India, of course, never had this choice, since its Europeans were agents of the Crown, and administered India for England. Schooling developed in line with British needs. In the capitalist period (after 1800), this meant schooling for Indians to fill British bureaucratic structures necessary to control Indian economy and trade and to promote British culture. In West Africa, after about fifty years of free-trade capitalist experimentation, direct occupation by Britain and France meant schooling for incorporation into African roles determined by economic relations with the two metropoli.[30]

Interestingly enough, formal schooling expanded in the colonies and in some Latin American countries *without* industrialization. But just as in industrializing societies, schooling served as a tool to *control societal change* in a time of stresses caused by important economic shifts. In the colonies, industrialization was prevented from occurring by metropole industrialists who kept manufacturing at home, yet schooling provided the moral and social guidelines for natives who tried to become Europeans (administrators were the main model).

In the United States and in those countries of Latin America where industrialization took place, schooling helped solve the institutional crisis caused by the development of the factory system.[31] Mass schooling as a socializer of the working class in response to the crisis generated by capitalism in the metropole and as a socializer of natives to bring them into social structures which had their origins in the metropole were one and the same solution to the problem of developing and maintaining class structures in the face of significant economic and social change. The solution occurred simultaneously because of the growth of schooling in the industrializing metropoli and the spread of metropole institutions throughout the Empire.

After World War II, when the United States gained hegemony in the capitalist world, the models used *within* the United States to control social change and to assign various groups their economic roles in a rapidly growing economy began to be spread to the Third World. Schooling played a key part in the postwar international system, just as it had been key to socializing immigrant workers in the Northeast, and to assigning blacks to agricultural labor and unskilled factory jobs in the South. The reforms pushed by U.S. assistance agencies to meet the threat of social upheaval in the Third World in the 1960s and '70s are the same reforms that were used to meet the threat of radical social change in the United States around the turn of the century. Both stress *individual* responsibility for success and failure, rather than the injustices of the organization of the economic system. Both blame inadequacies of schools on their inefficiencies with respect to managing students and to preparing students for the realities of the labor market. Such reforms direct themselves to the "ideology of efficiency" which has characterized U.S. capitalist development for the last hundred years.

Our historical analysis, therefore, not only stresses the past but also the present. It not only relates the role of schooling to fit Africans and Asians into European colonial structures, but also how schooling was called upon to colonize people in the United States, and how these methods and experiences were and are exported back to a now "independent" Third World. Schooling as an institution for colonization, social control, and hierarchical skill production was not in any sense limited to the formal empires of the nineteenth and early twentieth centuries. To the contrary, the more complex the division of labor in the United States and the Third World, the more sophisticated does internal and external colonization through schooling become.

An important purpose of the book is to show how schooling

changed to meet these changing needs of the dominant capitalist classes, and how such needs affected different groups in U.S. and Third World societies.

The use of schooling to promote and maintain class structures in capitalist development, whether in the colonies or in the metropole, was not the result of "conspiracy." We do not contend that certain men and women conspired to organize schools for colonizing little boys and girls. To the contrary, the theory spells out that powerful economic and social groups *acting in their common self-interest* succeeded through legislation and influence to use schooling to further their own ends. Important conflicts occurred in the power structure in times of economic and social change, and schooling often changed with the outcome of these conflicts to serve the needs of those who prevailed. But these conflicts were largely among powerful groups themselves, not between the mass of people and those who ruled. In imperial conditions, the struggles were centered on various colonial interests: for example, domestic manufacturers vs. merchants. Once colonies gained independence, conflicts emerged between metropole economic interests and the interests of at least part of the dependent country elite.

Within industrialized nations, struggles for political and economic power also shape the design and function of schooling. This is not a conspiracy of the powerful against the weak. It is the wealthy supporting institutions and ways of life which maintain their position of wealth and power in their own country and in the world. They are obviously not going to *help* the poor of the world take *control* of the world's resources for their own use, by schooling or by any other means. Schooling as a colonial and imperial institution is eminently reasonable once we understand who influences it and who controls the public funds which support it.

Is schooling inherently colonizing and imperialistic or can it serve to develop liberated, creative adults? The answer is not obvious and depends on the objectives of the society and its economic and social structure. We argue that, until now, formal schooling has helped a few to control more effectively the lives of many rather than the many to understand and control the nature of progress and changes in their own lives. In chapter 8 we review the evidence and discuss the implications of our analysis for action: Should we tear down the schools? Can school reform work? Can we get control of the schools? The historical analysis helps to resolve some of these questions.

Notes

1. M. Zymelman, "Labor, Education and Development," in *Education in National Development*, ed. Don Adams (New York: McKay, 1971), p. 99.

2. We define "liberation" as "freedom from bondage." Bondage here means that others control one's life economically, socially, and politically. Who one is and how much one gets of the things available in the society is a function of others' decisions. We stress the *relative* nature of the term liberation (and its antonym, bondage), and discuss whether education has significantly changed people's control over what they want, what they get and how they view themselves.

3. Like "development," "imperialism" and "colonialism" are charged terms, with different meanings for different people. Perhaps the most stereotyped is imperialism. It is clearly pejorative, full of political implications and ideological assumptions. So successful has the attack of the Left been on imperialism that admitting to being an imperialist falls in the same category as being a racist or a fascist. Does this make the term imperialism useless? As Tom Kemp points out, "The tendency to avoid a recognition or discussion of relatedness, and the suggestion that the term 'imperialism' is not a scientific concept but a radical slogan which stands in the way of objectivity, arises from a sensitivity to criticism of the phenomenon in question and a desire to evade discussion" (Tom Kemp, *Theories of Imperialism* [London: Dobson, 1967], p. 1). Surely the terms "racism" and "fascism" can be discussed and their causes analyzed if they are defined in some way that is understood and meaningful to both writer and reader. Similarly, we can deal with the concept of imperialism. In general, imperialism is connected with Empire, which is, in turn, thought of as the annexation or domination of territories and people both directly and not directly contiguous with the imperialist nation.

In the nineteenth century we run into a problem with the term imperialism. Until that time, the sense in which we used imperialism—the political domination of one state over another—became an inadequate explainer of what might be called "modern imperialism." Modern imperialism was "accompanied by so many new elements—particularly by an economic system so different from that of the past—that its explanation demanded either additions to the old ones, or entirely new theories. The Marxists accordingly developed and extended their own theory; non-Marxists also, to a very large extent, used the term and gave it an economic content which showed a similar recognition that there was something essentially new which had to be explained" (ibid., p. 2).

Whereas before the rise of capitalism, according to modern theories, imperialism could be largely explained by traditions of political power and the exercise of that power, after the industrial revolution saw an economic class imperative associated with the domination of other peoples and territories. Once the economic content of imperialism is recognized and accepted, we can identify the characteristics of the modern imperialist situation. While imperialism may follow old styles of political control and annexation (whether permanent or temporary) such as the U.S. invasion of the Dominican Republic in 1965 or the Soviet Union's occupation of Czechoslovakia in 1968, its form may also be more subtle: U.S. economic and cultural control of Cuba before 1959 was as complete as if Cuba had been a territory of the United States, although Cuba was politically defined as an independent nation. To a lesser extent, the same holds true today in countries like Venezuela, the Dominican Republic, and Micronesia in relation to the United States, and many of the former French and British colonies in relation to their former rulers. There continues to exist a conscious effort by the dominant class in many countries to influence and control other countries' economies for the economic and political gain of the dominating power.

4. As colonies sought their independence, the meaning of colonialism which emerged from the developing countries themselves was much broader than the occupation of territory and the abrogation of subjects' political rights. The colonialism of Fanon, Memmi, and Mannoni (see chapter 2) is the *psychological* relationship between human beings cast in various roles. The colonizer, as colonizer, regards the colonized as not only without political rights, but as a different *category* of being. All the terms used to describe the colonized—uncivilized, savage, primitive, traditional—convey the categorical separation of the colonizer and the colonized. The essence of colonialism in this literature is much more profound than military occupation. For true colonialism to take place—in contrast to old-style political imperialism—the colonized must be transformed from an individual with belief in himself or

herself as a capable human being to one who believes only in the capability of others. When the Europeans came to America, Africa, and Asia with superior military technology, they were able to degrade the local "savages" or "heathens" into believing that one must be European-like in order to be good, strong, able, and right. Naturally, once colonization is defined in this way, we move far from the definition of "a nation seeking to extend its authority over other peoples and territories" (*The American College Dictionary* [New York: Random House, 1958]). Colonialism becomes a description of relationships among people rather than nations. We therefore use the term to describe the way one individual behaves toward another (one individual's subjugation of another). Since human relations usually occur within the context of institutions (created and managed by people), these relations are shaped and mediated through institutional structures. "Colonial" institutions have clearly defined hierarchies: the institution defines each person's role in an authoritarian structure and there is great disparity between the control that various individuals have over its structure and operation. Such institutions are the family, the factory, the school, the hospital, etc. Colonial institutions can also be society-wide: a factory that is authoritarian and hierarchical has its counterpart in an economic system that tends toward centralization, concentration, and monopolization; a school that colonizes students and is rooted in inequality has its counterpart in a school *system* that provides one type of schooling for the wealthy and another for the poor.

5. Ivan Illich, "The Alternative to Schooling" (extended version), CIDOC document A/E 71/341, Cuernavaca, Mexico, October 1971, p. 6.

6. Ibid., p. 6.

7. Adam Smith did not see the necessity of public education for teaching people factory skills, which he considered so simple as not to warrant schooling. Nevertheless, he felt that "though the state was to derive no advantage from the instruction of the inferior ranks of people, it would still deserve its attention that they should not be altogether uninstructed. The state, however, derives no inconsiderable advantage from their instruction. The more they are instructed, the less liable they are to the delusions of enthusiasm and superstition, which among ignorant nations, frequently occasion the most dreadful disorders. An instructed and intelligent people besides, are always more decent and orderly than an ignorant and stupid one" (*Wealth of Nations* [New York: Modern Library, 1937], p. 740).

8. Jean Piaget, quoted in Charles Silberman, *Crisis in the Classroom* (New York: Vintage Books, 1970), p. 218.

9. Marx, who laid the foundations for later analyses of imperialism, was

himself a proponent of the necessity of capitalism as a stage in the development of non-European countries. He saw capitalism as a liberating force from feudalism. Capitalism would then, of course, generate conditions that would lead to socialism, but in the meantime, Marx considered that the role of imperialism was to spread capitalism and social change around the world. See Shlomo Avineri, *Karl Marx on Colonialism and Modernization* (New York: Doubleday Anchor Books, 1969).

10. To some extent, the same analysis can be applied to other economic and social organizations, particularly state bureaucracies. The primary difference between capitalist and state capitalist school systems is the focus of the former on individual mobility and achievement, and the focus of the latter on collective accomplishment. In practice, state capitalist schools do provide the means to individual status, but, until recent years, this status was not so clearly passed down from generation to generation through schooling.

11. T. W. Schultz, *The Economic Value of Education* (New York: Columbia University Press, 1964).

12. Alex Inkeles, *Becoming Modern* (Boston: Little Brown, 1974).

13. F. Harbison and C. Myers, *Education, Manpower, and Economic Growth* (New York: McGraw-Hill, 1964).

14. See James Coleman, *Education and Political Development* (Princeton, N.J.: Princeton University Press, 1965), pp. 19–20.

15. In 1940, the percent of the white male proprietors, managers, and officials with high school education or less was 70 percent in manufacturing industry; 76 percent in transportation, communication, and utilities; 56 percent in finance, insurance, and real estate; and 77 percent in wholesale trade. U.S. Dept. of Commerce, *U.S. Census, 1940, The Labor Force, Occupational Characteristics,* Table 3.

16. Zymelman, "Labor, Education, and Development," p. 110. This conclusion seems directly to contradict his earlier assertion that a country must educate its population in order to compete in international markets. However, he avoids this contradiction by settling on the compromise of vocational training and/or a marriage of the school and the work place. As we shall show, this marriage was impossible historically in societies which devoted a large part of their educational resources to training an academically oriented elite.

17. See Ivar Berg, *Education and Jobs: The Great Training Robbery* (New York: Praeger, 1970).

18. Average schooling increased rapidly in the United States between

1939 and 1969, but the increase did *not* contribute to equalizing incomes. See Barry Chiswick and Jacob Mincer, "Time Series Changes in Personal Income Inequality in the United States," *Journal of Political Economy* 80, no. 3, pt. 2 (May/June 1972): S34–66.

19. We can conclude one of two things from the apparent failure of increased schooling to lead to more equal distribution of income: (1) schooling is not a very powerful institution compared to family upbringing, access to physical wealth, and environment in changing the income structure; (2) the control of schooling is such that, while it may be a powerful institution, it is used to *maintain* the income structure rather than change it.

20. Ivan Illich, *Deschooling Society* (New York: Harper & Row, 1971).

21. See Jerome Kagan's recent work in Guatemala. Reported in *San Francisco Chronicle,* 27 December 1972, p. 4.

22. Considerable resistance to this interpretation of educational reality comes from those who grew up in low-income families and were able, through schooling, to achieve professional status. This is, unfortunately, evidence that the various institutions of our society which contribute to such mobility alienate the successful from the much larger percentage of unsuccessful members of the group that had low-income parents. Instead of trying to understand why so *few* of their income class moved up in relative social status, the successful congratulate the inequitable school system for allowing them to succeed (see the theory of colonialism in chapter 2). Nevertheless, it is important to view the resistance of this group in its proper perspective: as a group, successful low-social-class-background individuals generally have much less political power than the group who came from high-income families. It is this latter class that is responsible for perpetuating the inequities of capitalist development.

23. Again, the analysis can also be applied, with modification, to state capitalist bureaucracies.

24. This example is not an attempt to glorify the individually owned farm or shop, which is a difficult operation with obvious drawbacks. We use the example to show that the individual farmer, entrepreneur, or artisan has choices that the employee gives up, and that schooling in capitalist societies prepares children to be *employees,* dependent on others for work and livelihood. In that sense they give up important degrees of freedom of choice in their everyday lives.

25. Some would argue that the very existence of a capitalistic economic sector in a society transforms the entire society into a capitalistic-dominated

hierarchy. see Andre G. Frank, *Capitalism and Underdevelopment in Latin America* (New York: Monthly Review Press, 1969).

26. Paulo Freire, *Pedagogy of the Oppressed* (New York: Herder & Herder, 1970).

27. For an analysis of the similarities and differences between these various forms of colonization, see Albert Memmi, *Dominated Man* (New York: Orion Press, 1968). Memmi points out, for example, that the colonial relation between men and women differs from the white-black or European-African oppression because of the nature of the "couple" which binds men and women together. See Memmi's chapter 12.

28. There have always been groups in the colonies which were considered as "above" colonized citizens of the metropole. These are the professional elite and, more recently, the local managerial elite, especially those directly involved in the multinational corporations. However, those colonial elites aspire to equality with the metropole elite, not to be rated above the metropole working class. The theories of colonization are, therefore, just as applicable to these elites as to the people they, in turn, help colonize.

29. See the quote from Adam Smith in note 7 on why the state should support mass schooling.

30. For a good description of nineteenth-century African schools, see Desmond Bittinger, *Black and White in the Sudan* (Elgin, Ill.: Brethren Publishing House, 1941), pp. 185–90.

31. Michael Katz, *The Irony of Early School Reform* (Cambridge, Mass.: Harvard University Press, 1968).

EDUCATION FOR DEVELOPMENT OR DOMINATION?

2

A THEORETICAL FRAMEWORK

Interpreting the role of education in societal change requires a theory of development. Western social scientists and educators usually assume, for example, that the spread of capitalistic forms—the market economy and individual competition—increase everyone's well-being. They assume further that since capitalism is the most "efficient" organization for increasing the general welfare, capitalist expansion promotes development. Precapitalist, or "traditional," organization inhibits development and capitalist forms stimulate it.

This underlying philosophy also implies that the interchange of goods under free trade and the free movement of capital and labor contribute to the interchange of ideas and therefore to international peace. Obstacles to this interchange, such as tariffs, immigration laws, and controls on foreign investment, are defined as obstacles to international cooperation and understanding.

31

The capitalist view of development considers capitalism as the *antithesis* of imperialism: the likelihood that one people will dominate another is reduced by free trade and free capital and labor flows. To eliminate imperial and colonial relations, all obstacles to free movement must be removed. Where education contributes to the formation of a capitalist, "modern" society, it is contributing to the destruction of imperial relations and the elimination of future threats of imperial domination of one people by another. Those educated to be rational, competitive, market-oriented men and women are too committed to increasing their material well-being within the framework of market rules to resort to domination by physical conquest. Education is a force for rationalism and progress in this interpretation of societal change and international relations. Incorporating individuals and various groups into capitalist structures is in and of itself a *positive* function of the educational system.

But there are competing theories of capitalist growth which argue that capitalism *evolves* into monopoly and imperialism—that imperialism is an extention of capitalist forms—and that to discuss equal relations between large capitalist industrial powers and primary commodity producers is naive. If relations among nations engaged in trade tend to be imperialistic even in the capitalist framework, educational efforts that contribute to the growth of capitalistic forms must be analyzed within an imperialistic context. Incorporating groups into capitalist structures to exploit them is different from using education to train exploiters or revolutionaries. Obviously, education can be used to maintain imperial relations between nations or to break them. The theories which view capitalism as imperialistic deny that contributing to capitalist efficiency promotes peace and progress.

Thus, examination of relations between capitalist nations and the effects of such relations on the behavior of individuals and groups draws on a diverse and often conflicting literature. Before going on to analyze schooling in the context of these relations, it is crucial to understand the evolution of the intellectual discussion which deals with imperialism and colonialism. It is through that discussion that we are able to discover the sources of differences between our analysis and conceptions of schooling as "developmental." The major work in imperialism and colonialism therefore provides a necessary framework for the case studies that follow.

This chapter begins with a review of the two most important views of capitalism and imperialism—Schumpeter's and Lenin's—and their implications for the analysis of the function of schooling in a society. We argue that Lenin's theory and its recent modifications—with all their shortcomings—are much more useful for understanding international relations in the world capitalist system than is Schumpeter's nonexistent capitalist ideal. Analyzing the spread of Western schooling through imperialistic relations with an imperialistic theory of "development" therefore makes more sense than using a model derived from Western capitalist notions of improving social welfare.

Early theories of imperialism have given rise to their obverse: theories of dependency and colonialism. Lenin described the sources and effects of imperialism in the industrial countries. He was especially concerned in analyzing the roots of industrial-country domination of Asia and Africa and the causes of World War I. Writers from dominated countries are now writing on imperialism from *their* point of view. Schools (in the imperial context) are one of many institutions that produced the conditions of dependency and the psychological relations of colonialism. We review these writings to provide a framework for understanding the role of formal education in producing or maintaining "colonial" relationships both in the "underdeveloped" nations and in the industrial societies themselves.

These theories of dependency and colonialism complete the framework for our analysis. They carry Lenin's counter-view of capitalist development into the realm of relating institutions *within* countries to international relations and to the individual within the context of the international system. In later chapters, we apply these theories to education in different historical periods and different types of imperial conditions.

Theories of Imperialism

The domination of one people by another has taken place throughout history. This domination has been exercised for its own ends by a powerful group or class in a particular society. The goal of the class was usually to extend the numbers of "subjects" who would work for it. Thus, economic and political domination did not and does not take place in terms of one whole society dominating another, but of a *group* of people who are able to extend their power to other societies.

Before the industrial revolution, empires were based on slavery and/or extraction of tribute from peasants working land. The slave empires were designed to keep up the supply of slaves for a dominating, exploiting class. Peasant empires—such as China and India—lasted much longer than the slave empires and reached high levels of culture and innovation. All the major discoveries which, according to Francis Bacon, changed the face of the world—printing, gunpowder, and the magnet—were invented by the Chinese and brought to Europe by the Arabs.[1] The peasant empire extended the amount of land paying tribute to the ruling class of the dominant state. This tribute helped build and maintain a centralized bureaucracy which consumed on a lavish scale but also invested in public works. Although traders and artisans flourished in the peasant empires, manufacture and trade in scarce goods were state monopolies, so the surplus from these activities accrued to the centralized bureaucracy.[2]

These empires—slave and peasant—had a singular and simple rationale: the accumulation of wealth by the ruling class, either large landowners or the state bureaucracies. The larger the number of people under the domination of the ruling group (this included its own subjects), the greater the number of slaves available or the greater number of lands that could be taxed for tribute, or both (Rome and Greece, for example, were slave *and* peasant empires). Although there was a "culture" of war and conquest, in which warriors fought for "glory," an important element of glory also included tangible wealth. Indeed, the mercenary armies of many early empires lived off the booty of conquest. Throughout history, it is difficult to separate the "pure" drive for conquest from the booty which accompanied it.

However, Schumpeter stresses conquest for conquest's sake in his study of imperialism:

> It is evident that the king and his associates (Assyrians) regarded war and the chase from the same aspect of *sport*—if that expression is

permissible. In their lives, war occupied the same role as sports and games do in present-day life. It served to gratify activity urges springing from capacities and inclinations that had once been crucial to survival, though they had now outlived their usefulness. . . . War and conquest were not means but ends. They were brutal, stark naked imperialism, inscribing its character in the annals of history with the same fervor that made the Assyrians exaggerate the size of their muscles in their statuary.[3]

Schumpeter saw in many ancient societies the rise of a warrior class, whose very existence depended on continuous wars. He defined imperialism as the "objectless disposition on the part of the state to unlimited forcible expansion." [4] It was the ancient warrior states that most closely fit Schumpeter's imperialism. This was called "people's imperialism" because in a warrior nation the social community is a warrior community.[5]

Schumpeter's theory of imperialism, therefore, rests on the

unquestionable fact that "objectless" tendencies toward forcible expansion, without definite, utilitarian limits—that is, non-rational and irrational, purely instinctual inclinations toward war and conquest— play a very large role in the history of mankind.[6]

The explanation for this will to war lies

in the vital needs of situations that molded people and classes into warriors—if they wanted to avoid extinction—and in the fact that psychological dispositions and social structures acquired in the dim past in such situations, once firmly established, tend to maintain themselves and to continue in effect long after they have lost their meaning and their life-preserving functions. . . . The orientation toward war is mainly fostered by the domestic interests of ruling classes, but also by the influence of all those who stand to gain individually from a war policy, whether economically or socially. . . . Imperialism thus is atavistic in character. It falls into that large group of surviving features from earlier ages that plays such an important part in every concrete social situation. In other words, it is an element that stems from the living conditions, not of the present, but of the past—or put in terms of

the economic interpretation of history, from past rather than present
relations of production.[7]

Schumpeter finds the fundamental explanation of imperialism not in
the economic realm but in psychological forces that are left over from
past social and economic structures.[8] Imperialism is equated with war
and direct conquest. Based on this theory, Schumpeter tries to show
that capitalism is antiimperialist—that the relations of production
associated with capitalism are a force which counteracts the tendency
to dominate other people *by conquest* (this is his definition of
imperialism). He argues that capitalism generated antiwar and
antiimperialist sentiment on a large scale for the first time in history.
"As for a war to acquire territory, assuming free trade, forcible
expansion is pointless, because markets and raw materials are open to
all on equal terms." [9] Thus, Schumpeter explains away nineteenth-century British imperialism—which was undertaken largely under a policy
of free trade—as a holdover from past human behavior. Similarly,
World War I was, in the context of capitalist relations, an irrational
war, again the result of warrior tendencies left over from the dim past.

If the Schumpeter theory is correct, what does this imply for the
role of education in the colonies and at home from the eighteenth
century until now? Since the spread of schooling was certainly not part
of the psychological need for *physical* conquest (although it is unclear
whether Schumpeter would accept sublimated versions of conquest in
the same definition of imperialism—schooling, especially by the
missionaries, had and has many of the characteristics of man's need to
conquer), there was and is no relationship between schooling in the
colonies and imperialism. To the contrary, in Schumpeter's theory,
schooling is part of the antiimperialism of capitalist institutions. If
schooling indoctrinates young people in capitalist rationalism, to take
their aggressions out in healthy competition, schooling plays a central
role in *counteracting* the warrior tendencies of the past. This view
coincides with the Western, capitalist theory of development: that
capitalism has been and continues to be a force for rationalism and
antiimperialism. As people embrace the relations of production
associated with capitalism, they are less likely to try to dominate

others—less likely to make war—and will concentrate on making more personal and national income through interchange of goods and capital.

For Schumpeter, imperialism by trading and investment is an impossibility. So it is an impossibility that schooling of non-Europeans in schools that teach European capitalist norms and values could be part of an imperialist structure. Since "capitalism is by nature anti-imperialist," [10] all institutions associated with the spread of capitalism—European schools, for example—must be antiimperialist. We can begin to understand the essential elements of Western concepts of economic and social development: free trade and the spread of capitalist institutions are *antiimperialistic*. They combat the warrior elements in precapitalist man. The longer capitalism is around, the more antiimperialistic a nation will become. The more antiimperialistic a nation is, the less likely it is to attempt domination of others. Not only do free trade and capitalist relations in production lead to the highest possible rate of growth, but higher levels of ethical behavior are attained (antiimperialism). The logical extension of Schumpeter's theory is therefore that capitalism is a *civilizing* force coming from a civilization that rejects war and domination as a means of settling disputes and distributing economic and political power.

Schumpeter's concept of capitalism is a laissez faire, free-competition, free-trade capitalism. Although he described it as a beneficial mechanism which *could* act in textbook fashion, in the real world capitalism was

> a system of exploitation, based on disparities of wealth and power, which, although it made possible a great development of the productive forces, did not do so in direct response to social needs and inevitably was accompanied by socially disruptive aspects.[11]

Not only did the *reality* of capitalism differ from Schumpeter's rosy description, but his analysis does not provide an accurate picture of what occurred in the late nineteenth and early twentieth centuries: wars did not end, and imperialistic activity actually increased on Britain's part until 1914—in a free-trade context. While he ascribed this to the "irrational" need for conquest left over from the past, it is just as logical to argue that the world wars were the result of uneven capitalist development among the European powers. He considered, furthermore, that the growth of monopoly is the result of protection, and it is the intervention of the state in providing tariff protection that creates monopolies. If monopolies are allowed to develop, greater likelihood of conflict among nations exists, since monopolies identify with *national* protection and are identified with it. But even with protection, Schumpeter did not believe that monopolies will tend to expand into foreign countries. And he emphasized that protective tariffs

> do not automatically grow from the competitive system. They are the fruit of political action—*a type of action that by no means reflects the objective interest of those concerned* . . . the interests of the minority, quite appropriately expressed in support of a protective tariff, do not stem from capitalism as such. It follows that *it is a basic fallacy to describe imperialism as a necessary phase of capitalism, or even to speak of the development of capitalism into imperialism* (Italics in original).[12]

What all this boils down to is the view that whatever is wrong with capitalism is derived from noncapitalist elements in society. Of course, many traditional forces influence capitalism, but it is difficult to separate out these forces from capitalism itself. If aggressiveness and the need to do better than the next person make a successful entrepreneur, why should that entrepreneur not attempt to get the state to intervene in his favor? As long as Britain could produce more cheaply than anyone else and had a large colonial empire (in which Britain had enforceable preferences), she could indulge in free trade. Even with free trade, concentration in British industry increased markedly in the 1920s. Other capitalist countries' industry was well protected and concentration began earlier. Without protection, how-ever, industrialization outside Britain would have been much slower. How can we call Britain more capitalistic than France or Germany in the nineteenth century, just because the state erected tariff barriers in the latter to promote the development of their own capitalist institutions?

Perhaps the most important intervention of the state, aside from tariffs, was in education—in the preparation of a socialized labor force—an intervention, like tariffs, *supported* by the bourgeoisie.[13] It is difficult to argue that the striving for state subsidies, either direct or indirect, is not part of capitalism itself, but Schumpeter attempts to show that the state acts separately from the bourgeoisie, and that imperialism is a function of elements that are not only outside capitalism, but forced onto it against the interests of capitalists themselves. The crux of the difference between Schumpeter's and the Marxists' view of imperialism "lies in whether imperialism is an inevitable development of capitalism or something imposed on it, and running counter to its true nature, by political leaders and special interests able to evoke atavistic impulses found throughout society." [14]

Schumpeter's analysis was in large part a reaction to Lenin's work on imperialism which was written two years before.[15] Lenin argued that imperialism is a *necessary* phase of capitalism. He showed how, in the late nineteenth and early twentieth centuries, industry became increasingly concentrated into large oligopolies, controlling a high fraction of industrial production in the capitalist countries. In turn, industrial production came under the control of highly concentrated finance institutions, and this financial "oligarchy" determines which investments should be made or not, which firms will survive and which not, and so forth.

> Thus, the beginning of the twentieth century marks the turning point at which the old capitalism gave way to the new, at which the domination of capital in general made way for the domination of finance capital. . . . The concentration of production; the monopoly arising therefrom; the merging or coalescence of banking with industry: this is the history of finance capital and what gives the term "finance capital" its content.[16]

Lenin argued that uneven development of enterprises, branches of industry, and countries is inevitable under capitalism. He describes the development of Britain in the nineteenth century into the "workshop of the world," exporting manufactured goods to the world in return for raw materials. Other countries protecting their industry behind tariff walls developed into independent capitalist countries. Two levels of monopolies developed: at one level, monopolization of production within the capitalist countries; at the second level, a few rich countries occupy a monopolistic position in the production of manufactured goods.[17] In these advanced countries, an "enormous 'superfluity of capital' has accumulated." [18]

> It goes without saying that if capitalism could develop agriculture, which today lags far behind industry everywhere, if it could raise the standard of living of the masses, who are everywhere still poverty-stricken and underfed, in spite of the amazing advance of technical knowledge, there could be no talk of a superfluity of capital . . . if capitalism did these things it would not be capitalism; for uneven development and wretched conditions of the masses are the fundamental and inevitable conditions and premises of this mode of production. As long as capitalism remains what it is, surplus capital will never be utilized for the purpose of raising the standard of living of the masses in a given country, for this would mean a decline in profits for the capitalists; it will be used for the purpose of increasing those profits by exporting capital abroad to the backward countries. In these backward countries, profits usually are high, for capital is scarce, the price of land is relatively low, wages are low, raw materials are cheap.[19]

But Lenin does not limit his explanation of expansion of the capitalist countries into the "backward" countries to the declining rate of profit in the advanced countries. Imperialism strives to annex not only agrarian territories, but even industrialized regions. An essential feature of imperialism is the rivalry between the capitalist powers in the " 'striving for hegemony; i.e., for the conquest of territory, not so much directly for themselves as to weaken the adversary and to undermine *his* hegemony. . . .' In Lenin's argument these two factors combine, to produce a powerful force for overseas expansion." [20]

Following Hobson,[21] then, Lenin argued that imperialism has an economic base. In the competitive phase of capitalism, the advanced capitalist countries concentrated on the export of goods, but as concentration of production in monopolies, and particularly the control of decisions by financial interests became the main feature of capitalism in the advanced countries, "excess" accumulation of capital led to the export of *capital* to backward areas—the extension of the advanced country monopolies *directly* into the backward-country economies. This assured control over supplies of raw materials and their prices. There are a number of problems with the Hobson-Lenin thesis, especially in the way Lenin applies it to the British case. While concentration of production was certainly the characteristic feature of German, and to a lesser degree, U.S. production (which grew up behind tariff walls), monopoly concentration did not become important in Britain until after World War I. In other words, British imperialism made its greatest advances in a period of relatively competitive conditions.[22] Yet, there is little question that there was a shift in Britain, as well as in the other advanced capitalist countries, from trade in goods to capital investment, especially investment in those countries that were themselves industrializing, but also in the raw-material supplying colonies. Lenin's insights into the uneven development of capitalist societies, their striving for hegemony, and the conflicts this generates provide a much more reasonable explanation for the two world wars of the twentieth century than Schumpeter's "atavistic impulses." Furthermore, a great deal of evidence points to higher rates of return to advanced country investment in the Third World than in the advanced countries themselves.[23] Although the earnings from such investment may not be a large fraction of total income to capital in the advanced country, they may be a very large fraction of the earnings of a number of important domestic monopolies whose interests weigh heavily in the making of foreign policy.

More important for our purposes is the role that the spread of capitalism played in the "backward" countries. Schumpeter stressed the positive effects of capitalism. We inferred from his analysis that the extension of capitalism from the advanced to the backward countries of the world would increase economic output in both and would reduce the probability of peoples or nations dominating others by force. But the evidence shows that with free-trade relations, such as those between Britain and India since the middle of the nineteenth century,[24] only Britain gained. More and more of India was placed in jute and cotton plantations, reducing the amount of land available for domestically consumed foodstuffs. At the same time, there was not significant increase in agricultural production in the subsistence sector.[25] This same pattern was characteristic of the spread of capitalism under free trade within the British and French empires in Africa and Asia. On the other hand, in the lands of European settlement—North America, Australia, New Zealand, South Africa, Southern Brazil, and Argentina—capitalism did contribute to economic growth. In all these places, surpluses from agricultural production and mining were captured in part by the *local* population and invested in *local* industry. The United States and Canada raised tariffs early to protect their domestic industrialization and rapidly joined the ranks of the advanced capitalist countries. On a per capita income basis, Argentina was one of the richest countries in the world in 1910.[26] Japan remained outside the sphere of European trade, however, and also industrialized rapidly after the 1860s, based on production for military purposes, heavy taxation of the peasants, and protection against imports of manufactured goods.[27]

The spread of capitalism, therefore, benefited only certain countries, and these countries were either settled by Europeans, chose protection to achieve industrialization, or both. Except for Japan, industrialization before World War II was largely limited to European enclaves around the world. "Capitalism, which had grown from the tiny villages and valleys of England, had achieved world dominion and divided nations into rich and poor—advancing industrial manufacturers and declining primary producers." [28] It had created an international division of labor which benefited a small percentage of the world's population, and actually impoverished many of the world's peoples. As later studies of imperialism argue (see below), this unequal pattern of development reflected the nature of the "free trade" capitalism which both Lenin and Schumpeter describe.

Schooling as we know it today and as it was spread by the Europeans in the late nineteenth and early twentieth centuries was and continues to be part of the capitalist social and economic structure. Schumpeter's view proposes that schooling therefore contributes significantly to economic growth and world peace. Schooling brings people into the capitalist culture, makes them function more "rationally" and makes them more efficient producers than when they functioned and produced in traditional cultures. Lenin's theory argues that the spread of capitalism brought countries under the influence and sometimes absolute control of advanced-country monopolies. A primary purpose of schooling, as an extension of this theory, is to incorporate people outside the advanced countries into the sphere of influence and control of these countries and their monopolies. Going one step further, the role of schooling as introduced by the advanced countries is to bring people into a social and economic structure in which they can be more effectively exploited by the advanced-country monopolies. The degree to which this exploitation takes place depends on the degree to which the people or the nation have the ability to capture the fruits of capitalism for themselves. Although neither Hobson nor Lenin ever discusses the role of education in the imperial framework, the view of European education in the empire as channeling people into an exploitative hierarchy is consistent with Lenin's view of capitalism and the type of imperialism it generates. Likewise, Schumpeter never discussed education in his theory of imperialism, but European schooling as preparing people to participate in a hierarchy beneficial to them is consistent with his view of capitalism.

While this dichotomy may seem exaggerated, it represents the essence of the opposing views regarding capitalist development in the Third World. Although the assumptions have never been spelled out, the treatment of education and development has been limited to the Schumpeterian view of imperialism and its corollary development. No doubt, schooling helped some people in the colonies do better in the colonial situation, and, in that sense, the colonized reacted rationally in demanding more schooling which would help them succeed in the European hierarchy. This is not at issue here. The main question raised is whether people who were brought into the fold of empire (either the indirect free-trade empire of the British or the United States in Latin America, or the direct empire of the British, French, and other European powers in Africa and Asia) would have been better off under some alternative pattern of development. Obviously, the point is hypothetical. But its implications for the present are not, since much of the world is still part of capitalist commercial empires. The schooling that accompanied European influence and economic interests was and is part and parcel of empire. Would alternative systems of education serving alternative economic and political goals—independent of metropole norms and values—promote greater economic and moral growth? Again, a hypothetical question, but one with important implications for the present.

Some Recent Contributions

The Schumpeter and Lenin analyses still serve to define present work in the theory of imperialism. There is one school of thought today—primarily among U.S. social scientists—which looks to state bureaucratic behavior and political needs to explain imperialism. Those analysts assume that the State Department, military, and even the Congress choose war and imperialism independently of or against the economic self-interest of the United States or the self-interest of overseas investors, for example. The action of these agencies is based on the need to conquer—the "irrational" drive to war and domination or the cultural leftovers of the "frontier mentality." This is, of course, exactly Schumpeter's theory of imperialism. So we have a body of recent literature filled with statements like that of economic historian David S. Landes:

> It seems to me that one has to look at imperialism as a multifarious response to a common opportunity that consists simply in a disparity of power. Whenever and wherever such disparity has existed, people and groups have been ready to take advantage of it. It is, one notes with regret, in the nature of the human beast to push other people around—to save their souls or "civilize" them, as the case may be.[29]

At the same time, economists have attacked—with some success—the "pure" economic component of the Hobson-Lenin theory: the imperative for capitalist expansion caused by the declining rate of profit at home. Without going into all the data presented on both sides of the discussion,[30] enough doubt has been cast on this aspect of the theory that recent work which builds on Lenin regards profit differentials between the advanced and "backward" economies as a *contributing* rather than a key factor in understanding imperialism. The emphasis is shifted to Lenin's second point: "When the whole world had been shared out, there was inevitably ushered in a period of colonial monopoly and, consequently, a period of intense struggle for the partition and repartition of the world." [31] This is not a departure from the *economic* rationale for imperialism. It is rather a rejection of simplistic cause and effect explanations based on direct profit differentials. In addition, it is an adaptation of Lenin's work to changes in the nature of capitalism and to the political reality of an "independent" Asia and Africa, the Russian and Chinese Revolutions, World War II, the rise of the United States as the dominant capitalist power, and the cold war. Two examples of this shift are found in essays by Hamza Alevi and Harry Magdoff:

> What then becomes of the drive for imperialism expansion, if we now maintain that export of capital is not a necessary condition for sustaining the process of capitalist development and that its conditions for internal expansion are sufficient to provide an outlet for accumulating capital? The answer to this question must be sought in the drive of monopoly capitalism to expand and to extend its domination over the whole of the capitalist world and in the intensity of oligopolistic competition which demands such expansion for the survival of the giant oligopolies. . . . Furthermore, acquisition of overseas investments is by no means the only, or one may add even the main, form of penetration by monopoly capitalism based on the advanced capitalist countries into other market economies. It has developed a variety of instruments which it is able to bring into play, especially through the agency of the machinery of government which it controls.[32]

The structural difference that distinguishes the new imperialism from the old is the replacement of an economy in which many firms compete by one in which a handful of giant corporations in each industry compete. Further, during this period, the advance of transportation and communication technology and the challenge to England by the newer industrial nations brought two additional features to the imperialist stage: an intensification of competitive struggle in the world arena and the maturation of a truly international capitalist system. Under these circumstances, the competition among groups of giant corporations and their governments takes place over the entire globe: in the markets of the advanced nations as well as in those of the semi-industrialized and non-industrialized nations. The struggle for power by the industrialized nations for colonial and informal control over the economically backward regions is but one phase of this economic war and only one attribute of the new imperialism.[33]

The reaction to imperialism inherent in the Russian, Chinese, and other revolutionary movements plus the struggle for political independence by many other African and Asian nations introduce new variables into the relationship between the advanced and the less advanced countries. *Direct* control over another nation is no longer considered acceptable international behavior. Although military invasion and temporary takeover are still common methods of controlling a country which is in danger of being "lost" to the international capitalist economy (Dominican Republic, Greece, Guatemala, Vietnam), this is not the usual mode of keeping the less-developed members of the economy in the fold. Much more reliance is placed on working with groups within the less-developed countries who are willing to cooperate with the advanced economy and contain any movement away from the established dependent relation. This is the model developed in Latin America by both the British and the United States in the nineteenth century. Ironically, it was used by the United States after World War II to extend economic influence to Europe itself.

Galtung, building on Lenin and Andre Frank, defines imperialism as a

relation between a Center and a Periphery nation so that (1) there is *harmony of interest* between the *center in the Center* nation and the *center in the Periphery nation,*

(2) there is more *disharmony of interest* within the Periphery nation than within the Center nations,

(3) there is *disharmony of interest* between the *periphery in the Center* nation and the *periphery in the Periphery* nation.[34]

Galtung goes on to describe how the entire process benefits primarily the center in the Center nation, with the periphery in the Center nation and the center in the Periphery nation bought off by the center in the Center nation. Thus, there is disharmony of interest between the Center nation as a whole and the Periphery nation, but there is harmony of interest between the two centers. Galtung points out that imperialism is not merely an international relationship but a combination of intra- and international relations.[35]

This is not a new model, but it is now the prevalent model in imperial relations. The center of the advanced capitalist nation maintains the position of the center in the Periphery nation with military aid, technical assistance, and government to government "development" loans and grants. The center in the Periphery nation benefits from this relation: their disproportionate share of political power and national product is maintained by it. The center and, to some extent, the periphery in the Center nation profit from the relation because they maintain access to raw materials and markets in the periphery. By extending these kinds of relations to the world as a whole, one nation can in fact control the resources of the world through cooperating nationals in the countries themselves. The only threat to this control comes from other advanced countries attempting to woo the allegiance of centers in the Periphery to them and from the periphery in the Periphery nation, which finds itself in a relatively worse and worse position because of the arrangement.

The destruction of Europe during World War II enabled the United States to become the uncontested leader of the capitalist world. During the reconstruction of Europe, in which the United States played a major role, U.S. companies invested heavily and captured access not only to a significant portion of certain sectors in the recovering European market, but to the ex-colonial European markets in Asia and Africa. The United States moved quickly into the Middle East, previously a stronghold of British capital, sending troops into Greece and Turkey, and taking over as the single largest investor in petroleum.[36] In addition, during the 1940s and '50s, the United States obtained almost a monopoly on Latin American trade and foreign investment and replaced the Japanese, British, French, and Dutch as the dominant foreign power in Asia. When John F. Kennedy became President in 1961, the United States dominated a large fraction of the world.

In the period of U.S. hegemony, a number of Latin American countries and India continued attempts to industrialize through tariff protection and import quotas. Again, this was not a new feature of imperial relations, since the United States, Canada, and others had developed in this same way during the apex of the British Empire. But post-World War II protection accelerated direct foreign investment in manufacturing by the advanced countries. By the late 1950s, U.S. foreign investment in manufacturing was greater than in petroleum, and by the middle 1960s was almost as large as investment in total raw-material extraction. Much of this investment in manufacturing was in Europe and Canada, but even in Latin America, 1968 U.S. foreign investment was 33 percent in manufacturing.[37] While only a small percentage of total capital in most countries is held by foreigners, certain sectors are completely dominated by foreign investment and technology.

The attempt to industrialize in the Third World, then, has the effect of shifting new foreign investment from exploitation of minerals and plantation agriculture into manufacturing. At the same time, both to strengthen the relationship of the Periphery-Center country centers and to organize worldwide companies, *multinational* firms have become a dominant organization form of the advanced-country monopolies.

> The enormous investment in research and development required for these industries gives a special edge to the corporations which are large enough to be multinational in scale. Without trying to trace the causal interconnections, we should be aware of the happy blending of the new technology and the international corporations: (a) The United States has firms which are large enough to have, or be able to obtain, sufficient capital to develop the necessary technology and take advantage of pre-empting the field in other countries. (b) United States

firms are supported in this technical lead by huge government grants of research and development. (c) These same firms have had experience in international operations, either on their own or in cooperation with the United States government in the process of the latter's stretching its various military and foreign aid activities around the globe. (d) Along with generous government assistance has come an integrated apparatus of scientific research and technical development in the large corporation, one result of which is the considerable reduction of the lead time between scientific advances and the introduction of new products, thus giving the international corporation a global edge over smaller and less powerful rivals. Finally, (e) the technological advances embodied in the jet plane have made more feasible the coordinated management of the multinational corporation.[38]

In the last ten years, U.S. foreign policy has concentrated on building a flexible military force which could contain the Soviet Union, enforce hegemony over European rivals in the Middle East, and fight "brush-fire" counterinsurgency operations anywhere in the world. The Vietnam War—both as a result of domestic economic difficulties caused by the war and of domestic political reaction to sending American troops overseas in the future—has had a profound effect on U.S. capability to do any of these, and therefore on its capability to maintain its empire. Both Europe and Japan have made serious inroads into U.S. economic dominance in the capitalist world. Nevertheless, the technological and cultural effects of a generation of hegemony are only now beginning to be felt fully. It is this aspect of U.S. postwar imperialism which is of particular interest to us.

The role of formal schooling as an allocator of social roles had already become well established in much of the world by 1945. Even if there were few highly schooled people in the colonies, the concept of success through schooling was part of local culture wherever Europeans dominated the local population. As countries became "independent" of the European colonial powers, schooling was expanded rapidly. In an effort to "catch up" with European levels of development, Third World countries attempted to produce a literate, highly skilled population. They were aided in this effort by the United States and the former colonial powers, for both saw in schooling an important way to help the Periphery centers overcome political difficulties and at the same time to produce a skilled labor force which would serve the industrialization process. The United States' primary influence was and continues to be the stress on scientific and technical training, and the development of technical skills in the social sciences and business administration. The Third World has developed local markets and has chosen to protect local production. The response of the advanced countries has been to invest not only in the production of consumer durables in the Periphery (auto assembly, refrigerators, and so forth) but also in the processing of raw materials which formerly took place in the advanced countries themselves. All these investments tie into a world capitalist system, so their distribution and the kinds of goods produced are still a function of Center-center and Periphery-center needs. The schooling that accompanies this industrialization is therefore also a function of these needs. The best-paid professionals work for foreign, especially U.S., companies—the multinationals. The kinds of people needed by these firms are engineers, technicians, managers, and accountants. U.S. experts have stressed the need to fill these positions through university and secondary school reform. The United States has also stressed the need for education as a whole to be more "relevant" to the development process, which means that it should be less oriented toward traditional disciplines such as law and the humanities, and have a more science-oriented curriculum.

The changes in the nature of imperialism, then, had important effects on the expansion of formal schooling in the Third World. Yet, little or no change in the social structure accompanied this expansion. In Latin America, where economic growth had been taking place since the nineteenth century, the expansion of formal schooling accompanied increasing industrialization and the need for a socialized labor force. In some places—Argentina, Brazil, and Chile—this expansion occurred earlier, before World War I. In Africa and Asia, however, and especially in the former, school expansion is occurring independently of industrialization. Africa and parts of Asia seem bent on becoming European through formal schooling without being able or allowed to carry out a transformation to industrial capitalism. The resultant unemployment of even secondary and university graduates is the logical outcome of such colonial distortions.

The latest attempt by the advanced countries, particularly the United States again, to solve the "educational crisis" [39] is the introduction of educational technology. The stated purpose of educational television, radio, and computerized instruction is to substitute relatively "cheap" forms of instruction (TV, radio, computers) for "expensive" ones like skilled teachers (limited in supply) so that the world's children can all get formal schooling without loss of, and even increases in, quality.[40]

Implicit in this spread of formal schooling is a fundamental belief in the ability of capitalism to provide everyone with work through the market, and in the ability of schooling to turn traditional, unproductive human beings into productive elements in capitalist development. Neither of these premises seems to hold up empirically. The failure of capitalist development, particularly in the Periphery countries, to enable everyone to participate in economic growth, especially in the face of increasing average schooling and resultant expectations, creates important contradictions in these countries.

Imperialism and Dependency

The post-1929 Latin American attempt to industrialize gave rise to the theory of "dependency." Dependency is the obverse of imperialism: imperialist nations—the "metropole" or "center" nations in Frank's and Galtung's terminology [41]—dominate and exploit the periphery areas of the world, but the Periphery nations are exploited and *dependent*. Dependency theory creates a framework in which to analyze economic, political and social change in the *dependent* countries. Although this theory is derived from Lenin's theory of imperialism, it is not concerned with describing and predicting the effects of imperialism on the metropole countries—as Lenin was—but rather on the Periphery countries.

> Dependency is a situation in which a certain group of countries has its economy conditioned by the development and expansion of another

economy. . . . The relation of interdependence between two or more
economies, and between these and world commerce, assumes the form
of dependency when some countries (the dominant ones) can
themselves generate their economic expansion, while other countries
(the dependent ones) can only expand as a reflection of dominant
country expansion, which can, in turn, be a positive and/or negative
effect on their immediate development. In any case, the basic situation
of dependency leads to an overall situation for the dependent countries
which places them behind and under the exploitation of the dominant
countries.[42]

Dependency theory also provides an alternative to the theory of
capitalist development and change which emerged in both the United
States and Latin America in the 1950s. Neoclassical development
theory regards changes in the Periphery countries as connected to but
independent of changes in the metropole. In effect, the capitalistic
structures of Latin American countries are subject to the same
possibilities of expansion and change as the capitalistic structures of
the metropoles. The primary difference between the developed and
underdeveloped countries is their stage of development. If the
underdeveloped countries pursue "rational" economic policies, they can
develop to the same levels of consumption per capita, equality of
income distribution, and political democracy as the developed
countries. It is only a question of achieving a certain growth rate and
of copying the institutions of the developed countries.[43] Thus, social
scientists working with this theory concentrate on measuring the rate
of change of institutions, political characteristics, and social structures
from a "traditional" mode to a "modern" one. The change of the
economy is measured in terms of the national product per capita.
Development is defined in terms of these measures.

We can summarize these assumptions as follows:

1. It is assumed that development means moving toward a set of
predetermined general goals which correspond to a certain level of
man's and society's progress whose model is drawn from more
developed societies in the present world. This model is called by such
names as modern society, industrial society, mass society.

2. It is assumed that underdeveloped countries will move toward these (developed) societies once the former eliminate certain social, political, cultural and institutional obstacles. These obstacles are represented by "traditional societies," or "feudal vestiges," depending on the different schools of thought.

3. It is assumed that it is possible to distinguish certain economic, political, and psychological processes that permit mobilization of national resources in a more rational form, and that these means can be catalogued and used by planners.

4. To this is added the necessity of coordinating certain social and political forces that would sustain a development policy. Thus, it is necessary to have an ideological base that organizes the national will of the various countries to undertake the "work of development." [44]

Dependency theory rejects this view of development. It argues that historical time is not linear, that it is impossible for societies today to duplicate the process of change which took place in the developed countries in another historical period. The developed capitalist societies grew as a result of exploiting world trade through their technological advancement and military power, in addition to their well-developed internal markets and relatively highly skilled labor. The combination of these conditions is not possible to duplicate for the underdeveloped countries of the world. Neither is the Soviet experience relevant for these economies. Dependency theory also points out that many of the obstacles which impede development in the underdeveloped countries are not the result of a lack and a lag of development-oriented institutions of a "traditional society"—but rather of the *relationship* which these societies have with the metropolitan powers:

. . . between the developed and underdeveloped economies there not only exists a simple difference of stage or state of the productive system but also of function or position inside the same international economic structure of production and distribution. . . . [This is] a structure defined by relations of domination.[45]

It is this relationship which determines to a large extent the development process and the capability to develop in the Periphery country. In the historic situation in which dependency takes place, the structure of the world economy, to which the dependent countries belong, is favorable to the developed countries and unfavorable to the dependent countries. The social and economic structure of the dependent countries is geared up to fitting into this unfavorable world economy, and this in and of itself contributes to slowing development. In addition, attempting to develop within the constraints of an unfavorable world economic system creates distortions in the dependent societies, such as burgeoning urban centers accompanied by the marginalization of large parts of the labor force, highly unequal income distribution, control of dynamic sectors of the economy by foreign capital, and so forth. These are not the result of traditional elements in the society, but of the manner in which the society modernizes.

The dependent relation between the periphery and the center is transmitted through the dominant group in the periphery (which, in turn, is dominated by the center group in the metropole). The imperialist relationship that Europe and the United States have had with Latin America was based on this model since Latin America got independence from Spain and Portugal in the 1820s. Unlike the direct colonization of Asia and Africa, Latin American dependence on Europe and the United States was and is "voluntary," that is, a powerful group within each Latin American country maintains a close commercial and cultural relationship with the metropole, structuring the periphery economy to suit the needs of the international capitalist system. The dominant group in the periphery profits from this relationship much more than the average member of the periphery society. When there were wars among industrial countries and when the world economy temporarily collapsed in the 1930s, Latin American dominant groups turned inward to develop local industries and autarkic economies. Nevertheless, as dependency theory shows, they did so in a way that preserved their own position in the economic structure, and, in fact, left the Latin American economies just as tied into the international capitalist system. The type of goods traded changed as a result of local industrialization, but the type of goods *consumed,* the way the goods were produced, the social structure, and the distribution of income and consumption did not change. For the most part, these economies depend on a few raw-material exports for the bulk of the foreign exchange which finances their industrialization. Changes in the prices of these exports are responsible for important economic fluctuations in the periphery, even economic crisis.

Consequently, dependency theory argues that long-run and permanent improvement of the human condition in the dependent countries must—by the nature of the dependent situation—be largely limited to the dominant group in the Periphery country. This is not the result of obstacles left over from a feudal or traditional society, but the result of social, political and economic relationships prevalent in the international capitalist system: a stratified social structure, the political institutions necessary to maintain that social structure, and an economic system which produces goods to satisfy a small high- and middle-income group and is able to employ only a small fraction of the labor force in its dynamic sectors.

The theory tells that this structure creates a "cultural alienation" in Latin America which is manifested in the need to copy everything in the developed metropoles. Desired values and norms are taken from the metropole, not from the local experience. "This alienation was the key to the continued existence of the underdeveloped situation." [46] Cultural dependency, which includes dependence on technology, concepts, and art forms, severely limits the possibility of new forms of institutional development emerging. This is what Dos Santos calls the "conditional situation": "A conditional situation determines the limits and possibilities for human action and behavior. Faced by it, there exist only two possibilities: (a) to choose between the distinct alternatives within the situation . . . ; (b) . . . to change this conditional situation in order to permit other possibilities of action." [47]

In the dependent society, all these characteristics result in disharmony between the interests of the dominant group (voluntarily tied to the interests of the metropole) and the peasants, the marginal urban population, and even the employed urban workers. If democratization of political institutions occurs or is maintained, the dissatisfied majority could become increasingly powerful, and, if allowed, would eventually

take power and ultimately have to create institutions that break with
the metropole centers and with the international capitalist system in
order to develop without "conditions."

> If the situation of dependency is one which configurates an internal
> situation to one with which it is structurally bound, it is not possible to
> break (the situation) by isolating the country from external influences
> since this would simply provoke chaos in an internal structure which is
> essentially dependent. The only solution to breaking it would be, then,
> to change these internal structures, which leads necessarily, at the same
> time, to a confrontation with the international structure.[48]

We observe that internal movements which show any signs of
breaking the dependency relationship, and which consequently also
destroy the power of the dominant group in the periphery, are usually
met with force. In the internal confrontation, the dominant group has
the direct or indirect aid of the metropole power.

To speak of "democracy" in a dependent society implies that the
possibility of breaking the dependent situation is a permissible choice
for the masses. That there may be an inherent contradiction between
democratic political institutions in dependent countries and the
international capitalist system is not discussed in development theory,
but becomes clear in dependency theory.

There may be an inherent contradiction as well between the
function of an educational system as seen by metropole educators and
its function in the dependent society. Neoclassical development theory
views schooling as being a "liberating" process, in which the child is
transformed from a "traditional" individual to a "modern" one. This
transition is supposed to enable the child to be creative as well as
functional. Schooling is also supposed to enable the graduate to
contribute to the economy, polity, and society. But in dependency
theory, the transformation that takes place in school cannot be
liberating, since a person is simply changed from one role in a
dependent system to a different role in the same system. While the
latter may be more economically satisfying, it still leaves the individual
in a conditional situation, one dominated by the metropole culture,

technology, and goods through the dominant group in the periphery. The graduate cannot contribute to the society to his or her full potential, since the dependent society is limited in its ability to provide work to everyone. Much of the labor force is not even able to enter the "dynamic" sector, which is dominated by metropole technology, which uses a lot of capital but little labor. The "inefficiencies" of the school system as related to the social and economic structure are not inefficiencies at all, but direct derivatives of the dependent situation.

Just as development theory describes education in underdeveloped countries as inefficient, many indicators used also describe it as "backward." A high percentage of illiterates, a low percentage of children in school, and a low average level of schooling in the labor force, all point to low educational development.[49] But in the dependency context, these measures of backwardness are very misleading: the school systems are copies of metropole country school systems and serve copies of metropole country economic structures. Since the country is in a dependent situation, the "modern" economic structures serve only a small proportion of the population; schools oriented to those economic structures can also only function for a small proportion of the population. Rather than being the means through which individuals fulfill their potential, then, schools are reduced to being largely selectors and socializers. The large number of dropouts and illiterates in a particular society may, in fact, be accompanied by an *overdeveloped* school system, in which numbers of children go to school, but are henceforth unable to find employment different from that which they had before. This is not the result of irrelevant or low-quality schooling, as is often claimed, but the result of a dependent economic system that is dominated by the international division of labor. The kind of economic structure able to absorb all the educated is not possible under the conditions of the dependent situation. Thus, a system of schooling that complements all people's social utility is also not possible.

Yet, schooling does have a certain autonomy within the political, social, and economic system. Despite its primary functions of selection and socialization, it does produce individuals who are not only agents of change within the dependent system, but also some who want to break the dependent situation. Through increased schooling (as one of many educational institutions), the dominant groups in the society may unintentionally create forces opposed to dependency and the dominance of the groups who live off the dependent system. This is one of the major contradictions which occurs in a dependent society: the institution of schooling, part of the imported capitalist system, is *capable* of (although not programmed to) generating awareness of the dependent relationship of one society to another and of the role of the dominant groups in maintaining that dependency.

Theories of Colonialism

Lenin's theory of imperialism argues that there are economic imperatives which promote the domination of some peoples by others. As a Marxist, he also states that the *form* of domination is determined by economic-historical forces. In the period of financial imperialism that Lenin discusses, domination was shaped by the struggle among financial oligarchies in several technologically advanced countries to carve and recarve the world. The economic imperative behind this struggle is the pressure to seek outlets for capital accumulating in the advanced countries. Unlike earlier periods, in which the economic imperative was the drive for raw materials and markets to feed domestic industry in the advanced countries, the financial phase resulted in the establishment and promotion of industrialization outside the metropole. The relationship between people from the metropole and those from the periphery are, according to the Marxist-Leninist theory, shaped by the economic institutions which bind the two together. Since the metropole dominates these institutions—periphery economic, political, and social structures are defined to meet the needs of the metropole's monopoly power—people from the metropole dominate those who live in the periphery. In addition, since the economic structure brought in by the metropole is capitalistic, this defines certain hierarchical social relations in production and consumption among those who participate even marginally in that structure. These relations are universal, independent of the society on which they are imposed. Once introduced and adopted, they do not need the *direct* presence of the metropole. African nations that obtained political independence after World War II, for example, but retained capitalist production structures (with their well-defined command hierarchies and division of labor) and remained in the world capitalist system, also retained European norms and values. In theory, Europeans would not have to be directly present to perpetuate the social structures and social relations that derive from these production relations; however, the propensity to continue to accept Europeans in the highest positions of that social structure is obviously increased if capitalist production relations exist.

The psychological view of colonialism, developed in its extreme form by Mannoni,[50] stresses the particular nature of the colonial relationship among individuals in the colonial situation. Although this theory is not a direct derivative of the Schumpeterian model of imperialism, it has in common with it the abstraction from the capitalist mode of production as the main feature of imperialism and colonialism and stresses the psychological makeup of those who are the conquerors and those who are conquered.

Mannoni's view is not that colonialism is the result of "objectless tendencies toward forcible expansion" [51] but that the colonial relationship is derived from universal psychological drives among different kinds of people to dominate others or to be dominated.[52] Mannoni stresses child-rearing practices among Europeans and Africans as differentiating their predisposition to be colonizers or colonized. Such child-rearing practices in colonized societies were initially directed toward ancestors. The resulting feelings of dependency and inferiority were easily transferred upon the colonizer.

The key to Mannoni's analysis is the *previous* psychological condition of the colonizer and the colonized which permits the colonial situation to occur and which shapes the relations between the two. This previous condition is independent of the colonial situation itself. Mannoni therefore puts the blame for the colonial relationship (though not for colonization) on the colonized as well as the colonizer. Since the relation is a *psychological* one, independent of structure, there is no way out of it for the actors, according to Mannoni, except through intensive individual psychotherapy. Social action by the colonized is only a response to the colonizer not fulfilling his expected role.[53]

Memmi and Fanon[54] reject Mannoni's view but do incorporate the psychological dimension of his analysis and combine it with the economic-political universality of the colonial relationship.

> Let me take this opportunity to reaffirm my position: for me the economic aspect of colonialism is fundamental. The book itself opens with a denunciation of the so-called moral or cultural mission of colonization and shows that the profit motive in it is basic. I have often noted that the *deprivations* of the colonized are the almost direct results of the advantages secured to the colonizer. However, colonial privilege is not solely economic. To observe the life of the colonizer and the colonized is to discover rapidly that the daily humiliation of the colonized, his objective subjugation, are not merely economic. Even the poorest colonizer thought himself to be—and actually was—superior to the colonized. This too was part of colonial privilege. . . . Does psychoanalysis win out over Marxism? Does all depend on the individual or on society? In any case, before attacking this *final analysis* I wanted to show all the real complexities in the lives of the colonizer and the colonized.[55]

Memmi therefore concentrates on the condition of the colonizer and the colonized in the colonial situation. He produces a picture of the relationships among people in that situation and what this relationship implies for economic, social, and personal development of the colonized. The colonizer for Memmi may indeed be predisposed to be a colonizer before he arrives—Memmi argues that the mediocre tend to leave the home country for the colony—but even those who are liberal and want to see the colonized become "free" (he defines these liberals as "colonials" rather than "colonialists") end up either having to leave the colony or joining the colonialists in the ranks of the colonizers. They cannot join the colonized because they do not share their "lack of culture" or their "lack of history." The colonial has a well-defined past, while the colonized have had their past (their identity) destroyed by the colonizers. To become colonized, the colonial must accept the suffering and degradation of the colonized, something that few colonials are willing to do.[56] The only choice left to the colonial is to accept the role of colonizer or return to the metropole.

> . . . accepting the reality of being a colonizer means agreeing to be a non-legitimate person, that is, a usurper. To be sure, a usurper claims his place and, if need be, will defend it by every means at his disposal. . . . He endeavors to falsify history, he rewrites laws, he would extinguish memories—anything to succeed in transforming his usurpation into legitimacy . . . the more the usurped is downtrodden, the more the usurper triumphs.[57]

There are two very important points here: First, the colonizer needs the poverty and degradation of the colonized to justify his own place in the society. After all, where would he be if it were not for the colonized? He would not be able to do as well economically, since the colonial system exploits the colonized to the profit of the colonizer. He also would lose much of his self-importance if he were simply one among many of his own kind. Second, the colonial situation manufactures colonialists, just as it manufactures the colonized. It is not just the predisposition to become a colonizer or colonized that produces these roles (the Mannoni argument) but the colonial situation itself. The colonial comes with power into the colonial context: he has the economic and military might of the metropole behind him. The colonized has no power. If he attempts to fight, he is physically conquered. The colonized is not free to choose between being colonized or not. The colonizer can enforce his usurpation with great punishment. The colonized adjusts to this situation by developing those traits with which the colonizer characterizes him. The colonized is seen as lazy, vicious, dishonest, uncivilized, and so forth. Many of these traits are incompatible with each other, but that doesn't bother the colonizer, because the general traits are designed to destroy any culture or history that the colonized brings to the relationship. "At the basis of the entire construction, one finally finds a common motive; the colonizer's economic and basic needs, which he substitutes for logic, and which shape and explain each of the traits he assigns to the colonized." [58]

Eventually, the colonized accepts this caricature. All the institutions of society are shaped by the colonizer to fit *his* view of the colonized. Since the colonized is forced to function within those institutions, he begins to accept the colonizer's conception of him. If the colonized resists that image, he is punished; if he is aggressive, refuses to work like an animal, or to be an object, the colonizer's law is used to find him guilty. According to Memmi, the adherence to the caricature is part and parcel of colonization and not its cause.

> In order for the colonizer to be a complete master, it is not enough for him to be so in actual fact, but he must also believe in its legitimacy. In order for that legitimacy to be complete, it is not enough for the colonized to be a slave, he must also accept his role. The bond between colonizer and colonized is thus destructive and creative. It destroys and recreates the two partners of colonization into colonizer and colonized. One is disfigured into an oppressor, a partial unpatriotic and treacherous being, worrying only about his privileges and their defense; the other into an oppressed creature, whose development is broken and who compromises by his defeat.[59]

The relation between Memmi's analysis and dependency theory is obvious: the colonial relation determines the pattern of development or nondevelopment in a colonized country. On the one hand, the colonialist is more tied to the metropole than to the colonial country in which he resides. He is not interested in developing the colony in the image of the home country because that would destroy the social structure which ensures his privileges. The colonized, in turn, is removed from participating in the development of his own country. The legitimization of the colonialist's role requires the destruction of the colonized sense of culture and history, so the colonized is removed from all social and cultural responsibility. He deals only with the present, not with the past or future. The present he is forced to deal with are those institutions that the colonizer brings to the colonized country. The colonized therefore experiences a double alienation: the first alienation comes from having his own culture destroyed in the process of legitimizing the usurpation of the colonizer; the second alienation comes from the selective nature of the elements of the metropolitan culture with which he is confronted. The machinery, the books, the movies, the curricula, and the labor force exported to the colonies reflect the specific needs experienced by the segments of the metropolitan society present on the local scene. As such they offer a distorted image of the metropolitan culture.[60]

Under these conditions, it is unlikely that economic, political, and social development will take place among the colonized. Memmi argues that whether the European presence has made the colonized better off than without the European or not is irrelevant. The result of colonization is the condition of poverty without the responsibility for that condition in the hands of the colonized. The services produced are made to serve primarily the needs of the colonizer. The colonized cannot be mobilized for change because they have been led to believe that they are incapable of it. "To subdue and exploit, the colonizer pushed the colonized out of the historical and social, cultural and technical current." [61] The colonial situation inhibits change.

Dependency theory emerged from the Latin American condition of the 1950s and '60s, 130 years after independence from colonial rule. What does Memmi's analysis have to do with underdeveloped countries ruled by their own nationals? For the extension of his analysis to postcolonial colonialism and to the revolutionary imperative that colonialism generates, we must turn to Fanon. Fanon argues that the transference of power from the colonialists to the national bourgeoisie maintains colonial institutions and often even increases the economic and social power of the ex-colonial country. With independence, the cost of administrating the colony is left in the hands of the national parties, while the advanced-country capitalists continue to reap the rewards of the old colonial relationship. The national bourgeoisie after independence "discovers its historic mission: that of intermediary." [62] It attempts to take over where the Europeans left off, but it does not have the history, power, and wealth of its European counterpart:

The national middle class which takes over power at the end of the colonial regime is an underdeveloped middle class. It has practically no economic power, and in any case it is in no way commensurate with the bourgeoisie of the mother country which it hopes to replace. In its narcissism, the national middle class is easily convinced that it can advantageously replace the middle class of the mother country. But that same independence which literally drives it into a corner will give rise within its ranks to catastrophic reactions, and will oblige it to send out frenzied appeals for help to the former mother country.[63]

According to Fanon, this weak national middle class is the "transmission line between the nation and a capitalism . . . which today puts on the mask of neo-colonialism." [64] But this role is not the same that the bourgeoisie played in its earlier stages in Europe, that of discovery and invention. Rather, the national bourgeoisie imitates the present stage of the European elites without going through the more creative stage of capitalist development.

More important, the national bourgeoisie maintains the colonial institutional structure: the ex-colony's economy is not integrated into that of the nation as a whole. It is still organized to complete the economies of the different mother countries. This, of course, is the essence of dependency theory. In the dependent economy, the bulk of the population remains outside the dynamic sectors of the economy. But it is the culture of the national bourgeoisie which is least cognizant of the forces in its midst and, like the colonial regime before it, alienated from the national culture which is the means to liberation. Fanon argues that the return to primitive culture is part of the colonizing syndrome. The colonizer convinces the colonized that his culture is barbaric and bestial.[65]

Under colonial domination, the national culture is a contested culture whose destruction is sought in systematic fashion. After a long period of colonization, constantly under attack, all that is left from the old culture are its most rigid forms; because it was not allowed to develop in any way, it is completely unsuited to the present and is extremely conservative. With the emergence of a new national culture in the struggle against colonialism, it is the colonialists who become the defenders of the native style. That is their image of the colonized's culture: the colonizer is as much the creator of the colonized culture as the colonized himself. Fanon shows that the only route to a new national culture is through a national struggle for liberation from domination.

In Fanon's terms, formal liberation—the turning over of government to a national bourgeoisie by the metropolitan power—does *not* create a national culture. Fanon argues that the absence of struggle, or even of participation, by the colonized masses precludes the possibility of forming liberated cultural forms. The colonized retain their traditional practices, which are the product of colonization, and the national bourgeoisie adopts the culture of the metropole. In this situation, "development" only occurs within the constraints of the metropole culture. This is a continuation of the colonial model. For Fanon, there is no going back; his solution is neither the rigid form of what is left of precolonial culture nor the "developed" culture of the metropole. Through the struggle for liberation, a new, revolutionary culture, which is the product of both of these rejected cultures will emerge.

> We believe that the conscious and organized undertaking by a colonized people to reestablish the sovereignty of that nation constitutes the most complete and obvious cultural manifestation that exists. It is not alone the success of the struggle which afterward gives validity and vigor to culture; culture is not put into cold storage during the conflict. The struggle itself in its development and in its internal progression sends culture along different paths and traces out entirely new ones for it. The struggle for freedom does not give back to national culture its former value and shapes; this struggle which aims at a fundamentally different set of relations between men cannot leave intact either the form or the content of the people's culture. After the conflict there is not only the disappearance of colonialism but also the disappearance of colonized man.[66]

Fanon draws his observations primarily from the African scene, but they apply directly to Latin America in the nineteenth century and, in an altered form, today. For Fanon, as well as for Memmi, there is only one way out of the colonial (and neocolonial) situation: revolt. In Memmi's analysis, the revolt is necessary to do away with colonization, both its source—the colonizer—and its result: the dependent mentality produced in the colonized. But Memmi does not describe what such a liberation entails beyond the need for a radical change in colonies' political and economic power structure. He implies that liberation (decolonization) requires a number of sequential steps, passing through national independence. Fanon insists that such a revolution must be violent. The colonial relation is a violent one; it must therefore end in violence. The compromise of independence under the national bourgeoisie must be opposed:

> The observations that we have been able to make about the national bourgeoisie bring us to the conclusion which should cause no surprise. In underdeveloped countries, the bourgeoisie should not be allowed to find the conditions necessary for its existence and its growth. In other words, the combined efforts of the masses led by a party and of the intellectuals who are highly conscious and armed with revolutionary principles ought to bar the way to this useless and harmful middle class.[67]

The main contributions of Memmi and Fanon are the extension of imperialist theory to the *results* of imperialism in the colonized country, and the dimension of psychological effects added to the economic exploitation stressed by economists. Memmi gives us the concept of universal roles which are played in the colonial situation: the colonizer who accepts his role as a colonizer; the colonizer who does not want to be a colonizer, and the colonized who accepts being colonized. He shows us the contradictions in each of these roles and of the colonial situation. Fanon goes further and discusses the roles of various groups in the political struggle against colonialism, and the resulting contradictions of formal independence and the nature of the colonial relations which continue after formal independence. Most important, Fanon shows how traditional culture as observed today is the *product* of colonization rather than something left over from precolonial times. Similarly, the culture of the national bourgeoisie is also the product of colonialism. Neither is "developmental"; both are the result of a dependency relation. Only through liberation struggles, Fanon argues, can a new national culture of freedom emerge.

Yet these theories and analyses of colonialism concentrate on the underdeveloped countries, and more specifically on those nonindustrialized countries that were colonized.[68] Raskin[69] attempts a general political theory of colonialism and applies it to a highly developed nation, the United States. His analysis shows the United States, as other nations, governed by a few for a few. The lives of most members of the society are shaped by the pyramidal structure that characterizes the political, economic, and social institutions in the society. People orient their lives to satisfy needs that are not theirs but those of the hierarchic other—the needs of the hierarchy itself.

> The implication is that the many live their lives for the few, and political and economic institutions operate in such a way as to make this situation either bearable (liberal authoritarian) or painful (totalitarian). Whether the institutions are socialist or capitalist, the pyramidal structure operates to reinforce the pyramid and the sense of living the life of the hierarchic other.[70]

Raskin describes the pyramidal authority in America through four overlapping colonies. "Each colony, through its dynamics and processes, hollows out man and objectifies for the purpose of running the colony." [71] The Violence Colony is the military and police arm of the national security state. In consort with the few who sit at the top of the pyramid, the Violence Colony commits society to war and even self-annihilation without its explicit consent. Raskin uses the Cuban missile crisis in 1962 as an example of how a few men (fifteen) sitting around a table in Washington could decide for all humanity whether it should live or die.[72] This is the logical end of a colonized society that puts its fate in the hands of a few who are committed to violence and imperialism. The social contract is destroyed and the masses are alienated from decisions which affect their very lives. In the Plantation Colony, corporate monopolies produce goods which are "surplus" goods in the sense that they do not meet people's needs. Capitalist production sustains a pool of unemployed or underpaid at the very same time that it is producing a surplus of consumption goods. People find that "they work at meaningless and unreal jobs to obtain what they are led to want. Yet their work does not help them satisfy human needs." [73]

In his analysis of the Plantation Colony, Raskin concentrates on the type of alienation inherent in the corporate form as it exists in the United States, and its relation to the reaction of workers to capitalism. He tries to develop from this analysis the necessary transformation of the Plantation Colony as part of the reconstruction of the pyramidal state.

> A conflict will develop between the worker as one who is no longer necessary or who is worse off through automation because of time studies based on speed-ups to the machine, and the worker as consumer who is necessary to the successful and stable operation of the profit and social system. [74]

The Plantation Colony depends on the Violence Colony for its survival: government defense contracts employ an increasing number of workers and a high fraction of the labor force. Magdoff and Sweezy estimate that more than 20 percent of the U.S. labor force has been either unemployed, in the armed forces, or in defense-contract employment since 1938. [75] The percentage has shifted from unemployment to the Violence Colony over time. Only during wars (World War II, Korea, and Vietnam) has the unemployment rate fallen to near-full-employment rates. The average rate during nonwar years since 1946 has been 5.6 percent. The Violence and Plantation colonies are imperialistic, and the colonized become part of their imperialism: cities and lives at home decay while armaments are produced to colonize others.

The Channeling Colony (the educational system) and the Dream Colony (the media) serve the national security state and the economy. The schools are designed to get children to accept authority structures: the media provide "a surrogate of action and passion for the colonized, replacing their own actions and passions, which could stem from human feeling." [76] We shall have much more to say about the schools, but it is important to point out here that Raskin's analysis shows the colonizing effect of schooling in a developed high-income society that is supposed to be *change*-oriented. He also shows the contradictions that the Channeling Colony can generate: since the American ideology of education (and indeed most other Western ideologies of education) "assumes the right . . . of an individual to shape reality in terms other than those in which it is presented, the school's long term effect is to create a consciousness among many students and professors which stimulates the need for decolonization and reconstruction." [77] In the pyramidal society, however, this right is distributed only to those who are least likely to want to change the pyramidal structure.

Raskin's work brings us full circle: imperialism is derived from the decisions and needs of a handful of people in the advanced economies; this results in a colonization of the militarily weaker countries and those peoples who, in the precolonial period, are not conditioned to live in a world of threat and counterthreat; colonization creates the colonized, who are shackled with the chains of dependency and degradation; but institutions in the highly developed countries which are geared to the colonization of others must, by their very nature, also colonize the people in the developed country itself. Thus, imperialism colonizes everyone but those who make the decisions at the center of the metropole. The nature of the colonial relationship varies from situation to situation, but it also has universal traits: the dehumanization of men and women to fit them into the colonial structure; the incorporation of all culture and history into the colonializer's view of culture and history, and the development of institutions that serve the colonizer, not the colonized. The acceptance of the colonial situation by the colonized is crucial to the colonial enterprise. In the modern pyramidal state, and the modern imperial relation, schooling plays an important role in obtaining this acceptance. But if schooling and other forms of moral suasion (including the media) are not sufficient, force is still a very real option for the colonizer.

The Role of Schooling in Colonialism

All the authors who write about colonialism deal, explicitly or implicitly, with education. Memmi shows how the similarities and differences between the metropolitan and colonial school systems both work against the colonized. The curriculum and language of the colonial schools is not surprisingly the same as that of schools in the metropole countries, especially schools for the poor. Primary schools stress socialization into European language, values and norms (Christianity), and the degradation of all that is native.

> The history which is taught him [the colonized] is not his own. Everything seems to have taken place out of his country. . . . The books talk to him of a world which in no way reminds him of his own. . . . His teachers do not follow the same pattern as his father; they are not his wonderful and redeeming successors like every other teacher in the world.[78]

At the same time, schools are provided for very few among the colonized. There is not a general increase in scholarization in a European sense, and the previous ways of education are denigrated because of their association with the colonized culture. Foster points out that the African soon realized where the power lay, and in his colonized condition wanted only European academic education even though this education had little to do with his own reality. It was the only way out of the poverty and absence of culture which the colonial situation assigned him.[79] However, going to European academic schools creates a permanent duality in the colonized. Memmi argues that linguistic dualism causes a cultural catastrophe in the colonized which is never completely overcome.

> Possession of two languages is not merely a matter of having two tools, but actually means participation in two psychical and cultural realms. Here, the two worlds symbolized and conveyed by the two tongues are in conflict; they are those of the colonizer and the colonized.[80]

The high percentage of nations that chose to stay in close relations with the former colonial country after formal independence attests to the success of colonial education in "assimilating" the educated colonized into the developed-country-dominated world cultural and economic system. As Clignet states: " 'Assimilation' becomes the ideological framework within which the colonizer stresses the universality of his own culture, and reduces the aspirations toward upward mobility experienced by the colonized into individual rather than collective terms." [81]

The change in the ex-colonies from a raw-material-based economy to some industrialization (in Latin America in the 1910s and 1930s and in Asia in the 1950s and '60s) increased the demand for skilled labor and, therefore, for schooling. By this time, the colonies were formally independent and so schooling should have been much more oriented toward national culture and toward national development. Yet, the schools remained in the European or U.S. model, often teaching or stressing the colonial language, and using a curriculum largely drawn from the former colonial countries. History books were changed, and the beginnings of national culture were instilled in children after independence. But this national culture was based largely on its interpretation by the national bourgeoisie, and so the school system was (and is) still available primarily to those who have come into contact with European or North American values and norms.

Raskin's analysis of schooling as a channeling colony is as valid for the postformal-independence situation in a nonindustrialized country as it is for the United States. The primary difference is that children are not being channeled into an authority structure in which the decisions are being made by a group of *nationals*, but into one which extends to the center of the empire. The school in a nonindustrialized country teaches children to respond to standards, qualifications, and records that are set in other countries as well as by other groups in that particular country. Even after independence, for example, ex-British colonial higher secondary schools send their exams to be graded in Britain. The "best" universities are abroad, and the best opportunities are also abroad for those who succeed in school. Often the teacher is a foreigner, implicitly or explicitly extolling the virtues of the home country. So the school teaches allegiance to authority but the authority may not be national, or at best is a combination of cultures.

In a dependent country, the channeling colony alienates the child from his culture and the economic and social needs of his people. This process, recognized by Memmi as part of the colonial situation, continues after formal independence as long as the local hierarchy is hooked into a hierarchy that extends to the metropole center. Raskin concentrates on the role of schooling in preventing the individual from attaining self-definition:

> Once the student accepts the school treadmill, profilism, and the informal lesions of the pyramidal structure, he usually finds that to survive he must become a master at the strategy of faking or totally internalize the channeling colony's view of where he will fit into the colonized reality.[82]

In the nonindustrialized country, the school is an institution that not only keeps the individual from self-definition, but keeps the entire society from defining itself. The schools are an extension of the metropole structure, just as are the economy, polity, and social structure. As long as the national bourgeoisie in its colonial role dominates the domestic pyramidal structure, we can expect that the school will prevent liberation on two levels: liberation from the definition of culture and development by the high-income imperial nations, and liberation from the domestic pyramidal structure.

The Raskin analysis also leads us to the primary contradiction of increased schooling in the dependent societies: schools are organized to fit children into predetermined roles in the pyramidal structure, but education is also committed to teach children to question. When the questioning cannot be controlled, the pyramidal structure and the international system come under scrutiny too. Colonial institutions may raise consciousness in spite of themselves and those whose consciousness is raised require increased rewards to stay in the roles assigned to them. When the system cannot bribe them sufficiently, they begin to attack it. Increased marginality in the periphery countries may pose an important threat to the postcolonial structure.

Notes

1. Michael Barratt Brown, *After Imperialism* (New York: Humanities Press, 1970), pp. 26–27.

2. Ibid., pp. 27–28.

3. Joseph A. Schumpeter, *Imperialism and Social Classes* (New York: Augustus M. Kelley, 1951), p. 44.

4. Ibid., p. 7.

5. Ibid., p. 34.

6. Ibid., p. 83.

7. Ibid., pp. 83–84.

8. The Roman Empire, on the other hand, was—according to Schumpeter—the best example in history of "imperialism rooted in the domestic political situation and derived from class structure. The ruling class was always inclined to declare that the country was in danger, when it was really only class interests that were threatened" (Schumpeter, p. 69). Roman large landowners depended on slaves to work their extensive holdings; the state depended on tribute to maintain the court and the army.

9. Tom Kemp, *Theories of Imperialism* (London: Dobson Books, 1967), p. 95.

10. Schumpeter, *Imperialism and Social Classes*, p. 96.

11. Kemp, *Theories of Imperialism*, p. 91.

12. Schumpeter, *Imperialism and Social Classes*, p. 118.

13. "Indeed, it was the manufacturers themselves who suggested the adoption of an embryonic sort of formal education system for the Act of 1833" (Neil J. Smelser, *Social Change in the Industrial Revolution* [Chicago: University of Chicago Press, 1959], p. 287).

14. Kemp, *Theories of Imperialism*, p. 105.

15. V. I. Lenin, *Imperialism, The Highest Stage of Capitalism* (New York: International Publishers, 1939).

16. Lenin, in *The Essential Works of Lenin*, ed. Henry M. Christman (New York: Bantam Books, 1966), p. 203.

17. Ibid., p. 215.

18. Ibid., p. 216.

19. Ibid., p. 216.

20. Lenin, quoted in Hamsa Alevi, "Imperialism, Old and New," reprint published by the Radical Education Project, Detroit, Mich., pp. 3–4. In an aside, Lenin argues that another force for imperialism is the need to alleviate population pressure at home. The export of capital accelerates the development of capitalism in those countries to which capital is exported but may tend to arrest development in those countries exporting capital. In order to avoid "civil war," an outlet for the unemployed at home would be necessary. See Christman, *Essential Works*, p. 217.

21. J. A. Hobson, *Imperialism* (3rd ed.; London: Allen & Unwin, 1938).

22. Brown, *After Imperialism*, chap. 3.

23. For example, ibid., p. 248.

24. Up to the middle of the nineteenth century, India was worked by the East India Company, a royal monopoly.

25. Brown, *After Imperialism*, pp. 58–59.

26. Per capita national income in the United States was about $300 in 1910 compared with $60 in exports/capita in Argentina in the same year. Assuming that exports represented one-third of national income in Argentina, Argentine income per capita was 60 percent of the U.S. level, a much higher percentage than fifty years later.

27. Barrington Moore, Jr., *Social Origins of Dictatorship and Democracy* (Boston: Beacon Press, 1968), chap. 5.

28. Brown, *After Imperialism*, p. 48.

29. David S. Landes, "The Nature of Economic Imperialism," *Journal of Economic History* 21 (December 1961): 496–512; as quoted in Harry Magdoff, *The Age of Imperialism* (New York: Monthly Review Press, 1969), p. 13.

30. See, for example, Mark Blaug, "Economic Imperialism Revisited," *Yale Review* 50 (Spring 1961): 335–49; Brown, *After Imperialism*; R. Palme Dutt, *The Crisis of Britain and the British Empire* (London: Lawrence & Wishart, 1953).

31. Christman, *Essential Works*, p. 266.

32. Alevi, "Imperialism, Old and New," p. 13.

33. Magdoff, *Age of Imperialism*, p. 15.

34. Johan Galtung, "A Structural Theory of Imperialism," *Journal of Peace Research* 8, no. 2 (1971): 83.

35. Ibid., p. 84.

36. The immediate postwar policy of the U.S. in the Middle East is documented in detail in Richard Barnet, *Intervention and Revolution* (New York: World Publishing, 1968), chaps. 6 and 7. Magdoff, *Age of Imperialism*, p. 43, shows how, between 1940 and 1967, U.S. oil reserves controlled rose from less than 10 to almost 60 percent, while British control over reserves fell from 72 to 29 percent of the total.

37. Fernando Fajnzylber, "Estrategia Industrial y Empresas Internacionales: Posicion Relativa de America Latina y Brasil," Economic Commission for Latin America (November 1970), p. 21.

38. Magdoff, *Age of Imperialism*, p. 45. The multinational firms have also created an underdeveloped country national who identifies more with his *international* company than with his country.

39. See Philip Coombs, *The World Educational Crisis* (New York: Oxford University Press, 1968).

40. In fact, however, the "cheap," capital-intensive technology usually turns out to be more expensive than teacher training. See Martin Carnoy, "The Costs and Returns to Educational Television," in *Educational Television: A Policy Critique and Guide for Developing Countries*, ed. Robert Arnove (Stanford University, School of Education, May, 1973). Mimeographed.

41. Andre Gunder Frank, *Capitalism and Underdevelopment in Latin America* (New York: Monthly Review Press, 1969); Galtung, "Structural Theory of Imperialism."

42. Theotonio Dos Santos, *Dependencia economica y cambio revolucionario* (Caracas, Venezuela: Nueva Izquierda, 1970), p. 38. (My translation—MC.)

43. This is the essence of Rostow's theory of the *Stages of Economic Growth*.

44. Dos Santos, *Dependencia economica*, p. 9.

45. Fernando Enrique Cardoso and Enzo Faletto, *Dependencia y desarrollo en America Latina* (Mexico: Siglo Veintiuno, 1969), p. 23.

46. Dos Santos, *Dependencia economica*, p. 20.

47. Ibid., p. 40.

48. Ibid., p. 45.

49. See, for example, F. Harbison and Charles Myers, *Education, Manpower, and Economic Growth* (New York: McGraw-Hill, 1964).

50. O. Mannoni, *Prospero and Caliban*, first published as *Psychologie de la Colonisation* (Paris: Le Seuil, 1950).

51. Schumpeter, *Imperialism and Social Classes*,

52. See also Sigmund Freud, *Civilization and Its Discontents* (New York: W. W. Norton, 1962).

53. Remi Clignet, "Damned if You Do, Damned if You Don't; the Dilemmas of the Colonizer-Colonized Relations," *Comparative Education Review* 15, no. 3 (October 1971): 300.

54. A. Memmi, *The Colonizer and the Colonized* (Boston: Beacon Press, 1965); and F. Fanon, *The Wretched of the Earth* (New York: Grove Press, 1968).

55. A. Memmi, *Colonizer and Colonized*, pp. xii–xiii.

56. In *Black Like Me* (Boston: Houghton Mifflin, 1961), John Griffen, a Houston journalist, dyed his skin black and traveled throughout the South for a year. His experiences describe vividly what is in store for the colonial who chooses to become colonized.

57. Memmi, *Colonizer and Colonized*, pp. 52–53.

58. Ibid., p. 83. In a recent conversation with a neighbor, he explained to me the great difficulty he was having with his black employees. "They just don't want to work. We have to fire them after a couple of weeks on the job." He then went on to discuss how blacks were not sufficiently well trained to get available jobs. Later in the conversation, however, it turned out that there was an equally high turnover among white employees; his point about the blacks was simply a way of reaffirming the white-black relationship in a colonial society. He also used the term "they" when referring to blacks, which is a typical depersonification used by the colonizer when speaking about the colonized.

59. Ibid., p. 89.

60. Clignet, "Damned if You Do, Damned if You Don't," p. 303.

61. Memmi, *Colonizer and Colonized*, p. 114.

62. Fanon, *Wretched of the Earth*, p. 152.

63. Ibid., p. 149.

64. Ibid., p. 152.

65. This was especially true in Africa. See chapter 3.

66. Fanon, *Wretched of the Earth*, pp. 245–46.

67. Ibid., pp. 174–75. The group to be counted on to lead such a national revolution is the peasants. They are least touched by the colonial experience and so are least tied to the colonial culture and the economy of the former mother country. The peasants are the least likely to have internalized the colonized mentality and so will be the first to bear arms against it. However, the consciousness of the peasants is also very low, so Fanon counts on the intellectuals and the urban proletariat to raise the consciousness of these masses.

68. In a later work, *Dominated Man* (New York: Orion Press, 1968) Memmi does extend his discussion to blacks, women, and servants in industrialized countries.

69. Marcus Raskin, *Being and Doing* (New York: Random House, 1971).

70. Ibid., p. xiii.

71. Ibid., p. xiv.

72. Ibid., p. 63.

73. Ibid., p. xv.

74. Ibid., p. 103.

75. Harry Magdoff and Paul Sweezy, "Economic Stagnation and Stagnation of Economics," *Monthly Review* 22, no. 2 (April 1971): 1–11.

76. Raskin, *Being and Doing*, p. xvi.

77. Ibid., p. xvi.

78. Memmi, *Colonizer and Colonized,* p. 105.

79. Philip Foster, *Education and Social Change in Ghana* (London: Allen & Unwin, 1965).

80. Memmi, *Colonizer and Colonized,* p. 107.

81. Clignet, "Damned if You Do, Damned if You Don't," p. 307.

82. Raskin, *Being and Doing,* pp. 116–17.

EDUCATION AND TRADITIONAL COLONIALISM

3

INDIA AND WEST AFRICA

Between 1500 and 1900 most of the world was under the control of Europeans. Only a few societies such as China and Japan were able to resist colonization. Two kinds of traditional colonies emerged in this period: European *settlements*, where the immigrants conquered the natives, took their land, and developed the country for the enclave European community; and *occupied* and *administered* colonies, where a few European colonists, primarily traders and soldiers, controlled the colony for the home country. Initially, both kinds of colonies served the mercantile needs of the imperialist powers. Taxes and primary goods flowed into Europe from the colonies under tight trade monopolies. The United States was the first of the settlements to break away from Europe. Soon European settlements in Latin America struggled with Spain and Portugal for the right to trade with other countries.

Independence movements were organized by European bourgeoisies living in the colonies. Their demand for autonomy coincided with the Enlightenment, the rise of capitalism, and new views of economic relations among countries and among individuals. The first breakthroughs were armed confrontations, but other European settlements—Canada and Australia, for example—won peacefully the right to make economic decisions.

But these changes did not extend to non-Europeans. India was conquered by Britain in the mercantile period. Her taxes and exports—traded for simple manufactures—helped finance the growth of industry in Britain. The colonial independence movement passed over India.[1] Independence for some colonies made the control of markets for British textile and other goods in remaining colonies more important: as soon as textile production became important in England, Britain protected her own manufactured goods against Indian imports and forced India to accept British goods in free trade. Thus, India remained an exploited and tightly controlled extension of Britain throughout the "idealistic" years of early capitalism.

West Africa's role in the mercantile period was to provide slaves for sugar, indigo, and cotton plantations in the Americas. Occupation of African territories was unnecessary in the slave trade. Accustomed to a domestic slavery governed by tribal laws, Africans sold other Africans to Europeans for guns and alcohol. When Britain decided to end the slave trade in the early nineteenth century, West Africa became less important to England economically, but remained interesting as an area where theories of moral and economic transformation could be tested. The juncture between Christian morality and capitalistic rationality was nowhere clearer than in the efforts to Westernize the Africans.

Since there was no competition from African industry, trade and proselytization went on without much military intervention and with little European jurisdictional control. But because traders and missionaries did not themselves have the power to force African acceptance of European civilization, their proselytization efforts were not very successful. Earlier promises of commercial riches and hordes of converts did not materialize. The slave trade was ended by gradually abolishing slavery in Cuba and Brazil, not by British gunboats, missionaries, or the attractiveness for Africans of more "legitimate" trade. Yet, these failures did not cause Europeans to leave West Africa. France's drive to recover prestige, the rise of Germany as a competitor to British and French capitalism, and British protection of her routes to India opened a new era of territorial annexation by European powers. It was only then, with a permanent European presence, that large numbers of Africans adopted European ways.

India and West Africa, therefore, played very different roles in European development. India was a European-administered colony in the eighteenth century, before British capitalists gained control of Parliament and foreign policy. India was rich and her wealth was easily accessible. Agriculture and industry were well established when the Europeans arrived to trade. Whites could tolerate the climate and could live and travel in India without difficulty. So India was occupied early. Her riches fueled English industrial hegemony which, in turn, destroyed India's industry and impoverished her people for more than a century.

The West African Coast, with which Europeans made initial African contact, had little in common with India. White men died quickly from disease; there were artisans, but none of the fine products demanded in European markets. The main export was people. Europeans never settled. They stayed in their boats offshore, or in some of the healthier spots, where they erected forts, or "factories." It was only in the 1820s and '30s that interior exploration began, and it was not until the 1850s that the discovery of quinine made interior travel safe. By this time, Britain—now the most important imperial power—was in the throes of capitalist free-trade rationalism and efficiency. The British government wanted the fruits of trade without the cost of territorial administration. Thus, a combination of factors which induced Britain to conquer militarily 150 million Indians in the eighteenth century did not exist in Africa. This forestalled colonization until new conditions in the world capitalist system at the end of the nineteenth century compelled Britain and France to abandon the ideals of capitalism for outright annexation of almost all West Africa.

The different economic relations between each of the two regions and Europe produced different local educational histories. But in both, educational policy was made by European countries in the interest of European capitalists, traders, and missionaries.

Schools in Africa were intended to convert Africans from barbarians into civilized humans, to prepare them to fill the role of agricultural producers instead of slavers in the European-run world economic system. This was a European decision—Africans could only accept it or not. Ultimately, even the choice of accepting European values and norms was taken away from them. In somewhat different ways, both the British and the French viewed their education of Africans as fulfilling the goals of transforming Africans into certain social roles.

India, on the other hand, did not have the destruction of centuries of slaving; her cultures were intact when the British conquered her. Religions were strong in India and conversion difficult. The primary purpose of schooling was *control*, not change. Britain did not want India to become an independent capitalist country. British manufacturers wanted the Indian trade (Indian primary goods exchanged for British manufactures) but not Indian competition. Preparing a skilled labor force was unnecessary and undesirable from the British manufacturers' point of view. The British first concentrated on winning over the cooperation of already well established and well-defined elites. Missionaries were excluded because they offended the religious beliefs of these elites.[2] Once the British were well established, however, they began developing an English-speaking, Europeanized elite who could serve as middlemen between the British high administration and important elements of Indian society. Although changes were made in education over the next century, this policy remained the backbone of British education in India.

Missionaries were allowed to teach again in India in the 1830s where they paralleled closely the work of missions in Africa. But in India, elite training was so much more important than in Africa that primary school was seen early by Indians as a means to get to secondary education and university, which in turn was the key to administrative positions in the government bureaucracy. Fees charged in primary schools were relatively high, since primary schooling was left to private enterprise (including the missionaries), so lower castes and poor artisans could not afford to send their sons to school.

Quite the opposite happened in Africa. In the early years of the missions, families were often bribed to send their children to school. The children of domestic slaves and the poorest villagers were the first pupils in most missions. Tribes who had contact with the Europeans were among the weaker tribes, and they got more schooling than more powerful inland groups who were able to resist the European incursion.

Once Britain and France conquered West Africa, they pursued policies similar to British policy in India. More stress was put on elite formation and preparing lower-level administrators to fill British and French colonial bureaucracies. Even so, primary education played a relatively more important role in Africa than in India.

The European powers used education to effect change, but only those changes that solidified their influence and control over the peoples of India and Africa. Although the policy was not altogether successful, it did manage to bring these areas into conditions of economic and cultural dependency which few of them have overcome with political autonomy.

Many have stressed the contribution that education made to the Europeanization of Africans and Asians and have argued that Europeanization enabled these backward nations to enter the modern world. But out of context this line of reasoning is beside the point. European education in India and Africa was designed to fit *some* of the people in these areas into roles defined for them by Europeans, and the individuals who took schooling generally profited from assuming these roles—both in status and income. But the *intended* function of education was to help Europeans transform the local economic and social structure in ways which strengthened *European* commercial and political control over the region. Education was used to develop regions to meet European needs. The pattern of modernization evolved in this *dependent* context, and benefited few Indians and Africans.

Education in Colonial India, 1700–1930

British educational policies in India were designed to control politically the Indian subcontinent and to keep its people economically dependent on Britain. In the early days of British rule, when conditions could turn against the conquerors at any time and the purpose of occupation was mercantile, educational policy centered on the pacification of native elites: the Orientalist phase gave native elites their native colleges under British control. When capitalists began to gain control of the British government at home and to change the role of India in its relation to the metropole, the educational system changed as well: for Indians to become consumers of British goods and to become more capitalistic required a reconstructed educational system based on British values and norms. The Anglicist policy was implemented in India: Indians were to be taught in English. There was resistance to this policy at first because of deep-seated traditions. But the British created a demand for English-language education by hiring English-trained Indians to serve as low-level bureaucrats in the colonial government. Once this new social structure was imposed, secondary and higher education expanded gradually and then rapidly. At the same time, however, primary schooling was neglected. To reach the "masses," education in the vernacular was used in primary school; nevertheless, funds were limited and relatively few children went to primary school.

The case of India illustrates clearly how changes in the educational system of a colonized country were made to suit the perceived needs of the colonizer. English rule did eventually break up the traditional structure and replace it with a European-oriented hierarchy. So there may have been some value in India's "Westernization." But the cost to her of British policies was apparently enormous. The British had to force a cultural transformation on part of the Indian population to develop loyalty to Britain and to serve as intermediaries to uneducated and unassimilated Indians. A top-heavy bureaucracy and educational system was created to carry out this project. Cottage industry was destroyed without incorporating artisans with their skills into the new structure. For the British, "development" in India meant controlling Indian resources for British use, and education was structured to achieve that goal.

The Economic Context of British Conquest and Colonialism

Indian society in the sixteenth century was headed by the Muslim absolute monarchy of the Mogul Empire. The most famous Mogul ruler was Akbar (1556–1605) followed by Jahangir (1605–27), Shah Jahan (1627–58), and Aurangzeb (1658–1707). The monarchy was followed in turn by Hindu persecution, warfare, chaos, and decline. The basis of the Mogul rule was a strict bureaucratically centralized system that did its best to inhibit the growth of a trading class and of independent centers of economic power. Peasant agriculture produced a large surplus that was appropriated directly by the state through the military apparatus, local revenue officials (Zamindari) and (in some areas) cooperative Hindu chiefs.[3] The nobles and tax gatherers had no stable and independent sources of revenue or property rights of any sort. Their entire income came either through cash payments from the royal treasury or by being assigned a certain percentage of the royal share of produce in a particular geographic area. They held their privileges at the uncertain whim of the state, and could be (literally) removed at any time. Worse still, they were absolutely forbidden to pass on their wealth through inheritance, and when they died, all they had accumulated went right back into the royal treasury.[4]

Under such circumstances, with all the wealth concentrated in the center and the officials denied any long-term responsibility for the productivity of the land, economic parasitism became rampant. Officials and nobles squandered all the money they would lose at death on conspicuous consumption (gambling and sport). The emperor also indulged in building useless but expensive monuments (Taj Mahal), but more importantly, the main part of the surplus (especially by the time of Aurangzeb) was eaten away through costly wars of conquest in an effort to try and extend the base of taxation by adding new lands.

As a result of this attitude, the officials were constantly squeezing the peasants out of ever higher amounts of produce, to the point of the devastation of the land or the flight of the peasant himself. By the seventeenth century this intolerable exploitation led to massive and bitter revolts, tempered only by the conservatism of the caste system.[5] Pressure from the Zamindar forced the peasants to resist and seek protection from the local chieftains, anxious to encourage a breakdown of central authority. The net result of the peasant revolts was just such a breakdown, and the West European trading companies (by the eighteenth century) were operating in somewhat of a political vacuum.

Economically, the time of Akbar was one of expanding market relations and commodity production. The textile industry was the best in the world; silk, spices, and indigo were prominent export items. Technology even to the point of metallurgy was developing. Artisans in the towns produced many items for luxury consumption. But the government did not look with favor on these activities, imposing restrictions on the trader to render ineffective any attempts to accumulate wealth and power. No contracts were enforced; besides, on the trader's death the whole concern's property was seized.[6]

The crucial obstacle, however, was one that even the emperor was powerless to overcome: a lack of seapower. India's peculiar land-base forced it to rely almost exclusively on sea trade, and yet the lack of invasion in the early centuries had led to a neglect of shipbuilding. Thus, the emperor had to rely on foreigners for transport, as they were powerful enough to pirate any ships he might set sail himself. Initially, the Portuguese monopolized this sphere, earning huge profits from the European trade while leaving the emperor with but a small portion of the revenue. The British had to fight their way through this monopoly, using competitive bargaining techniques as a means to win concessions from the emperor. During a war in 1687 an enraged Aurangzeb tried to expel them and cease all trade, but in the end he had to call them back and deal as "they were supreme at sea and . . . the loss of his custom revenue was serious." [7] By 1700 the British East India Company had its own military base and trading center at Fort William, which became known as the port city of Calcutta. Fifty-seven years later, the company's army had defeated both the French

Company (Battle of Plassey) and the Nawab of Bengal's legions to become undisputed ruler of Bengal.

The *initial* impetus for conquest in India did not come from manufacturers, but from the old-line aristocracy and from mercantile policies. Pursuit of monopoly profits through plundering India's goods and selling them in Europe was the original design of such policies. The trader would march or float into a village, steal what he could from artisan or peasant, and even force them to buy from him unneeded products at outrageous prices. The traders had the British flag behind them, and even organized their own police forces for the purpose. A collector in Dacca, 1762, describes the process:

> In the first place, a number of merchants have made interest with the people of the factory, hoist English colours on their boats, and carry away their goods under the pretence of their being English property. Secondly, the Gomastahs of luckypoor and Dacca factories oblige the merchants [Indian] etc. to take tobacco, cotton, iron and sundry other things, at a price exceeding that of the bazaar, and then extort the money from them by force; besides which they take diet money from the peons, and make them pay a fine for breaking their agreement. By these proceedings the Aurngs and other places are ruined.[8]

Bengal, once the most prosperous province, soon became the most impoverished. The tax-assessing methods of the British were even more brutal and overbearing than what preceded, and the peasant was left with nothing to replenish his family or the land. Between 1765 and 1770 the company took out ten times what it put in.[9] In 1770 a bad harvest caused one of the most massive famines in world history, and one-third of the Bengali people (about 10 million) died. Despite this, the drain of resources flowing from India to the coffers of aristocarts and adventurers in Britain continued. After the famine the governor of Calcutta, Warren Hastings, wrote to the East India Company's directors (November 3, 1772):

> Notwithstanding the loss of at least one-third of the inhabitants of the province, and the consequent decrease of the cultivation, the net collections of the year 1771 exceeded even those of 1768. . . . It was

naturally to be expected that the diminution of the revenue should have kept an equal pace with other consequences of so great a calamity. That it did not was owing to its being violently kept up to its former standard.[10]

The drain was enormous, and some have even argued that the Indian surplus, coming at the time it did, helped fuel the beginnings of the industrial revolution in England, through the expansion in shipping and infrastructure and the richer home market. But ultimately the power of the East India Company became an obstacle to industrialization.[11] The rising Lancashire capitalists did not want goods imported from India as luxury items for the profit of aristocratic traders; they wanted to be able to sell *their* finished products in India and get Indian raw materials. The native Indian industry had to be destroyed (which it was) and the monopoly powers of the company as well. This battle took place in the beginning of the nineteenth century, and the industrialists eventually won. India became a free-trade area for British export. The East India Company was transformed from a commercial body to an administrative one; it became (under parliamentary supervision) *the* Government of India. The growth of official state-aided education arose from the changes that took place in this period.

In order to destroy the Indian textile industry the British Parliament had to impose a 70 to 80 percent duty on all cloth imported from India; at the same time the East India Company allowed Lancashire goods to come pouring into India with (at most) 3 percent charges.

It was stated in evidence (in 1813) that the cotton and silk goods of India up to this period could be sold for a profit in the British market, at a price from 50 to 60 percent lower than those fabricated in England. It consequently became necessary to protect the latter by duties of 70 and 80 percent on their value, or by positive prohibition. Had this not been the case, had not such prohibitory duties and decrees existed, the mills of Paisley and Manchester would have been stopped in their outset and could scarcely have been again set in motion, even by the powers of steam. They were created by the sacrifice of Indian manufacture. Had India been independent, she would have retaliated;

would have imposed preventive duties on British goods, and would thus have preserved her own productive industry from annihilation. This act of self-defence was not permitted her; she was at the mercy of a stranger. British goods were forced upon her without paying any duty; and the foreign manufacturer employed the arm of political injustice to keep down and ultimately strangle a competitor with whom he could not have contended on equal terms.[12]

This is the basic imperialist relationship that developed. From an exporting country India became an importing one; from a budding manufacturing potential she retreated into a pure agricultural nation, cities depopulated, peasants falling back on small plots with low productivity, barely above starvation. The surplus from all this was utilized to build "liberal" Britain. By 1850 the Indian market took up one-fourth of Britain's entire foreign cotton trade: the cotton industry employed one-eighth of England's population and contributed one-twelfth of the national revenue.[13]

Early Efforts at Western Education

In the first stages of British involvement, prior to their accession to power, missionary work was actively encouraged. At this stage the East India Company was facing heavy competition from the Portuguese, Dutch, and French, all of whom had relatively more privileged positions as sea traders with the Mogul ruler. The British were trying to win concessions from the Mogul as a "fair-minded" alternative to Portuguese shipping and were just beginning to feel their way into the country. Under the military protection of the company, missionaries could get to know a geographic area more intimately and provide essential information about the social structure, culture, economic production, and trading habits of the people. They helped to legitimate foreign presence among the natives (demonstrating the superiority of Christianity). They were able to establish some point of contact with the land other than that of the Court, a procedure necessary in building a firm base. Missionaries were the first people to try to learn the vernacular languages and to try to communicate directly with the people. They had the first printing presses, and set about translating the Bible and other books into the native tongues, attempting to introduce a Western perspective and religion to accompany their commercial counterpart. Much of the missionaries' work was done in the cities—instructing and serving the English community, getting to know the native Hindu and Moslem elites, and exchanging the printed and spoken word. In addition, they made direct attempts to convert natives to Christianity by working in the villages.[14] They would set up a house of worship and perhaps a hospital or school to try to relate to the poor, impoverished, and socially degraded lower castes (out-castes or depressed classes) who had the least to lose from putting on a coat and tie, reading the Bible, and accepting the tight discipline and self-denial of Protestantism in the hopes of improving their condition. The missionaries were very much concerned with social reforms, with eliminating the customs and habits that formed the basis of the caste system, and thus with "civilizing" India.

Aside from laying the basis for future efforts at Western education, the primary importance of missionary work in this period (and indeed throughout the history of British imperialism) was to *legitimate* the drive for expansion *within* the home country (Britain itself). Committing resources, manpower, and energy to seizing new lands and building huge trading operations overseas was not possible without the ideology of the "white man's burden," and it is missionaries and their reformist zeal most of all that confirmed this ideology.[15]

The missionaries were the only Europeans at this time who were setting up schools directly for Indian children, using their native languages and also teaching them English "to 'facilitate dealings.'" Up to 1770 the company was doing all it could to give protection to the missionaries and to assist them financially (help build and repair schools, provide personnel, etc.) and in other ways to advance their educational endeavors.

However, once the rule of the East India Company had been established on a more firm footing—once it had become a *political power*—Warren Hastings and the other leaders began to take a much more hostile attitude toward the work of the missionaries in English education, Christian proselytization, and social modernization. The company was attempting to win cooperation from the native Moslem and Hindu elites in establishing its legal and governmental powers, and the missionaries' attacks on these religions and their customs offended these elites and made them fearful that foreign presence would cause them to lose standing and privilege within their own communities. Srinivas describes the effects of missionaries on the Hindu (Brahmin) elite:

> For their part the missionary publications drew attention to the defects of Hinduism, the evils of the caste system, etc., and pointed out the truth of the Christian religion and the superiority of Western learning and science. Active missionary propaganda had now been in Northern India for over a quarter of a century, and Lord Minto had noticed in 1807 that its effect was not to convert but to alienate the followers of both Hinduism and Islam . . . resentment was roused by invective launched against the revered order of Brahmins. . . . Similarly, converts to Christianity from Hinduism did not exercise much influence in Indian society as a whole because, first, these also generally came from the *low castes,* and second, the act of conversion alienated them from the majority community of Hindus.[16]

The East India Company decided to ban missionary education entirely, and did everything possible to keep missionaries out of its territory in Bengal. Instead it introduced the policy of Orientalism, a policy designed to strengthen and pacify the traditional Indian elites.

It was under this political opposition that the famed Serampore Trio had to operate. Dr. Carey of the Baptist Missionary Society in England arrived in Calcutta in 1793 hoping to preach but was driven out. He then began working in North Bengal (Malda) as a superintendent of an indigo factory, and in his spare time translating the Bible into Bengali, holding religious services for the servants on the estate, setting up a school, and so forth. In 1799 two others, Marshman and Ward, arrived in Calcutta to join him. When the government ordered them to leave, they persuaded Carey to go with them to the Dutch settlement of Serampore—fifteen miles from Calcutta—where they would be under the jurisdiction and protection of the Dutch government. (Many missionaries took refuge at Dutch settlements.) At Serampore, Carey, Marshman, and Ward set up a printing press, and between 1800 and 1810—together with colleagues in various parts of India—they translated extracts from the Bible into thirty-one different native dialects, and printed tracts and pamphlets in twenty languages, and even schoolbooks for children and for colleges.[17] Later, they established their own college for boys, and in 1818 founded the first daily English-language paper, *Friend of India,* which was very influential. (It provided moral justifications for government policy and was widely quoted in the vernacular press.)

During the early days there was much conflict with the East India Company. In 1808, for example, a pamphlet of theirs was prohibited in company territory because it was a religious tract which offended Moslems and Hindus. In fact, the company tried to have them removed from Serampore, but to no avail. But it was more than Christianity that was in dispute. English or Western education itself was under attack by the authorities. There was plenty of opposition from native chieftains to the British rule: wars were fought, and even within the company native-soldier ranks there was a mutiny. The British were afraid of revolt, as Marshman, in his 1852 testimony before Parliament, records:

> For a considerable time after the British Government had been established in India, there was great opposition to any system of instruction for the Natives. The feelings of the public authorities in this country were first tested upon the subject in the year 1792, when Mr. Wilberforce proposed to add two clauses to the Charter Act of that year, for sending out school masters to India; this encountered the greatest opposition in the Court of Directors, and it was found necessary to withdraw the clauses. . . . On that occasion one of the Directors stated that we had just lost America from our folly, in having allowed the establishment of schools and colleges, and that it would not do for us to repeat the same act of folly in regard to India; and that if the Natives required anything in the way of education, they must come to England for it. For 20 years after that period, down to the year 1813, the same feeling of opposition to the education of Natives continued to prevail among the ruling authorities.[18]

In this period the British were not attempting to make any major economic transformations in the countryside, in the development of markets, or in new forms of production. Rather, using trade and military power they had seized control of a new territory but had not yet established a firm basis for their rule, not even to the extent of securing minimal cooperation from the landowners, privileged classes, and religious leaders. Neither did they have any means of communication with the people through language or tradition or law. Thus, English education and Western reform seemed an unnecessarily energetic and antagonistic undertaking. Ultimately, education was what the colonialists would like, but for the time being they were content to be cautious and distant in their approach, falling back on their superior armies as a last resort.

The (British) Government of Bombay, which was established in the early part of the nineteenth century, faced the same conflicts as did the Bengal rulers in the first days of their rule. This caution of the British approach was very well characterized by a statement of a member of the Bombay government in 1838, J. Farish:

> We are here in India, in a very extraordinary position—a small band of aliens totally unconnected by colour, religion, feelings, manners, or any one single tie—have established their despotic rule over a vast people, whose affections must be with their Native Princes, and all whose prejudices are arrayed against their conquerors. This supremacy can only be maintained by arms, or by opinion. The Natives of India must be kept down by a sense of our power, or they must willingly submit from a conviction that we are more wise, more just, more humane, and more anxious to improve their condition than any other rulers they could have. If well directed, the progress of Education would undoubtedly increase our moral hold over India, but, by leading the Natives to a consciousness of their own strength, it will as surely weaken our physical means of keeping them in subjection.[19]

A second view of this same phenomenon is the following:

> . . . [I]n order to understand their attitude, we must realize that their only object was trade, and that it was purely for the safeguarding of

their trade that they had interfered with the politics of the land. . . . They had won their territory by means of an Indian army composed mainly of high-caste Hindus, who were exceedingly strict in keeping all the rules of caste and religious practice. . . . In consequence, the government believed it necessary, for the stability of their position, not merely to recognize the religions of India but to support and patronize them as fully as the Native Rulers had done, and to protect their soldiers from any attempt to make them Christians. . . . They were convinced that rebellion, civil war, and universal unrest would certainly accompany every attempt to promote missionary enterprise, and, above all, that the conversion of a high-caste native soldier would inevitably mean the disbanding of the army and the overthrow of British rule in India.[20]

Orientalism: The Initial Phase

The purpose of the Orientalist policy, which strengthened and pacified traditional elites in British controlled areas of India, was to perpetuate British political power at a time when it was still weak. Education was provided for native elites in their own language and largely under their control.

In 1772 Warren Hastings took over as governor of Bengal and endeavored to make it a full-fledged government. Two years later he was made the first governor general of the East India Company's entire dominion in India. His first act in his new capacity was to establish a Supreme Court in Calcutta and to begin to codify Indian law for British administrative use. In accord with solidifying British rule, he saw that British power had to be based on Indian compliance. He began enlisting traditional Brahmin and Moslem scholars to codify and translate laws based on the most extreme religious separatism and orthodoxy (thus to a certain extent setting back the secularization and liberalization that had been taking place under Akbar and for the previous three hundred years). The Hindus got the Gentoo Code in 1776. Later came a separate Mohammedan code. In 1781 the Act of Settlement proclaimed the legitimacy of the two codes in all family and religious matters (inheritance, succession, contract) as enforced by

Hastings (a provision which meant that there were always many "exceptions"). Hastings actively encouraged Brahminism as a means of breaking Mogul power (although he later courted Moslems), and Brahminism even spread into areas which had been previously casteless.[21] The Gentoo Code endorsed polygamy, widow-burning (*sati*), and child marriage, banned widow remarriage and divorce, and generally upheld all of the most reactionary customs. Not only were missionaries banned from the territory, but native Christians were actively discriminated against: for example, they were not allowed in the army, a source of good pay and status. The Brahmins and Zamindars became landlords, an act which simultaneously reinforced hierarchical stability and created a base of support for British imperialism that lasted right up to the mid-twentieth century.

In 1780 Hastings founded the Calcutta Madrassah with his own private capital in order "to conciliate the Mahommedans of Calcutta . . . to qualify the sons of Mahommedan gentlemen for responsible and lucrative offices in the State, and to produce competent officers for Courts of Justice." [22] He was incurring hostility from the Moslem community, and this was one way of conciliating them. In fact, the effect was very favorable and the college got such a wide response that he immediately had to expand the institution and ask the Court of Directors for funding. This was granted (by assigning land revenue annually) and so it became the first state-supported school in India.[23]

Soon to follow was the Benares Sanskrit College in 1791, also with an annual financial grant and a European director. Jonathan Duncan, the founder, explained its purpose:

> Two important advantages seemed derivable from such an establishment, the first to the British name and nation in its tendency towards endearing our government to the Native Hindus; by our exceeding in our attention towards them and their systems, the care shown even by their own native princes. . . . The second principal advantage that may be derived from this institution will be felt in its effect upon the natives . . . by preserving and disseminating a knowledge of the Hindu law, and providing a nursery of future doctors and expounders thereof, to assist European judges in the due, regular and uniform administration of its genuine letter and spirit to the body of the people.[24]

Once again Bombay followed in the footsteps of its sister, Bengal. The British first conquered Bombay in 1818, and Mountstuart Elphinstone's first act was to adopt the Orientalist policy in education (he later also encouraged the vernacularist policy). He translated the law into a Hindu code and won the assistance of the educated classes in its enforcement through dispensing economic privilege and by training their sons to work in the government bureaucracy. Later, the government could take more positive steps in the direction of the law and in shaping the sons' education, but the first task was to establish solid political control. (Once the Indian resistance was totally crushed, the Orientalist policy was doomed to wither away.) Elphinstone founded a Hindu college at the city of Poona in the Bombay Presidency in 1820. Its first commissioner was William Chaplin, installed on November 24, 1820;

> The immediate motive with which the College was founded was more a political than an educational one—namely, to conciliate the learned Brahmin class who had suffered severely by the change of government on the overthrow of the Peshwa by the British in 1818. . . . To ensure its popularity with the Hindu community, stated Mr. Chaplin, he had provided for instruction in the college in "almost all their branches of learning," though he considered many of them worse than useless. The college in its inception was intended to be a purely Sanskrit one, and no measures were taken to introduce any sort of European learning. "I have however endeavoured," said Mr. Chaplin, "to direct the attention of the college principally to such parts of their own Shasters, as are not only most useful in themselves, but will best prepare their minds for the gradual reception of more valuable instruction at a future time. *When we have once secured their confidence, but not till then,* will be the time to attempt the cautious and judicious introduction of those improvements in the education of our Hindoo subjects, by which alone, joined with good Government, we can hope to ameliorate their moral condition." [25] (Italics added.)

Toward Anglicism

But the missionaries were not quite as patient as Mr. Chaplin, and neither was the new generation of townsmen in England, growing up in the industrial revolution and full of the reforming spirit. The industrialists wanted to smash the East India Company's trade monopoly and open up India as a market for selling goods; the British Protestant nation (or at least those small sectors of it that were concerned with these distant problems at all) wanted to see India educated and morally cleansed from its own religious decadence and from the company's corruption as its "just" reward for British rule. Together the industrialists and the Protestants initiated far-reaching changes in India policy.

In 1784 Pitt passed in the House of Commons an India Act which purported to regulate the East India Company's activities. (He was forced to pass the India Act under threat of more radical bills.) A year later Warren Hastings resigned as governor-general, and three years after that he was impeached and put on trial for corruption and scandal. It was these political stirrings within England and hostility to the company's regime which afforded the missionaries the protection they needed and gave a general spur to educational activities. In 1800 the Marquis Wellesley founded the Fort William College in Calcutta, despite bitter protests from the Court of Directors who attempted to halt its operations but were finally overruled by Pitt himself. This school was merely for the training of European youth and company officials in Indian languages, history, and law. Wilberforce's attempt to introduce an education clause into the charter in 1792 was mentioned earlier, but despite that failure, he kept on struggling. This religious leader of the "Clapham sect" finally succeeded in 1813, when the new Charter Act directed the East India Company to set aside a minimum of one lakh of rupees annually for Indian education. Also, missionaries were to be allowed free movement and activity throughout the territories. The charter abolished the company's trading monopoly and gave British industrialists free access to Indian markets. The provision to set aside the lakh of rupees is noted in every history of Indian education as heralding a major advance in educational policy, but *none* of the money was spent on any education until 1820.[26]

Yet the entrance of the colonial government into native education was the culmination of a long struggle: Charles Grant had written as early as 1792 that education should be used to improve native morals.

Grant, a Scotsman and member of the "Clapham sect," who later became a company director (1797–1818), member of Parliament (1802–18), and founder of the Church Missionary Society in 1799, argued strongly for education in *the English language,* thus foreshadowing Macaulay by forty-three years. He wanted English to be the language of administration, courts, and revenue and the basis for the teaching of European culture and science and the Christian religion. He wanted printing presses, and he wanted free schools to be set up throughout the Presidencies to teach reading and writing, using native Hindu instructors trained in the English language.

Grant understood both sides of imperialism (the cultural and the economic) very clearly:

> To introduce the language of the conquerors, seems to be an obvious means of assimilating a conquered people to them. The Mahomedans from the beginning of their power employed the Persian language in the affairs of government, and in the public departments. This practice aided them in maintaining their superiority, and enabled them, instead of depending blindly on native agents, to look into the conduct and details of public business as well as to keep intelligible registers of the income and expenditure of the State. Natives readily learnt the language of Government, finding that it was necessary in every concern of Revenue and Justice; they next became teachers of it; and in all the provinces over which the Mogul Empire extended, it is still understood and taught by numbers of Hindoos. *It would have been in our interest to have followed their example.*[27] (Italics added.)

> In every progressive step of this work, we shall also serve the original design with which we visited India, that design still so important to this country—the extension of our commerce. Why is it that so few of our manufactures and commodities are vended there? Not merely because the taste of the people is not generally formed to the use of them, but because they have not the means of purchasing them. The proposed improvements would introduce both. As it is, our woolens, our manufactures in iron, copper, and steel; our clocks, watches and toys of different kinds; our glass-ware, and various other articles are admired there, and would sell in great quantities if the people were rich enough to buy them. . . . How greatly will our country be thus aided

in rising still superior to all her difficulties; and how stable, as well as unrivalled, may we hope her commerce will be. . . . This is the noblest species of conquest, and wherever, we may venture to say, our principles and language are introduced, our commerce will follow.[28]

Grant's pamphlet projected the basic logic of subsequent events quite well, although, as with all political manifestos, it was too ambitious. Expenditures on education were to remain very small up to the twentieth century. By 1847, there were less than 10,000 students enrolled in government-sponsored English-speaking schools: in 1845 there were 2,186 students in the Northwest provinces; 7,036 in all (36) institutions of Bengal Assam and Orissa; 8,138 in Bombay; and 156 in Madras. Not all of these were English-speaking. There were also 92 English schools run by missionaries with 13,000 students.[29]

Important educational changes occurred in the early nineteenth century, as the English felt their way toward absolute political power. In order to get schools established and accepted at all, the Orientalist policy continued in a modified form after 1813. The Anglo-Indian Vidyala College was founded in Calcutta in 1816, followed by a Sanskrit College (for translations of literature and law) in 1823, and a college at Agra studying Arabic, Persian, Sanskrit and Hindu in 1823 (about 100 students). But the British soon took over these colleges. The government took control of Vidyala in 1824 by paying rent and appointing a European Professor brought from London to teach mechanics, hydrostatics, pneumatics, optics, electricity, astronomy and chemistry. The Sanskrit College got an English class in 1827, and Bentinck even ruled that they must have a course in human anatomy at the Medical College and dissect cadavers. This constituted a violation of Hindu religious custom and was the object of great controversy among the students. Agra College also got an English class in 1827.

In Bombay, the story is similar. Elphinstone's early years in power were on very precarious footing and as a result he wisely took a very active role in promoting vernacular education. He helped pioneer the Bombay Native Education Society, a private group of native leaders who cooperated with Elphinstone in setting up primary and secondary schools and colleges to teach law and literature, translate books, and hopefully introduce some Western concepts in the vernacular. Besides Poona, Elphinstone set up an Engineering Institute in Bombay. There European boys were trained to be surveyors and natives were trained in mechanical arts and lower sciences to help European engineers supervise public works. Natives were taught in the vernacular at the Engineering Institute with translation work done by its director, Lieutenant George Jervis.

But by the time Macaulay was causing a stir in Calcutta, the pressure was on for changes in the Bombay Presidency as well. Sir John Malcolm, who took over from Elphinstone in 1829, pushed very hard for English education, both as part of the ideology of the successful dominance of imperial rule and (in his case) more importantly as a source of civil servants for the government. There weren't enough Europeans to go around, especially outside the major cities, and the cost of importing them plus the huge salaries and special privileges they commanded were an enormous drain on the budget.[30] It seemed much simpler and politically wiser to create a class of cheaply paid but loyal Indian *low-level* bureaucrats to help staff the provincial offices and act as a buffer or intermediary class to stand between the government and the masses. Malcolm's successor, Lord Clare, set up an English college in Boodwar Palace (Poona) in 1833 and called it Elphinstone College (63 students). In addition Lord Clare abolished the Engineering Institute in 1832 as a waste of money,[31] and in 1843 all that was left of it was one professor at Poona. The Native Medical School of the 1820s was also abolished in 1832, and a decision made to teach in English. And, finally, the Poona Sanskrit College was abolished as a vernacular institution and some of its curriculum was merged into the English school (Elphinstone) in 1851.

By the 1820s, the policy of cultural conquest was already bearing fruit in the person of Raja Rammahon Roy. Nurullah and Naik describe him as "The Father of Modern India." [32] Roy, a beef-eating Brahmin, was the first leader of a movement of Hindu religious reformers (Brahmo Samaj) who accepted British rule as a good thing and the British as an ally in an attempt to reform the Hindu traditions in a more secular and Western direction. He fought for Western schools,[33] for the abolishment of customs like widow-burning, for property rights for women, and for the use of English in the law courts. Roy originally started out as a civil servant and revenue officer for the East India Company and spoke English fluently. He died in 1833, and one gets the sense that had he lived longer he would have been knighted by Queen Victoria.

In 1832 the first Reform Bill was passed in Parliament and the middle classes with their laissez faire capitalism had seized political power. A year later, when the Charter of the East India Company came up for renewal, its trading powers were abolished and it was constituted as a purely administrative body (the government of India). Provision was made in the charter that natives by religion, birthplace, descent, or color could not be barred from holding offices in the company. The stage was set for hiring Indians to work (cheaply) and become loyal to British administrators on a governmental level. For this, English education was required, and Macaulay came to India in 1834 to push for it.[34] Macaulay's Minute stated:

> In India, English is the language spoken by the ruling class. It is spoken by the higher class of natives at the seats of Government. It is likely to become the language of commerce throughout the seas of the East. It is the language of two great European communities which are rising, the one in the South of Africa, the other in Australasia; communities which are every year becoming more important and more closely connected with our Indian Empire. . . . We must do our best to form a class who may be interpreters between us and the millions whom we govern . . . a class of persons, Indian in blood and colour, but English in tastes, in opinions, in morals, and in intellect.[35]

This is the key: more than the need to have a cheaper, more extensive, and more efficient (English law) administration, more than the desire to have a greater body of consumers through economic development, the primary purpose was to build a cultural dependency among the educated and ruling classes so that revolutionary overthrow would never be a likely alternative. As Sir Charles Trevelyan, Macaulay's brother-in-law, wrote in his book *On the Education of The People of India* (1838),

No effort of policy can prevent the nations from ultimately regaining their independence. English education will achieve by gradual reform what any other method will do by revolution. The nations will not rise against us because we shall stoop to raise them. . . . We shall exchange profitable subjects for still more profitable allies . . . and establish a strict commercial union between the first manufacturing and the first producing country in the world.[36]

What is crucial here is the *form* that the education took for the elite. The British did not try to instill in the natives a deep grasp of the fundamental principles of economics, technology, science, and politics; rather they were content to force their pupils to ape and recite English literature, philosophy, and metaphysics in the most slavish imitative fashion. The purpose of this kind of training was for them to get some sense of vocabulary as used in law and administration. More importantly it instilled in them a respect and awe for the aristocratic virtues of the majestic English language and culture, and a corresponding contempt and disdain for their own background. Even today it is very difficult for educated Indians to break this pattern. They feel much closer bonds with British professors than with Hindu peasants, to whom they are unable even to speak. The students, for example, would read an Oxford text and do a recitation on some fine point of historical debate concerning King Alfred and the Norman Conquest. Of their own background they learned nothing, and by the time they were educated, they knew English as a first language, unable even to translate it into vernacular sentences or vice versa.

As Governor-General Lord Hardinge wrote to Queen Victoria in 1844:

The literature of the West is the most favourite study among the Hindoos in their schools and colleges. They will discuss with accuracy the most important events in British history. Boys of 15 years of age, black in colour, will recite the most favourite passages from Shakespeare, ably quoting the notes of the English and German commentators.[37]

Historian H. N. Brailsford also takes this view:

In short, the Brahman intellectual and the classical scholar of the I.C.S., bred in Public School, were equally indifferent to science and technology. The result was that Indians rushed into the legal profession and neglected the studies and careers which might have ended Indian poverty by the development of scientific agriculture and modern industry. This land was cursed with an unemployed proletariat of intellectuals.[38]

There was a split in policy directions over the Macaulay issue between Bengal and Bombay. There also was much discussion over Macaulay's celebrated "downward filtration theory." The "theory" was simply an elaborate rationalization for the fact that at this stage education involved very little in the way of financial expenditures and was confined almost exclusively to the instruction of a tiny elite group of future civil servants. Macaulay therefore argued that rather than the government taking direct responsibility for the education of the mass of the people, if it did a good enough job imparting Western values and concepts to this Indian elite, then *they* would in turn share their knowledge with their own people and somehow eventually it would all "filter down." K. C. Vyas, in the following quote mistakes the stated goals for the actual goals, but otherwise accurately describes the final outcome:

> The theory of "filtering down" was an evident example of wishful thinking on the part of the Government. After intense English education, the educated were practically cut off from their surroundings. For all practical purposes, in manners, clothes, language and tastes they became English-minded and developed a dislike for those who, unlike themselves, had not taken to an English education. *Obviously, such persons would never return to the illiterate masses.*[39] (Italics added.)

On November 23, 1844, Lord Hardinge informed Queen Victoria:

> In order to reward native talent and render it practically useful to the state, Sir Henry Hardinge, after due deliberation, has issued a Resolution, by which the most meritorious students will be appointed to fill the public offices which fall vacant throughout Bengal.

It is impossible throughout Your Majesty's immense Empire to employ the number of highly paid European civil servants which the Public Service requires. This deficiency is the great evil of British administration. By dispensing annually a proportion of well-educated natives, throughout the provinces, under British superintendence, well-founded hopes are entertained, that prejudices may gradually disappear, the public service be improved and attachment to British institutions increased.[40]

The key to the whole Anglicist policy was contained in Hardinge's memo. The growth of English education had been very slow, and there was no clear way to impose it on the population. Hardinge found the way. He made them want it, because it was the only way that they could get any sort of a job with the government. These were lucrative jobs by Indian standards. The net result was that almost the whole system of education, particularly in Bengal, became geared toward training for government service.[41] As there were not enough jobs to go around, many of these educated Indians became mere clerks ("Babus"), unable to use their literary and legal skills for any business, industrial, or scientific pursuits. This kind of bias still exists in the Indian educational system today, which is probably the main reason why India has such a huge state bureaucracy and patronage system and why there are so many Indian students attending foreign universities. Government schools provided a veneer of English and a good job that certainly helped "increase their attachment to British institutions." H. Woodrow, a school inspector in East Bengal, complains in an 1856 report that students in governmental schools value education

solely as a means of getting money. People have gradually forced themselves to acknowledge the English school as a necessity; not that they have at present any value for our learning, but they consider the acquisition of our language as necessary for the advancement of their children in this life." [42]

Vernacular Education

If "downward filtration" achieved its purpose in coopting the elite, Vyas was still correct in pointing out its absurdity. At some point the government had to assume responsibility for the education of the entire population, both for political and economic reasons. Economically, the changes came during the 1850s and '60s, when England was coming to rely much more heavily on India as a source of cotton and other essential raw materials due to the losses in trade caused by America's Civil War. This was a period when the colonial government was beginning to feel its substantial power and to make major reforms in the countryside: to try to break down the caste system, to establish a labor market, and to increase trade; to conquer and annex new land and expand agricultural productivity and tax revenues; to build railways, telegraphs, organize a postal system and generally carve out an infrastructure that would help unify the country's communications and trade and strengthen Britain's military and political power. Vernacular education came very slowly; much was undertaken under formal guidelines such as the Wood Despatch, but some (as with all previous policies) was undertaken informally, and the impetus for it came primarily from the newly settled provinces (Bombay and the Northwest) which were concerned with expanding the production of raw cotton for export to Britain. They attempted to construct much more efficient systems of land settlement and taxation than the Bengali Permanent Settlement and its parasitic Zamindari. They had to deal directly with the peasantry (Ryotwari), and (at least in the Northwest) used this as an opportunity to build up an indigenous system of education which would teach the peasants accounting and farming techniques and (hopefully) win more political support from the colonial government at the same time.[43]

In 1853, when the East India Company's Charter was up for renewal, a select committee of the House of Commons held a thorough inquiry into educational developments in India. The result of that inquiry, called the Wood Education Despatch, formed the theoretical basis for British educational policy in India over the next seventy years. In summary, the Despatch declared that

> . . . our object is to extend European knowledge throughout all
> classes of the people. We have shown that this object must be effected
> by means of the English language in the higher branches of instruction,

and by that of the vernacular languages of India to the great mass of the people. . . .

The higher classes will now be gradually called upon to depend upon themselves; and your attention has been more especially directed to the education of the middle and lower classes, both by establishment of fitting schools for this purpose and by means of a careful encouragement of the native schools which exist, and have existed from time immemorial, in every village.[44]

The inquiry created an education department in each province of British India, but the Wood Despatch and all that happened subsequently did nothing to alter qualitatively the Anglicist policy. Teacher-training colleges were established and it introduced the system of grant-in-aid. It also gave an impetus to secondary education and to some extent, primary schooling. But the plans of mass education visualized by the Despatch were not realized, nor were the high schools imparting education through native languages for more than seven decades afterwards. Higher education was taken more seriously and expanded, although the three universities established in 1857 at Calcutta, Bombay, and Madras were simply aggregations under British administrative control of *already existing* colleges and schools. The purpose of the reform was to *rationalize* the system of selecting educated youth for civil service appointments, not to change it. The universities simply standardized and made more selective the examination procedures, so that the number and types of labor available could be more centrally controlled. It was only during the time of Lord Curzon that the universities (then five) became actual teaching institutions. In 1857, also, a policy was formulated for mass education. Mass education had to be carried out in the spoken native languages. English would be impossible to administer in terms of time, books, and personnel available.

Thus, a two-tiered approach evolved: English for the elite, vernacular for the masses. Lord Falkland of Bombay as early as 1849 (five years before the Wood Despatch) laid out the essential four points of this policy:

a. Provision for superior education through the medium of English strictly limited, however, to the education of the wealthy who can afford to pay for it, the highly intelligent among the native youth who can establish their claims to admission into the English schools by a standard of acquirements, and the class of young men who are trained up as masters of the vernacular schools (the upper 10,000).

b. The production through the same medium of a superior class of district school masters and the providing for them of an adequate scale of salaries.

c. The education of the people under these masters in vernacular schools.

d. The systematic encouragement of translations into the vernacular from works of science and general literature.[45]

The provinces that were conquered by the British after Bengal tended to place more emphasis on vernacular education and primary education. Aside from being much more unsure of their position than Bengal, they were also making direct land settlements (tax assessing the peasants directly). Thus, by 1852, Bombay had 233 vernacular schools with over 11,000 pupils and 14 government colleges and English schools with 2,000 pupils. Bengal, on the other hand, had 30 colleges with 5,000 pupils but only 33 primary schools.[46] Elphinstone himself had been in favor of elementary education:

. . . the dangers to which we are exposed from the sensitive character of the religion of the Natives, and the slippery foundations of our Government, owing to the total separation between us and our objects, require the adoption of some measures to counteract them, and the only one is to remove their prejudices, and to communicate our own principles and opinions by the diffusion of a rational education.[47]

Similarly, James Thomason had developed a system of indigenous primary education in the Northwest (Agra Province) based on the existing village schools. He did this in the process of arranging revenue collection, and was even able to appear as the people's friend by getting them to agree to pay a portion of their tax directly for education, which he then levied as a grant-in-aid. The schools were organized in geographic bunches (Circles, or *Halkabandi*) with one traveling teacher-overseer among them. It should be noted that this scheme was set up *after* a scheme for higher and English education had failed to win the support of the people,[48] so there must have been great hostility.[49] Bombay, it seems, was also able to set up a direct tax (*cess*) for education. In Bengal, because of the Permanent Settlement and the fact that Indians already had established their own education system, the colonial government had a much harder time getting the people to pay for primary education.[50] It seems that the mode of agricultural production and what was produced—like cotton and other export crops—brought different responses to vernacular primary education in the various provinces.

Table 1

India: Enrollment by Level of Education, 1881–82 to 1936–37 (thousands)

Years	Primary[a]	Secondary	College/ University
1881–82	2,061,541	214,077	—
1901–2	3,076,671	590,129	23,009
1911–12	4,806,736	—	—
1921–22	6,109,000	1,106,803	66,258
1936–37	10,224,288	2,287,872	126,228

[a] Includes recognized primary schools only.
Source: Syed Nurullah and J. P. Naik, *A History of Education in India* (London: Macmillan, 1951).

Very little was actually done in mass education. In 1881–82 there were about 2 million pupils in primary schools incorporated into the departmental system in British India (see table 1). This represented about 7 percent of the school-age population (taking school-age population as 15 percent of the total population). About 14 percent of male children were in primary school, and less than one percent of female children. By 1921–22, the number of children in primary school had increased to 6 million, which represented about 17 percent of the school-age population. So, seventy years after the Wood Despatch, only one in six Indian children was in primary school (learning in the vernacular) in British-administered India. Although most native-Indian-administered states had very few children in school, two states, Travencore and Baroda, had almost 60 percent of school-age children in primary school by the 1920s.[51] These two were governed by "progressive" rulers who put a great deal of emphasis on education, more than the British. Total government expenditures on education in British India in 1921–22 were 13.2 rupees per pupil (about $4 *per pupil*). Since only one-sixth of school-age children were in school, this meant an expenditure of about 67¢ *per school-age child.*[52] Educational expenditures did climb from 6 percent of military expenditures in 1882 to about 9 percent in 1920.[53] The result of this policy was an almost stable literacy rate of the population between 1835–38 and 1931:[54]

	1835–38	1911	1921	1931
Percent of adult literates	4.4	4.4	5.2	6.0
Percent literates > 5 years old	5.8	5.3	6.3	7.0

The British government simply did not like to spend money on Indians.

> In these days of centralization, the sanction of the Government of Bengal was necessary for all new items of expenditure. Consequently, when the Government of Bombay put up proposals for the expansion of primary education, they were generally not sanctioned by the Government of Bengal on the grounds of heaviness of their cost and sometimes even advised the Government of Bombay to concentrate on English education because it was less costly to the government.[55]

A key provision of the Wood Despatch was that grants-in-aid would be given only to primary schools which charged a monthly fee to all their students,[56] and that the local community had to help pay part of the costs of the school. This was in part a reflection of capitalist ideology (British influence) that the state should not take the whole responsibility for education. It was believed that education should be left largely to private enterprise, and, conveniently, with such a policy the British government did not have to spend very much on education. As a result, only the more affluent were able to organize and pay for their children's schooling. By adopting grants-in-aid the government also bypassed thousands of indigenous informal village schools already in existence, most of which disappeared in subsequent years. By 1902, almost no village schools were left in British India. Instead, the British insisted on training their own teachers and having the schools be strict about class schedules and charging fees. The government tended to deemphasize the Halkabandi system of roving instruction in favor of using certified teachers from normal schools.

The school system was therefore organized to keep a tight *control* over whatever education existed. This once again confirms the political goals of British educational policies as practiced in India. The old social, economic, and educational system was broken down, and a very tightly controlled and not very extensive new system was put in to replace it. Education was developed to provide Indian subadministrators and clerks for the British government service—thus, the higher secondary and university system developed after 1854. Indians trained as subadministrators were thoroughly anglicized by the curriculum and selection process of the higher levels of schooling. At the same time, a primary school system was installed which was limited in the number of children it reached and was controlled to prevent an independent base of power and ideas to develop. Because of the fees charged, only families from higher-income brackets could afford to send their children to school. As late as the 1920s and '30s, few girls went to school at all.

In 1857, concurrent with the educational reform, and in the last year of rule of the East India Company, an attempt was made to reform the tariff structure through higher import duties and elimination of export duties. But the Indian Mutiny of that year raised revenue requirements, and under the newly imposed direct rule of the Crown, proposals were made to raise import duties without eliminating export duties. This reform was met with stiff resistance from both British manufacturers and British merchants in India, and they succeeded in reducing import duties and abolishing export duties. Yet, revenue needs continued to press administrators, and by 1871, they had reestablished higher tariffs on both exports and imports.

The main objection to raising tariffs was based on the competition of Indian manufactures with British imports. Even the slightest sign of manufacturing in India created pressure by British producers on the House of Commons.

> There is this difficulty that the interests of India and of England on that point [import duty on cotton piece goods] seem rather at variance. No doubt some considerable increase of revenue might be realized by increasing the import duties, say upon piece goods and yarns, but the direct result of that would be too diminish consumption and to stimulate production on the spot.[57]

> I say they are protective duties [5 percent on cotton piece goods]. I do not advocate their abolition solely for that reason. I do not know whether you are aware that, for instance, in the Bombay Presidency there are 12 cotton mills, employing . . . 319,394 spindles, 4,199 looms, and 8,170 hands, consuming, I think, 62,000 bales of cotton of 400 lbs. each annually.[58]

The struggle between British administrators in India—joined later by manufacturers in India—and British manufacturers and merchants went on until the 1920s. Until World War I, the Lancashire manufacturers won this battle, keeping tariffs low. In 1896, for example, when a duty of 3.5 percent was placed on cotton textile for revenue purposes, the government laid an equivalent excise tax on all cotton textiles manufactured in Indian mills. This remained in force until 1925.[59] The low tariffs imposed on India not only stifled manufacturing but reduced the revenue available for public works, including education. An increased part of the revenue had to be raised from land taxes.

Nevertheless, there was limited industrial growth between 1871 and the 1920s. From the 12 cotton and textile mills employing 8,200 workers in 1871, the number grew to 94 mills in the Bombay Presidency and 137 in all India, employing 110,000 workers in 1890. Another 60,000 worked in jute mills principally in Bengal, and 30,000 more in coal mines. Total factory workers increased from 317,000 in 1892 to 1.4 million in 1922 and stayed almost constant until 1931.[60] Even so, this represented less than one percent of the labor force in 1922. In 1890 there were more workers on tea plantations than in all factories combined.[61]

There seems to be little relation between this industrial expansion and the expansion of primary schooling, except that at the beginning of the twentieth century the lack of primary schooling among factory workers was identified as a major problem of low labor productivity.[62] Apparently, factory workers came from the lowest castes in the villages—largely landless untouchables:

> In 1916, in a large mill in the Central Provinces, 51 percent of the hands were *Mahars* alone. At other times this figure had been higher. This caste, along with the *Holis* and the *Dheds,* make up the principal "untouchable" group in Bombay Presidency and the Central Provinces. . . . At Sholapur, Ahmedabad and Bombay, it is always the lowest section of the village community that is shaken off to try its fortunes in the factory.[63]

The literacy of factory workers was therefore much lower than even the low literacy rate among the Indian population as a whole. Among the *Mahar, Holis,* and *Dheds* in the Bombay Presidency, for example, the literacy rate in 1921 was 1.5 percent (as compared to 6.3 percent in the population as a whole).[64]

Limited industrial growth plus small-holding plantation agriculture combined to limit the demand for primary-school-trained labor. The percentage of Indians living in urban areas remained almost constant between 1872 (8.5) and 1921 (10.2). The factory system did not get large enough to attract Indians outside the lowest castes into working in industry. Since British policy was one of limiting the growth of industries, duties, and therefore public revenue, were kept low. Since the British also had a policy of limiting the expansion of primary education, most of these revenues were spent on the military (to keep internal stability), and within the small education sector, on higher levels of schooling.

Consequently, the opportunities for educated Indians were almost entirely as bureaucrats in the colonial government. This is the sector that the British wanted to expand. Thus, at the same time that primary schools were limited in accessibility, secondary schools, largely private and primarily preparatory to college education, were expanding rapidly, doubling the number of pupils every twenty years. Once the taste for English education had been developed as a result of the anglicist policy, the demand for secondary education increased rapidly. As secondary education grew, the demand for university training grew also, and the number of universities increased. Both at the secondary and university levels, English was used almost exclusively as the language of instruction. For those who reached these levels, the separation from Indian culture and people was almost complete.[65] In 1919, when it was proposed that the Department of Education be transferred to the control of Indian ministers, a great controversy arose over the control of secondary and higher education. The government of India felt that

> . . . there is a compelling case for the transfer of primary education. . . . We may say that in our minds there is an equally compelling case for retaining secondary and university education in the hands of the official and more experienced half of the Provincial Governments. India stands today in a critical position; and her immediate future, apart from her slower political growth, depends on the solution of social, economic, and industrial problems to which a good system of secondary education is the chief key.[66]

All but a few colleges and the education of Anglo-Indians and Europeans were turned over. However, the resistance to giving Indians control of secondary and higher education shows again that the British considered these levels far more important to their colonization policy than the disregarded primary schools.

Education and the Colonization
of West Africa

The Slave Trade

For more than three hundred years, West Africa's relationship with mercantile Europe was the slave trade. From the time of Portuguese coastal exploration in 1441, slaves were a principal commodity of European traders. At first they were taken in small numbers to Portugal and to the islands of the African coast such as Saõ Tome and Fernando Po, but with the beginnings of mining and plantation agriculture in the Caribbean, slaves were taken to America. At first, the settlers enslaved native Indians, who were numerous on many of the islands, but they died of diseases, were massacred, or ran away. On the mainland of North America, Indians refused to work on the plantations and fought against the English and Spanish settlers. When it was discovered that slaves could be imported from Africa to work in the mines and plantation agriculture, the trickle of human trade reached enormous numbers in the seventeenth and eighteenth centuries. Although the Portuguese had a virtual monopoly on this trade until the end of the sixteenth century, they were eventually challenged by other nations. The French, Dutch, and, finally, the English became the dominant slave traders. In 1712, with the Treaty of Utrecht, the British secured a thirty-year monopoly of the slave trade, so that the eighteenth century saw Britain become by far the most important slave-trading nation.[67]

The European slave trade transformed West African society. Slavery existed in Africa before the European became involved with it, but from all available evidence, *it was of a completely different nature than the slavery of the Americas.* First, a slave in Africa was usually a household servant; he or she was a *member* of the household. Second, the rights of slaves were protected by tribal law and custom: "They seemed in many instances practically the ordinary privileges of any [Ashanti] free man, with whom, in these respects, his position did not seem to compare so unfavorably." [68] The European demand for slaves changed all this, even in West Africa itself. This difference in the role of slaves in African and European society and the subsequent effect of the slave trade is a key to understanding European-African relations in the colonial period. The European impact on African society through the slave trade was tremendous. In order to provide the large number of slaves demanded by the coastal traders, tribe raided tribe to get slaves. People captured in these raids were not protected by laws and customs; they were merely goods that had to be taken to the coast, there to be picked up by European vessels going to America, or handed over to middlemen who in turn traded them to the Europeans. The primary goods traded to Africans in return for slaves were rum, guns, powder, and cloth. This was the basis for the triangular trade: slaves went to the Caribbean; sugar, indigo, coffee, and tobacco to Britain; and rum, guns, powder, and cloth to Africa.

The slave trade depopulated large areas of West Africa. In more than 350 years, millions of people were taken from the coast, and many times their number died either in the raids, the marches to the sea, or the voyage en route, all of which were marked by incredible cruelty and hardship. "For each slave that reached the West Indies or America, it is variously estimated that from three to five perished en route." [69] Responsible estimates of the total who were exported range from 10 million to more than 20 million.[70] This implies that from 30 million to 100 million—primarily young men and women—left West Africa or were killed between 1450 and 1850.

The European trade, exchanging simple manufactures for human beings, also stunted the growth of metal casting, agriculture, and leather and cloth fabrication, all of which were well established in the sixteenth century.[71] The trade of the Sudan, to the north of the coastal region, turned from the trans-Sahara trade to the slave trade on the coast. The new European goods and the presence of Europeans, however, did not generate more production; rather, European goods were consumed in place of local products while the productive domestic labor force was greatly reduced. Those tribes that were successful because of the slave trade consumed much of their output in rum and firearms. Firearms were the new basis of power in West Africa, and the means to get more slaves.

The European stock in trade, down to recent times, consisted of trinkets and rum, which did not benefit the African but rather degraded him. Speaking of a West African factory, Herbertson said, "Nothing is manufactured in these places; and they are when all is said, shops, in which cotton prints, rum, gin, powder, beads, and cheap muskets are bartered for native produce." Of the trading products Ferryman said, "The trader saw nothing wrong in flooding the country with gin; it had become the stable import." In receipt for these things the whites desired, on their part, mainly slaves.[72]

As a result of the increased warfare among African states, new centers of wealth and power emerged. Coastal peoples and people just off the coast controlled the slave trade and profited from it. They were the intermediaries between the Europeans and the interior. The Sudanese, who controlled trade to North Africa and the Western Sudan, turned from the northern trade to slaving. At various times between the seventeenth and nineteenth centuries, Benin, the Oyo, Dahomey, the Fanti, and the Ashanti were powerful African states which grew out of the slave trade. At the same time, African social structure gradually changed:

> The slave trade weakened traditional African social relationships and sapped the moral fiber of African societies. The old order was undermined and power structures were altered. Slave traders of Afro-English, Afro-Portuguese, or Afro-Brazilian origins frequently replaced the former ruling classes. Social units were redefined. More and more servile class distinctions came into existence. Slavery became the punishment for less and less serious offenses. Kidnapping and ambushes uprooted families, clans, and tribes. All along the West African coast, African daily life became precarious. Ever present was the nagging fear that one would fall victim to the slave trader.[73]

The nature of slavery also changed within Africa; some plantations, owned by mulattoes, were manned by slaves. In the interior and across the desert to the North, the slave traffic also flourished. Slaves came to be used as currency in trade and as revenue or taxes paid to rulers of African states.[74] Thus, the demand for slaves created by the Europeans turned people into the main objects of trade in West Africa (and later in Central and East Africa, as well)—into a valuable good to be traded among Africans, and eventually into a currency.

At the beginning of the nineteenth century, the slave trade by Europeans began to end. In 1802 the Danish government declared the trade illegal; in 1804, the United States prohibited further importation of slaves; in 1807, slave carrying was made illegal in British ships. The British then tried to stop the trade: they made treaties with coastal chiefs to abolish the slave trade and to promote trade in other goods; they also tried to enforce the abolition of the trade either by treaties with Spain and Portugal (who continued to carry slaves until after 1850) or by seizure and search of vessels of all nations.

The slave trade was abolished by Britain because of a number of forces, including humanitarian sentiment and the rise of the free-trade philosophy exemplified by Adam Smith's *Wealth of Nations*. But the main factor which abolished British slaving was the competition of French, and then Cuban and Brazilian sugar:[75] The British West Indies supplied too much sugar to be absorbed by English consumers alone. The sugar trade was profitable to English merchants only if sugar could be sold to the rest of Europe. At the same time, British sugar refiners obviously wanted the lowest price on sugar that could be had. The French colony of Saint Dominque could produce sugar at a cost 20 percent lower than Jamaica or Barbados. The French, however, depended on British shipping for many of her slaves and for sugar exports to Europe. With the loss of the American colonies in 1783, British planters lost the U.S. market for sugar, which went to France, and lost control over French exports to Europe.

> Denied the British West Indian market (because of British Navigation, which prohibited the shipment of British colonies' imports or exports in foreign ships), the Americans turned increasingly to the foreign islands, where the outbreak of war between England and France (in 1793) and the destruction of the French navy and marine made the United States the great carrier of French and Spanish produce.[76]

American independence had other effects on the slave trade, and, in the longer run, on mercantilism: Since the U.S. Constitution of 1789 provided that Congress could legislate an end to the slave trade in 1808 (which it did as of January 1, 1808), the trade lost one of its important markets. The free trade between Britain and the newly independent American states became much larger and more profitable than the mercantile monopoly trade with the colonies had ever been. This increased the power of the industrial capitalists in England and reduced the importance of the West Indian planters.

William Pitt, the British prime minister, wanted to recapture the European sugar market from Saint Dominique by planting sugar in India, and by abolishing the slave trade internationally.[77] This plan failed because he was unable to reduce duties on sugar that was not British West Indian, and the French, Spanish, and Portuguese refused to stop carrying slaves. Even after the British destroyed Saint Dominique in six years of warfare (1793–99), Cuban and Brazilian sugar dominated European markets. Abolition of the slave trade in 1807 and attempted enforcement by the British Navy—including treaties with African tribes—was the only recourse left to save the increasingly less important West Indian colonies. The plan did not work, and led to an even worse situation for the British planters.

The abolition of slave trade in British ships therefore did not end the slave trade (although it was intended to), nor did it abolish slavery in English colonies. Despite the act of 1807 and British pressure on other countries, foreign slaving, primarily to Cuba and Brazil, rose to its greatest volume ever in the 1830s.[78] Slavery was abolished in British colonies only in 1833, when the increased power of the capitalists found the West Indian monopoly on sugar trade intolerable to their commercial interests, much as they had found the East India Company inconsistent with their needs in the India trade twenty years earlier and in the China trade one year later. Abolition of West Indian slavery was the first step in the destruction of West Indian monopoly. The capitalists ignored the same slavery in Cuba, Brazil, and the United States.

Europe in West Africa

Throughout their relationship, West African societies and economies were subservient to European social and economic needs. Part of
this domination came from the sheer size of European demand for any
product relative to African economies. Slavery, for example, existed in
Africa when the Portuguese arrived, but it was limited to domestic
servants and covered by societal laws. Labor-intensive sugar production
in the Caribbean demanded so many slaves that European trade
overwhelmed West African and later, all African society. When
British sugar plantations ceased to be competitive, British traders
turned to other goods, such as palm oil, and the French, to ground
nuts.[79] Again, the production of these goods was the dominant
economic activity wherever the European trader went.

The abolishment of the slave trade by Europeans, good as its
intentions may or may not have been, was not just a change in goods
traded, but a change in the concept of man as well.[80] European
missionaries came with the trader to spread a philosophy and moral
code which derived from European historical development. They
attempted to transport to Africa the ideal of the individualistic,
capital-accumulating small farmer who raised goods demanded in
European markets. Africa was to be saved from Europe (the slave
trade) by becoming part of the European economy and European
culture (just as the African as a slave had been part of that economy).
Whenever Africans resisted, missionaries and traders found it reasonable and imperative to crush this resistance with arms. In this they
consistently received the help—and in the case of the French, even the
leadership—of European military power.

Apparently, according to Robinson et al. and Foster,[81] the British
government in this period of early capitalism was reluctant to take on
additional colonial responsibility. Its main thrust was to try to end the
slave trade without getting involved in directly administering African
territories. In the theory of free-trade capitalism, the benefits of trade
could be obtained without direct colonization. But the theory of free
trade was one thing and its practical application was another:
Europeans established a clear presence on the coast from which traders

and missionaries consciously spread European *values* as well as goods. When necessary, both British and French relied on their military power to enforce the right of these traders and missionaries to operate.

> . . . British humanitarians were powerful enough to conscript their government into the anti-slaving crusade, and the politicians built a network of colonial footholds along the coast, Sierra Leone in 1808, the Gambia in 1816, the Gold Coast in 1821. They were intended as bases from which legitimate commerce and civilization would drive out the slave traffic.[82]

In a very narrow definition of imperialism, then, the British and French did not intend to build an empire in Africa. The British thought they could *convert* Africans to Christian, free-trade capitalism, and get them to accept the gains of integrating into the British system. They did not have a conscious policy of *occupying* and *administering* African territories. Strong antiimperialist forces existed in both England and France. Africa was not occupied until the 1880s.

But occupation is not the only form of imperialism. The British and French felt it was their right to impose and protect their commercial interests in Africa (and elsewhere). The early Victorians protected free trade; their successors operated from the fear that Britain's power was waning and that they had to preserve what they held. Early and later Victorians were willing to enforce trade if the trade was profitable for Britain or if it was necessary to support British capitalism. When the palm-oil trade on the Niger warranted it, British gunboats threatened tribes who tried to prevent Europeans from carrying it out. To protect the Gold Coast trade, the Ashanti were militarily defeated in the 1870s. Trade protection produced the Lagos colony in 1861 and Cape Coast in 1874. Competition with French and German economic power led to the annexation of all British West Africa by 1904.

That one people *must* trade and interact with another is imperialistic. Trade and interaction, contrary to Victorian and modern interpretations of nineteenth-century European "civilization," was not beneficial to Africans:

> The debauchery of the early trader had an effect on West Africa which several generations of British administration will not entirely remove.

. . . For this condition the trading whites are chiefly to blame. "The wealth and importance of various villages," wrote Joseph Thomson in 1886, "are measured by the size of the pyramids of empty gin bottles which they possess." [83]

However, "free trade" relations with Africa lasted a relatively short time. Britain abolished the slave trade in 1807; France, in 1815. Britain occupied Lagos and Cape Coast about fifty or sixty years later. France, faced by Muslims around Senegal, did not convert Africans to European culture through missionaries. French penetration into the interior was much more direct. It began with Louis Faidherbe, governor of Senegal from 1854–61 and again in 1863–65.[84] He was apparently inspired by a vision of French influence extending into the rich lands of the middle Niger. By the end of the 1870s, France was engaged in a full-scale military invasion of the Western Sudan, which culminated in total French occupation by the 1890s.[85]

The Suez crisis of 1882 and British policy on the Nile and East Africa was closely connected with the protection of her Indian interests. West Africa had little to do with this security, but trader and missionary pressure promoted the Franco-Anglo-German imperial struggles in West Africa.[86]

Even though the styles of conquest by the French and British differed, and the influence on and administration of African territories bore the stamp of differences in French and British culture, the results for the African were very much the same: he was subject to European power and commercial incursion and control. His life began to depend on the price of goods in Europe rather than their demand and supply among Africans. Under the British, commercial treaties determined who owned African land; under the French, it was military treaties. In both cases, African control over land was lost.

Along with European military and commercial power came the destruction of important African values, norms, and traditional hierarchies, and their replacement by European social stratification systems.[87] For many tribes, acting as middlemen between Europeans and interior tribes gave them power and wealth inaccessible before the European came. Coastal tribes such as the Fanti drew their status from association with the European trader. As Foster points out, however, European stratification and African social hierarchies were completely incompatible. Since European trade dominated economic activity whenever it interacted with Africans, European social structure gradually replaced the tribal hierarchy. Economic wealth depended increasingly on an African's integration into the European structure, so those best integrated wielded increasing political power among Africans.

But the relationship between Europeans and Africans was not simply one culture and economy peacefully interacting with another. Many Western writers [88] give the impression that European and African cultures encountered each other like two immigrant groups living in adjoining neighborhoods of the same city. While in some coastal settlements this model was accurate for a time, the adoption of European values and norms was *forced* on most Africans. Before the period of major conquest and colonization (1880–1900), few Africans who had not been taken as slaves had *direct* contact with Europeans. Interior tribes fought to resist European incursion.[89] Most Africans were eventually made to interact with Europeans through European institutions. The pattern of colonizer-colonized relations described by Memmi followed quite naturally under these circumstances. Africans who were least like the Europeans were defined as least civilized and human. Their resistance was paid with defeat and punishment. Survival in the colony meant learning to deal with the European or the Europeanized African on his terms.

The Role of European Education in the Colonization of Africa

European education came to Africa with the church and conversion, but it did not reach Africans on more than an occasional basis until the abolition of the slave trade. In the nineteenth century, widely held beliefs about the French *mission civilisatrice* in Africa notwithstanding,[90] the French efforts in providing schooling for Africans were minimal. The Catholic Orders in Senegal did not undertake, as did other missionary groups in Sierra Leone, to train African agents for the conversion of Africans in the interior. French missions in Senegal faced the hostility of Moslems and the appeal of their traditional Koranic schools. In Saint Louis, Goree, and, later, Dakar, the French government gradually provided primary education for the *habitants'* children and some local Africans, but progress was slow.[91] By 1910, there were only about 15,000 children in French schools in all of French West Africa. This represented less than 2 percent of the school-age population.[92]

Thus, in the nineteenth century, British-aided missionary work dominated Western education in West Africa. (Missionaries operated primarily in Sierra Leone, Gold Coast, and Nigeria.) Early schools existed in the Gold Coast European settlements in the eighteenth and even seventeenth centuries, but their pupils were probably recruited largely from castle mulattoes.[93]

> Unlike Sierra Leone, the Gold Coast never contained any proportion of transplanted slaves, and school enrollment consisted largely of the offspring of European garrisons and the local population. These recruits were supplemented by the children of some of the wealthier African traders in the urban centres, but there is no indication that the schools were successful in obtaining pupils from any wider segment of African society or that local chiefs were particularly interested in sending children to school.[94]

The function of schools during the slave-trading period was therefore not to train ordinary Africans, but to provide education—primarily religious—to children of those mulattoes and traders connected with the European forts. Even though conversion of the heathen was church policy in the eighteenth century, there was relatively little effort to do this in Africa on the part of missionary societies until much later. Part of the failure of early missionary attempts was lack of interest by Africans, but missionaries also came few and far between. Although the Spanish church saw in slavery the opportunity to convert Africans, British planters opposed Christianity in their slaves. Missionaries did not provide schools for slaves anywhere in the colonies, and many West Indian churchmen kept their own slaves until slavery was abolished.[95] Under these circumstances, the slave trade and missionary activity in Africa were not compatible, and schools in British spheres of influence were limited to teaching some freed slaves (Sierra Leone, after 1787),[96] or to dealing with mulattoes and non-Africans. The African functioned as plantation or domestic labor in European economies. As long as they were necessary only as slaves, they needed no education, religious or otherwise. On the other hand, those relatively few Africans who as slave traders had contact with Europeans had little demand for learning the European ways, since their livelihood was based on traditional trading skills.[97]

After the slave trade in British ships was abolished and Britain had a policy to interrupt the trade entirely, the role of the missionaries changed. The abolition of the trade gave the missionaries and traders an important impetus to stimulate trade in other products, such as palm oil, cocoa, and ground nuts, to "civilize" the "savage" (make him into a producer of "legitimate" trade goods), and to end the human trade continuing in the interior. The missionary societies that gained strength at the end of the eighteenth century took the abolitionist cause to Africa.

The abolitionists had a particular view of the civilizing mission: in order to stop the slave trade which had been brought to Africa by the Europeans and to convert Africans into palm-oil and cocoa producers, Europeans had to bring the advantages of "legitimate" trade to Africans. The English trader, on the one hand, had to be induced to come to Africa, and the African had to be induced to cultivate. The missionary would serve as the agent of civilization, teaching the African the moral codes of Christianity, which forbade slavery, and showing him the advantages of agriculture. From the beginning of their efforts in Africa, then, the missionary societies were dependent on the trader and the capitalist for success, since their objective of halting the slave trade depended on the development of a new trade that would replace slaving. Also, transforming African society was as important to the missionary as converting Africans to Christianity.

An attempt was made to implement this view in Sierra Leone in the 1790s using freed slaves brought from England and the American colonies. The agricultural part of the program was not very successful, but the mission schools did appeal to freed slaves who had been exposed to European society. These educated freedmen later played an important role in the colonization of Nigeria.

Despite the difficulties faced in implementing the civilizing mission in Sierra Leone, this same model continued to serve the missionary societies throughout the century. Most missionary groups discovered that the demand for their services was contingent on economic incentives to learn European ways. Therefore, the demand for education by Africans was a demand for learning English (to take better advantage of trading opportunities) and, later, for European academic education which could be translated into higher status and jobs in the European dominated urban social structure.[98]

A corollary of this demand was that missionaries would not begin their work until a European presence was already established. After Freetown, which was a town *created* by Europeans using Europeanized ex-slaves, the mission societies came to Gold Coast. In 1824, the British and their Fanti allies were crushed in the fourth Ashanti war. By 1829, the government decided to withdraw from the coastal settlements. Foster claims that the "[British government] was only prevented from so doing by the opposition of the London merchants. A compromise was reached by which effective control of the coastal forts was to remain in the hands of a committee of merchants." [99] Robinson et al. cite another source of opposition: "But the British government had to go on dragging these burdens [the colonies] because public opinion would not give up these symbols of the fight against the slave trade." [100] In any case, the political agent of the company, Captain George MacLean, illegally extended British jurisdiction over the Fanti tribes inland, far beyond the limits of the forts. He reopened the trade routes to the interior, but to keep peace with the Ashanti, agreed to keep European merchants from trading directly in the interior. MacLean's successes were the basis of a renewed government involvement. In 1843, the Crown again took control of the forts and continued to exercise jurisdiction among the tribes on the coast. "Although these groups were in no sense British subjects, the voluntary acceptance of such jurisdiction marked the real beginning of

British hegemony and control; the way was now open for direct British intervention in the internal affairs of the native states." [101]

Missionaries did not arrive in Gold Coast until well after MacLean had reestablished British control. The first Basel missionaries arrived there in 1828, and the Wesleyan Methodists followed in 1835. The two groups interpreted the abolitionist ideal very differently. The Wesleyans located their schools in the Fanti coastal towns, and like the government schools, taught in English. "They were able to take advantage of an already growing urban demand, a demand that was closely associated with the occupational structure of the towns and where . . . the vocational implications of formal education were already apparent." [102] In 1841, after many of its missionaries had died in Accra, the Basel mission went some miles inland to locate where the climate was healthier than in Accra itself. The missionaries taught in the vernacular and concentrated on boarding institutions to pull individual pupils away from the traditional milieu. Bribes had to be used to attract children into their schools.[103] The Basel mission attempted to follow strictly the civilizing model: the missionaries moved inland to teach vocations and to give the African an alternative to the slave trade. The Wesleyans in Gold Coast served Africans who were already "civilized"—those who were willing to go to school because they understood the advantages of a European education and were already tied to British jurisdiction. Although both missions attempted to proselytize among the Ashanti, they were not successful. In general, the schools recruited from nonelite groups. Tribal chiefs sometimes embraced Christianity, but even among the Fanti, educated Africans formed a "new" elite parallel to the old.[104]

With the end of the slave trade, Liverpool merchants began to trade in palm oil, and slowly it replaced slave trading among the Africans in the Niger delta. The delta became a model for the free-trade capitalism of the early nineteenth century. In order to keep the slave trade from continuing, British gunboats were stationed along the Guinea coast. The slave trade continued anyway, but British influence and power was everywhere evident with the presence of the navy.

Legally, the authority of the British government might be restricted to the formal colonies, but in fact its power was supreme along vast

stretches of the coast whenever it suited British interests. . . . This
official activity was important. The palm oil ruffians disliked state
intervention on the coast; but in fact their trade often relied on official
support. The influence of cruisers and the consuls helped to spread free
trade and quell strife.[105]

By the 1830s other groups of English merchants, particularly those
from London, were taking increased interest in finding routes to the
interior trade. They supported explorations to the interior, especially to
find the outlet of the Niger to the sea. The Lander brothers discovered
the mouth of the Niger in the Oil rivers in 1830. The Landers had no
sooner published the report of their findings than a Liverpool
merchant, MacGregor Laird, equipped an expedition to go up the
Niger to the supposed riches of the north.[106] The inland trade also
attracted the abolitionists. T. F. Buxton, a leader of the antislavery
movement, took up the merchants' argument that the Niger waterway
would enable Britain to bring civilization to the interior of Africa. He
combined the abolitionists' experiences in Sierra Leone with the
attraction of Africa as a trading partner for Britain to develop a
comprehensive rationale for intervening directly in African affairs to
stop the slave trade.[107]

Buxton argued that Britain's efforts to enforce the abolition of the
slave trade by diplomacy with the Spanish and Portuguese and naval
patrols off the Guinea coast had failed. The number of slaves shipped
to the Americas (Cuba and Brazil) had increased between 1807 and
1839. The only effective remedy was to attack the slave trade at its
source. To achieve this, Buxton outlined a four-point plan:

1. The British government should supplement the naval squadron
patrolling the coast.
2. The government should undertake expeditions into the interior
through the large rivers to make treaties with chiefs and to show
British merchants the opportunities for investment.
3. Industrialists and merchants should invest in Africa to develop a
new trade that would replace the slave trade. The new trade must be
carefully organized to stimulate agriculture and to civilize. The new
trade must be free. It must produce both a free peasantry and a new
commercial and industrial class.

4. Because of the climate, the government and merchants should rely on Africans from Sierra Leone and the Americas as their agents.

These Africans, protected by Britain, guided by the missionaries, and working with capital from European merchants, would not—like European merchants—stay shyly away from the people, in hulks along the coast, but move inland and man factories at every strategic point. . . . They would be commercial agents to encourage the cultivation of crops like cotton and indigo, which they would buy for the European market in return for European manufactures. They would teach new arts and new ideas and in every way bring down the old society on which the slave trade was based and set up in its place a new social order.[108]

The government adopted the plan and outfitted an expedition up the Niger in 1841. Although the expedition failed, largely because of the high deathrate among the Europeans, Buxton's ideas were taken up by the missionary societies. The naval squadron was reinforced, and wide publicity was given in Sierra Leone to resettlement efforts for Nigerian-born freedmen. Treaties were signed with some chiefs to halt the slave trade. After the Niger expedition, and after merchants and navy had been operating along the coast and in the Niger delta for some time, the first English-speaking missionaries began to arrive in Southern Nigeria. Thomas Birch Freeman and Henry Townsend arrived at Badagry in 1842 and the Church of Scotland Mission under Reverend Hope Waddell was started at Calabar in 1846.[109]

It is difficult to say how much individual missionaries were affected by Buxton's plan, but the pattern of their work in Nigeria followed it almost literally. Hundreds of Sierra Leone and later Brazilian and West Indian liberated slaves resettled in Nigeria in the 1840s and 1850s. These communities of Europeanized Africans formed the major constituency for the missionaries in the inland areas. Abeokuta was such a community and was also the main center of missionary activity off the coast. Although the African "émigrés" did not fulfill the role that Buxton had envisaged for them, they did provide the entrée for the missionaries who followed them. Neither did the émigrés settle along the Niger. Rather, they returned to their Yoruba country, and this is where the first missionary work began. But Samuel Crowther, a liberated slave and the first enrolled in Freetown's Fourah Bay College (West Africa's first postprimary institution, 1827), eventually did set up a trading company and a string of missions along the Niger in the 1850s along the lines of the Buxton plan.[110]

W. B. Baikie's 1854 expedition up the Niger established that, with the help of newly discovered quinine, the white man could live on the Niger. It also opened the country to trade and made it clear that the interior could be reached by way of the Niger. Crowther's Niger missions were particularly important because they, along with the West Africa Company he helped form (1863) kept the British involved commercially in Nigeria during a period when there was pressure from the House of Commons to withdraw from all the West Coast except Sierra Leone.[111]

> Since Crowther regarded it as vital to the success of the Niger Mission that the company should succeed, he placed the resources of the mission at their disposal. Although the company's depots were usually physically separate from the mission stations and the management of their affairs entirely independent of the mission . . . the company and the mission realized that the growth of one depended on the growth of the other.[112]

Missionary work in Africa and the schools connected with the missions were therefore born of a civilizing purpose, a purpose that not only involved religious conversion but the acceptance of new economic and social organizations. The origin of these organizations was, of course, European, primarily British. The missions tried to stop a European-induced slave trade by replacing it with agricultural products. The agricultural products to be produced by Africans were to serve European needs, just as the slave trade had served European needs. It must be understood that Buxton and his contemporaries in the antislavery societies, layman and missionary alike, regarded the civilizing mission in imperialistic terms, even though they believed that the mission could be accomplished without force.[113] The idealism of early capitalism is very much present in Buxton's and other writings of the period: if production and trade are shown to be *profitable,* people will change their life style and even become like the European in order to take advantage of the high economic returns. There was enough realism in capitalist ideology (many Africans did adopt European ways) to maintain the free-enterprise civilizing mission until 1861 in Lagos, 1874 in Gold Coast, and until the 1880s and 1890s in other parts of Nigeria.

Neither Buxton nor his fellow abolitionists considered boycotting Cuban and Brazilian sugar as part of the plan to halt slave trading in Africa. British capitalists argued that Brazilian sugar was necessary to keep British capitalism going, and the abolitionists took the side of the capitalists. So, on the one hand, abolitionists were fighting the West Indian planters to end slavery in the West Indies—which they accomplished in 1833—but on the other, they supported imports of Brazilian slave produced sugar to keep British refiners in business and maintain British trading interests in Brazil.

> Buxton took a curious position. If it could be shown that the foreign sugar to be imported would be consumed at home, instead of being exported, he would vote no (against importation). But it required one-third more labor to refine sugar in Brazil and then import it into Britain in a refined state. In permitting, therefore, foreign sugar to be refined in Britain, they were substituting British machinery at home for slave labor abroad, and consequently to that extent diminishing slave labor and discouraging the slave trade. Parliament was astonished. Well might it be.[114]

Buxton's remedy to the slave trade was therefore one that appealed to British capitalists on double grounds: it did not interfere more than nominally with their sugar imports from Brazil and Cuba—prices of slaves may have risen slightly as a result of increased British interference after 1840 with Portuguese and Spanish slavers—and it had possibilities of opening up new lines of trade with Africa. From the standpoint of stopping the slave trade, however, the plan could have only minor influence compared to a boycott of sugar imports from slave plantations.

In the period between the abolition of the slave trade and the direct administration by European centers of African areas, the missionaries and their schools played an ambiguous role. They had come to Africa primarily to convert and civilize the heathen and to stop the slave trade in the interior. Even though missionaries generally found traders vulgar and noncontributing to the welfare of the African, the fate of the missionary was inexorably intertwined with that of the trader, both in theory (the "remedy" to the slave trade) and in practice. Africans linked missionaries to other Europeans, including traders and officials, and missionaries—even Africans such as Crowther—identified with other Europeans rather than with Africans. If Europeans were not welcome in an area, African hostility was applied to missionaries and traders alike. The Ashanti did not permit traders inland; neither did they allow missionaries to set up schools.[115] In 1861, when the British made Lagos a colony, the Egba reacted by destroying everything *European* in their region and forcing both missionaries and traders to leave. Christian, Europeanized Africans were not affected by the Egba uprising.

> The general effect [of the annexation of Lagos] was to create the fear of impending annexation in the states around Lagos, fear and suspicion and hostility towards all European penetration, philanthropic, mercantile or consular. Where missionaries had before been welcomed, and schools and trade asked for, the people began to draw back, pointing to Lagos, *where schools and trade led to annexation*.[116] (Italics added.)

During this period, Europeans and Africans were on somewhat equal terms. European governments were unwilling to get involved in direct military conquest. Missionaries and traders knew that the squadron would help them along the coast, but inland their fate depended on the good will of the Africans. Also, the civilizing mission in this period was based on the *voluntary* acceptance by Africans of European values and norms; missionaries tried to convince Africans to accept Christianity in the belief that the advantages of Europeanization simply had to be revealed to be understood. And although early missionaries looked down on the Africans as ignorant and superstitious, they considered them redeemable, and once educated, able to take their place among the "civilized and Christian nations." [117]

But the voluntary nature of educational expansion during the early capitalist period had its limitations. First, if a tribe did not want mission education, missionaries could not proselytize. Second, even if the chief allowed missionaries to set up a mission house in his village, unless the usefulness of European education were apparent to people in the village, there would be little demand for missionary services. In Gold Coast, for example, the Basel mission operated in areas that had less contact with Europeans than the coast, and the missionaries initially had to pay families to send their children to school. Third, the type of education demanded by Africans was different from what was intended by Buxton and the missionary societies. Foster tries to show that Africans did not *accept* vocational training.[118] Rather, they went to school to learn English so that they could deal more effectively with the European. In the towns, where jobs were available with European trading firms, a European academic education gave some Africans access to those jobs. Later, with European annexation of African territory, academic training led to administrative posts. Apparently, the missionaries were able to compromise African demand for academic schooling with the missionary ideal of the "Bible and the plough." The most important goal was to educate the African in Christian values and norms and to stop him from trading in slaves. This was achieved by academic education just as well as by vocational training. If the mission school could not attract Africans, then this primary goal would not be attained.

> . . . in general, neither mission nor government was in a position to create a demand for education directly, and the principal way by which children could be attracted to school was by providing a form of education for which a limited demand *already* existed. As we shall indicate, this existing demand was essentially for an academic education.[119]

The phyiscal limitation put on missionary activity by hostile tribes and often lack of strong government support caused missionaries to push for increased British intervention in the 1860s and '70s. In Nigeria, they meddled in the affairs of Lagos, and, in general, approved of its annexation in 1861.

> The reaction of Venn to the annexation was to regret the violent way in which it was done, but to attempt to take advantage of the increased British interest and influence at Lagos for the philanthropic desires of the mission.[120]

When in 1865 the House of Commons proposed the withdrawal from all colonies except Sierra Leone, the missionaries combined with commercial interests to prevent such a policy from being enacted. When the Ashanti threatened to wipe out British stations in Fanti territory in 1873 in an attempt to get access to the sea, the British attacked the Ashanti directly and then formed a colony on the coast under British protection. The missionaries pressed for abolition of domestic slavery in the new colony, and, in imposing European standards, destroyed a tribal institution vital to the Fanti economy. The Ashanti confederacy also fell to pieces as a result of their defeat and the formation of the colony on the coast. All this ruined the possibilities of expanding trade with the Ashanti, and committed the British to African colonization.[121]

The Yoruba and Ashanti wars in the 1860s and '70s were a turning point for missionary activity. The wars threatened the missionary enterprise. To preserve it, the missionary societies and traders—whose interests were also threatened—turned to increased government intervention, both military and civil.[122] Missionaries in Nigeria, confined to the coast by the Yoruba wars, began once more to move inland. "After being in the vanguard . . . missionaries were beginning to follow after the political officer." [123] In the next decade, competition in West Africa overtook the missionary movement and it became subordinate to British and French commercial and political needs.

Thus, the missionaries came to Africa in the first half of the century believing that they could transform the African from a slave trader into a capitalist and Christianize him in the bargain. The trader thought that he could operate without government interference to tap the riches of African soil and mines. Neither did particularly well under laissez faire, although the potential always seemed to be there. The missionaries reached very few Africans, confined largely to the coast in towns that were centers of trade, where the advantages of speaking English and having a Christian education were obvious.[124] Trade with Africa remained so small that neither Britain nor France was very interested in further involvement on behalf of the trader-missionary lobby. The African resistance to European incursion in Gold Coast and Nigeria put the survival of coastal European settlements in jeopardy and prevented the civilizing mission from moving forward. Rather than allow Africans to control their destiny, the missionaries helped push Britain into military support of the "civilization" of Africa. By the 1880s, the "scramble for Africa" had begun, both for security and commercial reasons. The laissez faire era had ended.

The new missionaries who came to Africa did not consider the Africans in the same way as those who had come forty years earlier. The missionary was no longer a "guest" in Africa, trying to convince natives to buy his product. Europeans were now conquerors and protectors, and their attitude toward Africans changed accordingly.

> From fellowmen and brothers, though not without rivalry, they were becoming part of a ruling caste. . . . The mission-educated Africans, in particular the missionaries on the Niger, were gradually discredited; European missionaries were introduced into the Niger, and, in the end, Crowther was forced to resign. The 1880s were a transitional period, a decade of conflict and bitter racial feelings.[125]

Once political annexation took place, the missionaries were subject to the will of political officers in the colony. The civilizing role took second place to the extension of commerce and the peaceful administration of the colony. Governor Lugard refused to jeopardize the success of political and commercial agents in Northern Nigeria by allowing missionaries in to propagandize against the Moslem faith. Lugard made agreements with the emirs to obey the laws of the protectorate, to aid British political representatives, to place no restrictions on traders, to impose no taxes without British consent, to assist in the construction of roads and barracks, to cede all mineral and uninhabited land rights in the Crown, all in return for military protection and no interference in religion.[126]

Table 2

Southern Nigeria:
Enrollment as a Percentage of School-age Population, by Province, 1921 and 1931

Province	1921	1931
Western Region:		
Lagos and Colony	28.4	39.5
Abeokuta	6.3	7.4
Benin	4.0	10.3
Ijebu	16.7	13.0
Ondo	4.8	7.3
Oyo	2.3	4.4
Warri	6.2	10.4
Eastern Region:		
Calabar	20.4	30.2
Ogoja	2.3	1.5
Onitsha	9.3	11.8
Owerri	5.5	13.5
British Cameroons	1.8	10.4
All Provinces	9.2	12.5

Source: David Abernethy, *Political Dilemma of Popular Education* (Stanford: Stanford University Press, 1969), p. 37.

Although missionaries were no longer in the vanguard, they continued to carry on the educational imperative in British colonies. In French colonies, except for Dahomey and Madagascar, Africans went largely to state-run schools. European curriculum itself changed little as a result of direct colonization. The British assisted an increasing percentage of mission schools in an effort to control the quality of schooling. In general, African demand for academic training became even more noticeable as the British and French political structure was imposed directly on the various regions. Getting higher status and higher-paying jobs was, as before, contingent on knowing a European language and being socialized into European culture. The schools taught these skills.

Table 3

Gold Coast:
Percentage of Population with Six Years of Education or More, in 1948

Area	Standard III or Above
All Gold Coast	4.0
(1) Colony	5.8
Accra	12.0
Akwapim–New Luaben	11.3
(2) Ashanti	3.9
Kumasi	4.7
(3) Northern Territories	0.2
(4) Larger Towns	
Accra	17.8
Kumasi	10.5
Cape Coast	24.9

Source: Philip Foster, *Education and Social Change in Ghana* (London: Routledge & Kegan Paul, 1965), p. 118.

By the 1920s—after more than a generation of direct European rule in West Africa—educated Africans almost all lived in the cities. In French areas, this was the result of centralized French administration and schooling policies: there was a polarization of power and influence, and the French brought children of elites to be schooled in the capital cities (see the discussion of assimilation below). But even in more decentralized British-administered areas, the farther from the original centers of British influence, the lower the influence of Western education (see tables 2 and 3). The overall level of enrollment was also very low before the 1930s, reaching about one-third of the school-age population in places like the Lagos area and 10 percent of the school-age population in Southern Nigeria as a whole (see table 2). In Gold Coast, the percentage was about 9 percent of the school-age

Table 4

Gold Coast:
Primary and Secondary School Enrollment,
1890–1950

Year	Enrollment[a]	Total Enrollment[c]	Approximate School-age Population of Primary (thousands)[d]	Total Enrollment as Percentage of School-age Population
1890–91	5,076(3,641)[b]	—		
1895–96	11,205(8,558)[b]	—		
1900	11,996(8,911)[b]	—		
1911	18,680	—		
1920	28,622	42,339	—	
1930	42,445	54,151[e]	630	9
1940	62,946	91,047[e]	700	13
1945	74,183	143,312	730	20
1950	209,303	281,020[e]	848	33

[a] Government and assisted schools only.

[b] Average attendance in parentheses.

[c] Includes enrollment in non-grant-aided institutions.

[d] Taken as 20 percent of total population. Total population is derived from estimates in 1937 (3,375) from United Nations, *Demographic Yearbook* and Foster's estimate (p. 117) for 1950 (4,241,000). As Foster points out, the 1948 census probably underestimated total Gold Coast population. Our 20 percent estimate for school-age population is probably also low. Total enrollment does not represent average attendance, so the percentage of school-age population enrolled is probably highly overestimated.

[e] The total enrollment in secondary schools was 600 in 1930, 2,600 in 1940, and 6,200 in 1950. Thus, secondary enrollment is a small part of total enrollment.

Source: Philip Foster, *Education and Social Change in Ghana* (London: Routledge & Kegan Paul, 1965), tables 2, 3, 5.

population in 1930. In 1920, the enrollment in Gold Coast secondary schools was 200, and in 1930, it was 600 (see table 4). The situation in French-administered areas was even worse (see table 5), since the French system strictly controlled the number of students attending school. In 1946, the two French *lycées* in French West Africa together had 174 pupils.

Table 5

French West Africa: School Enrollment, by Level of Schooling, 1936–37 and 1948–49[a]

	1936–37			Total Native School-age Population in 1936[b]	
Level of Schooling	Boys	Girls	Total	6–14 years old	Percent in Primary[c]
I. Total public primary	49,204	5,705	54,909	2,450,000	2.2[d]
A. Village primary	23,465	1,466	24,931		
B. Regional primary	18,935	3,006	21,941		
C. Urban primary	6,804	1,233	8,037		
II. Higher primary (junior high)	571	11	582		
III. Secondary (academic)	578	265	843		
Secondary (technical)	778	—	778		

1948–49

| | | | | Total Native School-age Population in 1948[b] | |
Level of Schooling	Boys	Girls	Total	6–14 years old	Percent in Primary[c]
I. Total public primary	88,265	16,184	104,449		
Total private primary	23,152	9,557	32,709		
Total primary	111,417	25,741	137,158	2,746,000	5.0
II. Secondary academic colleges	2,441	380	2,821		
moderns	1,169	176	1,345		
normal school	1,203	154	1,357		
technical	483	—	483		

[a] Includes Senegal and Dakar, Sudan, Mauritania, Guinea, Ivory Coast, Dahomey, and Niger. More than one-fifth of the total primary school students in 1948–49 were in Senegal-Dakar.

[b] Estimated as 16.7 percent of the total population.

[c] Total primary figure divided by school-age population.

[d] Does not include private primary students (dates not available).

Source: Annuaire Statistique de l'Afrique Occidentale Francaise, 1949.

By 1945 the educated elite of French West Africa included, besides 2000 or so alumni of (Ecole Normale William) Ponty and the Ecole de médecine, a few lawyers and veterinarians who had returned from France and a single, and justly celebrated, African professeur agrégé, born in Joal but long resident in France—the future President Senghor.[127]

The spread of schooling in West Africa was therefore not a function of industrialization, but of European commercial and cultural influence. Even in the 1950s both British and French West Africa imported all their manufactured goods (except for home-produced consumer goods which satisfied traditional needs) in exchange for cocoa, gold, palm oil, ground nuts, and other primary products. Foster points out that, in rural areas, schooling followed the spread of cash-crop production—in the case of Gold Coast, the spread of cocoa cultivation.[128] But schooling in rural areas was limited. The greatest demand for European education came in urban areas, where contact with Europeans was greatest. Apparently, in British areas, where education was much more widespread, it did not guarantee European-type employment; rather, it was a necessary but not sufficient condition for access to European institutions. Education distinguished people who were in the European mode from those who were African and traditional. It served largely as a social stratification device, although it was also a requirement for the best jobs. In French Africa, the correspondence between European education and elite jobs was much greater, because of French educational controls.

Educational reforms in West Africa were few and far between. French colonial schools took their cues from the French metropolitan system. British schools were much more decentralized and, especially in the unaided part of the system, catered more to local demands. There was no general rethinking of education in the British colonial office between 1847 and 1925. The results of that rethinking when it finally came were remarkably similar to the original 1847 formulation based on Buxton's concepts of the African's economic role.[129] The 1925 policy recognized that the curriculum of African schools was not adapted to the African context, and it did force some changes in the teaching of history and other social subjects at the primary level. But secondary schools, which trained the new African elite, continued to be distinctly British after 1925, and Africans themselves apparently continued to demand European academic education to put them on par with their British masters.

Adaptation and Assimilation

Once Britain and France annexed West Africa, they controlled educational policies in the areas under their jurisdiction. French colonial policy is usually characterized as "assimilationist"—a policy of having Africans conform to a highly centralized French education, using the same curriculum and language as in France. The concept of assimilation is said to stem from a French tradition of "equity" in education, which meant that students were to be treated and judged equally whether they were French or African, whether they were from one tribe or another. All Africans going to school were therefore educated to become "black Frenchmen." British policy, on the other hand, is characterized as "adaptive"—a policy that evolved through Buxton (see above), the Education Committee of the Privy Council to the Colonial Office in 1847,[130] and the Phelps-Stokes reports of 1922 and 1925.[131] The British believed that the African had to be transformed and that education would be the vehicle of this transformation. But the African was not to become British; rather, he was to be educated to be a cultivator, in keeping with the *British* view of local African conditions, present and future. By the 1920s, this nineteenth-century view had become more sophisticated under the influence of Americans like Samuel Chapman Armstrong and Booker T. Washington, who prescribed a similar educational approach to the needs of the American Negro:

> Education should be adapted to the mentality, attitudes, occupation, and traditions of various peoples, conserving as far as possible all sound and healthy elements in the fabric of their social life, adapting them where necessary to changed circumstances and progressive ideas, as an agent of natural growth and evolution.[132]

The difference in British and French educational policy did not stem from differences in colonial policies but from the differences in their own metropolitan systems. In both cases, the basic structures of the two systems were imposed in Africa. Thus, both were "assimilationist" since they forced the African to learn in the context of an imported European educational structure.[133] The French system, as it was in France, was highly centralized; it brought academic education to sons of the African elite and vocational education to sons of the lower classes. Education was state-subsidized, and the number of graduates tightly controlled, again as in France, not to exceed the jobs available for educated people.[134] As we have seen, this number in French West Africa was very small.

The British system in Africa, as in Britain, was highly decentralized, and was based on the concept of formal schooling as a privilege "to be privately acquired, or a duty to be individually performed." [135] The result is a system of private institutions, aided by the state, but relying largely on self-finance through school fees. There was public control of the grant-aided institutions, but it was not great enough to restrict the number of graduates as in French-administered areas. The decentralized British system was more subject to local demand than the French. Ironically, the British colonial policy had a philosophy of vocational education for Africans but, because of local demand, produced largely academic education,[136] while the French, who are characterized as producing academic, assimilationist schooling, actually had well-developed vocational education in Africa, as they did in France.

In both systems, the existence of European colonialists in positions of power determined the aspirations of Africans in school. Attempts at differentiating Africans from Europeans by providing less access to academic education which prepared Africans for European-type jobs was met with resistance by Africans themselves. Both systems ended up preparing Africans academically, but for diffrent reasons. Both systems tended to restrict the number of people receiving schooling as well: the French through conscious planning and control and the British through some control of aided schools, but largely through the self-support of schools through fees. As in India, fees were high enough to keep most students out of primary school. In British colonies, a higher fraction of school-age children did attend school, and the distribution of schooling was more dispersed—at least among cities—than in French West Africa. Nevertheless, as our previous figures show, schooling in all West Africa was concentrated in large towns and the percentage of people with schooling in the 1930s was low.

Some Conclusions

Africa emerged into the twentieth century colonized by capitalist, not by mercantile, European powers. The idealism of early capitalism had failed to transform Africa into a useful commercial appendage of Europe. Local interests (missionaries, traders, and colonial garrisons) and worldwide competition between established (Great Britain) and emerging (France and Germany) imperialist countries had brought European administration in to annex West Africa by force rather than persuasion. Sixty years later, most of Africa was politically independent again, although economically tied to the former colonialists.

Formal schooling developed a new elite in Africa, drawn in British areas largely from previously nonelite groups and in French areas from the old elite. The new elite has learned European ways, and often adopted them for the reward they offered. Many European and American writers and politicians also attribute to schooling the growth of nationalist movements in Africa (and in India as well):

> If there is unrest, and a desire for independence, as in India and Egypt, it is because we have taught the value of liberty and freedom, which for centuries these people had not known. Their very discontent is a measure of their progress.[137]

More indirectly, Foster and Abernethy have expressed the same view. Colonial education produced the unforeseen consequence for Europeans of fostering nationalism: "In any event the most significant consequence of colonial education was an unforeseen one: the demise of colonial rule." [138] This view admits that education was a tool of imperialism, an attempt to build commercial control or to strengthen the hold of the colonial power over the colony by developing a class of intermediaries. However, because of the inherently liberating nature of formal schooling, it could *not* be used effectively to colonize people and produce a nationalistic elite which opposed European occupation. This, plus the role of formal schooling in preparing Africans to modernize, it is argued, are the main *positive* outputs of European colonial education.

Actually there is little evidence that European education did teach the value of liberty and freedom from European colonization, even unconsciously. It is much more reasonable to believe that Africans continued to resist colonization *despite* European schooling. The story of West African resistance to the European in the nineteenth and early twentieth centuries is one of local and widespread fighting by uneducated tribesmen who valued their independence not only from European domination but also from domination by other Africans.[139] This feeling of independence was not brought to Africa by the European. In the 1920s, '30s, and '40s, when the present African nationalist movements developed, open warfare with the British and French was only one or two generations in the past.

Formal schooling produced a new elite who could deal with the European. This elite acquired the leadership of masses of people *already opposed to European occupation and jurisdiction.* The elites translated what had been tribal and group resistance to the Europeans into "nationalist" resistance. In this way, schooling may have made them more dangerous to European rule than their more local predecessors, but schooling also made these new leaders more European and often more willing to mediate the demands of the mass of people for European ouster [140] In the short run, particularly in the immediate post-World War II period, France and Britain may have seen schooling as a curse, but in retrospect, European education created "sensible" values of liberty and freedom, ones that were derived from European standards of conduct and were likely to produce a continuing cultural and economic dependency on the ex-colonial countries. As an alternative to the kind of resistance to colonization produced by the uneducated, schooling served Britain and France well.

Notes

1. An important rebellion in the Indian military in 1857 was crushed.

2. The French tried to follow a similar policy in Algeria and later in Senegal and French West Africa. At the end of the nineteenth century, the British again excluded missionaries, this time from Moslem Northern Nigeria. In all four places—India, Algeria, French West Africa, and Northern Nigeria—church and state clashed strongly.

3. Michael Barratt Brown, *After Imperialism* (New York: Humanities Press, 1970), p. 29.

4. Barrington Moore, Jr., *Social Origins of Dictatorship and Democracy* (Boston: Beacon Press, 1968), p. 319.

5. Ibid., pp. 328–29.

6. Ibid., p. 323.

7. Ramkrishna Mukherjee, *The Rise and Fall of the East India Company* (Berlin: Deutscher Verlagder Wissenschaften, 1958), p. 221.

8. R. C. Dutt, *The Economic History of India*, Vol. I (London: Routledge and Kegan Paul, 1950), p. 24.

9. Mukherjee, *Rise and Fall of East India Company*, p. 351.

10. Ibid., p. 353.

11. For this argument, see Barratt Brown, *After Imperialism*, pp. 44–48.

12. James Mill and Horace Hayman Wilson, *History of British India* (London: J. Madden, 1848), I: 385.

13. Karl Marx, "The East India Company," *New York Tribune*, 11 July 1853, quoted in Mukherjee, *Rise and Fall of East India Company*, pp. 404–6.

14. Syed Nurullah and J. P. Naik, *A History of Education in India* (London: Macmillan, 1951), pp. 60–61.

15. The first known Protestant missionary work began in Madras in 1706. There the Danish missionary Ziegenbalg began proselytizing at Tranquebar. (The Danish missionaries worked under the protection and active encouragement of the East India Company, as their own government had no foothold or commercial relations on the subcontinent.) Ziegenbalg set up a printing press in Tamil in 1713 and began printing the Bible in native language and Portuguese. In 1716 an institute for training teachers was set up, and a year later two charity schools were opened: one for Portuguese children and one for Indians. Schools were generally separated along these European/ Indian lines. In Madras, about 1717, Grundler started "a Portuguese school in the White town and a Malabar school in the Black" (Nurullah and Naik, *History of Education in India*, p. 62). Another Danish missionary, Kiernander, was called by Clive to work in cooperation with the company; he founded a charity-school in Calcutta in 1758. By 1785 another missionary (Schwartz) had pioneered the founding of three schools (Tanjore, Ramnad, and Shivganga) where English was taught to Indian children, with the assistance of the East India Company's agent, John Sullivan. Sullivan said he hoped the schools would "help the Company and the people to understand each other" and to "facilitate dealings of all kinds between them." The schools were not for expressly religious purposes, and thus had the company's enthusiastic support (the company was always wary about conversions arousing hostility). The directors even sanctioned a grant-in-aid to the enterprise: "The utility and importance of establishing a free and direct communication with the natives, having been sensibly experienced during the late war in India, and their

acquiring a knowledge of the English language being the most effectual means of accomplishing this desirable object. . . . Highly approving of institutions calculated to establish mutual good faith; to enlighten the minds of the natives and to impress them with sentiments of esteem and respect for this British nation, by making them acquainted with the leading features of our Government so favourable to the rights and happiness of mankind . . . we accordingly direct you to pay such schools, respectively the annual stipend of 250 pagodas, flattering ourselves that our example will excite the Native Princes in alliance with us to similar and more extensive benefactions." (Ibid; p. 63).

16. M. N. Srinivas, *Social Change in Modern India* (Berkeley, Calif.: University of California Press, 1963), pp. 59–60.

17. Nurullah and Naik, *History of Education in India*, p. 65.

18. Mukherjee, *Rise and Fall of East India Company*, p. 419.

19. B. K. Boman-Behrman, *Educational Controversies in India* (Bombay: Taraporewalla Sons & Co., 1943), pp. 236–37.

20. J. N. Farquar, *Modern Religious Movements in India* (London: Macmillan, 1919), pp. 8–12.

21. Mukherjee, *Rise and Fall of East India Company*, p. 321.

22. A. P. Howell, *Education in British India, prior to 1854, and in 1870–71* (Calcutta, 1872), p. 1.

23. However, a European controller came with the financing of the school.

24. Nurullah and Naik, *History of Education in India*, pp. 58–59.

25. Boman-Behrman, *Educational Controversies in India*, p. 499.

26. Ibid., p. 31.

27. Nurullah and Naik, *History of Education in India*, p. 72.

28. Mukherjee, *Rise and Fall of East India Company*, p. 431.

29. M. N. Das, *Studies in the Economic and Social Development of India, 1848–56* (Calcutta: Mukhopadhyay, 1959), p. 205.

30. Boman-Behrman, *Educational Controversies in India*, p. 540.

31. Ibid., p. 526.

32. Nurullah and Naik, *History of Education in India*, p. 192.

33. He founded the English-Hindu Vidyalaya College in Calcutta in 1816.

34. In fact, most of the changes had already been made *before* Macaulay ever arrived; the economic and political trends were there in India for a long time—all he did was to give them ideological content.

35. Nurullah and Naik, *History of Education in India*, p. 136.

36. Quoted in A. Mayhew, *The Education of India*, (London, 1926) p. 21.

37. Das, *Economic and Social Development of India*, p. 5.

38. H. N. Brailsford, *Subject India* (New York: John Day, 1943), p. 13.

39. K. C. Vyas, *The Development of National Education in India* (Bombay, Vora & Co., 1954), p. 49.

40. Das, *Economic and Social Development of India*, pp. 203–4.

41. See Brailsford, *Subject India*, and Aubrey Zellner, *Education in India* (New York: Bookman Associates, 1951), p. 64.

42. Boman-Behrman, *Educational Controversies in India*, p. 384.

43. See Das, *Economic and Social Development of India*, chaps. 6 and 7, for details on this policy.

44. Quoted in Nurullah and Naik, *History of Education in India*, p. 213.

45. Das, *Economic and Social Development of India*, pp. 216–17.

46. See Edward Thompson and Geoffrey T. Garratt, *Rise and Fulfilment of British Rule in India* (Allahabad: Central Book Depot, 1962). In 1843–44, the colonial government in Bombay spent almost as much on education as in Bengal, even though the former had a population about one-fourth the latter. However, the distribution among vernacular and English schools was very different.

	Bengal	Bombay
Population	37.0 million	10.5 million
Funds for education (rupees)	5.5 million	5.2 million
Pupils in government schools	5,570	10,616
Pupils in English education	3,953	761

Source: Boman-Behrman, *Educational Controversies in India*, p. 561.

47. Das, *Economic and Social Development of India*, p. 212.

48. Nurullah and Naik, *History of Education in India*, p. 126.

49. Dutt, *Economic History of India*, p. 44.

50. See Zellner, *Education in India*, p. 76.

51. Nurullah and Naik, *History of Education in India*, pp. 869–910.

52. V. V. Oak, *England's Educational Policy in India* (Madras: B. G. Paul & Co., 1925), p. 144.

53. Ibid., p. 143. But more than 25 percent of educational expenditures

went for university training. See Nurullah and Naik, *History of Education in India*, p. 288.

54. Nurullah and Naik, *History of Education in India*, p. 601.

55. Ibid., p. 152.

56. In 1921–22, the average fees paid were Rs. 7.2 per student per year. Fees therefore covered about one-third of costs in government schools. See Oak, *England's Educational Policy in India*, p. 144.

57. Sir Bartle Frere, as quoted in Dutt, *Economic History of India*, pp. 338–39.

58. Walter Cassels (1871), a Bombay merchant and member of the Bombay Legislative Council, quoted in ibid., p. 339.

59. D. H. Buchanan, *The Development of Capitalistic Enterprise in India* (New York: Augustus Kelley, 1966), p. 163.

60. Ibid., p. 139.

61. Ibid., p. 59.

62. Alfred Chatterton, *Industrial Evolution in India* (Madras: The "Hindu" Office, 1912), chaps. 1 and 12.

63. Buchanan, *Capitalistic Enterprise in India*, p. 297.

64. Ibid., p. 405.

65. There is some evidence that from the early 1890s onward, the supply of university graduates had already begun to exceed the demand. See Chatterton, *Industrial Evolution in India*, p. 4.

66. Nurullah and Naik, *History of Education in India*, pp. 608–9.

67. Desmond Bittinger, *Black and White in the Sudan* (Elgin, Ill.: Brethren Publishing House, 1941), p. 108.

68. R. S. Rattray, *Ashanti Law and Constitution* (Oxford: Clarendon Press, 1929); reprinted in Evelyn Jones Rich and Immanuel Wallerstein, *Africa* (New York: Random House, 1972), p. 176.

69. Bittinger, *Black and White in the Sudan*, p. 108.

70. Phillip Curtin, *The Atlantic Slave Trade: A Census* (Madison: University of Wisconsin, 1969), p. 269; Jones and Wallerstein, *Africa*, p. 184; Bittinger, *Black and White in the Sudan*, p. 112.

71. Bittinger, *Black and White in the Sudan*, p. 100.

72. Ibid., p. 107.

73. Jones and Wallerstein, *Africa*, p. 185.

74. Bittinger, *Black and White in the Sudan*, p. 111.

75. Eric Williams, *Capitalism and Slavery* (New York: Capricorn Books, 1966).

76. Ibid., p. 122.

148

EDUCATION AS CULTURAL IMPERIALISM

77. Ibid., p. 146.

78. Ronald Robinson, John Gallagher, and Alice Denny, *Africa and the Victorians* (New York: St. Martin's Press, 1961), p. 28.

79. In the 1830s, the French began to cultivate the ground nut (peanut) and even attempted to process it into oil for export into France. But the French government wanted to protect French olive-oil producers and refused to allow processing in Senegal. By 1852, Senegal sent almost 3,000 tons of ground nuts to France. J. D. Hargreaves, *West Africa: The Former French States* (Englewood Cliffs, N.J.: Prentice-Hall, 1967), p. 82.

80. Although the attempt to halt the slave trade was not completely successful until all sugar and cotton producers had abolished slavery at the end of the century, wherever the British imposed their will by treaty or colonization, African social and economic structure—geared to slave trading for 300 years—was severely disrupted. The timing of these new disruptions depended largely on European initiatives. "As it had been a European idea to start exporting African slaves across the Atlantic, so it was a European idea to forbid this. Africans, puzzled by the mutable morality of their white customers, did not all respond immediately or enthusiastically. Failing the presence on a particular coast of merchants ready to buy alternative produce, it was difficult to respond at all" (Hargreaves, *West Africa*, p. 78).

81. Ibid; Philip Foster, *Education and Social Change in Ghana* (London: Routledge & Kegan Paul, 1965).

82. Foster, *Education and Social Change in Ghana*, p. 28. Actually, the "legitimate" trade with Africa remained very small. British exports to West Africa in the 1870s and 1880s never went higher than about a million pounds annually, while exports to India in the same period averaged 20 million annually and total British exports, 200 million pounds. The West Coast colonies did not pay for themselves once the slave trade ended.

83. Bittinger, *Black and White in the Sudan*, p. 125.

84. The French had already conquered and occupied Algiers in 1830. Faidherbe's experience in Algeria with Muslims led him to allow Africans to become France's loyal subjects while remaining Muslims. He used this policy to consolidate a French empire in Senegambia which formed a secure base for inland penetration toward the Niger. "But, unlike successors who invoked his name to justify their military campaigns, Faidherbe hoped to achieve this penetration by negotiation backed only indirectly by force" (Hargreaves, *West Africa*, p. 95).

Despite Faidherbe's successes, further expansion into the Sudan was blocked by the Tokolor Empire, then in a state of ferment. The French government was not enthusiastic about extending their empire in West Africa. So governors who followed Faidherbe over the next eleven years restored deposed African chiefs to power.

85. Until the end of the 1870s, French influence was still felt only indirectly, even in the Senegal valley. The change in policy which led to the French conquest of the Sudan seems to have come not from France, but from the "initiatives of local military commanders or governors, taking advantage of opportunities for glory provided by changing political conditions in France. Expansion carried out this way tended to level out African authorities which failed to comply with the simple imperatives of military expediency, and so cause some rather sharp breaks in the continuity of African history" (Hargreaves, *West Africa*, p. 97).

These initiatives began with the Niger railway line scheme in 1878. Since the line implied political control, the French began a series of military campaigns which eventually brought them into conflict with the British and Germans in the lower Niger. The campaigns destroyed at least two important African military powers: the Tokolor Empire and the Mandinka Empire farther to the south led by Alimani Samori. Samori fought the French in the area stretching from Guinea to Upper Volta for more than a decade until his capture in 1898. Sekou Touré, the present president of Guinea, claims to be Samori's grandson.

Another French military expedition defeated the Dahomey Kingdom in 1892–93, and another, the Hovas in Madagascar (1895). By the 1880s, partly as a result of the Franco-Prussian War and French humiliation by the British in Egypt, economic competition between the great powers was translated by France into the military occupation of vast areas of West Africa. It is important to note that although Africans like Samori tried to stop the French by appealing to the British for modern arms, European solidarity asserted itself by partitioning areas of control in European conferences, and avoiding direct confrontations between the big powers in Africa. African states like Tokolor and Mandinka were dealt away among European diplomats, and the Brussels Treaty of 1890 agreed to restrict the sale of newly developed European weapons to Africans.

Civilian control of Sudan was not established in French West Africa until the twentieth century. In Niger and in the other military empire of Mauritania, French military government continued into the 1920s, and their military influence remained strong after that. Ibid., p. 106.

86. Once the French military based in Senegal began its conquests, and French traders began to move up the Benue toward Chad, the British reacted

to this "threat." With the help of George Goldie, a British trader on the Niger, British claims on the Niger were solidified for the Berlin Conference of 1884. Goldie bought out the two French firms trading on the Benue, and made treaties for Goldie's National African Company as far north as Sakoto and Gandu. The Berlin Conference put the navigation of the Upper Niger under French control, and that of the Lower Niger under the British.

After several attempts, Goldie managed to secure a charter (monopoly) for his National African Company in 1886 under the name Royal Niger Company, and thereafter the company assumed not only trading rights but the *rights of government and administration.* See Bittinger, *Black and White in the Sudan,* p. 123. The company had a judicial staff, a system of courts, and a constabulary force of one thousand. "In a short time the company had concluded treaties with two hundred and thirty-five riverside states and sent out missions to approach the inland emperors at Kano and Sokoto" (ibid., p. 131). These treaties transferred the entire tribal land rights on both sides of the rivers to the Royal Niger Company as far as the company desired. The company also fought successful military engagements with the Fulani, and made treaties with the Emirs, forcing them to accept British rule through the company.

The Royal Niger Company resisted pressure from missionaries to make Nigeria a colony, and from the Liverpool merchants on the Delta to dissolve its control over trade on the river. Similarly, German complaints that the company did not allow free Niger access to all countries' ships (as agreed in Berlin) also went largely ignored. But by 1897, Goldie confronted the imperial policy of the new Colonial Secretary, Joseph Chamberlain, who saw in West Africa a chance to develop tropical Africa as a state enterprise. He could do little to extend British territorial claims since these had been largely settled by 1895, but he inspired the beginnings of its modern administration and development. His model of development was based on government loans to provide infrastructure, such as roads, railways, and harbors, which would stimulate private trade and investment. At the same time, the imperial government would bring its spheres of influence under effective rule, impose peace and encourage the African to contribute labor and taxes.

" 'Scientific administration,' Chamberlain hoped, would create wealth and engineer progress for the African, as for the British urban and agricultural poor . . . he held that profit and social justice must go together. It was his special aim in tropical Africa to curb the liquor traffic, and to abolish slavery and forced labour. Otherwise, he explained, '. . . We should kill the goose that lays the golden eggs—the people we want to be our best customers.'

Chamberlain brought colonial 'development' and 'welfare' into the vocabulary of policy toward the African tropics." (Robinson et al., *Africa and the Victorians*, p. 398).

Chamberlain's policy was applied to Sierra Leone and Gold Coast as well as Nigeria. He unleashed an expedition to bring the Ashanti under control (1895) and get the gold in their territory. Sierra Leone was brought under much tighter colonial administration. In Nigeria, he created the West African Frontier Force to confront the French army in the hinderlands of the northern and western borders. Finally, at the end of 1899, Nigeria came under colonial administration. Frederick Lugard, who had organized the Frontier Force, became High Commissioner of Northern Nigeria. In the following seven years he conquered Northern Nigeria for the British and laid the basis for the Dual Mandate system, by which the British ruled the region indirectly through the Fulani Emirs until independence sixty years later.

87. Foster, *Education and Social Change in Ghana*.

88. See, for example, David Abernethy, *The Political Dilemma of Popular Education* (Stanford: Stanford University Press, 1969).

89. ". . . one of the reasons why the European occupation of West Africa took over twenty-five years was the strength of the African resistance. Parts of Ivory Coast, Mali, Niger, Eastern Nigeria, the plateau of Northern Nigeria, and Mauritania were not 'pacified' until the second decade of the twentieth century. Not only was resistance bitter, it was often skilful. It was provided not by a few states with well developed armies like Dahomey and Ashanti but by a very wide range of peoples. Indeed, it is rarely appreciated that a good majority of the states of West Africa, large and small, as well as most of the people living in segmentary societies, opposed European occupation with force" (Michael Crowder, ed., *West African Resistance* [New York: Africana Publishing, 1971], pp. 1–2).

90. For example, Abernethy writes. "Moreover the purposes of the British in colonizing Africa were not as closely related to the task of educating the African as was the French *mission civilisatrice*. A principal aim of French imperialism was to spread French culture; instruction in the French language was a major justification for the whole colonial enterprise" (*Political Dilemma of Popular Education*, p. 81).

91. "During the nineteenth century the term *habitant,* and the superior status it implied, seem gradually to have become restricted to persons born locally of part-European ancestry" (Hargreaves, *West Africa*, p. 84).

92. Ibid., p. 29.

93. Foster, *Education and Social Change in Ghana*, p. 45. The schools in

the Gold Coast were for a time a subsidiary function of the merchant companies—the Royal Africa Company and the Africa Company of Merchants. In 1712, the Royal Africa Company had been established by Parliament to keep up the coastal trade; in 1750, Parliament opened up the trade to all British merchants by enabling them to join the Africa Company of Merchants, which controlled the coastal trade until 1821. After a series of wars with the Ashanti, Parliament abolished the Africa Company of Merchants and transferred the administration of the coastal forts directly to the Crown.

94. Ibid., p. 45.

95. Williams, *Capitalism and Slavery*, pp. 42–43.

96. The coast of what is now Sierra Leone was a slave-trading area for more than two hundred years. After 1787 it played a strange role in African history: many Africans had been brought to England as domestic slaves. In 1772, when slavery was abolished in the British Isles by Lord Mansfield's decision in the case of the slave Somersett, these slaves were freed and became the "black poor." Abolitionists raised funds to care for these poor, and arranged to ship them—with enough supplies to begin a farming community —back to Africa. Sierra Leone was the site chosen. In 1787, the first shiploads arrived. After considerable difficulties, during which many died, the beginnings of a settlement were established. Soon, slaves freed to fight on the side of the Loyalists in the American Revolutionary War came to Sierra Leone by way of Nova Scotia. All these settlers were Africans who were already very Europeanized and did not originally come from Sierra Leone. They formed a black European settlement in Africa, fighting local tribes, and eventually serving to bring Christianity and European culture to other parts of Africa. Nevertheless, the eventual colony of Sierra Leone was administered by the English. For a detailed account of this history, see Christopher Fyfe, *A History of Sierra Leone* (Oxford, England: Oxford University Press, 1962).

97. The leading traders on the coast wanted their children, or selected slaves, to learn English and bookkeeping. This they did either in Europe or by apprenticeship on board a trading vessel. The traders preferred such a practical education to the type used by missionaries, memorizing the catechism and training to say the mass and administer the sacraments. J. F. Ade Ajayi, *Christian Missions in Nigeria, 1841–1891* (Evanston: Northwestern University Press, 1965), p. 6.

98. Foster, *Education and Social Change in Ghana*; and Abernethy, *Political Dilemma of Popular Education.*

99. Foster, *Education and Social Change in Ghana*, p. 47.

100. Robinson et al., *Africa and the Victorians*, p. 29.

101. Foster, *Education and Social Change in Ghana*, p. 48.

102. Ibid., p. 51.

103. Ibid., p. 57.

104. Ibid. The Fanti Federation (1871) was led by a group of Chiefs but had educated Africans as its officers. See G. E. Metcalfe, *Great Britain and Ghana* (Accra: University of Ghana, 1964), pp. 335–36.

105. Robinson et al., *Africa and the Victorians*, p. 34.

106. Bittinger, *Black and White in the Sudan*, p. 121. Although the main purpose of the expeditions was to open up trade with the Moslem states of the Sudan, they were also aimed at breaking the hold of the Liverpool merchants on the Niger palm-oil trade. By going upriver, other merchants got access to palm oil at much lower prices.

107. T. F. Buxton, *The African Slave Trade and Its Remedy* (London: Frank Cass & Co., 1967).

108. Ajayi, *Christian Missions*, pp. 11–12.

109. Abernethy, *Political Dilemma of Popular Education*, p. 26.

110. Crowther had been on the original expedition in 1041.

111. Bittinger, *Black and White in the Sudan*, p. 123. Another Ashanti war (Gold Coast) in 1863–64 caused a select committee of the House of Commons to recommend withdrawing from all the settlements except Sierra Leone, but again pressure from various humanitarian and comercial groups kept Parliament from taking any action (Robinson et al., *Africa and the Victorians*, p. 30).

112. Ajayi, *Christian Missions*, p. 211.

113. Buxton, quoting MacGregor Laird on the advantages of establishing a chain of British posts on the Niger: "British influence and enterprise would thereby penetrate into the remotest recesses of the country; one hundred millions of people would be brought into direct contact with the civilized world; new and boundless markets would be opened to our manufactures; a continent teeming with inexhaustible fertility would yield her riches to our traders; not merely a nation, but hundreds of nations, would be awakened from the lethargy of centuries, and become useful and active members of the great commonwealth of mankind; and every British station would become a centre from whence religion and commerce would radiate their influence over the surrounding country" (Buxton, *African Slave Trade*, pp. 420–21). Laird had the only trading company on the Niger (subsidized by the Crown) until his death in 1861.

114. Williams, *Capitalism and Slavery*, p. 191.

115. Foster, *Education and Social Change in Ghana*, p. 60.

116. Ajayi, *Christian Missions*, pp. 171–72.

117. Buxton, *African Slave Trade*, pp. 457–58.

118. Foster, *Education and Social change in Ghana*. Foster is convincing on this thesis, but he underestimates the impact of vocational education offered by the Basel missions, and overestimates the European commitment to vocational education. Although it seems clear that Africans would want to get education which made them most like Europeans, it is also clear that missionaries felt most comfortable offering a curriculum based on morality and academic learning (their own educational experience) than one based on skilled trades. The Basel mission was very successful in training Africans in the trades, but other missions did not push vocational education very hard.

119. Ibid., p. 58.

120. Ajayi, *Christian Missions*, p. 193.

121. Robinson et al., *Africa and the Victorians*, pp. 29–30.

122. After 1871, gunboats were sent on annual punitive sweeps upriver. "What had taken place in Sierra Leone and on the Gold Coast was repeated in the palm belt between Lagos and Niger country. The time-honoured bases of exchange, of inter-tribal politics, of the relations between producers and middlemen were upset by the presence of the European, by his innovations and by the play of the world market. Instead of spreading peace, commerce seemed to have encouraged unrest and corroded tribal authority" (Robinson et al., *Africa and the Victorians*, p. 39).

123. Ajayi, *Christian Missions*, p. 234.

124. In Gold Coast, for example, where there had been British administration since 1874, by 1881 there were only about 10,000 to 15,000 pupils in mission schools, both government assisted and unassisted. Foster, *Education and Social Change in Ghana*, p. 79.

125. Ajayi, *Christian Missions*, pp. 234–35.

126. Sonia F. Graham, *Government and Mission Education in Northern Nigeria, 1900–1919* (Ibadan, Nigeria: Ibadan University Press, 1966). Freed slave children from Northern Nigeria were sent to established missionary schools in Southern Nigeria.

127. Hargreaves, *West Africa*, p. 131.

128. Foster, *Education and Social Change in Ghana*, pp. 126–27.

129. Ibid., pp. 54–56.

130. Ibid., p. 54.

131. Abernethy, *Political Dilemma of Popular Education*, p. 89. The main agent in the commission was Thomas Jesse Jones, the white director of the Phelps-Stokes Fund: "Between August, 1920, and March, 1921, the African

Education Commission visited Sierra Leone, Liberia, the Gold Coast, Nigeria, Cameroons, the Belgian Congo, Angola, and South Africa. The report was written exclusively by Jones, the chairman of the Commission, and reads like the report on Negro education with a different locale. His general recommendations deal with the adaptations of education to meet local conditions, the incorporation of his four "essentials" of education (health, appreciation and use of the environment, effective development of the home, and recreation) into the curricula at all levels, the need to develop a sense of community consciousness among the indigenous people, the overriding importance of agricultural and simple industrial training, the need for better school supervision, the necessity for cooperation between missions and governments for African education, and the need to differentiate between education for the masses of Africans and their leaders" (Edward H. Berman, "American Influence on African Education: the Role of the Phelps-Stokes Fund's Education Commissions," *Comparative Education Review* 15, no. 2 [June 1971]: 132–45).

132. From *Education Policy in British Tropical Africa*, quoted in Abernethy, *Political Dilemma of Popular Education*, p. 89.

133. Remi Clignet, "Inadequacies of the Notion of Assimilation in African Education," *Journal of Modern African Studies* 8, no. 3 (1970): 425–44.

134. Ibid. p. 433.

135. Ibid., p. 430.

136. Foster, *Education and Social Change in Ghana*. There were important exceptions to this generality, such as the Basel mission in Gold Coast and the Leanes schools in Kenya.

137. Lord Lugard, quoted in Jones and Wallerstein, *Africa*, p. 273.

138. Abernethy, *Political Dilemma of Popular Education*, p. 16.

139. Crowder, *West African Resistance*.

140. The Mau-Mau rebellion in Kenya (conducted by uneducated Kikuyu), for example, was mediated by educated Kenyan nationalist leaders. Senghor, educated in France, has kept close ties between Senegal and France, while Touré, a self-made man, has followed a much more independent route for Guinea.

4

EDUCATION AND FREE-TRADE COLONIALISM

LATIN AMERICA IN THE REPUBLICAN PERIOD

At the end of the eighteenth century, after almost three hundred years of Spanish and Portuguese colonial administration and mercantile control, Latin American economies were opened to trade with other countries. Weakened by war, and themselves markets for Northern Europe's manufactured goods, Spain and Portugal gave up their intermediary position as marketers of Latin American primary goods. By 1820, the industrial power of Great Britain had gained free-trade arrangements with a group of politically independent Latin American primary goods producers.

The British found Latin America well suited to their new role in the world. As British industry grew, England became hegemonic militarily and economically. No longer was it necessary or even desirable to be burdened with the administration of other nations as long as they could be counted on to participate with the British in free trade. As we have seen, British occupation of India was in part a holdover from mercantile times, and in part was necessary to keep India from competing with the British cotton textile industry. African peoples were not willing to organize their production processes suitably for British commercial interests. This, among other reasons, "forced" the British to occupy parts of Africa. But in the Latin America of 1800, the British could deal with a local elite that was culturally European, and who had already accepted the liberal ideology of capitalism.[1] This elite was in charge of running the Latin American plantation/mining economies, and wanted little more than to get a share of the profits from trade with Europe. In return, they delivered the primary products needed by European industry and consumers and took care of native unrest where it existed.[2]

Through free trade, then, Latin Americans were tied directly into industrializing European economies such as England, whereas before they had to deliver and buy all their goods through Spain and Portugal. Although this change in partners would not appear to imply much alteration of economic and social structures, some changes did occur; perhaps most important, political independence and the end of mercantilism meant that a domestic bourgeoisie developed as a counterforce to the landed aristocracy and the church.

But there were also many things that the shift to free trade did not change. Despite capitalist influences on the bourgeoisie, it was largely their consumption habits which changed, not production. Unlike their counterparts in the northern United States, Latin American merchants did not move toward protection and local industrialization. It could be argued that they would not have been able to resist the British militarily if they had made such a move, but it is more likely that the structure of Latin American economies from which the bourgeoisie made their fortunes did not produce protectionist sentiments. Like the southern United States, whose ruling class remained distinctly free traders until they were destroyed, Latin American economies were geared to *export* the economic surplus rather than develop internal markets.

Furthermore, the change to free trade did not change Latin American social structures, even in the long run. Since the economic system remained largely the same as in the colonial period, the mass of people played the same economic roles they had played in the past. In those countries with large indigenous populations, Indians continued to farm on a subsistence level and to provide the mineworkers and some of the plantation labor force. Most countries had a slave population who remained slaves long after independence. Thus, realignments occurred among the elite—even in that class, power was *shared* rather than one group replacing another—but since production structures did not change, these realignments generally did not extend to other groups. In fact, the shift to a new system of law—the Napoleonic Code—probably made indigenous peoples worse off, since it removed protection from their communal lands, and increased the legal power of large private landholders. Although the concepts of free trade and private property emerged from a new view of man in seventeenth- and eighteenth-century Europe, this new view of man was itself the result of changing modes of production. The Latin American bourgeoisie, working with British merchants on the one hand and French ideas on the other, imposed some elements of capitalist forms on plantation economies. This distorted existing structures even more *against* the masses without necessarily setting up the preconditions for production changes like those which occurred in Europe.

Formal Schooling and Independence

In colonial times, within the mercantile system, schooling was largely limited to preparation of a small group for professional roles.[3] With independence and free trade, Latin American liberals incorporated educational reforms copied from France and England into their constitutions. These reforms reflected capitalist ideals of the benefits of public education, but in practice, Latin American educational systems did not change. University and secondary school curriculum were the same as in colonial times, and primary schooling remained in the hands of local, church-dominated municipalities. Thus, despite liberal rhetoric and even constitutional acts of reform, the lack of change in the economic and social structure precluded the need for educational change.

In previous analyses of educational change in the free-trade period of Latin American history, it is hypothesized that formal schooling was prevented from helping to create a modern mobile society by traditional, or conservative, elements in the elite. But this hypothesis assumes that the free-trade model and the society it was supposed to produce as envisaged by liberals was intended to be equitable, and was intended to permit the masses to participate in wealth accumulating to the local merchants from the export trade. This assumption has no empirical justification in the Latin American context: while it is true that the church and conservative landowners opposed educational reform and educational expansion because their vision of the ideal society was much more feudal than capitalistic, capitalist liberals, even when they obtained power, were themselves hooked into a dependency economic structure and were themselves elitists. Since Latin American economic and social structures did not change in the transition from colonial to free-trade capitalist economies, there was little need to change educational systems. Indeed, as long as the ruling groups got their income from the trade, it was not necessary to change anything. The liberal rhetoric of educational expansion and of social change was not put into practice, as much from their own reluctance to alter economic and social structures as from resistance by other factions in the elite.

Furthermore, it is implied in these analyses that the initial expansion of primary schooling in Latin American countries was in response to demands from working and indigenous peoples. Such demands may have taken place later, once schooling had been institutionalized as a means to increased income or to get urban jobs, but we find no evidence even in the writings of those elites who originally wished to expand schooling in each country that this was their response to mass demands.[4]

Rather, we propose in this chapter that educational expansion and reform were implemented in "independent" Latin American countries when the liberal faction of the local elite perceived that *its* interests would be furthered by "modernizing" the economy. In the two countries we analyze, this perception resulted from changed international trade conditions. Modernization in one case meant the beginnings of industrialization, and in the other, the turning over of the export sector to foreign investors. But in both countries, schooling was expanded to socialize marginal groups into the portion of the economic structure controlled by the liberal elite and under a set of rules developed by that ruling group and transmitted through the schools.

There are two important aspects to this expansion. First, it was limited by the structure of the economy itself. Since the ruling class was tied to the export trade, most of the economic surplus was invested in production of internationally tradable primary goods. The mobilization of the masses for increased domestic production and consumption of manufactured goods was only of secondary importance. Also, the domestic ruling class had itself only a share in the income from trade since it was a partner with metropolis merchants.

Second, in Peru and probably in Brazil, the expansion of public primary school was a response to a perceived threat of social conflict if marginal groups did not begin to participate in the economic surplus generated by the export trade. In the liberals' vision of society, class conflict would be avoided because there would be increased economic product and greater participation in it. This participation would be allocated rationally according to "ability." Thus, mass public primary schooling was imported from Europe and the United States as a bourgeois state controlled mechanism that would allocate roles in a "rational" way, a way acceptable to the ruling class because it *maintained the social structure* while diffusing social conflict and supposedly contributing to economic growth.

Those individuals from marginal groups who got a certain amount of schooling participated in the modern sector of the economy and thus got access to some of the surplus generated by the export trade. Whoever did not get that amount of schooling was deemed by the system *incapable* of participation at all, not by dint of birth, but because of lack of training.

This system, as it was brought to Latin America at the end of the nineteenth and beginning of the twentieth century, had already been used to maintain social order in the industrialized countries during periods of economic growth and change, and so, it was reasoned by the

Latin American bourgeoisies, it would do the same in Latin America. As we show, access to secondary and higher education, which greatly increased individual access to income and status, was very limited during the free-trade period (1800–1930), and the composition of enrollment in these higher levels of schooling was highly biased toward children of the wealthy.[5]

We do not try to illustrate these points by referring to historical data from many Latin American countries. Instead, we picked two case studies: Brazil and Peru. There is no typical Latin American country, and therefore Brazil and Peru are not "typical." Nevertheless, they allow us to make certain comparisons and contrasts which are useful for our thesis. Brazil was a Portuguese colony; Peru, a Spanish colony. Peru had a large and well-organized indigenous population when the Spanish conquered it; Brazil was populated by nomadic hunters and gatherers. Both countries had active Jesuit missions, and similar mercantile education systems. Both were export economies after independence, relying on mining and export agriculture (Brazil also had important wood export) to buy manufactured consumption goods for a small merchant bourgeoisie.

Around the middle of the nineteenth century, however, the two economies diverged: Peru went through a guano export boom which created new income for a small domestic merchant class. This merchant class invested in coastal sugar and cotton plantations, but lost its wealth in the Chilean war of 1879–81. After the war, the pieces of the ruined economy were picked up by foreign investors, who became the owners of Peru's export trade. Except in a very limited sense, Peru did not industrialize until World War II.

In contrast, Brazil's bourgeoisie invested their money in coffee plantations in the 1860s and '70s, and then turned part of their profits from that trade into manufacturing in the 1880s and '90s. At the time, a large wave of foreign immigration, primarily from Italy, was brought into Brazil to provide agricultural labor for increased food production. By 1920, a significant proportion of the Brazilian labor force was in manufacturing, while Peru was still almost entirely a primary exporter/subsistence agricultural economy.

Yet, primary schooling expanded in both countries at about the same time. In Brazil, it would appear that the expansion took place as a result of industralization and the need for an industrial labor force. Certainly, factories needed labor that was socialized to work with machines, to show up on time, and so forth. Another reason that public primary schools expanded in Brazil around the turn of the century was that the immigrants (who soon formed the bulk of the labor force) had to be incorporated into a Brazilian culture and fit into the social order. Schools fulfilled this function. The Positivist philosophy prevalent in Brazil at the time called for individual decisions about education and no state intervention; yet, the exigencies of potential disorder in the rapid changes taking place forced the state to intervene in spite of this philosophy. Public primary enrollment increased fivefold between 1889 and 1920 incorporating a high fraction of the school-age population in the southern part of the country.

In Peru, the expansion took place without industrialization; therefore, the role of schooling in controlling social change is much clearer. The Peruvian ruling class did not import European immigrants, but attempted gradually to assimilate its Indian population into the lower levels of a wage structure dominated by powerful foreign firms. The purpose of this assimilation was to civilize Peru, to make it attractive and safe for foreign investment. Specifically, the liberals wanted to avoid potential social conflict in a sharply divided society. Their vision of society was a "united" Peru, where Indians, mestizos, and whites worked together for order and progress. This society would be run by whites, but Indians and others would be prepared through education to participate in economic development at lower levels of the hierarchy. The Peruvian case shows that industrialization was not a necessary precondition for educational expansion, but that potential social conflict because of class divisions or cultural separation *was*.

Before turning to the case studies themselves, it is worth mentioning again that in both Peru and Brazil the expansion of primary school was limited to a relatively small percentage of the school-age population. We hypothesize that this limitation was a function of their dependent economies. Neither country was willing or able to mobilize its masses for development because economic growth was conditioned by growth of the export sector and by an economic system organized to supply the needs of a small group in the urban centers and the metropolis. Secondary and higher education remained enclaves of the well-off. When the secondary level did expand, as it did in Peru and Brazil in the 1920s, it expanded through vocational training, a concept of secondary schooling for the poor imported from the United States and Europe.

Indeed, throughout their colonized history, whether in the mercantile period or with British free-trade and foreign investment, Brazilians and Peruvians had to develop under conditions heavily influenced by foreign institutions. They went through foreign schools to work for foreign companies. The difference—and there is no question that the difference is important—between the free-trade colonialism of Latin America and the direct colonialism of India and Africa was the existence in Latin America of a politically independent local elite. Although this ruling class was more tied to Europe than to its own indigenous masses, it still had to deal directly with domestic political consequences of changes in international conditions. The manner in which the *domestic* ruling class chose to fit the economy into the international system was crucial to the characteristics of educational expansion. Significantly, Latin American elites continued to orient themselves to European and U.S. needs, and based the limited economic incorporation of their masses on European and U.S. models.

Education and Free-trade
Colonization: Brazil

From earliest colonial times, the Brazilian school system was designed to teach two kinds of students: children of the white ruling class and children that this ruling class needed to incorporate into the lower levels of its economic and political structure. Perhaps more than any other major Latin American country, Brazil managed to keep the two educational systems separate until very recent years.

Both parts of the system depended on the structure of Brazil's economy. Under Portuguese rule, Brazil was the main source of raw materials for Portuguese mercantilism: European manufactures flowed into Brazil in exchange for sugar and then gold. With independence, the Brazilian ruling elite inherited an economic structure already tied into a free-trade relation with the industrial power of Britain. Although Britain could not directly enforce the nature of trade between Brazil and Europe as Portugal had, the result was essentially the same: raw materials from Brazil to Europe, manufactures from Europe (primarily Britain) to Brazil. For most of the nineteenth century, that part of the ruling class which favored free trade (the large landowners, mining interests, and merchants) managed to maintain free trade and an economic structure almost totally dependent on Britain for manufactured consumption goods. Indeed, Brazil's history is described by the struggles between this group and other elements of the ruling classes to control the nature of Brazilian development. However, the struggle until very recent times revolved around the *nature* of the dependency relationship, not as to whether Brazil would attempt an economic development policy independent of the international system of trade.

Thus, first Britain and then the United States had the allegiance and cooperation of the dominant elite groups. Both imperial powers were willing to give Brazil military protection and foreign loans in return for her natural wealth. The ruling class served as intermediaries in these arrangements, altering the economic structure when it became profitable to do so. Establishing free trade with Europe and granting English concessions made more sense economically than Portuguese trade monopoly; protection, industrialization, and direct foreign investment were eventually more profitable for a significant part of the Brazilian bourgeoisie than depending on foreign commercial loans for primary goods production in a free-trade context. The mass of Brazilians had little to do with these changes, or with changes in the educational system used to complement altered economic structures. These were conflicts between imperial countries and colonizing elites and among the colonizers themselves.

As long as Brazil was primarily an agricultural and mineral exporter, the ruling-class part of the educational system formed administrators and professionals to service a "colonial" bureaucracy and military. Higher and secondary education grew slowly in response to limited demands. Even after the beginnings of industrialization, the dependent economic structure preserved its plantation export economy, restricting industrial growth and the expansion of agricultural goods for domestic consumption. Secondary (and primary) schooling did expand with industrialization, but the expansion was limited and class structured because the *Brazilian economy remained largely subservient to the needs of the developed country and Brazil remained a highly structured society.* Control of the academic secondary schools continued in private hands, acting as a ruling class screen for university eligibility. Thus, the highest social classes in Brazil held the upper levels of education for themselves in colonial times, during the more than two generations of British free trade after independence, and even in the period of industrialization. The curriculum of higher education changed somewhat over time, but the people who went to university did not.

Primary education served a similar function of integrating people into certain social roles. Besides providing access to secondary schools for a very small percentage of that small group who even got to primary school, lower schooling was a means of preparing certain groups of people to work for the plantation owners and then industrialists. In the colony, the native Indians formed a threat to Portuguese settlements. They were also a potential and needed source of labor for Portuguese plantations. The Jesuits schooled the Indians and taught them to give up their nomadic values and accept wage work on the plantations. Jesuit schools were a successful means of pacifying Indians to fit into the "new" society in Brazil at the lowest level of wage labor.

After the Jesuits were expelled from Brazil in 1759, the role of primary education did not change significantly until the coffee boom one hundred years later, accompanied by the abolition of slavery, the large-scale immigration of Europeans, and the beginnings of industrialization, created serious structural problems. With slavery abolished, and slave labor shifted into coffee production and subsistence agriculture, what had been the single cheapest source of labor for commercial food production decreased. The Brazilian government began promoting immigration to increase agricultural production, both for domestic consumption and for export (coffee). European immigrants were chosen rather than Asians to ensure that Brazil's population would be predominantly European. Primary education was not used to incorporate ex-slaves into the beginnings of an industrial labor force or to raise their agricultural productivity. Schooling was expanded to incorporate the new European immigrants into Brazilian society and also into factory work. Through schooling, immigrants were brought into a social order which was controlled by Brazilians, particularly an emerging Brazilian industrial bourgeoisie.

Most ex-slaves remained in the northern part of the country, working in the same general area in which they had formerly worked as slaves. These were *declining* agricultural areas, which had turned from plantations into meat producing and subsistence farming. Some slaves came south to work as wage workers on the coffee plantations, but they did not become the urban workers; skilled workers in industry were drawn from the new wave of European immigrants, especially the artisans. Besides primary schooling, the immigrants had access to secondary vocational or "professional" schools, a track parallel to academic elite secondary schools. The expansion of primary and vocational secondary schooling in the early twentieth century was a southern, urban phenomenon, and catered largely to whites. It is contemporal with tariff protection, the expansion of the industrial labor force, and the advent of autarkic capitalism. But it was also a phenomenon limited by the continued emphasis in the Brazilian economy on plantation export agriculture, and the continued appropriation of surplus by foreign merchants and financiers, and the high consumption Brazilian elites.

Brazilian educational reforms must be viewed in the context of these economic changes as well. With independence from Portugal in 1822, for example, the ideals of European philosophy produced a rhetoric of educational expansion and increased access to knowledge. Nevertheless, the educational system remained almost completely unchanged for the next three generations. After 1889, a number of reforms took place, but these dealt with academic secondary education and control over access to the university. Meanwhile, primary and vocational secondary schooling expanded with little rhetoric: it only became economically convenient and even necessary to put into practice earlier educational philosophies seventy years *after* independence. It was not political autonomy that produced these changes in education, but the emergence within the ruling class of a wealthy (and therefore powerful) group that promoted autarkic capitalist development. Even so, these changes affected only lower levels of schooling, and had little direct influence on the composition of the ruling class.

Colonialism (1500–1808)

The Portuguese colonization of Brazil was part of her mercantilist expansion in the sixteenth century. Although the colonizers' declared purpose was the propagation of Christianity and European culture, Portugal was sending explorers and settlers to Brazil to exploit natural resources for growing markets in Europe. The Jesuit Christian mission participated directly in this expansionist mercantilism. Planters, traders, and missionaries working together shaped Brazilian culture in the colonial period.

Typically, the Brazilian colonial elite is characterized as *separated* from Brazilian "reality" and therefore failing to develop a national culture.[6] But this analysis blurs the elite's role in the colonial structure: in that analysis, the people called "Brazilians" are characterized as Portuguese who happened to be born in Brazil, who looked to Europe for norms and values, and who did not attempt to create a new Brazilian culture. However, these same "Brazilians" did attempt to convert the native Indians—Brasilíndios—to incorporate them into the mercantile economy. Those Brasilíndios who were Christianized by the Jesuits were integrated into the lowest class of "freedmen" in the colonial structure. The Brazilians also imported millions of Africans as slaves. They were condemned to plantation labor and, unlike the Brasilíndios, did not receive any Jesuit education or protection, since Africans were apparently already socialized to work in agriculture.

The colonial elite therefore *did* create a Brazilian culture based on a well-defined exploitative hierarchy. The slave labor force and the *latifundio* (plantation) were the fundamental economic characteristics of this colonial system, and agriculture and mineral exports, principally sugar, and then gold, cotton, and tobacco, were its principal outputs for more than three centuries.

To build the colonial economy, the Portuguese colonizers needed labor: the Brasilíndios resisted expropriation of their land and few tribes submitted to slavery. Resistance resulted in Indian decimation. Thus, plantation agriculture expanded with imported slave labor. During the 400 years of slavery, more than 3.3 million Africans were brought to Brazil.[7]

The Portuguese eventually called in the Jesuits to civilize and Christianize the resisting Indians, with direct support from the Portuguese government. Jesuits were the only group in colonial times who learned Indian languages; they helped in expeditions inland and in capturing Indians. Brazilian political history views the Jesuits as Indian *protectors* against destruction by colonizers. But economic history, less concerned with church-state relations, shows that Indian nomadism was incompatible with plantation agriculture,[8] and that the Jesuits developed techniques for *incorporating* Indians into the colonial economy. Indian villages (*reduções indígenas*) were organized for protection against Brazilian raids; but at the same time, the villages served to prepare the Indians for wage labor. Jesuits and colonizers made agreements for Indian plantation labor.[9] Jesuit schools for Indians (*escolas de ler e escrever*) were effective instruments for the long-run integration of the resistant Indians into the plantation labor market. By 1798, of Brazil's total population of 3.2 million, more than 400,000 were "free" Indians; 250,000 were counted as uncivilized Indians; 1.5 million, black and mestizo slaves; and 1 million, whites.[10]

The Jesuits therefore built an extensive network of Indian villages and schools. They were used to bringing the Indians into a labor-short white-controlled economy at a low level of unskilled wage labor. Undoubtedly, the missionaries thought that they were serving the Indians by civilizing them; at the same time they were serving their countrymen by providing them with cheap labor. There was no similar Christian concern with educating Africans, since slaves were the property of the plantation. This dichotomy between educating Indians and ignoring the large number of blacks brought into Brazil casts doubt on the *moral* imperative of Jesuit educators and makes more reasonable the economic explanation for native schooling.

Besides their role in the territorial expansion and economic organization of the colony, the Jesuits were officially responsible for the spiritual life of the white settlers. After 1573, when modifications were introduced in the Jesuit Order's structure and functions, Jesuits slowly moved away from participation in mercantile expansion (Indian education) to fighting the Reform movement in the Catholic Church. Education (for whites) became the instrument for strengthening Catholicism against Protestant heresies. Strongly committed to orthodoxy, the Jesuits reinforced the medieval tradition that condemned free inquiry—culture for them meant humanistic and philosophical education as the basis for theological formation.

Jesuit schools for Brazilians (1549–1759) formed the other half of two separate systems, one for the "savages" and the other for the Brazilian elite. The latter were concerned primarily with preparation of priests but also admitted sons of landowners and mineowners not entering religious life. These schools were located in colonial villages along the coast. Postprimary education was for the few Brazilian children who would fulfill the limited number of available positions in the metropole controlled colonial administrative structure.[11] In this period, Jesuits had a monopoly on education in Brazil. The monopoly was granted and financed in part by the Portuguese government.[12] Anyone who wanted to attain high levels of education had to go through Jesuit schools and then on to Portugal for university training.

Restricted as it was to socializing Indians and forming a small, conservative colonial bureaucracy and church, Jesuit education was consistent with Brazil's export agricultural economy, organized to produce raw materials for Portugal, and "made up of isolated units directly linked to the exterior, and cut off from all other areas of the country, with the exception of the pastoral interior which developed as a dependency of the sugar economy."[13] This economy required cheap labor kept working long hours on plantations run by small numbers of

European settlers. The education system was designed and structured to serve the labor, administrative, and spiritual needs of the Brazilian elite and through them, of the Portuguese metropole.

By the middle of the eighteenth century, the anti-Enlightenment stance and independent power base of the Jesuit Order clashed with the increased strength of Absolutist philosophy[14] in Portugal and Spain. The Portuguese prime minister, the Marquis de Pombal, managed to have the Jesuits expelled from Portuguese territory under the accusation of intolerance to the advancement of science.

Jesuit expulsion brought collapse to Brazil's school system.[15] The Portuguese government reduced the little support it had given education, and the colony had few other teachers. During the half-century decay of colonial education, which was matched chronologically by a decline in sugar production and then gold mining,[16] the remaining small school system was reorganized from Portugal on the same lines as school reforms in the metropole. This was the period of greatest Portuguese control over the colony, both politically and economically. Brazil became a vice-kingdom, and this required greater sophistication in the Brazilian administrative apparatus (staffed primarily by Portuguese officials) and closer ties to the metropole. Heavy taxation, a continued monopoly of Brazil's trade, and prohibition of manufactures were efficient measures to curtail the accumulation of wealth and expansion of Brazil's economy. A strong system of police control destroyed independence movements organized by members of the European-educated elite and supported by the emerging urban merchant bourgeoisie, particularly those hurt by monopoly controls on trade and manufacturing.

England and Brazil

After 1600, the power of Portugal declined and was overtaken by that of her rivals. When the Spanish and Portuguese royal families joined, Spain's enemies attacked Portugal as well. Between 1629 and 1654, Holland occupied one-half of Brazil's sugar lands. In 1642, 1654, and 1661, Portugal signed commercial treaties giving Great Britain economic concessions in return for political protection, and in 1703, the Treaty of Methuen guaranteed Portuguese metropolitan and colonial markets to English manufactures in exchange for preferential markets for Portuguese wines in England. By the same treaty, an earlier Portuguese agreement to buy only English ships was renewed. These controls resulted in the withering away of emerging textile and ship industries in Portugal and Brazil. Portugal and the colony concentrated on agricultural production with Portugal as the commercial intermediary between Brazil and European markets.[17] The Portuguese that internally regulated these contracts abolished "all industries and factories—in order not to take labor from agriculture—and to differentiate production between the colonies and the metropolis, in order to foment commerce and increase the consumption or the metropolis' industries." [18]

By the beginning of the nineteenth century, Portugal had lost her principal colonies in Asia. During the Napoleonic Wars, Portuguese institutions themselves became weak, and England dominated her commercial life even more. When the Portuguese royal family left for Brazil in 1808, the English navy protected the royal party in exchange for a new series of concessions:[19]

1. Reaffirmation of the 1703 Treaty of Methuen.

2. The opening of Brazilian ports to the commerce of friendly nations (Great Britain).

3. Creation of a free port in South Brazil (Santa Catarina or Rio Grande do Sul) as an entry into the Platte River region.

4. Progressive steps toward abolishing the slave trade.

This agreement was signed in 1810. Besides the four points, English manufacturers received better tariff concessions in the Brazil trade than Portugal herself: the general import duty was 25 percent ad valorem, imports from Portugal paid 16 percent, and English manufacturers paid only 15 percent.[20]

Portuguese Kingdom (1808–21)

When the Portuguese Court transferred to Brazil, the new role of

Brazil as the center of the kingdom required changes in the kinds of services available to Brazilians (Brazilian-born Portuguese). The capital—Rio de Janeiro—got streetlights and garbage collection, a newspaper, a public library, a museum, a botanical garden, a higher school of art, two medical faculties, and two military arts faculties.

In these higher-level educational services, emphasis was put on professional schools, both because of ideological-cultural reasons and the immediate administrative needs to be filled. The ideas of the French Revolution had spread suspicion among the bourgeoisie of the "university" and "nonutilitarian" knowledge considered typical of universities. Such knowledge was condemned as a manifestation of the medieval concept of the universe and contrary to the "objectivity" of applied science. More important, there was an urgent need for trained personnel to administer the kingdom from Brazil and to serve in the military and the judiciary.

Other faculties were also created, according to Azevedo, as an expression of the king's concern with the absolute lack of technicians to fulfill the needs of urbanization and industrialization and a better organization of the agricultural economy as the main factors for sustaining and improving internal integration within the colony.[21] These faculties functioned as independent schools: economics, agriculture, chemistry (including industrial chemistry, geology, and mineralogy), technical design and an academy of sciences, and arts and crafts. However, the king's concern with industrialization could not have been very great because most of these faculties had a short life and few students. They lacked public funds (since they had low royal priority compared to liberal professional schools) and were low in prestige. Much more crucial to their failure was the lack of demand for their graduates: based on European functional higher education of that time, they had little to do with the Brazilian colonial economy. Extensive agriculture with new land easily available and worked by slave labor did not need agricultural experts to improve productivity or to study scientific farming. Mining had declined. Manufacturing was not prohibited after the administration of the Portuguese Empire moved to Brazil, but tariff concessions to low priced English manufactures effectively prevented any significant industrialization during the period.

Becoming industrialized was a concern of few of the educated elite, while the majority of the ruling class was committed to agricultural production and export-import trade. Although the Court's shift to Brazil imported with it a European model of higher education and some public services, the economic and social structure remained inherently colonial. The Crown did not provide primary schooling, because it did not need to incorporate the mass of blacks and civilized Indians into the wage structure. The maintenance of the plantation economy and the resultant social hierarchy worked for the colonial elite, who lived off the trade, and for the industrializing nations—particularly Britain—who wanted Brazilian agricultural products and markets for their manufactured goods.

Brazilian Independence

Independence came in 1822, but in an unusual way: Brazil had not depended economically on Portugal for the previous fourteen years, since it had had "free" trade. The metropole for Brazil was no longer Portugal but Europe. Independence simply meant the return of the royal family to Portugal and the legitimization of the 1808 break in the Portuguese monopoly of trade. The new nation maintained the international relations it had before independence—especially the strong commercial ties to England—and the same internal socioeconomic structure. A member of the Portuguese royal family was even proclaimed emperor.

After Independence, foreign trade interest remained in the hands of the Portuguese, protected by the continuity of the Crown, or were taken over by Englishmen. There was thus little change in the sugar region where the old structures were maintained under the more direct control of the English interests. The most significant changes occurred in the South, where the mining economy had been on the decline since the end of the 18th century. The dwindling gold output, which shrank to a third or a quarter of the quantity formerly produced at the same time as administrative expenses were rising sharply as a result of the transference of the Court and the subsequent establishment of independent government, created an overall imbalance in the economy. This was countered by contracting foreign loans and issuing paper currency which rapidly depreciated.[22]

The immediate postindependence period was marked by a struggle between liberals, who were inspired by the egalitarian ideals of the French Revolution, and the conservatives, tied to the Portuguese nobility and the latifundia structure. Liberals pushed for primary schools in each municipality, secondary schools in each province, and universities in the most appropriate cities.[23] Popular education was proposed by this branch of the educated elite as a basis for universal suffrage. The objectives of schooling were to "educate free citizens able to sustain the newly created representative system . . . well educated people are synonymous with a liberated, well governed, and rich people." [24]

Despite the European cultural ideals pushed by the liberals, the results of independence for the educational system were almost exactly the opposite of what the liberals proposed. The 1824 Constitution abolished whatever weak state control existed over education. The influence of British capitalist ideals prevailed: the same "no state intervention in private life" policy which characterized free trade and British education in the nineteenth century was adopted by Brazil. However, the British provided government aid to mission schools for the poor in England, since schooled labor was needed for British factories. No such labor was needed in the Brazilian economy. Although the liberals did manage in 1827 to approve legislation that made the state responsible for the "creation of 'first letter' schools (reading and writing) in all towns and villages and the same type of schools for girls in more populated areas",[25] no arrangements were made for financing this educational extension.

Thus, education did not expand much despite laws which called for large increases in the number of schools. The export agriculture slave economy did not require large numbers of qualified workers. The ideals of freedom and democracy promulgated by the liberals (and to be spread by education) may have been important to legislators, but did not mean much to small urban merchants, peasants, and slaves, on whom they had little effect. By 1889, even after slavery had been abolished, only 5 percent of the adult population was allowed to vote.[26]

In 1834, the federal government reaffirmed its commitment to financing higher education as a means of assuring administrators and professionals in the government, and gave responsibility for primary education to the provinces. Secondary education was left in private hands and was primarily a preparatory phase for professional training.[27] For the next four decades, until substantial changes occurred in the composition of the Brazilian population and in the economy, federal policy concentrated on higher levels of schooling. There was little interest in education as a whole, although considerable discussion took place in the legislature in the formation of a university. In the end, however, only two faculties of law and some improvement in the existing military and medicine faculties were added to higher education during the first forty years of independence.

The Brazilian economy continued to be closely tied to Britain. The 1810 treaty was renewed in 1827 on the same terms which enabled England to undersell nascent Brazilian industries.

> During the mercantile epoch the metropolis's monopoly was maintained by military force and commercial monopoly; it was thus that the metropolis developed its industry while the satellites underdeveloped their agriculture. During the liberal epoch, the same monopoly of the now industrially stronger metropolis was maintained and extended through free trade and military force. As Alexander Hamilton and Frederick List recognized, it was liberalism and free trade which guaranteed Britain its nineteenth century industrial monopoly over the satellites.[28]

Under British-Brazilian free-trade relations, the Brazilian economy produced raw materials for British industry and imported British manufactured products, many of which were luxury goods for the urban merchants (foreign and domestic) and large landowners. Brazil's terms of trade worsened by 40 percent between 1820 and 1850; the exchange rate fell steadily from 1808 to the 1880s, with only a brief respite during the American Civil War. The balance of payments was in constant deficit each year between 1821 and 1860. This deficit and other economic activity was financed by foreign loans; by 1850 service on foreign debt consumed 40 percent of Brazilian government receipts. At the same time, British merchants took over almost all foreign and domestic wholesale trade.[29]

But since political power was vested in merchants and landowners, reactions to free trade economic policies and foreign domination were small and distorted. The English ambassador during the 1830s reported that the Brazilian urban middle class hated the English. However, these complaints were directed much more against the personal behavior of English merchants and their special civil-judicial rights than against low custom duties on British imports and other concessions to Britain.[30] Until the 1930s, there continued to be important resistance to protectionist policy by powerful Brazilian merchants and growers.

In this context, the national elite was most interested not in education but in concentrating resources on other priorities such as national defense and in increasing the output of export goods. Increased education was not related to the attainment of these priorities: increasing production in agriculture meant increasing the *number* of laborers and the amount of land under cultivation (slave imports accelerated after independence), and national defense, particularly international "protection," was achieved through good relations with Britain. Those who ran the country profited from the intermediary role they played between the British and the natural riches of Brazil. The existing school system was needed only to provide educated people for administrative and political tasks.[31]

In this period of political independence before the gradual abolition of slavery, the Brazilian ruling class had an "idealized" capitalistic philosophy (despite the existence of slavery). Government entered little into education although it did promote infrastructure like railroads, which were largely foreign financed and used to expedite exports of coffee, iron ore, and other primary goods. The population lived off this export trade, and the trade served to define the social hierarchy of *latifundários* and mine owners, white farmers and traders, mestizos, Indians, and finally black slaves. In this economic system, education was needed only to meet minimum administrative require-ments. This Positivist philosophy stressed the "right" of the individual to take education if he wished it but left such decisions to *individual,* not state, responsibility.

Under Positivism, primary schools did get built to accommodate basic education for some white and mestizo children. About 5 to 6 percent of the school-age free population was enrolled (average attendance was about 4 percent) in primary school in the 1860s and 1870s (see table 6).[32] The imperial administration claimed it did not have the human and material resources to implement a large national system of education even though it had committed itself to such a system in 1834. Azevedo blames this dichotomy between ideal and action on Latin American romanticism and unwillingness to face reality;[33] however, it is more likely that there was little pressure from politically powerful groups before the end of the century to spend more on schooling. A demand for schooling may have existed, especially among mestiços who wanted to work in the government bureaucracy, but apparently this demand was all but ignored until Brazil began to industrialize.

Republican Brazil

Coffee growing had begun in the 1820s, and by the 1840s was moving inland from Rio de Janeiro. The capital in coffee was Brazilian—accumulated in mining and foreign commerce. Slaves brought in from the Northeast worked the plantations. There were strong efforts on the part of the Northeast ruling groups to halt the slave traffic south, but they failed to do more than put an export tax on the slave export.[34] Coffee production began to grow rapidly in the 1860s, the beginning of a new export boom. This latest crop had important effects on the structure of the Brazilian economy. First, although much of the increase in coffee production was foreign financed, it led to the accumulation of capital in Brazilian hands as well. Part of this capital was invested in small-scale industry, particularly textiles.[35] Second, the need for agricultural labor to work the coffee plantations led to the promotion of immigration. The

Table 6

Brazil: Primary School Pupils, 1867–1949

Year	(1) Number of Pupils—Effec- tive Enrollment (thousands)[a]	(2) Total Population (thousands)	(3) School-age[b] Population (thousands)	Effectively Enrolled (average attendance) Pupils as Percent of School-age Population
1867	91[c]	—		—
1869	99[c]	—		—
1872	118[c]	8,420[d]	2,270	5.2
1889	220[c]	14,199 (1890)	3,800 (1890)	5.8
1907	543[c] (448)[e]	20,860	5,975[f]	9.1 (7.5)
1920	1,063[c] (855)[e]	27,404	8,484	12.6 (10.1)
1929	1,750[c] (1,602)[e]	32,894	9,654[f]	18.1 (16.6)
1939	2,652 (2,150)[e]	40,289	11,086 (1940)	23.9 (19.4)
1949	4,158	50,769	13,323 (1950)	31.2

[a] Effective enrollment is taken as 85 percent of enrollment at the beginning of the year (based on 1929–49 figures).
[b] 5–14 years old (from census data).
[c] Figure derived as 85 percent of total enrollment given in *Anuário*.
[d] "Free" population (nonslave).
[e] Figures in parentheses represent *average attendance*.
[f] Estimated by linear interpolation.

Sources: Column (1) 1867: Santa Anna Nery & Barão de Tefé, "A Educaçao ao fim do Império" in *Le Brésil en 1889* (Paris: Librairie Charles Delagrave, 1891). 1869: Roberto Moreira, *Educação e Desenvolvimento no Brasil* (Rio: Centro Latinoamericano de Pesquisas em Ciencias Sociales, 1960), p. 57. 1872–1949: *Anuário Estatístico do Brasil*, p. 1397. 1939, 1949: Werner Baer, *Industrialization and Economic Development in Brazil* (Homewood, Ill.: Richard Irwin, 1965), p. 244.
Column (2) 1872: *Anuário Estatístico do Brasil*, 1939/40, p. 87. 1890–1949: Baer, p. 242.
Column (3) 1872, 1890, 1920: *Anuário Estatístico do Brasil*, 1939/40, p. 87. 1940, 1950: Baer, p. 243.

combination of northeastern obstacles to bringing slaves south (coffee growers needed the blacks to work *their* crop), British pressure to end the African slave trade, and a domestic abolitionist movement,[36] also led to the gradual abolition of slavery, a legislative process which took almost twenty years, from 1873 to 1889.[37] The slave population of 1.5 million blacks was gradually integrated into the lowest class of "free" men primarily as agricultural (landless) labor in the *latifundio* structure, but many came south to work the coffee, and some became urban workers in the nascent industrial sector.

As slavery was being abolished, the government promoted European immigration as a way of increasing the labor force in agriculture (since slave importation had ended). Some of these new immigrants could buy their own land on easy terms through the government, while the freed slave population could not. The ex-slaves became wage labor in the north and the European immigrants became small land holders, largely in the South. The broad cultural impact of the immigrants on the Portuguese elite was attenuated by settling the immigrants in uninhabited areas. They formed clusters of European life within the country as a way of avoiding integration with the "tropical" Brazilians and as a way of providing infrastructure for the communities in which they lived. The Germans especially kept to themselves, building their own schools and cultural life. Ultimately, these German islands formed a "threat" to the economic and cultural power of the Brazilian ruling class, and their autonomy was destroyed.

The declaration of the Republican state in 1889, like the proclamation of independence in 1822, cannot be characterized as a popular political movement. *República* resulted from an elite group sharing a new philosophy and economic-political ideology brought about by important changes in the national and international sphere. In 1822 the so-called *elite ilustrada,* representing commodity exporters and English interests in Brazilian commerce, created the conditions for political change without popular participation. In 1889, the urban middle class and antislavery groups forced a change.

During the 1860s and 1870s, new industrial enterprises were helped partially by favorable terms of trade during those years and by the occasional tariff protection resulting from increased revenue needs of the government.[38] The rise of a group of industrialists combined with the abolitionists to gain power by the end of the 1880s. They claimed that Brazil had to foster import substitution industrialization to gain

economic independence. High-level legislators and military commanders, who were leaders of the Republican movement, represented the
urban merchants and industrialists who wanted to expand the internal
market, particularly among the immigrants. Abolition was supported
as a political ideal, consistent with a republican form of government,
but it was also a way of creating a large pool of potential wage labor,
and of creating a new basis of political support behind the industrial
bourgeoisie.[39]

The military rebellion against the emperor was transformed into a
Republican overthrow. It established "Order and Progress" as the basis
for freedom. The Catholic Church was separated from the state in
order to free the Republican government from any religious commitment in the face of other religions brought in by European immigrants
and to pull economic and political power away from the Catholic
hierarchy. The Republicans pushed for and obtained increased tariff
protection[40] and financial assistance from the government to new
industries.

> During the last decade of the nineteenth century Brazil also undertook
> a series of successive currency devaluations in order to deal with
> balance-of-payments problems. This also provided a certain amount of
> protection for new manufacturing enterprises. Thus, behind a protec-
> tive wall, Brazil's number of industrial establishments increased from
> 636 in 1889 to 1,088 in 1895. Throughout the last decade of the
> nineteenth century, industries catering to the rising export sectors and
> to the internal consumption sector made their appearances.[41]

The population increased from 10.1 million in 1872, to 14 million in
1889, to 17.3 million in 1900, and to 30 million in 1920.[42] (Table 7
shows the population by race.)

Between 1891 and 1914, about 2.4 million immigrants entered
Brazil, primarily in the South.[43] Railroads increased in length from 3.4
to 21.3 thousand kilometers between 1880 and 1910.[44] Coffee exports
were approximately 4 million 60 kilogram bags in 1880, rose to 10
million bags in 1900 and to over 16 million bags on the eve of World
War I.[45]

Table 7

Brazil: Population by Race, 1872–1950 (percent)

Race	1872	1890	1940	1950
White	38	44	63	62
Black	11	15	15	11
Mestiço (colored)	42	41	21	26
Asian	—	—	—	—
Total population (millions)	10	14	41	52

Source: Anuário Estatístico do Brasil, census years.

Although the Republic and abolition of slavery brought about problems of labor force shortage in agriculture and some political instability, the overall economic situation in the Republican period was good. Government loans for stimulating production and foreign loans did bring on a high rate of inflation, and the consequences for industrialization would have been serious had not the export sector continued to produce a large favorable balance of payments:

	Exports (in £'s)	Imports (in £'s)
1901–10	50 million	32 million
1911–20	70 million	55 million[46]

This first phase of industrialization (1889–1920) was the result of an emerging bourgeoisie, an expanding internal market (immigrant groups) and shocks from the external sector. These shocks consisted either of interruption of supplies from overseas due to wars (although industrialization probably slowed by 1917–18 when material imports were severely restricted) or of reduction in imports due to declines in foreign exchange. In periods of lack of employment in agriculture, labor came to the cities. Immigrants tended to remain in the cities if they had not agreed to work in agriculture in order to get their passage paid by the government.[47] By 1920, more than a million persons were working in the secondary sector (including construction), primarily in the textile industry, which had little multiplier effect on the rest of the economy.[48] Table 8 summarizes the approximate percentages of the total labor force in manufacturing between 1900 and 1950. Even though the estimated 1920 percentage is much too high, substantial growth of the manufacturing sector did take place between 1900 and 1920.

Table 8

Brazil: Total Labor Force and Labor Force in Manufacturing[a]

Year	Manufacturing Labor Force (thousands)	Total Labor Force (thousands)	Percent in Manufacturing
1900	196	6,800[b]	2.9
1920	1,189[c]	9,566	12.4
1940	1,400	13,868	10.1[d]
1950	2,231	17,070	13.0

[a] Manufacturing includes construction.

[b] Approximate.

[c] Includes small workshops and rural handicraft (even home needlework). An alternative approximation of the labor force in manufacturing based on manufacturing enterprises only is the following:

	No. of Enterprises	Labor Force	Approximate Percent of Total Labor Force
1907	3,258	150,000	2
1920	13,340	280,000	3

(Nilson Werner Sodre, História da Bourgesia Brasileira (Rio: Civilização, 1964), p. 243).

[d] Borges and Loeb show 14 percent for 1940 (see Baer, p. 18).

Source: Werner Baer, Industrialization and Economic Development in Brazil (Homewood, Ill.: Richard Irwin, 1965), tables 3A-9A; 3A-10A.

The period of the end of the nineteenth and the beginning of the twentieth centuries was also marked by continued and even growing involvement of foreign companies in all sectors of the economy, particularly mining and railroads. Between 1899 and 1910, for example, there were 160 national *sociedades anônimas* (corporations) formed, and 41 foreign corporations.[49] By 1916 the total capital of foreign corporations was 2.6 million contos de reis, while total capital of national enterprises was only 1.7 million contos de reis.[50] In 1920, foreign and national banks had almost equal deposits of 1 million contos de reis.[51]

Economic growth promoted the expansion of national economic groups related to the production and marketing of export goods, particularly coffee and mining; and those in manufacturing. Foreign investment continued to be an important part of the Brazilian economy. All this increased urbanization and cultural interchange with the new immigrants. Within thirty years of abolition of slavery, Brazil had a white majority and the South was industrializing.

Education, 1889–1930

Positivism continued to be the most influential philosophy of education in the early Republican period. Its proponents held teaching positions in all the major middle and higher schools. Although educational reforms in the first generation of the Republic reflected this philosophy, stressing "free instruction"—noninterference by the State in school finance, orientation, or taxation for education—these reforms concentrated on secondary and higher education or elite formation.[52] At the primary and secondary "professional" (vocational) levels, which were sources of skilled workers for industry, the state increasingly intervened to expand the number of children attending school, especially in the South.

Thus, two philosophies of education worked side by side: On the one hand, through policies of keeping secondary schools in private hands without state subsidies, secondary school and university were restricted to a very small group of students (see table 9) coming almost

Table 9

Brazil: Secondary and Higher Education Enrollment, 1889–1949

Year	Secondary Academic Enrollment (thousands)	Normal (thousands)	Other Post-primary Enrollment (thousands)	Higher Enrollment (thousands)
1889	10.4	—	—	3.3
1907	30.4	5.0	20.5	5.8
1929	83.2	23.8	86.5	13.2
1939	155.6	26.7	179.6	21.2
1949	365.8	36.7	462.4	37.6

Sources: 1889: Roberto Moreira, Educação e Desenvolvimento no Brasil (Rio: Centro Latinoamericano de Pesquisas en Ciencias Sociales, 1960), p. 57. 1907–49: Werner Baer, Industrialization and Economic Development in Brazil (Homewood, Ill.: Richard Irwin, 1965), p. 242.

entirely from the highest social classes. The private secondary schools therefore acted as an effective screen which essentially permitted only the wealthy to attend university. Since only this high-income group got to a university, the universities were subsidized by the government. On the other hand, those pushing for industrial expansion saw the need for a socialized industrial labor force and the Brazilianization of immigrants, and supported state participation to expand the primary level.

> Production . . . is the direct result of intelligence: it is, around the world, directly proportional to popular education. All protectionist laws (tariffs) are ineffectual in generating national economic greatness. . . . Popular education is the most creative of all economic forces, the most profitable of all financial measures.[33]

This was a significant departure from educational policy during the

Império, when Positivism applied to primary as well as secondary-level schooling. In addition, the state also provided, after 1889, more support to normal (teacher-training) schools and craft schools at the postprimary level. The normal schools (4 years) were for women, and the craft schools (3–5 years) for men. They were free (financed by each state) but did not allow access to the university. This dual system of education helped maintain the class structure while training teachers and artisans—skilled workers for roles in capitalist expansion.[54]

The result of transmitting the class structure through the educational system while attempting to satisfy industrialization's demands for workers and social integration are shown in tables 6 and 9. At the end of the empire, both primary and secondary schooling were limited. Only 200,000 pupils were effectively enrolled in primary school in 1889 and about 10,000 enrolled in secondary. Only a few thousand students attended university. Furthermore, primary enrollment increased very slowly in the last twenty years of empire, by about 5,000 annually, which was only slightly more than the increase in school-age population.

After 1889, there was a rapid increase in primary school enrollment, which corresponds directly to the labor force increase in manufacturing between 1889 and 1920 (see table 8). The number of pupils enrolled in primary school was less than 6 percent of the school-age population in 1889 and 12.6 percent in 1920, during a period of rapid population increase. Starting from a much smaller base, the relative increase in academic secondary school students kept pace with primary, but the absolute increase in number enrolled was small. Higher education was even more limited. In 1929, out of a population 15–22 years old of about 5 million, only 83,000 students were enrolled in academic secondary school and 13,000 in university. More than 100,000 students were enrolled in normal and nonacademic secondary training.

This was, in effect, a compromise reached by the conservative elements in the ruling class tied to free trade dependency with the rising industrialists: primary schooling, normal schools to service primary schools with teachers, and nonacademic secondary training were expanded, while academic secondary and university, which gave access to the liberal professions, were severely restricted. Expanded

primary and "vocational" training was used primarily to incorporate
new immigrants into the industrial labor force. The increase in pupils
took place largely in the South of the country, and even at primary
level, whites had a disproportionate number of children attending
school. Although some blacks got jobs in the manufacturing sector,
most stayed as wage labor in agriculture. The educational expansion
was largely a southern phenomenon, connected with the growth of
manufacturing in the South[55] and with the incorporation of immigrant
whites into the new industrial working class.

Schooling expanded rapidly, but it still only reached a small
percentage of school-age children. Table 6 shows that in 1920 only 10
percent of the school-age group was effectively enrolled in primary
school, and even in 1949, only 31 percent of children went to primary
school. This limited incorporation of children into the emerging
capitalist structures was the direct result of the limited extension of
those structures themselves.[56] Most laborers were still producing
export goods or living off subsistence agriculture. There was no
attempt to mobilize these masses of blacks, mestiços, and poor whites.
The economy was still structured as a dependent part of the world
system of trade, despite its protected industrial sector, and that
dependent structure prevented the participation of most of the
population in the "development" sectors.[57]

Foreign schools played an interesting role in educational expansion.
Schools run by German immigrant communities posed a political
"threat" to national "unity" during World War I and were closed by
the government.[58] This led to a national conference in 1922 to plan the
expansion of federal financing of primary education to incorporate
schools of all cultures in the interest of national solidarity.

But at the same time that the government was eliminating attempts
at internal cultural pluralism, it was tolerant to considerable influence
on Brazilian education from the United States. During the last years of
the imperial government, the "free instruction" system, created in 1879
as a result of slave abolition and migration policies, permitted the
accreditation and expansion of schools run by foreigners—both
religious and nonreligious groups. An American woman, together with
a Brazilian woman trained in Massachusetts, were responsible for

expanding the normal schools, reorganized on the lines of the Massachusetts schools and financed from the United States.[59] Mackenzie College, today a large private university in São Paulo, was founded in 1890 with private U.S. funds. The agricultural school in Viçosa (Minas Gerais) and women's professional schools in Rio and São Paulo were also financed and organized from the United States, and the teaching and orientation of these schools followed U.S. patterns. The differences between European and U.S. educators were apparent from their stated objectives: European educators were primarily moved by religious principles and by the preservation of culture and traditions in their communities transplanted to Brazil. U.S. educators were interested in transforming *Brazilian* culture, by spreading U.S. ideals[60] in Brazilian economic and political organization.

The U.S. contribution to Brazilian education became more apparent after the 1920s, when several Brazilian educators began to apply U.S. doctrines in educational reforms. Although U.S. educational philosophy and psychology have been important influences on teaching methodology since the 1920s,[61] it has only been recently, with important changes in the Brazilian economy (particularly the influx of U.S. technology and investment in manufacturing) that the U.S. schooling structure and concepts of economic development and social control are beginning to be adopted. During the 1960s, the movement toward work-oriented education on a mass scale and college-level short careers (an extension of vocational training to develop technicians) were defined as part of the U.S. development model.

In this Republican period, we find all the elements of later educational developments in Brazil. The struggle within the elite over the expansion of schooling in the first decades of the century reached its climax in 1960–61, when exactly the same issues formed the basis of the controversy over the expansion and control of secondary schooling.[62] Again, the private/public control issue masked the different economic and political ideologies of the opponents and their views of the role of education in the country's development. The earlier influence of the United States became increasingly important once the Brazilian economy became increasingly tied to the United States after World War II and particularly after 1964.[63] Despite that earlier influence, the Brazilian ruling class allowed changes in the structure of their educational system only when they themselves identified with the industrial society promoted by U.S.-type economic structures.

Education and Free-trade Colonialism: Peru

Like other Latin American countries, Peru passed from Spanish mercantile monopoly to political independence in a free trade international system dominated first by Britain and then by the United States. While some of the larger Latin American republics managed to begin protectionist industrialization by 1914 even within a dependent economy, Peru's ruling groups since colonial times were primarily concerned with participating in the foreign-controlled export surplus.

This section traces the history of Peruvian education from the precolonial Incaic period to the *oncenio* (1919–30) of Augusto Leguía. In that long history, through mercantilism and free-trade capitalism, schooling was always organized on a rigid class basis—performing primarily two basic functions: to preserve the economic and social differences among Peruvians rather than reducing them, and to *control social change.*

The crises in the Peruvian economy were generally caused by *external* events, such as the rise and fall in the demand for certain goods, or by shifts in power among metropoli on which Peru's elite was dependent for income. As each crisis occurred, the ruling classes struggled for access to Peru's export surplus in a new alignment of power. By 1875, formal schooling had become part of this struggle. As one group within the ruling class tried to reorganize Peru's relationship with the external powers for its own long-term political control, the group gave formal schooling an important role in setting the internal conditions for those relationships.

Peruvian education, whether Spanish colonial or Republican, until recent years was organized in the context of an export economy, dominated in both the mercantile and capitalist periods by foreigners. Internal economic structures served the export trade or subsistence agriculture, but *not* a growing internal market. Foreign culture greatly influenced the consumption habits of the wealthy (though not the productive habits), and schooling, especially at the secondary and higher levels, reflected these consumption patterns.

But it is the expansion of primary schooling which is of particular interest to us. That expansion, which began just before the ruinous Chilean war (1879–81), was to be the basis of a new kind of Peruvian economic development: an important segment of the ruling class wanted to create a "modern" Peru which would attract foreign investment. An integral component of this modernity was the assimilation of Peru's indigenous population into the lower levels of the dependent economy's wage structure; primarily to avoid the possibility of future class conflicts and to create a politically stable, "progressive" economy.

At best, the purpose of education in the most liberal of these models—that of the *civilistas*—was to "develop" the poorest Peruvians in ways that would somewhat increase their income, but more important, would create the conditions whereby the local elites could expand their own wealth. The *civilistas* believed that a primary schooled indigenous population would make Peru safe and attractive for foreign capital, and therefore, would promote economic growth.

In part, this vision came true: after the Chilean war, foreign investors rapidly took over almost all Peru's exportable wealth and the railroads with which to move it to ports. But rather than increasing the demand for skilled labor, the plantation structure of Peru's dynamic sectors *limited* the expansion of education. Primary export activities did not require skilled workers, only the peaceful and controlled conditions in which to exploit local resources. In practice, despite some vague *civilista* desire to elevate the poor, even by 1930 primary education was extended to only a small percentage of the school-age population. It can be argued that this limited expansion resulted from resistance by "traditional" elements in Peruvian society, such as the church, which previously controlled schooling. Although church resistance *was* a factor in educational reform, the dependent structure of the economy and the *civilista* project itself were as important in defining educational change as any compromise made with conservative groups. Thanks to the *civilista* bourgeoisie's cooperation with the British in free trade, for example, domestic manufacturing had to compete with foreign imports and could not develop until World War II. The *civilista* project also was intimately connected with foreign control of resources and later, of manufacturing. Furthermore, the *civilistas* had no intention of changing the class structure; the expansion of primary schooling was implicitly used to modernize Peru through preserving the social order.[64] Opposition to expansion was only mollified when the conservatives were convinced that schooling's socializing function would benefit the elite rather than threaten it.

Because of its social-maintenance function, schooling was concentrad in Lima and Callao, and the composition of enrollment in primary and secondary school reflected the class nature of these two schooling levels. Far from mobilizing the Indian and urban masses to participate in their project, the liberals, like the Spanish and the church before them, used schooling to organize Peru largely for the benefit of their own class. Thus, although the church also tried to keep the poor and rich in their proper places, it was not only the "traditional" elements in Peruvian society who were responsible for social structural rigidity, but the liberals themselves. The primary difference between the two was that the church and its allies were trying to maintain a precapitalistic social order, while the liberal *civilistas* were attempting to create a more capitalist Peru, with a similarly structured, but more "modern" hierarchy.

Inca Education

Before Francisco Pizarro came to Peru in 1532, the native Andean Indians built an extensive and sophisticated empire under Inca rule. The empire's economy was based on a regimented communal agriculture which depended, in turn, on a highly developed irrigation system.[65] Different areas of the empire specialized in different crops. These were exchanged through strict government control and a good system of transportation. Common people had to work in community jobs assigned by the state; in turn, they were guaranteed the minimum necessities of life (food, dress, and shelter). Those who could not work or who lived in famine areas were supplied their food needs from public granaries.[66] The Inca state was therefore all-powerful: it demanded labor and allegiance and provided security.

Although this regimented society had rank distinctions among nobles and occupational differences among commoners, it was basically a two-class social structure. At the head of this structure was the Inca god-king. "His power was total and absolute, and every member of the empire, lord or commoner, was his vassal." [67] Below the god-king, Inca nobles served as senior civil administrators, generals, and priests. They were responsible for control over production and distribution of goods and services.

> Although private property, currency, or the possibility to accumulate wealth were non-existent, the nobles received a variety of privileges in exchange for total loyalty to the Inca. They lived in large palaces staffed with commoners obtained under the *mita,* or draft-labor law. As a class, the nobles were exempt from taxes and agricultural work and were richly supplied with both staple and luxury items. They were sharply distinguished from commoners by their fine dress and jewelry, their right to take more than one wife, and by numerous other privileges.[68]

Commoners lived in agricultural villages and were entirely at the disposal of the nobles to carry out the state's demands; however, they were not slaves and could not be bought and sold. Slaves were not needed in an economy where all the commoners had to serve the state.[69]

The two-class society seemed to have a dual educational system. There is not much informatiion about Inca educational practices, but historians think that the Incas had a formal education system for the elite (the *cacique* family, the military, and the priests), administered by the priest caste. The purpose of these schools was to give nobles an understanding of the foundations and reasons for Inca laws, and the art of government and skills of warfare.[70] Commoners' children were educated only informally through labor in the *ayllu*—the agricultural community—and through participation in civic and religious activities left over from pre-Inca times.[71] This dual education system reflected

> the needs of the empire for well-trained workers and for leaders in public administration, the Church, and the military. All knowledge was seen to fall into three major divisions: the moral, the intellectual, and the physical. The Inca class alone was exposed to all three, as were the sons of conquered chiefs whom the Inca called to Cuzco for formal schooling.[72]

The Colonial Period

In 1532, the Spanish, under the command of Francisco Pizarro, occupied the apex of the Inca government structure and rapidly extended their power over the Inca empire. Pizarro maintained the tribute and *mita* system used by the Incas so as to maintain traditional control patterns, but it was now the Spanish, not the Inca state, who appropriated the productive surplus. Very rapidly, the Spanish shifted Indian labor from indigenous agriculture to silver and gold mines, and silver and gold provided the limited commerce that replaced the domestic Inca economy.

Besides shifting labor to mining, the Spanish introduced the *encomienda* system: the Crown granted large tracts of land to deserving Spaniards (usually ex-soldiers) for one or two generations. Through the *mita* system of requisitioning Indian labor, the Spanish made Indians into serfs on these large landholdings. Because of the shift of Indian labor away from traditional agriculture and the introduction of Spanish-owned livestock, which took large amounts of land out of agriculture altogether, Indian agricultural output declined greatly. Irrigation systems and roads were neglected, and the entire Inca organization of exchange began to disappear. The Indian population declined from 4 to 6 million in 1532 to 1.5 million in 1570 to its all-time low of 700,000 in 1796.[73]

In forty years, the Spanish destroyed the Indian economy and turned Peru into a supplier of minerals to Spain—this despite the turbulence

of Indian revolts. Crops changed from Indian staples to grapes and
wheat needed by the Spaniards. Later in the colonial period, sugar
began to be grown on the coast for export (slaves were imported to
work the sugar plantations). The destruction of the Indian economy
was so complete that the Peruvian Indian population almost disappeared.

At the same time, the Spanish settlers in Peru were closely tied to
Spain's mercantile system. Although Pizarro had initiated trade with
Spanish settlements in Mexico soon after conquest, Spain moved to cut
off such intercolony trade: all settlements had to send their exports to
Spain and get all their goods from Spain. Spain's mercantile monopoly
also exercised control over Peru's domestic economy: Through the
viceroy—the official representative of the Crown—tracks of land were
granted only for one or two generations. This kept settlers from
developing a power base of their own. Since there was little commerce
between colonies, local merchants were made completely dependent on
the metropole. The mercantile system was designed to prevent any
local group from getting enough power to question subordination to
Spain herself.

> . . . the land as such did not have the same attraction and importance
> at different times during the colonial period. For the most part, during
> the mineral boom, the agricultural surplus as well as indigenous labor
> had to be devoted to mining and transport. This perhaps is the
> explanatory context of two of the fundamental institutions of colonial
> exploitation: the *encomienda* (and later the *corregimiento*) and the
> colonial *mita*.[14] (Authors' translation.)

Education was an important part of both the appropriation of Indian
surplus by the Spaniards and of the control of Spanish settlers by the
Crown. Unlike the Portuguese in Brazil, who had to contend with
"savage" nomads, unsocialized in the ways of hierarchically organized
work, the Spanish conquered an established social structure in Peru.
There were similarities between Inca and Spanish institutions: both
the Inca and Spanish church and state were closely linked; the Inca
religion, like Catholicism, had a hierarchical priesthood, a belief in a

superior being and life after death, and used images in worship. The Spanish saw, correctly, that Inca structures could be controlled through the Inca leaders (*caciques*) if the caciques could be made loyal to Spain.

The *escuelas de caciques* were organized specifically for this purpose. Run by the Jesuits, the schools brought the sons of Indian nobles to Lima, Cuzco, and other cities to be taught Spanish language and "to banish the sin in which they live." [75] The children were kept at school, isolated from their communities, learned Spanish, and enrolled under Spanish names received through baptism. They had a strict study schedule and wore uniforms with the Spanish royal arms.[76]

The schools were a complete success. The Spanish converted Indian nobles into Spanish intermediaries. In his new role the cacique continued to be responsible for collecting tribute as under Inca rule, but had to turn a large part of it over to the Spanish rather than to the Inca state. The Spanish increased the tribute and the cacique was responsible, in addition, for providing labor to the mines.

> The cacique was the intermediary between Spain and the "Indian republic" for communicating orders and tasks; the work shifts in the mines; the levies to the *encomenderos;* the persecution of the guilty or of fugitives.
>
> The cacique was also responsible . . . for making sure that the communities (in his province) gave the priests and convents the sustenance that the latter needed while converting the Indians. . . .
>
> The power that the caciques acquired was really very great, so that if their subjects did not comply with the goods which they owed for tribute, the caciques became cruel persecutors of their own race without making allowance for widowhood, hunger, or misery. In this way they increased their fortunes.[77] (Authors' translation.)

Jesuit education for caciques was therefore designed to make Indians use their positions of power as a kingpin of the Spanish colonial administration. The caciques, in turn, were dependent on the colonial system for their personal position and wealth. They served the Spanish, not the Indians, and were usually loyal to the Spanish during the Indian uprisings.

Some Jesuits also tried to organize planned rural towns (*reducciones*) like those in Brazil, in order, according to Paulston, to "protect" the Indians from the excesses of economic exploitation. The attempt "failed" to achieve that goal, but once the scattered Indians were centralized in the towns, Spanish officials "came to use these relocations as easily governed and controlled sources of manpower to be exploited economically." [78]

Education for children of Spanish settlers or their descendants (*criollos*), administrators, and military was very limited in the colonial period and designed to keep them subjugated to the Spanish Crown. Primary education, for all practical purposes, was available only through tutors privately hired by upper-class families. The Jesuits had seminaries to train clergy and later these became the colony's first secondary schools for university preparation. The colonial government opposed mass public education: "the nobility of the metropolis and those in charge of power in the colony saw a great danger in the diffusion of teaching and culture in general . . . 'for the good of the people and social peace,' came orders from the Viceroy, it was better to have no public education." [79] Thus, aside from a few parish schools and orphanages run by the clergy, there was no primary schooling for the masses, either Indian or European.

In contrast, higher education for the local upper classes developed rapidly. The *criollos* wanted a university in Peru so that their children could gain access to a professional career and therefore into the upper strata of colonial society. The Crown supported universities as a way to supply the professional needs of the colony and to increase its hispanization. The church wanted universities to train priests and to implant scholastic theology in the colonies. With the support of these groups, San Marcos University was created in 1551, and later, other higher level institutions were founded at Chuquisaca, Huamanga, and Cuzco. [80]

These "universities," all under church control, supported secondary schools that frequently shared the same teachers, premises, and courses. The distinction between the two institutions, therefore, is frequently not clear. Only San Marcos developed into a university on a par with its predecessors at Salamanca and Bologna in Europe. [81]

The universities were nothing more than an imperfect copy of higher education in Spain. The main characteristics of Peruvian colonial universities was their religious orientation dominated (as in Brazil) by the anti-Enlightenment position of the Jesuit Order—their high selectivity along class and racial lines, and their teaching method—dogmatic, memoristic, authoritarian, and unsystematic.[82] They also disregarded everything concerning Peru as such.[83] History was that of the metropolis, and the present was based on the obedient and subordinate relationship of colonials to Spain.[84]

All three groups who brought the university to Peru—creoles, church, and viceroyalty—ensured their interests by restricting access to it and having complete control over the curriculum. The creoles passed laws that excluded from the university mestizos and all others with mixtures of European, American, African, or Asian blood. Illegitimate children were also prevented from entering. The church tried to use the university as an additional means of conversion and control of the Indian population by requiring that Indians be allowed free admission to the university. Of course Indians rarely got to the university. Neither could anyone whose father or grandfather had been punished by the Inquisition attend.[85]

From the seventeenth century onward, Spanish mercantilist policy faced British (and to some extent, French) industrialization. Because Spain did not expand her industrial production, she ended up exporting colonial gold and Spanish wool to England, Holland, and France in order to import manufactured goods needed by Spain and Spanish America. Spain became an intermediary between other European countries and her own colonies. Peru's position in the colonial system also declined in the eighteenth century because of the creation of other viceroyalties—Neuva Granada (Venezuela and Colombia) and Rio de la Plata. Thus, where in the past, all Spanish South American trade had gone through Lima, now Buenos Aires, Cartagena, and many other ports shared the trade.

By the end of the century, Spain was at war (Napoleonic Wars). Incapable of supplying her colonies with manufactured goods, and unable to control the monopoly trade, Spain decided in 1797—as a temporary measure—to open its American ports to neutral ships.

When she tried to revoke that decree two years later, it was too late. The colonies themselves would not close their ports to other countries.[86]

All these changes, including the decline of Peruvian mining beginning at the end of the seventeenth century, reduced Peru's income substantially. English influence and the liberalization of commerce in South America primarily benefited Buenos Aires, not Lima. So the end of Spain's mercantile power came at the same time that Peru was in a difficult economic situation herself. Peruvian political independence from Spain, achieved not by Peruvians, but by outside troops and leadership, was not entirely welcomed by the Peruvian ruling class.

> Many of the *peninsulares, criollos,* and clergy had become fantastically wealthy through Crown grants of land and rights to exploit Indian labor in the fields and mines. The idea of revolution, quite understandably, had limited appeal to this small ruling group whose power and riches derived from the crudest forms of colonial exploitation. They successfully limited the independence movement to the removal of Spanish power and its replacement by the Creole element.[87]

Along with economic decline, a new dynasty gained the Spanish throne in Spain in the eighteenth century. The Bourbons brought with them fragments of French technical administration, and much more sympathy for the Spanish bourgeoisie.[88] Although Bourbon reforms had little effect on the Spanish economy (the production of manufactured goods increased slightly), they did open Spain and the colonies to the influence of the European enlightenment. Baran attributes the change in the characteristics of the colonial education system to this change in environment.[89] In the period until the end of the seventeenth century, according to Bazan, education was effectively an instrument of domination, not only because it was dictated in every detail directly from the metropole, but because *submission* was the essence of education at all levels: external submission to the monarchy and internal submission to the moral-spiritual and intellectual prescriptions of the church. But during the second half of the eighteenth century, education (university) became "infiltrated by reformist ideas, noble inspirations which found the strength and direction to protect rights unrecognized until then." [90]

The Republic–The Guano Period

Despite the liberalism that emanated from San Marcos and the ensuing independence from Spanish authority, the universities and the socioeconomic structure were changed little by the Enlightenment.

> When the ties with Spain were broken, the fundamental Peruvian linkage to the international system—gold and silver mining—was undergoing a grave crisis. If we add to this Peru's geographical position, the political-administrative vacuum because of centuries of metropolis control, Peru's structural heterogeneity, the absence of a bourgeoisie who wanted to take national power—the result of a dependent commercial capitalism—we will understand the character of the first twenty years of Republican life. [91]

Peru found itself at independence without very much to export and far from European markets. The Spanish had transported Peruvian goods across Panama; with the break in the Spanish trading monopoly, Peruvian commerce either went around Cape Horn or overland to Cartagena and Buenos Aires. The effect of this long transport haul to Europe was to price Peruvian sugar out of the market and to limit her exports before 1840 largely to her remaining minerals, hides (alpaca), and wool.

Independence did bring liberal views of legal structure imported from France. The Napoleonic Code protected individual ownership of property, but did not recognize communal lands. In Peru, this led to the rapid aggrandizement of already large landholdings. Indian communal land holdings were broken up because the new laws in effect turned communal lands over to individual Indians. They were given the right to sell their piece of land, and large landowners got the right to buy communal land, which opened the way for illegal expropriations. The superimposition of bourgeois reform (French law) on Peru's socioeconomic structure led to a strengthening of the traditional hacienda system. Since Indians were increasingly separated from the land, it also strengthened feudal institutions like the *mita* system.

> Liberalism, which in the European democratic bourgeois revolution served the bourgeois offensive against the landed aristocracy, in Peru came in as a sophisticated product imported by the landholders, mine owners, and foreign merchants, who first utilized its political content to confront Spain, but then after independence, conferred on it a completely different content than originally defined by the European industrial bourgeoisie.[92]

Under these conditions, the powerful groups in the country wanted as little interference from the state as possible. They pushed for free trade, little taxation, and the state's passive acceptance of their actions at the local level. During the first half of the nineteenth century, then, the new state's life was marked by a laissez faire type of precapitalist economy. The commerce of the economy was handled by foreigners, primarily English. The word "foreigner" became synonymous with "merchant." Foreign capital also began to develop large coastal estates (sugar) and took over mines which had been closed during the war of independence.

The merchants were the one group who could have accumulated the surplus to begin industrializing Peru and who had the political power to organize a political and administrative reform. But the merchants were foreigners and had no interest in doing so. While they realized the importance of keeping Peru solvent, they also wanted to extract as much income from the raw-materials trade as possible. In that sense, they were the allies of the *hacendados:* both opposed tariffs and all other taxes which affected imports and exports; both opposed any stimulus by the state to a national bourgeoisie.

The government therefore had to rely heavily on covering its expenditures through taxation of Indians and other individuals. The colonial Indian tribute remained intact after independence, and Indians paid about 60 percent of the total individual taxes collected, and about

33 percent of all taxes, including customs duties.[93] Peru already owed one million pesos to Colombia, and one-half million to Chile as a result of having armies from those countries fight Peru's war of independence. Besides, her balance of payments was negative in the 1820s and internal debt increased rapidly as the limited taxes collected could not cover costs of maintaining an army and a corrupt bureaucracy. In 1822, Peru took her first loan from England, and by 1826, her English debt was almost 2 million pounds. The interest on this debt was 100,000 pounds annually, an amount Peru had great difficulties paying.

Thus, to continue land acquisition and to maintain serf (and slave) labor, the large landowners threw Peru into enormous debt and shared part of the surplus from the land with foreign merchants and financiers. But almost the entire surplus ended up either in luxury consumption by the landowning class or in England—invested there by British interests in Peru.

Under these circumstances, no group in the country wanted to expand education, and there was no money with which to do it. Even though provision was made in early constitutions for the state to provide public education equally to every citizen, the pattern of colonial education continued largely unaltered and the masses received no schooling whatsoever. Before independence, San Martín created the first teacher-education institution in Lima, and under the directorship of a British missionary, San Martín also introduced the Lancaster system at the secondary level. That system was designed to teach hundreds of pupils at one time through a monitorial system and one master teacher. Four years later, Simón Bolivar, another of the liberators of Peru, established two more monitorial normal schools in an effort to stimulate Peruvian education. These efforts failed because they were an attempt to implement a European bourgeois vision of society on a traditional, plantation economy. There was no national bourgeoisie in Peru who would support these efforts.

With the failure of the Lancaster system, education continued to be organized around the *conventos;* a public system of primary education did develop slowly, but never got the financial and human resources necessary to make it available to more than a few middle-class students.

The selection of students was carried out by each region's bishop, which implied that non-Catholics (primarily Indians) were excluded. Financing schools was legally a responsibility of the municipal and provincial governments, which would annually select six students to go to the federally financed secondary schools.

This, then, was the situation in "independent" Peru twenty years after the formal break with Spain. Powerful landowning and church interests controlled the structure of Peruvian society and the educational system. But in the late 1830s, the industrial revolution in Europe—particularly England—had a profound effect on Peruvian trade. The reintegration of Peru into the international system, this time through England and France instead of Spain, determined the course of the Peruvian economy and politics until the war with Chile in 1879–81. The educational system was reformed somewhat in this period under the influence of part of the ruling class—the *civilistas*—who remained largely outside the export boom and used the vision of a modernizing Peru as a means of coming to power. Nevertheless, as we shall show, the *civilista* project had to wait until the turn of the century to be realized, and then only in the context of a Peruvian economy largely controlled by foreign investors.

The necessity of higher agricultural productivity in Europe to feed the growing number of urban workers coming from the countryside, created a demand for fertilizer. Huge Peruvian coastal guano deposits, which had been used earlier in the century to promote domestic agriculture, began commanding high prices in European markets and brought Peru its greatest wealth since the mining boom. The guano export came on suddenly, and given the size of the undertaking, the nature of the risks, and the new scale and demands of the international system, none of the local elites could assume direct and exclusive exploitation of the guano export. Instead, a system was devised in which powerful London and Paris corporations were granted the right as consignees to sell the guano in designated regions of the world.[94]

The absence of a Peruvian capitalist group able to undertake foreign trade on a large scale meant, therefore, that the guano exploitation fell into foreign hands. Yet, a part of the local bourgeoisie managed to participate in the guano boom through the Peruvian state beginning in the late 1840s. For the next thirty years, Peruvian politics revolved around the struggle by local elites over the guano surplus. Control of the state apparatus was the key to this surplus, and the role of the state was almost entirely that of an intermediary between European guano markets and local elites.

In the 1850s, the Lima bourgeoisie obtained access to the guano revenue by getting the state (Ramón Castilla was the first president to perform this role of imtermediary) to expand ("consolidate") the internal debt by recognizing numerous past (and imaginary) claims against the government. This arrangement provided a source of high interest and commissions for this part of the Peruvian elite through its control of the government.[95] The elite, in turn, converted much of the internal debt into external debt by discounting internal debt in foreign banks and investing the money abroad. But part of the money stayed in Peru: little by little, enough capital and commerical technology accumulated so that Peruvian companies could make profit on guano contracts.[96] Peruvian groups in the late 1850s received contracts for areas outside consignments to foreign corporations. When the Gibbs contract—the major consignment for Britain and all Europe but France and Spain—expired in 1861, Gibbs' area was given to those Peruvian capitalists who had made their fortunes on the internal debt.

The guano trade was extremely profitable for these capitalists, and with the profits, they began the first domestic financial houses. The banks could have been the source of funds for Peruvian industrialization, but since the internal market had been unaltered by the guano boom—it had not at all been used to mobilize local agriculture or even small-scale artisan-type industry[97]—the new domestic financial interests invested their capital in export agriculture, primarily in coastal cotton and sugar plantations, as a response to the rise in prices of those goods because of the American Civil War and the Cuban political crisis.

Until the mid-1860s, coastal haciendas had been (since colonial times) producing for local food consumption. Once they were shifted into export agriculture, more sierra land was taken out of subsistence agriculture and turned into haciendas for urban food production. This continued the process of concentrating land holdings. Since most of those Indians whose land had been expropriated did not get work on the coastal plantations imported Chinese chattel slaves and some black ex-slaves got the jobs, and since increased internal debt was accompanied by rapid domestic inflation, we can assume that despite the guano boom and the subsequent cotton and sugar boom (1861–75) the bulk of the population was *worse off* in terms of real consumption in the 1860s than they had been in the 1840s.[98]

It is in this context that we should analyze the minor educational reforms which occurred in the third quarter of the century. During Ramón Castilla's first term as president (1845–51), the mestizo general turned to education for national integration and the expansion of Peruvian crafts within a free trade economic system. In a speech to the Congress in 1850, asking for the approval of the education reform law, Castilla said that "the abolition of the protectionist system and the lack of professional education prevent our handicrafts from competing with foreign goods . . . This can be remedied by establishing art schools." [99]

His policy reflected, in general, the European liberal sentiment of the time, which believed in the benefits of free trade and, at the same time, in the equality of men. Castilla apparently wanted to integrate Indians, mestizos, and blacks into a Peruvian nation, but he was also obligated to the economic needs of the Lima bourgeoisie. Instead of instituting protectionist tariffs to encourage the artisans, he argued that Peru could have the benefits of both free commerce and increased artisanal production through art schools. He helped blacks and Indians by working for the abolition of slavery and removing the Indian tribute, but redistributed wealth to the already higher-income bourgeoisie through the consolidation of the internal debt.

Castilla's second term (1855–62) continued to exhibit these contradictions. The first educational reform (1850) had defined education as a public service, had established a central educational authority, and a Code of Schooling which differentiated between public and private education, and recognized the state as responsible for offering education. The second reform (1855)

> organized Peruvian education into three functional divisions that are still used today. At the bottom of the educational pyramid, *educación*

popular represented the State's first limited commitment to provide
elementary schooling for the masses. During the primary grades, the
curriculum included reading and writing Spanish, arithmetic, catechism,
and training in "pious and decent manners." The upper grades of the
"people's" school offered courses in the areas of technical and normal
school education. Four years after their founding, primary schools, free
to the poor, enrolled some 15,573 children throughout the nation.[100]

By 1856, there was a newspaper campaign favoring compulsory
primary education: it stressed Castilla's commitment to public
instruction as an instrument of national progress.[101] This conception of
education as an instrument for socializing people into the characteristics of a modern society, also conceived of education as the means to
bringing this society into existence:

> The acquisition of the learning fundamentals is beneficial for productiv-
> ity. He who doesn't have these fundamentals will not leave his daily
> routine, nor will he understand the machines which will open the doors
> of progress for him.[102]

These concepts closely paralleled contemporary educational philosophy in the United States (chapter 5), but whereas in the United States,
the educational system was expanding to provide socialized workers for
industry, in Peru, capital was being invested in coastal plantations
which required slaves rather than artisans or workers trained in "pious
and decent manners." Thus Castilla's liberalism produced educational
reforms that could not be realized within the economic structure which
that liberalism supported. Indeed, it can be argued that the reforms
resulted in rhetoric and some token favors for the poor while leaving
them no better or even worse off economically during a period of great
wealth accumulation by a small class of Lima merchants and of foreign
consignees.[103]

The Civilista Period and the Expansion of Schooling

Far from constructing a national bourgeoisie to replace foreign
merchants, however, the local guano capitalists of the 1860s main-

tained the process of decapitalizing Peru. They invested in export crops, kept Peru in a state of debt, and used much of the surplus in the consumption of luxury goods. Lima, as an intermediary, grew affluent while the rest of the country stagnated. Lima's urban privileged groups tried to copy the styles, values, and institutions of Europe, but this importation of institutions was limited to consumption goods and did not extend to the production values of the European bourgeoisie. Furthermore, the local guano merchants did not build a power base through which they could maintain and consolidate their economic hegemony. They lent money to the government against exploitation of the guano deposits, but they did not build a political infrastructure through which they could control the government. Although the elements of a political philosophy around which they could organize were present in the Castilla terms of office—liberalism and national integration—the guano group's economic base was destroyed before they used this philosophy to regain power.[104]

Nicolas de Pierola, the minister of hacienda under Balta (1869), represented a sector of the provincial aristocracy marginal to the guano boom. Pierola wanted to give the guano exploitation directly to foreign firms, so that the surplus could be taken away from local guano merchants and redistributed by the State to other dominant and dominated factions.[105] In 1869, he signed a contract with Dreyfus Bros., a French firm, which consigned to Dreyfus all European distribution of Peruvian guano. Dreyfus, in turn, took over servicing the Peruvian external debt and greatly expanded guano output. But in order to destroy the powerful local guano-based merchant-financial-export crop interests, Pierola had to come up with a project which would capture the imagination of the heterogeneous groups marginal to the guano trade: this project was the construction of two major railroads (Mollendo to Cuzco and Lima to Cerro de Pasco). With Dreyfus as Peru's banker, Pierola borrowed abroad heavily in 1870–72 to finance the railroads. Meiggs, the American adventurer,[106] received incredible amounts for construction ($40,000 per mile), much of which went for bribes and personal profit. By 1872, the external debt was up to £35 million, and the service on the debt was so large—£2.7 million—that all guano sales went for servicing the debt and the government was unable to meet the *internal* debt, creating a new crisis. Pierola had managed in three years to plunge Peru into a financial situation from which it would not recover: his policies created the conditions for foreign takeover of the country's resources and established the context of Peruvian development to the present day.

When Pierola took their economic base away from them, the Lima merchants finally understood the necessity to establish political institutions through which they could maintain alliances with other groups. They formed a party with a program: the basis of the "Civilista" party, as they called themselves, was a state which would be the expression of a new relationship between the metropolis (England) and the hegemonic faction in Peru.[107] In order to get their power back (and hopefully, the guano trade), the guano capitalists of the 1860s adopted a liberal platform which promised to "modernize" Peru by attracting foreign investment and promoting free trade, popular education, and an electoral system. Manuel Pardo, a prominent member of the Civilista party, although not one of the guano capitalists himself, became the first Civilista president in 1872.

Pardo saw the guano income as an artificial inducement to consumption which did not raise other local production. His solution to the mono-product economy was to bring in foreign capital and *to create favorable conditions for it*,[108] including insuring a high rate of return through subsidies and concessions. In other words, the *civilista* model was a project that expanded the international system by getting foreigners to invest in hardware like railroads, which would promote exports, while the state invested in social infrastructure, like education, which would insure a high return to that foreign investment.

But the guano capitalists founded their program and their model too late. They could not use the state to make money because the state had pledged the guano deposits to pay for the railroads; the service charges on the external debt took all the guano income. They could not get the guano trade because Dreyfus and Co. had the consignment for European markets. To add to these difficulties, in 1875, sugar and cotton prices began falling drastically, and Peruvian exports of these products collapsed. In 1875, Dreyfus suspended amortization of the external debt, so Peru got a loan (over the objections of the 1870–72

British lenders) from an English firm, Raphael and Co. The guano output of both Dreyfus and Raphael competed for the falling demand of the world market. The situation was so serious in 1876 that the Peruvian government suspended payment of the public debt and began expropriating the nitrate lands in the South. The war in 1879 with Chile completed a decade of ruin for the Peruvian ruling class and destroyed the whole power structure built up since the beginning of the century. The failure of the *civilistas* led to international capitalists assuming direct control of Peruvian natural wealth—not simply investing in Peru, as the *civilistas* wished.[109]

In the pre-Chilean war period, the *civilistas* had an important influence on Peruvian education, but the extent of their reforms was determined by a number of overriding factors: first, there was very little money available in the Peruvian treasury; second, Pardo's ambition of establishing a system of popular education, universal and free, controlled and supported by the state, was not approved by Congress, which was still heavily influenced by church/landowner interests, and primary education stayed in the hands of the church-dominated municipalities; finally, the nature of the reform, where it did occur, was not intended to change the social or economic structure in Peru or to develop internal markets, but simply to establish the preconditions of a dependent economic growth through foreign investment and foreign institutions.

Thus, although Pardo had a well-conceived plan of using education to "modernize" Peru through Order and Democracy (as a counterforce to anarchy), the church successfully blocked an important part of his reforms. The clergy viewed his plans as being "too practical, too liberal, and more scientific than orthodox in orientation." [110] Although the church felt (correctly) that any change in the educational structure was a threat to its power base, the church's opposition to the reforms was not addressed to a possible alteration of a "natural" order of the Peruvian class structure, for the reforms had no intention of doing so. For example, at the secondary level, where substantial reform did take place, the change was primarily one of replacing Spanish with French influence. With the new organic law of education in 1875, the University of San Marcos was patterned after the University of Paris, and secondary school administration was reorganized on the lines of the Frency *lycées*.[111] But both the universities and secondary schools remained centers of elite formation:

> The secondary curriculum retained its marked upper-class value orientation and continued to stress humanistic and universal culture, while practical and scientific courses were virtually non-existent.[112]

If the secondary schools were designed for the upper classes, primary schools were intended to fit the masses into the lower levels of a modern, industrial hierarchy. Indeed, one of the important elements of Pardo's reform was to found a few vocational schools to educate and assimilate Indians into Peruvian society as industrial workers. Although this reform was eventually successfully opposed by the church, Pardo's intentions were clear:

> Because of his interest in *preparing the Indian for assimilation into Peruvian society,* he ordered the founding of Peru's first workshop school. Located in the sierra community of Ayacucho, its purpose was to *teach Indians industrial skills.*[113] (Italics added.)

The announcement of Pardo's Lima industrial school in *El Comercio* of January 1873, also made clear that these lower levels of schooling were to serve a concept of progress defined by social order: "In January, 1873, The Municipal Industrial School is being inaugurated in Lima to increase the worker's productive capacity and to guarantee order, which is the basis of progress." [114]

The war with Chile interrupted these reforms. It ruined the Peruvian rich, and after the war, the government had income only from taxes and import duties. All the guano income was appropriated by Peru's creditors. With the collapse of the coastal agriculture which had depended on the local banking interests, foreigners like William Grace took over the sugar plantations and mechanized them and their sugar mills. Sugar growing became greatly concentrated into three large holders—Grace, Gildermeister, and Larco; this concentration improved the marketing of sugar and knocked out the small producers.

In 1889 the Peruvian government settled British lenders' claims on the 1870–72 debt by turning over the railroads, the exploitation rights to 3 million tons of guano, and cash to the Peruvian Corporation, formed to act for the lenders. The Peruvian Corporation, with Grace on the board of directors, also gained control of Peru's copper mines. Thus, the coastal sugar plantations, the railroads, and the mines were all owned by foreigners. Effectively, the export trade was out of Peruvian hands, and local producers were relegated to secondary exports or to production for local markets.

But the role of the Peruvian elite was much more important than just producing goods that the foreign companies did not. Direct control of the state continued to be held by a select and aristocratic group of *civilistas*. Their role in the postwar period was to develop a stable country whose modernized institutions would make it viable to do business in the new international system. For Peru, that system differed radically from the 1870s: now foreign corporations were not being encouraged to invest in Peru by a domestic elite who owned the resources of producing export goods; rather, it was the foreign corporations who owned the resources, and the elite was seeking the means to participate in the income those resources produced. The Peruvian elite chose to be the intermediary in imposing the new rules of the game on the mass of Peruvians, hoping in return to be able to negotiate the conditions of elite participation in the benefits.[115]

In the new system, the Order and Progress of European Positivism had to be spread to the Peruvian population. Development (progress) signified, as before the war, the development of capitalist economic institutions in a free trade and free enterprise system.[116] The war accented the need to incorporate all Peruvians into these capitalistic institutions: internal defeat was blamed on inferior naval power, financial mismanagement, and by the non-involvement of marginalized Peruvians (Indians) who lacked *national feeling and minimal skills for participation*. The neo-Positivists like Javier Prado and Manuel Villarán argued that these ideas of Order and Progress and of material development would elevate Peru among nations, and would form the basis of a new Peruvian culture and society. The majority argued (Prado dissenting) that Indians were not racially inferior as held by the upper classes, and unless the lower classes were educated, any increase in wealth would go to the already rich, *thereby serving to create greater social tension.*[117] Thus, the neo-Positivists generally expressed a faith in the ability of Indians to contribute to Peruvian development, and pushed for a popular education which stressed practical knowledge and scientific thought as a means of incorporating the marginal population into Peruvian development and of preventing social strife.

In 1895, when the *civilistas* fully regained power, most people in Peru were illiterate. Although Pardo's reform effort in the 1870s had increased primary school enrollment so that about 70,000 children enrolled in 1890 (see table 10), this represented only 10 percent of the school-age population, and average attendance was only 50 percent of enrollment. Nicolas de Pierola, the first Positivist president (1895–99) of the new era, undertook a number of reforms of Peruvian government administration and tax collection, and also began to push public-financed, universal primary schooling with emphasis on practical knowledge. Educational expansion moved slowly because the government wanted to avoid budget deficits,[118] but as table 10 shows, there was still a 25 percent increase in primary enrollment (and average attendance) during this period.

In José Pardo's first term (1904–8), the Congress passed laws making primary education free and compulsory and further centralized administration by removing control of primary education from the provincial and municipal councils and placing it in a National Ministry of Justice and Instruction.[119] Pardo, a true *civilista* like his father, continued his father's work in educational expansion, increasing the budget for the Ministry of Justice and Instruction from 9.6 to 17.2 percent of total public expenditures during his four year term.[120] In addition, he established a school of arts and crafts and expanded the school of medicine. The greatest expansion of primary school enrollment in the *civilista* period occurred between 1898 and the end of Pardo's first term (1908), and during his second term (1916–19) (see table 10).

Primary education *was* expanded by the *civilistas,* and by 1920 almost 20 percent of the school-age population was enrolled in primary school (although average attendance was only 12 percent). But as in

Table 10

Peru: Primary Enrollment and School-age Population

Year	Enrollment	Average Attendance	Total Population[a]	School-age Population (6–14)[b]	Enrollment (average attendance) as Percent of School-age Population	
1890	71,435	35,718[c]	3,443	689	10.4	(5.2)
1898	91,853	45,926[c]	3,886	777	11.8	(5.9)
1902	134,658	67,329[c]	4,107	821	16.4	(8.2)
1906	150,506	73,086	4,328	866	17.3	(8.4)
1908	168,184	89,009	4,438	888	19.0	(10.0)
1910	146,400	79,331	4,549	910	16.1	(8.7)
1915	165,774	94,992	4,826	965	17.2	(9.8)
1920	195,701	120,562	5,102	1,020	19.2	(11.8)
1930	342,016	217,215	5,656	1,274	26.8	(17.0)
1940	565,932	384,377	6,208	1,486	38.1	(25.8)

[a] All population estimates before 1940 are based on interpolation between the two census years, 1876 and 1940. There were no complete Peruvian censuses taken between those years.

[b] The 5–14 age group represents 25 percent of the total population in 1940. We assume a linear distribution age between 5 and 14, so the school age group (6–14) is 22.5 percent of the total population. Since the population was probably growing more slowly between 1876 and 1920 than between 1920 and 1940, we take the school-age population as 20 percent of the total for 1890 through 1920, and 22.5 percent for 1930 and 1940.

[c] Average attendance is approximated as 50 percent of enrollment based on 1906–15.

Sources: Enrollment, 1890, 1898: Ministerio de Justicia, *Estadística de la instrucción pública del Perú correspondiente al año 1890; 1898* Anexo a la *Memoria* del Ministerio (Lima: Imprenta Torres Aguirre, 1891, 1899). Enrollment, 1902: Dirección de Primera Enseñanza, *Estadística escolar del Perú Correspondiente al año 1902* (Lima: "El Lucero," 1904). Enrollment and Average Attendance, 1908, 1910, 1915, 1920, 1930: Ministerio de Instrucción Pública, Dirección General de Enseñanza, cited in Dirección General de Estadística, *Anuario Estadística, 1937* (Lima, 1939). Enrollment and Average Attendance, 1940: Ministerio de Hacienda y Comercio, Dirección Nacional de Estadística, *Estado de la Instrucción en la Perú según el Censo Nacional de 1940* (Lima, 1941). Population, 1876: Ministerio del Gobierno, Dirección General de Estadística, *Censo general de la república del Perú formado en 1876* (Lima: Imprenta del Teatro, 1878). Population, 1940: Dirección General de Estadística, *Censo general del Perú, 1940* (Lima, 1942).

contemporaneous Brazil, educational expansion was still very limited (as the enrollment figures indicate) and—despite Villarán's and the other Positivists' feelings about Indians—was highly class structured. For example, total enrollment in public primary schools was 236,000 students in 1925, in public secondary schools, (*collegios nacionales*) about 5,000 students, and in all unversities, 2,300 students. The racial composition of enrollment (not average attendance) in public primary schools was 52 percent mestizos, 33 percent Indians, 12 percent whites, or *criollos,* and a very small number of blacks or Asians. Average attendance was 59 percent of enrollment, and it is probably safe to assume that absenteeism was higher among mestizos and Indians than among *criollos.* The racial composition of secondary *public* schools (children from wealthy families went to private schools) was markedly different: the percentage of whites was 25 percent of total enrollment; mestizos, 61 percent; and Indians only 12 percent. Since private secondary schools had as many or more students than public, and the racial composition of private schools was probably much more white/mestizo, only about 6 or 7 percent Indians went to secondary schools, even though in 1940 (the first year since 1876 for which such data are available) Indians represented 46 percent of the population while whites and mestizos together represented 55 percent.[121] Thus, not only did a very small number of students get to secondary school or university, but almost all of them were from white and mestizo families.

Despite the popular and nationalistic concern of the neo-Positivists, there is other evidence that in practice the *civilistas* were interested primarily not in the welfare of the masses, but in maintaining social control for foreign investment-induced growth. By the Supreme Resolution of September 1903, owners of mines were authorized to "establish rules and regulations for the places of work which are necessary to preserve order and respect for property and life . . . and to adopt the disciplinary measures or the indispensible security to prevent any disorder or danger to political authority." [122] Most workers in the mines were debtors, or *enganchados,* to the miners, so the law also gave the mine owner the right to "keep" the *enganchados* as chattel slaves. This was the main source of labor for the foreign corporations in mining, the coastal sugar plantations, and the rubber plantations, and the *civilistas* were committed to giving these corporations all rights over the indigenous Peruvian work force.

Quite clearly, the *civilistas* were committed to assuring the rights of capitalists to profits, not the rights of Indians to their land nor of workers to higher wages and decent working conditions. The expansion of primary schooling has to be viewed in this context: schooling would assimilate some Indians into a society run by the rules of the bourgeoisie for the bourgeoisie and their colleagues, the foreign companies. The advent of mass public primary schooling in no way increased the control of Indians or workers over their own country, nor over the schools themselves. To the contrary, schooling was supposed to socialize Indians and other marginal groups to *accept* the power of the owners and the social structure of society as a *rational* means of organizing production and distributing output.

Furthermore, although the "popular education for development" philosophy of Villarán and Prado generally prevailed in government policy, there was an important counter-educational philosophy within the *civilismo* movement: Alejandro Deustua, an influential San Marcos professor, reacted against the "rationalism and utilitarian-materialism" of the neo-Positivists and stressed "the importance of intuition and liberty of will." [123] He opposed the policy of educating the lower classes to enable them to contribute to the increase of national wealth, and instead, advocated education for only a small number of the elite. Schools and universities would develop this intellectual and scientific aristocracy who would properly govern the masses. He considered domination by a paternalistic ruling class necessary because of the insurmountable ignorance of the masses. Deustua felt that universal popular education brought on "the materialistic appetites of the masses and make them less content with the lowly place they were destined to occupy in the properly ordered society." [124] The dispute between the two educational philosophies was *not* about what the social structure of society should be: both Deustua and the neo-Positivists agreed that the ruling class would continue to be largely drawn from the already wealthy families, and that the working class would be formed from the masses. Neither did the two philosophies clash on the role of Peru in the international system. Free trade and development based on foreign exploitation of Peru's resources was fundamental to both. Disagreement hinged on whether education of the masses did or did not provide the *social order* necessary for economic growth (progress) in the *civilista* model; Villarán, Prado, and others arguing that popular education was *necessary* for social order, and Deustua arguing that it bred anarchy.

The Civilista Republic of the post-Chilean War period imposed national order, organized a rational state administration, which used its available public resources carefully, and converted Peru into a country where the most "able" governed a prosperous export economy. The perceived role of education in this period was to integrate marginal elements of society—particularly Indians—as contributors to national income. Civilista philosophers like Villarán foresaw correctly that unless these marginal elements began to participate in increased income, class strife in Peru would destroy social order. Thus, universal primary schooling was intended to uplift the poor into the lower levels of a growing national economy and at the same time, to control the conditions under which that uplifting occurred.

But the *civilista* model generated its own downfall. The primary contradiction of the model was that Peruvian prosperity depended completely on the excess of exports over imports, and the export sector was largely in the hands of foreigners. Thus, the surplus from foreign trade was controlled by Europeans and North Americans. The surplus remaining in the country was distributed among the dominant elite who, in turn, spent it mainly on imported consumption goods. There was no domestic basis for economic development and little expansion of or attention paid to internal markets. Some domestic industry did grow up at the beginning of the century, particularly cotton and woolen textiles, vegetable oil, and food processing plants. Most of these were in Lima, and most were controlled, again, by foreign corporations like Grace and Duncan Fox, or by immigrant families who had little roots in the country.[125] Even in 1918, with shortages caused by the war, about 50 percent of Peru's cotton textile consumption and almost all woolen textiles were imported.[126]

The first year of World War I caused a crisis in Peru, as the European trade was interrupted. But Peru's exports recovered rapidly, and copper, sugar, rubber, petroleum, and cotton all boomed in 1915–18. Both Presidents Leguía (1908–12) and Billinghurst (1912–15) represented splinter groups in the Civilista party, and attempted to deal with the growing unrest of the urban proletariat and the contradictions of export dependency.[127] But with the war boom, José Pardo came back to rule over a new Civilista coalition. During his second term (1915–19), although it appeared that the *civilista* model was working again, the beginning of the end was taking shape. The rise in prices of sugar and cotton led to an expansion of sugar and cotton plantations at the expense of small local producers. Also, with the rise in prices of export agriculture goods, food production for local consumption did not increase and the price of food rose. From 1913 to 1920, the cost of living doubled.[128] As a result of this rise in prices and the expropriation of local agricultural producers, the middle class and working class suffered during what should have been an unprecedented prosperity for all. The *civilista* model concentrated the gains from this prosperity in foreign hands and among a few rich Peruvians. However, limited industrialization had created an urban proletariat and a small group of local entrepreneurs who produced for the domestic market and even for export. Export capitalism produced a periphery with consciousness; when members of this periphery began to lose the gains they had made during a period of prosperity, they threatened and then destroyed the *civilista* project.[129]

Simultaneously, the United States replaced Great Britain as Peru's main trading and investment metropolis. In 1914, Britain had about $170 million invested in Peru, and the United States, $63 million (up from $6 million in 1897). By 1919, the U.S. Cerro de Pasco Corporation had taken over the copper deposits from English investors, as well as gained complete control of the oilfields by 1921. In 1913, 44 percent of trade (exports plus imports) went to Great Britain and Germany, and 31 percent to the United States. In 1917, 61 percent went to the United States and 18 percent to Britain (none to Germany).

The Oncenio

At the end of the war, Peru was racked by a series of strikes and peasant uprisings organized by increasingly militant urban labor and peasants. Beginning in 1918 Indians staged bloody uprisings aimed at retrieving their land in the Sierra. There had been some strikes on plantations in 1917, but the major stoppages occurred in Lima in December 1918 to January 1919 and centered around demands for an eight-hour day. Middle-class university students joined the strikers, asking for university reforms. The combination of these groups who had not participated in the *civilista* project successfully achieving their demands ended the era and brought to power former president Augusta Leguía on a pro-university student, worker, and Indian reform platform.

But none of these groups benefited much from his eleven years in office. Leguía maintained the prosperity of the export economy, now based on trade and investment with the United States.[130] He also increased the participation of the domestic bourgeoisie and white-collar workers in the export surplus by the tried and true method of borrowing abroad (this time from the United States) and transferring the debt to particular groups in the economy. Public works and government bureaucracy expanded, railroad construction boomed, and primary education attendance almost doubled, representing 17 percent of Peru's school-age children by 1930.

In the initial years of Leguía's rule, it appeared that he would live up to the reforms he had promised. He supported the university reform of 1919 which called for the modernization of the university, extending its studies to themes of the present national reality, the establishment of a system of seminars and active teaching, free attendance at classes, participation of students in university government, and the extension of the university into an active participation in social problems.[131] When Leguía took power, he "went through the motions of rewarding the university youth who had enthusiastically supported his presidential bid." [132] But he used the reform law of 1920 to get rid of professors who were his political opponents. Within two years, San Marcos became a center of radicalism which tried (unsuccessfully) to appeal to the bastion of Leguía's support: the middle class. Most student and faculty leaders of the APRA (Alianza Popular Revolucionaria Americana) movement and other university-based opposition were exiled by 1924.

Similarly, Leguía cracked down on two other sources of support: the Indians and the workers. As already mentioned, the Indians had staged a series of bloody uprisings in 1918 and 1919 to get back their land in the sierra. Leguía appointed a commission with pro-Indian land reform directors. The Roca Commission prepared and submitted for congressional approval a comprehensive legislative code which provided for the protection and education of the natives.[133] The landowners reacted to these developments by appealing to Leguía, who dissolved the commission and prevented the Congress from considering its proposals. He then sent in the army to put down further disorders. After several Indian massacres, the area was safe again for the landowners.

Organized labor suffered the same fate. After initial prolabor moves, Leguía began to destroy anarchist labor groups, whose possible violent actions against the bourgeoisie were a direct threat to the Leguía government. Since the labor movement was still small in the early 1920s and poorly organized (despite its victory in the 1919 strike), and since the other sources of opposition to Leguía were more moderate than the anarchist-syndicalists, the strategy worked. There was little reaction to Leguía's repressive actions.[134] Thus, Leguía was able to deal with popular movements much more effectively than the *civilistas*. On the one hand, he coopted certain elements of these movements to his own cause by allowing them to participate in the expansion of the export economy. He did this by appropriating public resources in a way which was inherently not acceptable to the *civilista* model of careful budget management. On the other hand, he severely repressed other elements of the movement which directly threatened him. He was able to do that because there was strong opposition in the middle class and ruling bourgeoisie to any form of violence; indeed, most of Leguía's opposition, who were not anticapitalist, also opposed violent change.[135]

It is in this context that popular education expanded as part of

Leguía's public works programs. We argued earlier that the expansion
of enrollment was highly class structured, even in primary schools,
where only 33 percent Indians were *enrolled* in 1925 out of a population
which was probably more than 50 or 60 percent Indian. In 1925, about
4,500 students were enrolled in public secondary schools, and nine
years later, in 1934, about 6,000, all this expansion coming from the
increase in women students. In the meantime, there was a large
increase in vocational school enrollment.[136] University enrollment also
increased slowly, from 2,000 students in 1918 to 2,300 in 1925 to 2,900
in 1930.

Leguía was a great admirer of the United States. In the new
organization of Peru's economy, in which the United States had taken
over as the primary holder of Peru's export-sector wealth, it was logical
that U.S. influence on education should replace Europe's. Leguía had
already attempted as president in 1908–12 to introduce some U.S. ideas
in educational reforms. One of his first acts in 1919 was to recall Harry
Bard, director of an earlier U.S. mission, to resume the work he had
interrupted in 1912. Bard drafted a new educational law that attempted
to introduce U.S.-style innovations into Peruvian schools.[137] The 1920
Ley Orgánica de Enseñanza, as drafted by Bard, called for a new corps of
professional full-time teachers, modern (U.S.) methods of teaching and
study, including vocational training, and universal primary instruction;
required mine, farm, and industry owners to offer free coed primary
schools for their employees' children; and created three regional
educational agencies to be administered directly by members of the
U.S. mission. Leguía not only gave Bard a free hand to write this law,
but also to hire the personnel to put it into practice. Despite this, the
mission failed: at the end of 1924, only six months after the U.S.
advisers had left Peru, "not one significant trace of its influence
remained." [138]

There are a number of reasons given for the failure of the mission,
from Victor Belaunde's, "the lack of cooperation on the part of the
United States Government and, in some cases, the unsuitability and
inadaptability of some of the personnel brought here" [139] to Paulston's
"overemphasis placed on the importance of sound administration as a
reform device and the near-total disregard or ignorance of deep-seated

cultural patterns, and education's functional relationships with an authoritarian, hierarchical society." [140] But most important is that there was no group in Peru to support reforms which were useful in maintaining the social structure in an *industrial, corporate* society like the United States.[141] The church obviously opposed the reform, as it had opposed all reforms which put more people in school, particularly coed schools. Although bourgeoisie and middle-class support would have been enough to have overcome church opposition, the reform did nothing for these latter groups while it offended conservatives.

Since the Peruvian bourgeoisie was not tied to industrial capital, their need for skilled workers was not very great; rather, they saw popular education at best as a means of social control and, in a vague sense, as contributing to national development. The expenditure of large amounts of public funds on *universal* primary education was unnecessary to achieve social control in a country where still only a fraction of the labor force lived in urban areas, and much of the labor force was already under the direct control of mine and plantation owners. Some educational expansion was useful, but not to the extent implied by the 1920 reform. The middle class was much more concerned about secondary and university education, and the law dealt with these levels only on secondary *vocational* training, irrelevant to middle-class aspirations. Thus, Bard and his associates attempted to build an educational system which would expand literacy and technical training on a grand scale, but did not give anything to the groups that counted in the power structure. This does not mean that the reform was opposed because it "democratized" education. To the contrary, as Mariategui saw clearly, the reform was fundamentally conservative. It was more conservative than mid-nineteenth-century reforms in the United States because it was framed in the vocational concept of equality of the early twentieth century: children would go as far in school as was appropriate to their future vocational station.[142]

> The failure of the educational reform of 1920 was not due to excessive ambition or to the ultra-modern idealism of its supporters. In many ways this reform was restricted in its aspirations and conservative in its point of view. It maintained in education, without the slightest

substantial alteration, all the privileges of class and wealth. It did not provide free education on the higher levels for children selected by the primary schools. On the contrary, it relegated children of the proletariat to special organized schools and made it impossible for the children of workers to enroll in secondary or higher schools . . . it is impossible to consider the reform of 1920 as a democratic reform.[143]

Table 11

Peru: Public Primary School Expenditures, 1906–26

Year	(1) Total Primary Average Attendance	(2) Total Amount Budgeted (thousand soles)	(3) Expenditures per Average Attendance (soles)
1906	73,086	22,615	309
1910	79,331	20,442	258
1915	94,992	22,942	242
1920	120,562	35,174	293
1921	125,909	63,961	508
1922	136,973	48,616	355
1923	128,438	50,421	392
1924	133,875	49,821	372
1925	141,638	51,978	367
1926	165,723	59,765	361

Note: Expenditures per average attendance are in current prices. Between 1910 and 1921, wholesale and consumer prices more than doubled, a fact which means, in effect, that there was no change in real expenditures per pupil.

Sources: Column (1): *Anuario Estadístico*, 1937.

Column (2): Ministerio de Instrucción, Dirección General de Enseñanza, *Extracto de Estadística Escolar*, 1926.

— Column (3): Column (2) divided by column (1).

In the 1920s, Peru did not have the appropriate capitalist structure, with its attendant sociopolitical configuration, to import even half-breed U.S. reforms. In any case, these reforms were never intended to promote equality or more political power for the masses. Peru had a completely dependent economy, which in order to provide income for local elites had to have social stability, with everyone in the structure accepting his role. An expanding public educational system was part of the implementation of this social order, but the ruling classes even in the high-spending 1920s were not about to devote enough public monies to public primary education to make it universal, nor enough to secondary to open it to the poor (see table 11 for expansion of expenditures). Until Peru began significant industrialization in the 1950s and '60s, and a new crisis occurred in Peruvian dependent capitalism, formal education continued along essentially the same path it had followed since the beginning of the *civilista* era and the *oncenio* of Leguía.

Notes

1. There were other factions in the elite, such as the Catholic Church, that were opposed to scientific thought. But on the economic front, these factions could not, or did not wish to, resist the new arrangement.

2. Generally, the local bourgeoisie did not have the technology and capital to market their own goods in Europe. This was handled by European merchants in Latin America.

3. Even during the mercantile period, however, "schooling" of the poor, particularly by Jesuits, resulted in pacifying (or preparing) indigenous peoples to be incorporated into the lowest levels of the wage structure.

4. In chapter 5 we present more detailed data for the United States which show that the working class probably *resisted* public school reform in the mid-nineteenth century.

5. Of course, education was only one mechanism to maintain order, and the most subtle. Liberals and conservatives agreed on the need to suppress violence which threatened the societal order, but they themselves used violence frequently to quell peasant uprisings, workers' strikes, and slave revolts.

6. See, for example, Fernando de Azevedo, *A Cultura Brasileira,* vols. 2 and 3 (Rio de Janeiro: Editorial Melhoramentos, 1958).

7. Celso Furtado, *Formação Econômica do Brasil* (7th ed.; São Paulo: Companhia Editôra Nacional, 1967), pp. 125–126.

8. Although the issue of "accepting" slavery is complex, apparently Africans did and Indians did not, but not because of African passivity or Indian pride. Rather, Africans had already experienced agricultural societies; Indians were nomads, unsocialized to work on the land.

9. Roberto C. Simonsen, *História Econômica do Brasil* (*1500–1820*) (4th ed.; São Paulo: Companhia Editôra Nacional, 1962), p. 316. The Indians were paid "duas varas de pano" monthly.

10. Contriras Rodrigues, *Traços da Economia Social e Política do Brasil Colonial,* as reported in Simonsen, *História Econômica do Brasil,* p. 271.

11. Azevedo, *Cultura Brasileira,* p. 36.

12. Some educational historians (Fernando Magalhães, M. D. Moreira Azevedo) call this the first experience with public education in Brazil; however, the financing was provided as a payment for taking care of orphans sent by the Portuguese government to Brazil. Secondly, the financing seemed to be small compared to the total cost of Jesuit education. The Jesuits mentioned their financial difficulties (since colonizer enrollment was low) in all their letters to the Order's heads. The letters recommended in 1564 that the king use part of the royal taxes to build schools in Bahia, Olinda, and Rio. E. V. de Morais, "Qual a influencia dos jesuitas em nossas letras?" *Revista do Instituto Histórico e Geográfico Brasileiro* 1 (Tomo Especial, parte 5): 635.

13. Celso Furtado, *Latin American Economic Development: From Colonial Times to the Cuban Revolution* (London: Cambridge University Press, 1971), p. 18.

14. Modern Absolutism had rapidly become the prevailing type of government in Northwestern Europe by the beginning of the sixteenth century, the period of the development of nation-states. It was based on "a revision of the long-standing belief in the divinity of civil authority" (George H. Sabine, *A History of Political Theory* [New York: Henry Holt, 1950], p. 391). The rising sense of national independence and unity gave new force to the old argument of the divine right of kings. It was proposed and reinforced as a defense of order and political stability against a view widely believed to augment the danger implicit in religious civil war (pp. 391–92) as well as an instrument of avoiding clerical influence over secular government.

Royal legitimacy, represented in terms of natural processes, had its origins in the changes of medieval institutions. Since the merchants expanded the trading organizations beyond the power of the guilds, conditions of trade and resource exploitation had to be regulated by government larger than the medieval municipality. The new merchant class had both money and "enterprise" and for obvious reasons was the natural enemy of the nobility.

The merchants' "interests were on the side of 'strong' government both at home and abroad, and hence their natural political alliance was with the king" (p. 332). "For the time being they were content to see his power increase at the expense of all checks and limitations which had surrounded medieval monarchy . . . from every point of view the bourgeoisie saw its advantage in concentrating military powers and the administration of justice as much as possible in the hands of the king. On the whole, the gain in orderly and efficient government was probably considerable" (p. 333).

The republican movements of the eighteenth century resulted from both the controversy about the origin of power—God or the people—and the growing power and prestige of the merchant and industrial bourgeoisie.

15. In 1759, at the time they left Brazil, Jesuits controlled 25 parochial houses, 36 missions, and 17 schools and monasteries. Azevedo, *Cultura Brasileira,* p. 47. There is no information about the existence of other lay or religious schools.

16. At the end of the seventeenth century, after expulsion from Brazil, the Dutch and later others established sugar plantations in the West Indies. The supply of sugar grew rapidly and prices fell by one-half. After 1680, the Northeast of Brazil fell into decadence and involuted into a subsistence economy. Beginning in 1720, and reaching its apex between 1740 and 1760, the next primary export was gold from Minas Gerais. The gold went through Portugal to England. Some slaves were brought from the Northeast to work in the goldfields, but the boom ended quickly, around 1760. Just as mining decayed, cotton production increased rapidly in the Northeast during the Napoleonic Wars. By 1815, with peace in Europe, this export crop declined as well, and no more export booms took place until the coffee expansion of the 1880s. As each area declined from the heyday of its export economy, it was left with large numbers of workers (or slaves) who were used in local, low productivity agriculture and mining. See Andre Frank, *Capitalism and Underdevelopment in Latin America* (New York: Monthly Review Press, 1969), chap. 3.

17. See Furtado, *Formação Econômica do Brasil;* and Simonsen, *História Econômica do Brasil.*

18. Simonsen, *História Econômica do Brasil,* p. 385. See also Frank, *Capitalism and Underdevelopment in Latin America,* pp. 161–62 for the full text of the queen's decree.

19. "Do not worry that the introduction of British goods might hurt your industry. . . . For now your capital is best applied to the cultivation of your lands . . . later you will advance to manufactures. . . . Experience will

show you that expanding your agriculture need not totally destroy your manufactures; and if some of them are of necessity abandoned, you may rest assured that this is proof that this manufacture did not rest on a solid base and was of no real advantage to the state. In the end, there will result great national prosperity, much greater than you could get before" (Dom João VI, king of Portugal, as quoted in Simonsen, *História Econômica do Brasil,* pp. 405–6).

20. Nicia Vilela da Luz, *A Luta pela Industrialização do Brasil* (São Paulo: Dif. Europeia do Livro, 1961), p. 17. See also, "Tradado de Comércio e Navigação entre o Principal Regente de Portugal e El Rey do Reino Unido do Grande Bretanha e Irlanda" (Rio de Janeiro: Impresas Regia, 1810).

21. Azevedo, *Cultura Brasileira,* pp. 327–28.

22. Furtado, *Economic Development of Latin America,* p. 25.

23. Primitivo Moacyr, *A Instrução e o Império* (Rio de Janeiro: Cia. Brasileira de Educação, 1936), 1: 79.

24. Statement of constituent congressman in 1825, as quoted in ibid., p. 81.

25. Ibid., p. 190.

26. Azevedo claims that the failure of popular education programs at this time (1820s and 1830s) was due to the type of teaching methods adopted immediately after independence. The Lancaster Method was being used in Europe and in the United States, and the argument for its adoption was based on the success it was achieving in those countries: "its [the Method's] effects on the habits, character, and intelligence of youth are highly beneficial; disposing their minds to industry, to readiness of attention, and subordination, thereby creating in early life a love for order, and a preparation for business" (Quoted from a commission of evaluation in 1828 in Joel Spring, "Education and the Corporate State," *Socialist Revolution* 2, no. 2 (March/April 1972). The Method was also very low-cost per student: it required one teacher working with a group of monitors who in turn transmitted the lessons to several groups. Azevedo thinks that the Method was the most disastrous example of several attempts to solve the complex problems of education in Brazil through simplistic methods or solutions. He blames Lancaster for lowering quality and spreading distrust for public education. But Azevedo's analysis assumes that there was more than a passing commitment to primary schooling through the Method. In order for a mass education method like Lancaster's to be successful, there had to be a payoff to those who took this education and a reason for the government to invest in it. Both these conditions seemed to be lacking in Brazil in the early independence period.

NOTES: EDUCATION AND FREE-TRADE COLONIALISM

27. For example, the only public secondary school (Colégio Pedro II) in Brazil up to the middle of the century stressed literary studies (*estudos disinteresados*), as a necessary base for *further* education.

28. Frank, *Capitalism and Underdevelopment in Latin America,* pp. 163–64.

29. Ibid., p. 165.

30. Vilela da Luz, *Industrialização do Brasil.*

31. Public and private teacher-training institutions were also built to service the small school system.

32. In 1869, there were fewer than 11,000 children in secondary school, of which more than 8,000 were in private secondary schools (Moacyr, *A Instrucão e o Império,* pp. 108–9.

33. Azevedo, *Cultura Brasileira.*

34. Frank, *Capitalism and Underdevelopment in Latin America,* p. 168.

35. By 1889, there were about 200 industrial enterprises in Brazil with 400 thousand *contos* of invested capital. See Caio Prado, Jr., *História Econômica do Brasil* (São Paulo: Ed. Brasileira, 1967), p. 258. Capital was distributed in the following way: textiles, 60%; foodstuffs, 15%; chemicals, 10%; wood, 4%; clothing, 4%; metallurgy, 3%. In 1907, foodstuffs represented 26% of the total invested, and in 1920, 40%.

Industry became progressively more concentrated over time. In 1881, the regional distribution of industrial production was: Rio, 55%; Bahia, 25%; and São Paulo, 5%. By 1907, Rio had fallen to 30% and São Paulo had 16%. In 1914, São Paulo had 20%; in 1920, 33%; in 1938, 43%; and in 1959, 54%. Bahia fell by 1959 to 1.7%. See Frank, *Capitalism and Underdevelopment in Latin America,* pp. 170–71.

36. As in Britain one-half century before, the abolitionists were philosophically tied and politically allied to the same vision of society as the new capitalists: "There are still other classes whose development is retarded by slavery: the laborers, the industrialists, and in general the commercial classes. Slavery does not permit the rise of real industrial workers, nor is it compatible with a wage system and the personal dignity of the artisans. . . . Furthermore, working classes are not strong, respected and intelligent in countries where those who employ workers are accustomed to ordering slaves around" (Joaquim Nabuco, "Negro Slavery in Brazil: The Chief Obstacle to Development," in *A Century of Brazilian History Since 1865,* ed. Richard Graham [New York: Alfred Knopf, 1969], p. 73). Nabuco (1849–1910) was one of the leaders of the abolitionist movement. This is an excerpt from his book *O Abolicionismo,* 1883.)

37. Slave population as a percentage of total population: 1850, 31%;

1872, 15% (1.5 million); 1887, 5% (64 thousand). See Nelson Werner Sodré, *História da Bourgesia Brasileira* (Rio: Civilização, 1964), p. 179.

38. Werner Baer, *Industrialization and Economic Development in Brazil* (Homewood, Ill.: Richard Irwin, 1965), p. 13.

39. Vilela da Luz, *Industrializacão do Brasil.*

40. "As one of the objects of the new tariff is to foster the infant industries of Brazil, it is probable that the customs revenue will increase very considerably during the latter part of October and the first fortnight of November (1889), just as it did during the month of June last in anticipation of the payment of the duties in gold.

"The duties on cotton and woolen goods are generally raised in the new tariffs" (British Foreign Office, Consular Reports, "Brazil, Report for the Years 1888–89–90," no. 807, London, 1890) p. 8.

41. Baer, *Industrialization in Brazil,* p. 15.

42. Roberto Moreira, *Educação e Desenvolvimento no Brasil* (Rio: Centro Latinoamericano de Pesquisas em Ciencias Sociales, 1960), p. 58.

43. Ibid., p. 65.

44. Furtado, *Economic Development,* p. 35.

45. Ibid., p. 36.

46. Moreira, *Educação e Desenvolvimento no Brasil,* p. 60.

47. Baer, *Industrialization in Brazil,* p. 16.

48. Furtado, *Obstacles to Development in Latin America,* p. 141.

49. Vilela da Luz, *Industrializacão do Brasil,* p. 87.

50. Sodré, *História do Bourgesia Brasileira,* p. 248.

51. Ibid., p. 248.

52. This series of educational reforms—all in line with Positivist thinking—did not alter the school system substantially. They were essentially struggles within the ruling class about the kind of education higher social class children were to have. The main themes were the number of years of secondary school (varying from 5 to 7), and whether or not each State should be allowed to organize its own educational system. The 1911–14 reform (*Lei Orgânica do Ensino*—Rivadavia Correa) is considered as sectarian Positivism and reinforced "free instruction" by prohibiting state participation in education and eliminating diplomas. Under the reform, the requirements for entrance in higher education would be an entrance examination held in each higher secondary school. In 1915, the Carlos Maximiliano reform reinstalled State financing of private education, entrance to higher education after 5 years of secondary school plus passage of an entrance examination. For a complete description of Positivism's role in the *República* from a Positivist's point of

view, see Ivan Lins, *História do Positivismo no Brasil* (São Paulo: Cia. Editôra Nacional, 1964).

53. *Obras Completas de Ruy Barbosa* (Rio de Janeiro: Ministério de Educação e Saude, 1941), vol. 10, tomo I (1883), p. 143. Ruy Barbosa (1849–1923) was one of the most influential Positivists. He was minister of justice in the Republican government (1889) and the most famous Brazilian foreign minister of the late nineteenth and early twentieth centuries.

54. The dual system also had its counterpart in the struggle between humanistic and utilitarian views of education. The humanists condemned the partial understanding of reality conveyed by technical training; the utilitarians stressed direct role of education in social function. Those who were to be workers needed a certain type of schooling, and those who were to be intellectuals needed another. Utilitarianism was expressed in the "close relations between instruction and the needs and concerns of the elite group, who, in turn, state these concerns as being the needs of the whole society" (Azevedo, *Cultura Brasileira,* p. 148).

55. In 1907, almost 40% of manufacturing (by invested capital) was in Rio de Janeiro and the states of Rio de Janeiro, São Paulo, and Rio Grande do Sul. By 1960, the four southern states of Rio Grande do Sul, Santa Catarina, Paraná, and São Paulo, produced 60% of the country's income from industry.

56. ". . . the different sectors of the Brazilian industrial sector did not develop as a function of each other, adjusting to each other to form a harmonious whole. Each industry was born in fortuitous circumstances and had as its objective to attend to some necessity that couldn't be satisfied by imports; in this way it remained isolated, with a continued dependence on imports" (Caio Prado, Jr., as quoted in Paulo Cannabrava Filho, *Militarismo e Imperialismo en el Brasil* [Buenos Aires: Editorial Tiempo Contemporaneo, 1970], p. 41).

57. Despite some tariff and increased industrial production, Brazil continued to import most of its manufactured products. Apparently, the rich consumed foreign goods despite their rise in price, while local production was sold to lower income groups. This applied particularly to Brazilian textiles which were heavily protected but still were faced by increasing imports of English cottons and woolens. See British Foreign Office, "Consular Reports for the Year 1899," p. 9.

58. Azevedo, *Cultura Brasileira,* pp. 650–51.

59. See chapter 5 for a description of the Massachusetts school reforms.

60. See chapter 5.

61. In the 1920s there were school reforms in several states (Pernam-

buco, Rio, Bahia, São Paulo, Ceará) all within the framework of the *escola nova* or *escola ativa*. The main concepts of the new formulation dealt with teaching techniques which emphasized understanding over memorization; adaptation of education to the characteristics of the modern society in expansion; and the role of individual differences in the learning process. The movement was not a global and homogeneous one. It had at least two broad and divergent conceptualizations of the educational task. One tendency stressed less authoritarian techniques in order to provide more free and spontaneous activities as basic elements of the child's natural development—respect for the child as a person called for very individualized attention. The other group was more concerned with the school's role as a social institution—not only the development of the individual child, but also his initiation into social life. These principles were taken from John Dewey. Indeed, some of the main activists in the reforms studied with Dewey at Columbia University.

62. See Isaura Belloni Schmidt and Osvaldo Kreimer, "Educational Ideologies in Brazil, 1959–1961" (Stanford University, Political Science Department, February 1972). Mimeographed.

63. U.S. influence was promoted financially through the MEC-USAID contracts, as well as by Brazilian adoption of U.S. teaching techniques and U.S. training of teaching personnel.

64. Public secondary schooling was not expanded, and it was only under Leguía in the 1920s that the university was moderately expanded to meet the demands of a small middle class.

65. Roland Paulston, *Society, Schools, and Progress in Peru* (Oxford: Pergamon Press, 1972), p. 25. By the sixteenth century, according to Paulston, irrigation farming had reached the limits of its productivity and all available land was in cultivation.

66. Ibid., p. 24.

67. Ibid., p. 23.

68. Ibid., p. 24.

69. Ibid., p. 25.

70. Reyna M. Barzan, *Contribución a la Historia de la Educación en el Perú*, tesis doctoral, Pontífica Universidad Católica del Perú, Lima, 1942, p. 11.

71. Paulston, *Society, Schools, Progress in Peru,* p. 25.

72. Ibid., p. 25.

73. Ibid., p. 29.

74. Ernesto Yepes del Castillo, *Perú, 1820–1920* (Lima: Instituto de Estudios Peruanos, 1972), p. 27.

75. Juan Castro Fernandini, *Legislación Escolar del Perú* (Lima: Editorial Auteria, 1939), p. 18.

76. Ibid., p. 18.

77. Emilio Romero, *Historia Económica del Perú* (Lima: Editorial Universo, 1949), 1:174.

78. Paulston, *Society, Schools, Progress in Peru*, p. 31. The results of the *reducciones* were exactly the same as in Brazil. The Jesuits "protected" the Indians by serving as direct intermediaries between them and secular Europeans who used the planned towns as an efficient way of drafting cheap labor. Paulston calls this a "failure" of Jesuit intentions, although it is difficult to understand why Jesuits, if their intentions were really to protect the Indians, used this method repeatedly since it always had the same result.

79. Fernandini, *Legislación Escolar del Perú*, p. 26.

80. Paulston, *Society, Schools, Progress in Peru*, p. 35.

81. Ibid., p. 35.

82. Ibid., p. 36. Paulston points out that instruction in Jesuit institutions was based on the Scholasticism of Aristotle as interpreted in the *Ratio Studiorum* of Loyola. This method used oral explanation, repetition, memorization, and formalistic debate in an unvarying modus operandi. Knowledge came from God through the Church and the authoritarian instruction of the clergy (pp. 34–45).

83. Paulston claims, however, that Indian languages were part of all universities' curriculum.

84. This was also true for Brazil, where textbooks were brought from Portugal and Europe up to 1808.

85. Ibid., p 37.

86. Yepes del Castillo, *Perú*, pp. 29–30. The United States was the main beneficiary of the trade.

87. Paulston, *Society, Schools, Progress in Peru*, p. 38.

88. Yepes del Castillo, *Perú*, p. 29.

89. Barzan, *Educatión en el Perú*.

90. Ibid., pp. 32–33.

91. Yepes del Castillo, *Perú*, p. 33.

92. Ibid., p. 39.

93. Ibid., pp. 42–43.

94. Since British lenders wanted to get back the money they loaned Peru between 1822 and 1825, their government got an agreement from Peru that one half the guano income would go to pay the external debt. But this seemingly simple arrangement put Peru into a perpetual debt situation: to pay

off the claims of the British lenders of a previous generation, the Peruvian government borrowed large sums from the consignees, using future shipments of guano as collateral. The guano contracts undervalued the guano and charged exorbitant interest and commission rates. Peru's difficult financial situation was also the result of conscious expansion of internal debt so that the local elite could participate in the guano revenue. As a result, guano shipments never seemed to be large enough to cover ever-increasing external plus internal debt. See Frederick Pike, *The Modern History of Peru* (New York: Praeger, 1967), p. 97; also see Enrique Araujo, "La Historia del Guano en Perú" (Thesis, Universidad Mayor de San Marcos, Lima, 1920). According to Araujo, Peru's foreign debt to England grew from 8 million pesos in the early 1820s to 15 million pesos in 1836 to 19 million in 1845.)

95. Part of the expended debt was due to emancipation of 20,000 slaves in 1854. Former owners were promised 300 soles for each liberated black. See Pike, *Modern History of Peru,* p. 112.

96. Earlier, in 1850, a Peruvian company got the guano consignment for North America, China, France, and Spain. But within one year, the company was bankrupt.

97. Some industries were created at the end of the 1840's, but without protection, most of these failed. See Yepes del Castillo, *Perú,* p. 78.

98. Ibid., p. 78.

99. R. MacLean y Estenos, *Sociología educational del Perú* (Lima: Libreria y Imprenta Gil, 1944), pp. 209–10.

100. Paulston, *Society, Schools, Progress in Peru,* p. 43.

101. MacLean y Estenos, *Sociología educational del Perú,* p. 227.

102. *El Comercio* editorial of April 1856, as quoted in ibid., p. 233.

103. It should be mentioned that at the end of the seventeen-year period dominated by Castilla (1845–62), the church still controlled secondary education. That level of schooling continued the tradition of the colonial *colegios* by serving the upper classes and offering a curriculum designed to instill general culture and prepare students for higher, or professional, education.

104. Yepes del Castillo, *Peru,* chap. 3.

105. Ibid., p. 85.

106. For a favorable description of Meiggs' operations in Peru, see J. Fred Rippy, "Henry Meiggs, Yankee Pizarro," in Lewis Hanke, *History of Latin American Civilization,* vol. 2 (Boston: Little Brown, 1967).

107. Yepes del Castillo, *Perú,* pp. 95–96.

108. Ibid., p. 100.

109. Ibid., chap. 4.

110. Paulston, *Society, Schools, Progress in Peru,* p. 45.

111. Ibid., p. 44.

112. Ibid., p. 44.

113. Francisco Garcia Calderon, quoted in Pike, *Modern History of Peru,* p. 135.

114. Quoted in MacLean y Estenos, *Sociología educational del Perú,* p. 263.

115. Yepes del Castillo, *Perú,* p. 127.

116. Manuel Candamo, president in 1903–4, summarized this policy: "The welfare and prosperity of Modern peoples are bound to their commerce, and, for Peru, the development of its foreign trade is a vital necessity. To protect it and foment it is one of the foremost responsibilities of public power. . . . In addition to its great economic importance, foreign trade has been and will continue to be, for Peru, one of the most powerful means of civilization and culture" (Quoted in Yepes del Castillo, *Peru,* p. 191).

117. Villarán, quoted in Pike, *Modern History of Peru,* p. 168.

118. Pike, *Modern History of Peru,* p. 174.

119. Paulston, *Society, Schools, Progress in Peru,* pp. 45–46.

120. Ibid., p. 46.

121. Dirección Nacional de Estadística, *Extracto Estadística del Perú, 1940* (Lima: Ministerio de Hacienda), pp. xxxvi–vii. In 1876, Indians were 58% of the population; whites, 14%; and mestizos, 25%.

122. Article 20 quoted in Yepes del Castillo, *Perú,* p. 210.

123. Pike, *Modern History of Perú,* p. 184.

124. A. O. Deustua, *Colección de artículos* (Lima, 1964), cited in Paulston, *Society, Schools, Progress in Peru,* p. 46.

125. Of 1,015 workers in the cotton textile industry in 1902, 490 were in mills owned by Grace and Duncan Fox. In 1918 there were a total of 3,049 workers in cotton textiles, of which 2030 were in mills owned by those two companies. Yepes del Castillo, *Perú,* p. 169.

126. Ibid., p. 172.

127. According to Emilio Romero, Leguía's most important contribution to the development of a capitalist economy in Peru was to spread the use of guano in domestic plantation agriculture (as cited in Pike, *Modern History of Peru,* p. 196). The Peruvian historian, Jorge Basadre called Billinghurst the precursor of Peruvian enlightened and demagogic capitalism (as cited in ibid., p. 198). Billinghurst was concerned that an unregulated economy would bring

about abuses which would provoke the masses to arise and destroy the capitalist society. In 1915, he agreed to an eight-hour workday for the Callao dockworkers (ibid., pp. 200–201).

128. Yepes del Castillo, *Perú*, 268.

129. Ibid., p. 282.

130. Pike quotes Dora Meyer de Zulen, one of Leguía's critics, as noting that this general prosperity was false because it was "not based on internal capitalization and improved labor habits, and therefore had not contributed toward a self-sustaining economy. Rather it depends on foreign capital lavished upon us because of the imperialistic interests of the United States" (*Modern History of Peru*, p. 229).

131. Yepes del Castillo, *Perú*, p. 284.

132. Pike, *Modern History of Peru*, p. 223.

133. Ibid., p. 222.

134. Payne, as quoted in Yepes del Castillo, *Perú*, p. 286.

135. "APRA's preoccupation with Peru's middle sectors explains why Leguía was so harsh and unrelenting a foe of its spokesmen at the same time that he was relatively tolerant of the Peruvian Communists who especially after 1928 grouped around Mariátegui. The dictator's hope to continue as the dominant political power in Peru, a position which he wanted to occupy indefinitely, depended to a great degree upon the support of the middle elements. This was the very socio-economic group which the APRA was seeking to proselytize. Leguía therefore rightly regarded the APRA as his most immediate and dangerous enemy, and was careful throughout his rule to keep most of its spokesmen in jail or in exile. Communists, even of the unorthodox variety of Mariátegui, purposely alienated the middle elements, contemptuously dismissing them as the *petit bourgeoisie* and advocating their liquidation. As a result, communism did not loom as an immediate challenge to Leguía's political aspirations" (Pike, *Modern History of Peru*, pp. 241–42).

136. All the enrollment figures are taken from Ministerio de Educacion Publica, *Estadística Escolar del Perú*, in appropriate years.

137. Paulston, *Society, Schools, Progress in Peru*, p. 53.

138. Ibid., p. 53.

139. Quoted in ibid., p. 60.

140. Ibid., p. 57.

141. See chapter 5.

142. See chapter 5.

143. J. C. Mariátegui, *Siete ensayos de interpretación de la realidad Peruana* (Lima: Amantua, 1952), quoted in Paulston, *Society, Schools, Progress in Peru*, pp. 59–61.

EDUCATION AS INTERNAL COLONIALISM:

5

EDUCATIONAL REFORM AND SOCIAL CONTROL IN THE UNITED STATES, 1830–1970

What is now the United States was one of several colonies (among others, Argentina, Canada, and Australia), that were virtual extensions of European society, with (eventually) a European immigrant majority and industrial growth parallel to that of many European countries. The original U.S. colonies were in many ways separate societies, and they developed separately until the early nineteenth century. The northern colonies were populated by small landholders who raised food products largely for consumption in the colony. Artisans also produced for local consumption, and traders brought goods such as molasses from the West Indies to be processed into rum and exported to Europe and Africa. The southern colonies, on the other hand, after an initial period in the seventeenth century of small holdings, rapidly became dominated by large plantations, tobacco and cotton exports, and the import of manufactured consumption goods and African slaves. Thus, the northern colonies began early to take on the economic and social

233

structures of their parent metropoles, while the South developed a plantation economy similar to that of the West Indies and Brazil.

The evolution of education closely followed these economic and social structures. Both in the North and in the South, educational systems were decentralized: each colony, and usually each community, was in charge of its own children's schooling. As in England, schools were usually established privately, although some colonies passed laws in the seventeenth century governing primary school provision by communities; after independence different states treated schooling differently. Nevertheless, certain educational trends are apparent. Until the end of the Civil War (1865), southern schooling was limited to the formation of an elite white society. Schooling was private and provided the small number of professionals needed for a plantation economy. Since the South remained agricultural and precapitalist, relying on England and the North for industrial goods, an institution such as public schooling was not necessary to maintain societal order. There was little social change. Much of the labor force were slaves, kept away from schools and even from churches because owners believed that any gathering of blacks bred sedition. Poor whites lived on small holdings in rural areas, as they had before independence. Only with the northern victory in 1865 was public education imposed on the South.

But in the northern states, primary education—although it consisted of little more than learning how to read and write and religious instruction—became an important issue as early as the beginning of the nineteenth century. Besides the New England community schools and the private primary schools for wealthier children preparing for university education, church groups organized public school societies for educating the poor. These public school societies paralleled similar groups in England, all of which formed the model for British (and American) missionary efforts in Africa and Asia.

> With minimal administrative expense, scrupulous financial integrity, and commendable efficiency, the [New York Public School] [s]ociety maintained for decades an extensive network of schools that taught thousands of children a year.
>
> But make no mistake about it: This was a class system of education.

> It provided a vehicle for the efforts of one class to civilize another and thereby insure that society would remain tolerable, orderly, and safe.[1]

The public school societies made poverty a condition of free schooling, a stipulation that clashed with the interests of those who wanted to extend primary schooling to all. As long as public schooling was associated with being poor, the children of those who were neither wealthy nor paupers would not attend. Wage earners were a rapidly growing group in the North, and social change wrought by industrialization and the immigration of large numbers of Irish into northern cities threatened social order in the young Republic. Visionaries such as Horace Mann saw schools as the means to produce economic change without disruption and chaos. With Adam Smith, he believed that state support (and control) of public schooling would help maintain morality and decent behavior, and would contribute to economic growth. But to achieve this, it was necessary to get everyone in school. The Public School Society, or "paternalistic voluntarism," as Katz calls the Society's organization of schooling, was not suitable for the task. It stood in the way of universal public schooling because it set the condition of poverty for access to it. Decentralized control in the districts was also not suitable because it often left the conduct and curriculum of schools in the hands of the very working class that had to be transformed into moral and decent members of an industrializing economy.

In the place of the Public School Society and the decentralized district control of schools, reformers like Mann—beginning with the Massachusetts Board of Education in the 1840s and '50s—organized public education centrally under their control and their philosophy. This was the first major reform in U.S. education and it set the pattern for school expansion for the next two generations. By that time, another wave of immigrants was entering the United States and large enterprises were in the process of consolidating their position in the economy. To meet these new conditions, a second important period of educational reform took place between 1900 and 1920. But that reform was an *extension* of earlier structures built in Massachusetts, and simply reinforced trends established earlier.

Thus, the movement for public education in the United States began in the industrializing northern states under pressure from reformers who represented the views of a growing bourgeoisie.[2] Local industrialists saw schooling as a means to offset the disruptive social conditions of factory life; some institution was necessary to provide the moral guidance and control which the family and church had supplied in precapitalist society.[3] Schooling was imposed on a working class who viewed schooling (correctly) as largely serving the children of higher-income groups.[4] The South did not participate in this movement until northern capital took control of its institutions.[5] Public education as it developed in the United States was the reformers' answer to the growth of industry and the crisis it caused in the traditional social structure. Schooling was seen by reformers and industrialists alike as promoting their common vision of an ordered, purposeful, and progressive society. In conjunction with this view, it also helped preserve a class structure in the face of economic and social change.

Since Massachusetts was the first state with state-run public education, and since that case served as the model for others and is so well documented, we use it as a detailed example of mid-eighteenth-century educational reform. The chapter then discusses the reform period around World War I and the present problems in American education.

The Early Reform Era: Public Schooling in Massachusetts

The most detailed analysis of early school reform in America is found in Michael Katz's work.[6] Katz shows how the first generation of professional educators, who emerged in the northern, industrializing states, faced a society in the process of rapid social change. The agrarian economy that had characterized the colonial and immediate postcolonial period was being transformed into an urban one. Even more important, children of small farmers came into the towns to become wage earners. They were joined by a wave of Irish immigrants. Decision making in production passed from the one-family farmers and artisans to capitalists with many workers in their factories. The extended-family system which pervaded rural life began to break down, and with it, controls on social behavior.

One answer to the feelings of powerlessness and dislocation caused by capitalist industrialization was to adapt rural institutions to urban conditions. "Democratic localism," as Katz calls it, was a movement which tried to bring the district or community school into the cities. The people of the district would have the right to provide any kind of education they wished and they could not be overridden by the state. The democratic localists wanted to keep American government decentralized; they emphasized the virtues of variety and adaptability. They believed in public education for all, but also believed that each individual community (even within a city) should control its schools:

> The case of the democratic localists, then, rested ultimately on a combination of faith in the people and a point of view about the sources of social change   The imposition of social change would never work; changes in society, in habits and attitudes, came only from within the people themselves as they slowly, haltingly, but surely exercised their innate common sense and intelligence. By being left to their own devices, by perhaps being encouraged, cajoled, and softly educated, but not by being forced, the people would become roused to the importance of universal education and the regular school attendance of their children.[7]

The professional educators rejected this way of organizing the schools and opted for a centralized model in which a state-level bureaucracy, run by educator-reformers, would organize education, setting norms and enforcing them. The reformers argued that democratic localism was in fact undemocratic since 51 percent of the local parents could dictate the religious, moral, and political ideas taught to the children of the remainder. Katz adds that democratic localism also failed on other grounds: it was a rural transplant and could not function properly in the heterogeneous urban setting.

But the professionals' opposition to democratic localism was much more profound than their critique of its democracy. Their view of future American society was centralized, under the control of those who would transform it from agriculture to industry, avoiding the problems of crime and poverty prevalant in English cities. Because they perceived schools as the "key agencies for uplifting the quality of city life by stemming diffusion of the poverty, crime, and immorality that were thought to accompany urban and industrial development," [8] professionals argued for raising the quality of education by centralizing power over the educational system. Through that central bureaucracy, they could systematize and standardize structure, curricula, and teacher certification.

In order to achieve their goal, it was necessary to break the hold of the districts and masters (schoolteachers) over the schools. Once the Massachusetts Board of Education was created, Mann and his fellow members began their attack on district control by establishing and promoting public high schools, whose administration cut across district lines.

> All their plans had certain characteristics in common, most important among them centralization. This had two principal components: first, the modification and eventual elimination of the bastion of democratic localism, the district system, whereby each section of a town or city managed its own schools with a great deal of autonomy. . . . The ultimate remedy was the replacement of the district by one central board of education. In most cases, however, that was politically impossible, and reformers consequently turned to an interim measure, the establishment of high schools. In Massachusetts, for example, both the law and practical considerations required the high school to be a town school. . . . It was thus an administrative device for undercutting the power of the district.[9]

The reformers argued that the high school promoted mobility, contributed to economic growth and communal wealth, and saved the towns from "disintegrating into an immoral and degenerate chaos." [10] They were backed, not surprisingly, by the bourgeoisie, which had the same vision of society and perceived the same solution to the ills which the realization of that vision was creating.[11] Katz shows that in the vote on the abolition of Beverly High School in Massachusetts in 1860, the people of most wealth and prestige in the community, joined by those of middle-level position, supported the high school. They shared the view that cities and factories were good and should be promoted. The high school, they believed, would foster industrial growth by increasing communal wealth and creating a skilled labor force through replacing the apprenticeship system. At the same time, the high school would fight the accompanying social and family disintegration caused by industrial growth by civilizing the community and providing guidance to children usually lacking in the working class family situation. With the reformers, these wealthier members of the community looked to the state to "sponsor education that would help build modern industrial cities permeated by the values and features of an idealized rural life." [12]

Thus, the reforms were not the result of majority consensus, even though the educators' most important argument against democratic localism was that it fostered the tyranny of some of the parents over the education of all the children. The very reformers, such as Horace Mann, who proposed to protect the interests of all the people, *imposed* a system of education which served minority interests. The working class in Beverly opposed the high school and voted it down. Artisans saw in the new industrialization the destruction of their position in the community. The high school represented to them that new order. The artisans were the propertied, moderately well-off groups whose life was being altered by technological development. They were joined by citizens without children who protested the raising of taxes to finance the schools. Finally, many working-class people felt that the high school would not benefit their children.

> The underlying cause of both the establishment and abolition of Beverly High School was the shifting economic base and the consequent social division in both the town and the state. It was to keep pace with these changes that promoters urged an extension of the educational system; it was to assure opportunity for the individual within an altered economy that the high school was argued; it was to reunite a splintering community that a high school was necessary. [13]

Despite the Beverly case, the reformers prevailed. By 1861,

Massachusetts had 103 high schools, one for every three towns and cities. Public high school became the symbol and reality of the first major school reform in America, beginning in the 1820s and continuing into the 1880s and '90s. It represented the victory of the professional educators and the industrialists over the local power structures which had their base in rural areas and in the wards of the larger towns. Through the high school, the reformers effectively imposed their view of what Massachusetts and the rest of the industrializing North would be like in the coming generations. Other states developed high schools as they industrialized and urbanized, for the high schools accompanied the need to combat the destruction of preindustrial, agrarian social structures by large-scale capitalist enterprise. The impact of the reform was predictable: although the reformers had promised that the high school would promote social mobility and civilize communities, it did neither. Like other institutions associated with industrialization, it exacerbated divisions in the community by serving the well-to-do. Nor was it able to overcome the problems of poverty and crime which plagued industrial towns.[14]

One of the most important objectives of the centralized state school system was to form a new working class for industrial growth. Schools had to inculcate behavior patterns relevant to working in factories instead of on self-owned farms or as artisans. Crucial to factory work patterns was a sense of time and authority. Reformers realized that if children could be taught to attend school regularly and be taught the importance of punctuality, they would come on time to work. If they could be taught to respond to the reward system in the classroom and to submit to the authority of the teacher, they would be obedient workers. Industrialists also recognized that the school served as a means of preparing a disciplined work force:

> ". . . by diligence and a willing acquiescence in necessary regulations, to merit the good opinion of their employers and the community"; they "secure . . . by the same means, the respect and confidence of their fellows," and "oftentimes exert a conservative influence in periods of excitement of great value pecuniarily and morally." [15]

The main task of the educators, then, was to get the children into the schools. With the opposition of working-class parents to schools that did not serve their needs, truancy was rampant. If schools were to incorporate all children into the new society, school had to make schooling more appealing to children. This was a main purpose of the pedagogical reforms which accompanied the structural reform. The pedagogical reform was concentrated at the primary level, and it consisted of changing teaching methodology to excite the children's interest in learning. The reformers wanted to develop in students the "necessary intrinsic self-controls through leading them to internalize a love for knowledge." [16]

Simply enough, the reform was designed to make school a more pleasant place, so that children would be induced to like school. At the same time, however, the reform reflected changed views of the relation of the adult to the authority structure. "Soft-line" educators, as Katz calls them, could have pushed for less authoritarian structure in the schools, with more peer group reinforcement. But they wanted to replace the old style of teaching, which stressed *direct* obedience to external authority, with teaching which stressed obedience to *abstract* authority through internal controls. This change reflected the reality of the times. With the gradual destruction of the old authority structures—the family and the tight-knit community—which controlled members directly, the old forms of external authority were disappearing. Factory managers could not afford to hire new people every week and teach them their jobs; nor could they constantly watch the workers to make sure they were performing correct tasks. Urban communities were not cohesive enough to control directly the actions of individuals living in them. Also, large numbers of immigrants, particularly the Irish, represented an "untamed" group who had to be incorporated into new social values and norms without the benefit of a well-organized community to teach them. A new authority was needed to fulfill all these functions, but it had to be indirect. Thus, the soft-line educators wanted to reform the schools so that children would be taught to *internalize* external authority and become individuals who would follow rules because of society's reward for doing so rather than the fear of being punished. Although the soft-line educators claimed that they were concerned with the spiritual values of life, the stress on responding to external reward was precisely translated into the response to material gain, the quality most needed to succeed in the competitive capitalist society.

The pedagogical controversy had one other important aspect. It pitted the centrist reformers against local primary school teachers, who argued for strong discipline in the classroom and for teaching methods that were not particularly designed to try to interest the child. The teachers believed in an "absolute" curriculum which taught the child how to discharge the "duties of life." [17] But the curriculum issue represented the fight of the teachers against control by the state Board of Education, a fight for local autonomy against the state bureaucracy. In order for Mann and his fellow reformers to organize the educational system under their jurisdiction, they had to demonstrate their power over the teachers. The Board did this by changing the required curriculum and therefore changing how the teachers taught.

Other changes were pushed in schools in line with changes in the organization of society, particularly the organization of the production of goods. Just as processes in manufacturing were being increasingly subdivided, so the teaching process was subdivided in the high schools. Teachers, ideally, would be responsible for students' education, and the teachers would be trained in the new normal schools. Larger schools formed to eliminate overlap and to gain efficiency. Furthermore, partially because it was believed that women were better teachers for younger children, and mainly because they cost much less to employ than men, the feminization which occurred in U.S. industry between 1840 and 1860 was matched by a feminization of the schools. According to Katz's data, in that period, the percentage of males teaching in Massachusetts schools dropped from 60 to 14 percent.[18] In order to bring the large numbers of immigrant children into the schools—since their parents contributed little to taxes—it was necessary to cut down on the cost of schooling; this was done by hiring women. Thus, the same scarcity of labor that brought women into manufacturing and put pressure on manufacturers to increase efficiency, brought them into schools and put pressure on the schools to avoid duplication of effort and promote division of labor.

Soon after their establishment, it became clear that public high schools benefited the middle class. Boys gained entrance either into college or the business world from the high school while it prepared girls primarily for teaching. In theory, the high schools competed with the private academies, which had been established in the eighteenth century to prepare boys for university. But in practice, the academies drew their boys from a wealthier class than attended the public schools. Public education also offered nonacademic courses (some academies did too). Such nonacademic courses were the beginning of the tracking system which became prevalent after the turn of the century. Far from being a "thoroughly democratic institution since it fostered equality of opportunity," [19] the high school instituted a hierarchy of access to education which corresponded to the social hierarchy associated with capitalist industrialization. There were important socioreligious overtones to this hierarchy. The reformers had argued against democratic localism on the grounds that Catholics could impose their will on non-Catholics in the wards. The reformers' view was that the schools should be religiously and politically neutral. In practice, the schools were not neutral at all. "Protestant ministers, as David Tyack has shown, played active and important roles in common school promotion and management, and it is in fact impossible to disentangle Protestantism from the early history of the common school." [20] For the most part, the wealthy Protestants in the preindustrial order retained their positions in the new order. Catholics, at least in Massachusetts, were the immigrants, and they filled the new working classes. Schooling contributed to establishing the new social structure.

Once the high school was established, the children of wealthy parents continued to attend academies to prepare themselves in classic education, with the possibility of going on to university. Middle-class children gained entrance to public high schools (and some who could afford it also went to academies) and were tracked either into a college preparatory course or a nonacademic (business) course. Working-class children generally did not get into high school or their parents were not sufficiently convinced of the value of education to want them to go. The significant change introduced by the high school was that a free higher level of schooling now existed which, unlike the academies, did not require fees. The only criterion for entrance was *achievement*. Mann and his contemporaries probably believed that simply making a higher level of school *available* would guarantee equal access to all classes of society, as soon as all parents could be convinced of the value of education. Of course, this is not what happened. The stress on achievement is a fundamental criterion for reward in bourgeois democratic theory, and was an important part of the shift in the basis of social valuation from ascriptive (traits handed down from father to son) to universalistic ("objectively" measured achievement) norms. But when achievement in school became a measure of potential achievement in the economy, the class structure was preserved rather than democratized.

> Schoolmen who thought they were promoting a neutral and classless— indeed, a *common*—school education remained unwilling to perceive the extent of cultural bias inherent in their own writing and activity. However, the bias was central and not incidental to the standardization and administrative rationalization of public education. For in the last analysis, the rejection of democratic localism rested only partly on its inefficiency and violation of parental prerogative. It stemmed equally from a gut fear of the cultural divisiveness inherent in the increasing religious and ethnic diversity of American life.[21]

It is this class structure of the schools, the incorporation of white immigrant groups into the lower rungs of the education and economic ladder, and the growing centralization and bureaucratization of urban schools that marks American educational history in the rest of the century. In the 1880s and '90s, for example, the second generation of educational reformers were becoming superintendents of large-city school systems, after they, together with the leading industrialists and professionals of the cities, moved successfully to take control of urban schools away from political wards dominated by politicians and working-class ethnics and to transfer it to city-wide elected school boards controlled by business interests.[22]

Well before 1900, then, the schools were organized to promote capitalist industrial development—to produce a working class with desired behavior patterns, particularly the internalization of an authoritarian work structure and loyalty to a society which was run by the bourgeoisie. Reformers, industrialists, and the wealthier segments of northern society combined to impose centralized control on school systems; democratic localism, which tried to retain this control at the local level even in the cities, failed in this political and philosophical power struggle. Once their control over school systems was achieved, the reformers turned to the second phase of reform: helping the schools to serve these social and economic functions more *efficiently*.

The Consolidation of Capitalism and Twentieth-century Educational Reform

Important changes occurred in the United States after the Civil War. First, northern industry grew phenomenally as a result of the war, and by the turn of the century, cities began to dominate American life. There was also a great immigration to these cities from Eastern and Southern Europe. As the population grew and industry expanded, schools had an increasingly more important role in preparing people for incorporation into the industrial structure. As industry became more complex, the schools also had to change to meet its needs. Furthermore, enrollment in the schools increased and the percentage of primary school graduates going on to high school grew markedly. Compulsory schooling became more accepted by the working class, especially the new immigrants, and compulsory schooling age rose. The socioeconomic composition of the high schools therefore changed, creating serious conflict in the purpose and structure of public education.

Educators (and other "leading" citizens) met this crisis by gaining increased political power over urban schools, and then differentiating the high school curriculum to make it vocationally oriented. As we shall show, they accentuated the class bias of public education through striving for greater efficiency in preparing children for occupational roles in the expanding economy. Reform at the end of the nineteenth and beginning of the twentieth century has been named Progressivism, paralleling the so-called Progressive movement in politics. Yet, like its political counterpart, it was basically conservative, supporting industrial monopolies' (corporate capitalism's) influence on American life by using public institutions to help consolidate their power.[23]

The reform movement at the turn of the century built on the philosophy and structures established by Massachusetts fifty years before. As with earlier reform, it had strong class overtones, and was based on the attempt "to socialize the urban poor to behavior that will decrease crime, diminish expenditures on public welfare, promote safety on the streets and contribute to industrial productivity." [24] Later in the century, schools took on the added function of helping to find nonsocialist approaches to educational reform. With the new waves of migration, the growth of manufacturing, and socialist movements in Europe, schools had to ensure that the free-enterprise system worked: workers had to be made to identify with the growth and health of that system, even though it was inequitable, and not very healthy. People had to be sold on the idea that getting education would solve the problems of poverty and unemployment.

> The prescription, for one thing, unleashes a flurry of seemingly purposeful activity and, for another, requires no tampering with basic social structural or economic characteristics, only with the attitudes of poor people, and that has caused hardly a quiver.[25]

Despite the reforms in Massachusetts and the spread of high schools to many other industrializing states, democratic localism still flourished after the Civil War. The big-city political machines were based on control of political wards; municipal education systems were run by city school boards elected from the wards, and the wards got patronage from the city bosses in the form of education jobs, contracts and supplies. Thus, through political muscle people in wards continued to control the kind of education their children got. This system was corrupt and led to very uneven schooling, but it had the advantage of decentralized community control. The reformers attacked the boss and patronage systems in the 1880s and 1890s, and as part of that attack, they proposed the centralization of power in a small school board with members elected at large. A small board representative of the whole city, they felt, would be freer of political influence; it would standardize education throughout the city and would provide higher quality schooling more efficiently.

By 1900, the reformers were successful in almost every large city. The educators who led this movement often became big-city school superintendents. The new boards were controlled by old-stock first citizens, often professionals and big businessmen. They did standardize education, but as we shall see, standardized education was geared to differentiate children by the adult occupational roles they were measured to be fit for. The professionals and businessmen had an antiimmigrant and antiworking-class attitude which underlay most of their municipal reform.

> Their aim remained similar to earlier reformers: inculcating the poor with acceptable political attitudes. This has had important political implications. It has meant that the government of school systems has continued to rest on disdain for a large portion of students and their families. This has only widened the gulf between working class communities and schools that mid-century reformers had helped to create.[26]

One of the most important results of the alliance between the educational reformers and businessmen—an alliance that stemmed from the common vision that the two groups held of societal progress and their common class values (going back to the 1830s and '40s)—was an emphasis on school efficiency and the introduction of business-oriented curricula in high schools.[27] Efficiency was interpreted by schools as the effectiveness with which they prepared children for future work. Since schooling was conceived as preparation for work, schoolmen turned to factory efficiency studies and models to organize the schools.[28] "School superintendents saw themselves as plant managers, and proposed to treat education as a production process in which children were the raw materials." [29]

But as Michelson points out,[30] the application of "scientific management to factories and schools had less effect on workers and

students than the introduction of industrialization with its "fragmenta-
tion of jobs and life styles" had had fifty years earlier. Nevertheless,
scientific management in industry did differentiate production further,
and schools followed suit by differentiating courses. Differentiated
courses meant that educators were giving up the concept of equality of
opportunity. In that concept, rich and poor would attend high school
together exposed to a common curriculum and would participate
equally in the upward mobility of the community. Of course, as we
have seen, the poor generally did not go to high school until the end
of the century, just when course differentiation began in earnest. The
new concept of equal opportunity, developed to resolve the conflict
between equality and efficiency, was the "opportunity for all to receive
such education as will fit them *equally well* for their particular life
work." [31] Thus, as the differentiation of schooling spread, the notion of
equal school achievement for equal ability emerged. "Differentiation
was justified as a way of organizing education to conform with social
and economic realities, and this in turn was presented as a way of
providing meaningful equality of educational opportunity." [32]

This aspect of Progressivism was appealing because the single
academic track in high school led to retardation and dropouts.
Working-class and immigrant children could not meet the difficult
regimen of the middle-class-oriented program, for which standards had
been set at a time when only a small percentage of children went to
high school. Rather than change the nature of academic (or college
preparatory) training—a move which would have been inconsistent
with the class bias in the schools and in the work place—the reformers
stratified the curriculum so that working-class children would not drop
out but neither would they receive academic instruction. Once this
system of "equal opportunity" was implemented, its success could be
measured by the number of pupils who were kept in school, and how
well the schools trained people for available jobs.[33] The incorporation
of vocational training in the high schools alongside academic and
business courses during and after the First World War was the
triumph of the comprehensive high school.[34]

The National Education Association's 1910 *Report of the Committee on the Place of Industries in Public Education* summarized the rationale for educational differentiation:

1. Industry, as a controlling factor in social progress, has for education a fundamental and permanent significance.
2. Educational standards, applicable in an age of handicraft, presumably need radical change in the present day of complex and highly specialized industrial development.
3. The social aims of education and the psychological needs of childhood alike require that industrial (manual-constructive) activities form an important part of school occupations. . . .
4. The differences among children as to aptitudes, interests, economic resources, and prospective careers furnish the basis for a rational as opposed to a merely formal distinction between elementary, secondary, and higher education.[35]

Ultimately, in the 1920s, testing led to ability tracking in junior high and even primary schools. Because truancy and dropouts continued to be a problem even with vocational training tracks in high school, a new way had to be found at lower levels of school to keep children in school and more fully "individualize" their instruction. Thus, children were classified into ability groupings where members were fairly homogeneous in ability. L. M. Terman, the author of the Stanford-Binet IQ test, and one of the leaders of the testing movement, was also one of the founders of tracking. Terman and others believed that tracking ensured "educational democracy." By fitting the curriculum to the child, they thought that every child could be brought closer to the maximum achievement consistent with individual ability.[36] Proponents of tracking argued:

It is not social segregation. It is not a caste stratification. It is not an attempt to point out those who are worthwhile and those who are not. It is not a move to separate the leaders from the followers.[37]

But fifty years later, Judge Skelly Wright, in reviewing tracking in the Washington, D.C., school system,[38] concluded that "while in theory the tests which presumably measured ability and the track which were supposed to serve individual needs actually, in practice, measured past socio-economic advantage as much as presumed ability while the curricular track served to lock the child into the socio-economic class from which he came. Few children ever crossed tracks." [39] Once the child was tracked, the court found, he worked at the level expected from the requirements of the track. In fact, there is evidence that pupils' performance actually declines when they are in a low track. Since tracking was progressively moved downward from junior high to primary school, many pupils were (and are) locked into a prescribed pattern before they had (or have) a chance to develop their full mental abilities.

To function properly, differentiation among students needed an efficient mechanism to allocate them among the various course levels. There were two stages to this mechanism. The first stemmed from a dogmatic belief that adult success depends on school achievement. If the schools were in the business of transforming children into successful adults, they should—to be efficient—differentiate them on the basis of their achievement in school. Thus, the development and popularization of testing instruments that measured the educator's definition of school achievement contributed to the scientific management of the schools. Armed with a battery of tests, the educator could ensure that each student fit into his or her proper place in the school and, by inference, into the proper adult occupation. "Thorndike and his students developed scales for measuring achievement in arithmetic (1908), handwriting (1910), spelling (1913), drawing (1913), reading (1914), and language ability (1916)." [40]

The Alpha Test developed by the army during World War I to identify officer potential and those unfit for service showed a clear correlation between measured intelligence and occupational attainment.[41] At the same time, testing in school showed that people who had higher IQ completed more years in school. All these results reinforced educators' notions on the relationships between achievement and success, and helped rationalize the use of testing to achieve greater school efficiency, as defined by the successful incorporation of children into the differentiated school structure. By 1932, when President Hoover called a White House Conference on vocational education, about three-quarters of the 150 large cities surveyed were using intelligence tests to classify students.[42]

Vocational guidance represented the second aspect of the classification mechanism. Vocational guidance and the junior high school were, like the differentiated high school, a response to the increased complexity of American industry by the turn of the century. Skills were more diverse and skilled workers more mobile. Firms were less willing to invest in the more general skills that they needed, because workers could move to other establishments which could also use their general training. Schools were given the task of providing this general training. To carry out this task efficiently, the schools had to differentiate students according to vocational goals.

> The early vocational guidance leaders attempted to function as human engineers who matched and shaped individual abilities to fit a particular slot in the social organism. This gave them the dual responsibility of analyzing personal talents and character and planning educational programs in terms of future vocation. Junior high schools were designed to make educational planning and guidance possible at an early age. The original purpose of the junior high school was to divide students into separate courses of study in the hope that with proper guidance they would choose vocations early and follow a directed educational program through high school to the occupation.[43]

The guidance counselor was therefore an intermediary between corporate needs and students. In that role he classified students for the labor market. Armed with a variety of tests, the counselor decided which occupations the student was suited for. The student then was channeled into the high school program most relevant to his or her career. It was in junior high school that this testing and channeling began, so that by the time a student completed the ninth grade, it was determined whether he or she would follow an academic, business, or vocational career. High school courses were geared to prepare the student for his counseled occupation.

All this differentiation was class biased. The school "meritocracy" first depended on all children being able to do high school academic work which was oriented to middle-class culture and norms. The college preparatory curriculum (which included Latin and Greek) required behavior patterns alien to working-class children. Many working-class families, as Katz shows, chose not to send their children to high school at all. Once business courses were introduced, it was natural that those who were not "suited" to the academic track were prepared for lower occupational strata. Finally, with the advent of vocational courses, testing, and guidance, the efficiency of selecting the greatly expanded number of enrollees for the various courses increased. The schools' methods of measuring merit were therefore seriously biased by inherited status and culture. According to Bowles and Gintis, who have done work on recent data,

> . . . while one's economic status tends strongly to resemble that of one's parents, only a minor portion of this association can be attributed to social class differences in childhood IQ, and a virtually negligible proportion to social class differences in genetic endowments—even accepting the Jensen estimates of heritability. Thus, a perfect equalization of IQ's across social classes would reduce the intergenerational transmission of economic status by a negligible amount.[44]

Thus, there is evidence that the rating systems used by the schools were (and are) only in part related to childhood IQ. They differentiate children more on class-associated information and forms of expression, as well as behavior patterns. In designing the Stanford-Binet intelligence test,

> Terman developed questions which were based on presumed progressive difficulty in performing tasks which he believed were necessary for achievement in ascending the hierarchical occupational structure. He then proceeded to find that according to the results of his tests the intelligence of different occupational classes fit his ascending hierarchy. It was little wonder that IQ [as measured by this test] reflected social class bias. It was, in fact, based on the social class order. Terman believed that, for the most part, people were at that level because of heredity and not social environment.[45]

The Progressives therefore contributed to a system of schools which divided children, mostly on the basis of their class, into occupation-oriented course streams, and to a system that used (and still uses) ability tracks even at the elementary level. The schools prepared children for future work roles defined by class-biased "ability" tests and by the vocational guidance counselor. The tests and guidance served to "objectify" selection processes in a way that made people think that they were being given the fairest deal possible within *their own limitations.* Merit selection shifted the responsibility for an individual's productive capability to the individual himself and away from the structure and organization of the economy. If a person is convinced that he is *not able to do well,* he is less likely to rise up against the social system than if the person believes that the system is unfair and based on class. The Progressives institutionalized meritocracy as a means for social control, to insure that those with the "correct" characteristics got the highest positions in the society and that those who were not as suitable believed in the objectivity and fairness of the decision which put them in their place. America was the land of opportunity, where the best excelled and the inferior found themselves in the lowest status (and paid) occupation. The definition of democracy had changed from rule by the people to rule by the intelligent. The intelligent, as defined by the designers of tests and vocational guidance counselors, were those of higher social classes, who were at the same time more "moral" and had the characteristics necessary for leadership in America.[46]

It is worth discussing one other part of the Progressive education movement because it is so identified with the philosophy of the period. Already in the earlier reform era, the "soft-line"educators had argued for child-centered curriculum. In the first decades of this century, the child-centered wing of American education were advocates of play in schooling. They generally opposed market-oriented, extrinsic criteria of educational merit, although some justified play as the child's natural work and therefore as the most efficient method for producing good workers. It was this latter argument that permitted the formation of kindergartens and, later, nursery schools—primarily for middle- and upper-class children—during a period when the public schools were moving toward an increased occupational orientation. Nevertheless, public school personnel often argued that kindergarten children came to school poorly prepared either to learn or to behave properly.[47]

John Dewey rejected the work-play dichotomy. He believed that work and play were part of a continuum, and they differed only in that work required a longer period of concentration and a greater goal commitment. The lack of goal commitment in play made it an intrinsic activity, carried out for its own ends, thus keeping alive a creative and constructive attitude in the child. But Dewey's view of work and play could be consistent only if the nature of work in the society changed. He realized this and called for a change in the organization of work from an orientation to the needs of the economy—that is, the production of more goods—to the needs of the individual or society. Given the nature of work, Dewey wanted the school to provide a period for the child in which he could live and learn without economic pressure, carrying out activities for their intrinsic value. This would enable the young to learn for learning's sake, internalizing the joy of intellectual experience.[48]

Although Dewey's philosophy of education gave a boost to the child-centered orientation in education, it had little impact on public education until important changes occurred in the kind of work done within corporations in the 1950s and '60s. The movement to bring play into the classroom had its greatest following in middle-class private schools, where this type of education fit in with the trend in middle-class child rearing "away from repression and externally imposed discipline, towards greater freedom," and the idea that "happiness in learning seemed to be linked with higher levels of achievement." [49] While industry needed specialized and well-disciplined workers, and societal "leaders" saw schooling as a means to control social change (especially during a period of rapid immigration and urban poverty), it was not likely that public schools would stress intrinsic experiences as a form of learning.

The failure of Dewey's philosophy to have an effect on the nature of schooling at the time of his Chicago Laboratory School points out the flaw in those histories of societal institutions like schooling which stress the "man in history" view of institutional change. Dewey was obviously an important intellectual force in American education, but it was those educators who rationalized and made more efficient the role of the school as a provider of specialized and socialized labor to industries and as an agent of social control who made the greatest impact on the educational system during their time. Educators who worked to make the capitalist economic and social system—with its class structure and hierarchic organization—function more smoothly were the principal reformers of the early twentieth century. Thus, it was a particular economic and social system which shaped reform, not John Dewey.

This reform was not the result of conspiracy between business leaders and schoolmen, although there is ample evidence that business interests did control the schools through pressures on schoolmen and that schoolmen *were* businessmen.[50] It was the result of the same kind of sharing of societal views as occurred in Horace Mann's time. The key to understanding why schools were organized for the benefit of the few and the repression of the many is *enlightened self-interest*. Both reformers and business leaders were interested in maintaining a social order in which those who shared their view of societal change, not the immigrant and working-class rabble, came to power in the next generation.

The Problems of U.S. Education in the 1970s

The description of these two earlier reform periods should make clear that the structure of U.S. schools today is not an accident or the result of inefficiencies or of conservative administrators and teachers. Rather, schools are the way they are today because of *successful* reforms between 1850 and 1920, reforms which were designed to meet the needs of capitalist industrialization. The objective of schoolmen was to inculcate faith in the capitalist system, especially in its objectivity and rationality, and to prepare people to take their *proper* place in that system. This objective was derived from a particular and hierarchical view of society which in turn was derived from a particular and hierarchical economic philosophy: the rich and powerful are cleverer than the poor and weak, and therefore have the *right* to be rich and powerful. And society is better off for that division and ordering of power.

Alongside this view, however, there has always been an undeniable concern with equality in American society. Horace Mann saw the public high school as equally accessible to all, a place where different social classes would mix freely, exposed to the same curriculum and experiences, and with the same opportunities for success in a growing economy. The later reformers gave up this idea partly because all children were not getting into or finishing high school. They considered it more important to get all children into school and keep them there longer than to have children take the same courses. Of course, the differentiation of schooling also served changing industrial needs, and the necessity for stricter social control during a period of heavy immigration, labor organizing, and left-wing agitation in the labor movement. To satisfy the concern with social unity while preserving the class structure, differentiation was organized within the same school. As Spring points out, the concept of equality as interpreted by the reformers included the ideal of democracy which brought people from different classes together in the same institution —the comprehensive high school—to give them "Common ideas, common ideals, and common modes of thought, feeling, and action that made for cooperation, social cohesion, and social solidarity." [51] Since students were separated into different courses, other means of creating a sense of unity and equality among the groups was necessary; thus different social classes of students were mixed through extracurricular activities, such as athletics, social clubs, and school government.

But equality was only a façade and had little to do with the reality of the school or the reality of the economic and social structure. Once out of school, the sharing of common experiences by members of different social groups ceased. Furthermore, with the large internal migration of blacks and Mexican-Americans to Northern and Western urban areas after World War II, racial and ethnic conflicts became too great to overcome with a false sense of unity in schools.

The school system as reformed in the early twentieth century began running into serious problems in the 1960s. Twenty years of rapid postwar economic growth had produced little change in income distribution. Education was still distributed along class and racial lines, a situation that became increasingly unacceptable to blacks, Chicanos, Puerto Ricans, and American Indians, whom the Progressive definition of "equal opportunity" left at the bottom of the vocational ladder. To them, centralized control by Anglo school boards was to blame, and in some communities a struggle began for community control of schools—the democratic localism movement all over again. But in the 1960s, many upper-middle-cass whites were not satisfied with schools either: they rejected the corporate structure and the transmission of that structure and its values through the school. Those parents pushed for child-centered schools which stressed interpersonal relations rather than extrinsic rewards.

> In a more general framework, we see two significant challenges to the existing social order. First there are demands that the schools satisfy their rhetorical goals of providing equal educational opportunities (read as equal educational outcomes) for all groups in the society, rich and poor, black and white, Chicano and Anglo. This objective has implications for the financing, heterogeneity of enrollments, and educational offerings of the schools. Second, the schools are being pressured to be client-oriented rather than professionally oriented, child-centered rather than adult-centered. This goal has implications for the number and nature of alternatives that must be available to satisfy the needs of students with substantially different talents, personalities, abilities, and interests.[52]

Most blacks, Chicanos, and Puerto Ricans, as well as some Indians are demanding that the schools make them more *employable* in the present economic structure; that the schools increase their status within the colonial structure. Much of the community control movement fits into the challenge of equal school outcomes: minority groups believe correctly that white Anglo control has created schools in which their children *cannot* do as well as those of the controlling interest; therefore, control is essential to equal opportunity to learn in schools. "Control," however, is a tricky, many-leveled word. Where blacks have gained control of the boards of ghetto schools, for example, they have found that they do not control the state legislature, which distributes state aid to education and sets curriculum and other requirements. But even if blacks could get equal funds out of the legislature, even if they could alter curriculum, even if they could produce equal outcomes through community control, they still would not control the economy and requirements for jobs. They would remain dependent for the definition of social roles on a society that has continually ensured them the bottom rung on its ladder.

Winning at least some control over one's own destiny, however, especially for a people who have been oppressed during their entire history in this country, does have important psychological effects. Political and social learning as a result of community control may not be the end point of a liberation period, but the beginning of something much more extensive and profound, depending upon who controls the community control movement. Cooptation by establishment blacks and Chicanos would ensure that the building of self-identity and the use of the schools for real community social change and political development be subverted to the needs of the corporate structure. In that case, oppressed minorities would successfully maintain their undesirable social roles through their "own" school boards. The results of community control of schools, then, are inexorably tied to the dependency of the community on decisions presently out of its control.

Since most poor still believe that more and better schooling can get them out of poverty, both individually and *as a class,* the role of liberal reformers is to try to provide minorities (who have been most militant and most threatening to societal order) more mobility *without* giving them more control over the economic and social structure. Again, reformers in the 1960s turned to the schools to meet the challenge of serious disruption of the social order. In this most recent attempt at reform, "disadvantaged" children—children who come from homes that do not prepare them properly for middle-class education and hence, for college-level vocations—were to get (1) expenditures per pupil in their schools equal to middle-class children's schools, and (2) "compensatory" education—extra schooling such as Head Start and higher-quality instruction during the normal course of their schooling. The ultimate objective of the reform was to equalize the *school (test) performance* of all *groups* of children going to school: pupils entering with, on the average, different "endowments" in the first grade would leave high school with, on the average, equal endowments. The function of the state and the schools would be to allocate resources in a way which would fulfill this compensatory objective.

But, like Horace Mann's belief in equal opportunity, the underlying assumptions of compensatory education have fatal flaws:

1. It is assumed that the instruments used to measure equalization —for example, reading, verbal, or math test scores—are not class-, race-, or sex-biased, and at the same time, reflect employers' hiring criteria and society's status criteria. But in a society that practices racial, sex, or ethnic discrimination, tests will be better predictors of future economic success, if the tests are biased in the same way the labor market is. Terman's Stanford-Binet test (1960 version) reflected the reality of the economic system's class structure: those children who could identify the Nordic Anglo-Saxon child as the correct answer to the question, "Which is prettier?" best understand the values of their society.[53] If the tests are unbiased and the labor market is discriminatory, it is less likely that the test score will be correlated with economic success. The equalization of test scores in the face of a labor market that has a different set of rules from the school will not do much to equalize social and economic roles. Clearly, equal test scores for women and men does not translate into equal opportunity for women in the economy and society. Neither will blacks or Mexican-Americans coming out of school with scores equal to those of whites necessarily gain equal pay or status.

2. It is assumed that the choice of future roles among graduates with equal test scores is equal. The perception of "desirable" vocations for lower and higher socioeconomic class students may be very different at the end of high school despite equal test scores for the two groups. Women's test scores are equal to men's, but their choice of occupations has been clearly different: social-role perception correlated with social origin, race, and sex is reinforced by schools even if test scores are equalized. From this standpoint alone, public schools, organized by the state to service the goals of the state, cannot equalize different social, ethnic, racial, or sex groups' life possibilities at the end of a given period of schooling unless the society is itself egalitarian.

Public schools, as we have seen, reflect and reinforce rather than counteract the prejudices and perceptions of the outside world.

3. It is assumed that the relationship between the teachers and students in the school is such that improving the "quality" of the teacher will result in compensating low-performance pupils. Compensatory education models in the United States assume that this relation is capable of producing equal performance on the part of different groups of pupils. But most teachers use learning models that expect pupils to *behave* in certain ways while absorbing cognitive knowledge. Under the track system, lower-class children are usually in the lowest tracks, so they are expected to learn less than the higher-class children in the higher tracks. Even in tracks, however, lower-class children are supposed to learn in the same way (they may have to be more disciplined) as higher-class children, even though they come from different cultures. The learning environment in the classroom leads the teachers to treat much better those children with whom they can communicate well (and reward them more often) than children with whom they are having difficulty. Even today, with all our understanding of cultural differences and an increasing sensitivity to cultural pluralism, schools are preparing different social classes of students for different economic and social roles. Discipline is much stricter in lower-class high schools than in higher-class schools, and the hierarchical relationship in all the schools leaves the child no recourse but to take rewards and punishment from the teacher.

There is almost no evidence that increasing the dollar resources per student or the "quality" of teachers for "disadvantaged" pupils will equalize performance of "disadvantaged" and "advantaged" pupils. However, there is a growing body of empirical results which shows that compensatory education within the present societal and school structures will *not* equalize school outcomes even if more school resources are devoted to the poor than the rich.[54] The supposition that more resources would be devoted to poor children than to rich is obviously hypothetical, since if U.S. education followed that course, the state's decision would have to be preceded by a radical change in the state's view of inequality. Its decision would probably also imply a change in the organization of production, since it is unlikely that wealthy managers and industrialists would be willing to have public education organized in a way that favored the poor over their own children (and their own class) unless formal schooling had become an unimportant allocator of socio-economic roles. In fact, to have schooling reorganized in favor of the poor would mean that those who are at the head of the economic hierarchy would have to lose their political power, both their direct power and the implicit power that their class holds over the values and norms of U.S. society.

Reformers always believed in merit selection because they believed that they could reduce economic and social inequality through individual mobility. They reasoned that as more and more people got schooling—any kind of schooling that helped them to get work—the less unequal the income distribution would be. The notion that increasing the average level of education and other social services is a substitute for direct redistributive social change is the foundation of American liberalism.[55] Liberal reformers are committed to the idea that significant redistribution of income, wealth and power can occur in a society without confronting the distribution and ownership of property nor the organization of production.

The challenge to the liberal position is now devastating. Income distribution in the United States has not changed significantly since 1944, despite a rapid increase in the average level of schooling in the labor force and a significant decrease in the variance of years of schooling received.[56] Kolko argues that income inequality has not decreased significantly since 1910.[57] Chiswick and Mincer show that the decrease in income inequality they observe between 1939 and 1965 was the result of a large decrease in the dispersion of weeks of unemployment in the labor force, which occurred primarily in the five years between 1939 and 1944. Furthermore, they predict that even with full employment, income distribution will not change significantly between 1965 and 1985, assuming that the structural relationships estimated for the 1949–69 period continue to hold true.[58]

Yet it could be argued that although income distribution does not change, the people getting high incomes and low incomes change from generation to generation. Since there is a significant relationship between the number of years of schooling an individual has had and income earned (especially in younger age groups), we can easily check how the amount of schooling taken by those with low-education fathers has changed relative to the mean education of the adult population. Table 12 shows that *white* males whose fathers had less than eight years of school have not improved their position relative to the mean number of years of schooling since the early 1920s.[59]

Table 12

United States: Absolute and Relative Years of School Completed, White Males, by Age and Father's Education, March 1962.

Years of Schooling Completed by Father

Age of Son (years)	<8	8–11	12	College 1–3	≥4	Total Mean
20–24	10.6 (0.78)	11.8 (0.89)	12.8 (0.96)	13.4 (1.01)	14.1 (1.06)	13.3
25–34	10.8 (0.89)	12.1 (1.00)	13.0 (1.07)	14.3 (1.18)	15.3 (1.26)	12.1
35–44	10.6 (0.92)	11.6 (1.01)	13.0 (1.13)	14.0 (1.22)	15.1 (1.31)	11.5
45–54	9.9 (0.92)	11.6 (1.07)	12.4 (1.15)	13.0 (1.20)	14.2 (1.31)	10.8
55–64	9.1 (0.91)	10.4 (1.04)	11.8 (1.18)	11.9 (1.19)	13.6 (1.36)	10.0

Source: Bureau of the Census, *Current Population Reports*, Series P-20, no. 132, September 1964, table 4.

Even if we ignore the 20–24 age group, many of whom have not completed their college training, and even if we recognize that there is some bias in the average number of years completed by those with low-education fathers, it appears that those lowest two groups have not improved significantly relative to the mean years of schooling.

Distribution of schooling years has improved over time, but children of fathers with less than high school education still find themselves in a disadvantageous job-market position.

Table 13 shows that the greatest percentage increase in those who attended college between the mid-1920s and the mid-1950s came from families where the father had attended college, even though this group is much smaller than the group of fathers who had not attended college. Although of those who went to college in the 1920s an equal percentage were sons of fathers who had completed high school or attended some college, in the 1950s, sons with fathers who completed high school had a 30 percentage point lower probability of attending college than those with fathers who had attended some years (but not completed) college. Since at least some college in the 1950s was already considered necessary for entrance into the white-collar occupations, this spreading probability of access to college between those from families where the father had completed high school or less and where the father had completed some years of college indicates the kind of class division that still characterizes the public school system. Also, these tables are only for *white* males, which means that a high percentage of the lowest income groups in the United States are excluded. For example, in 1962, only 13.9 percent of nonwhite males 25–34 years old completed one or more years of college, compared with 32.3 percent of white males.[60]

The schools are also being attacked from another direction: by high-income whites. Alienation within this group, when it occurs, is not concerned with opportunity but with the *meaning* of opportunity. To this segment of the affluent, liberation means rejecting the employment mentality, rejecting the accouterments of success, and rejecting the concept that increasing the complexity and technification of society is progress. The "free schools" are the result of this white "liberation." The cost to affluent parents of experimenting with new educational forms is hardly high; surrounded by a learning environment outside the school, parents and children can always change their minds and be successful in traditional ways. Although no real research has been done on what happens to children after they leave the free schools, the desired result is to increase their propensity to choose life

Table 13
United States: Absolute Probability of Attending College, White Males, by Age and Father's Education, March 1962.

Years of Schooling Completed by Father

Age of Son (years)	<8	8–11	12	College 1–3	≥4	Total Mean
25–34	0.174	0.282	0.445	0.724	0.896	0.323
35–44	0.164	0.225	0.457	0.618	0.810	0.262
45–54	0.130	0.195	0.336	0.524	0.732	0.204
55–64	0.091	0.150	0.329	0.351	0.602	0.157

Source: See table 12.

rather than death.[61] This choice would manifest itself in the ways in which an individual works and lives, especially in the relations he has with those around him, as well as the kinds of products and services he produces and consumes, and the way he produces them.

As in the case of community control, however, the full impact of free schooling in its experimental and innovative forms may never be felt. Professional educators, along with foundations and industries, are incorporating elements of free-school style (child-centered classrooms) into the public schools. Silberman's interest in English open classrooms and the North Dakota "experiment" of child-centered classrooms as the solution to our schooling problem show the direction professional educators are taking to maintain control of the schools.[62] Children can undoubtedly gain as a result of North Dakota-type schools, with their sensitized teachers and more joyful atmosphere. But the end result will still be competitive achievement tests and socialization into capitalist, alienating economic organizations—organizations with needs that are somewhat less rigid than in the past, but which still require workers who respond to extrinsic rewards and who will follow implicit rules and regulations.

. . . when the rhetoric becomes so heated that people can be heard suggesting that we do away with the system or radically change it, Carnegie Foundation supported James Conant (1964), who, in effect, said the system was basically sound but then co-opted the rhetoric of the attackers to recommend limited change. It was, after all, the survival of the system which Conant had in mind when he spoke of social dynamite in the ghettoes. By the 1970's when most manpower projections clearly indicated surplus of labor for the next decade, the educational reform rhetoric shifted from training scientists and engineers to open classrooms. Again, critics could be heard suggesting that the system be radically altered if not abolished, and once again, the Carnegie Foundation supported a study by Silberman which, in effect said that the system was basically sound but needed some reforming.[63]

In concluding this chapter, it is worth noting that, as in the past, today's educational problems in the United States are a manifestation of a much more profound malaise in the economic and social order, particularly the hierarchical relations in production-consumption brought on by large-scale capitalist industrialization. In the past, educational reformers, many idealistic and with good intentions, imposed on the mass of urban workers an educational system which contributed to preserving social order, but did so while maintaining an inequitable class structure. In the 1970s, professional educators continue to try to rejuvenate this same educational system because they continue to believe in the existing economic and social structure, and in the corporations' view of America's future.

Notes

1. Michael Katz, *Class, Bureaucracy, and Schools* (New York: Praeger, 1971), p. 9.

2. Samuel Bowles, "Unequal Education and the Reproduction of the Social Division of Labor," in *Schooling in a Corporate Society*, ed. Martin Carnoy (New York: David McKay, 1972).

3. Michael Katz, *The Irony of Early School Reform* (Boston: Beacon Press, 1970), pp. 93–112.

4. Ibid., pp. 48–50.

5. For an analysis of black education in the South after the Civil War, see chapter 6.

6. Katz, *Irony of Early School Reform* and *Class, Bureaucracy, and Schools.*

7. Katz, *Class, Bureaucracy, and Schools,* pp. 19–20.

8. Ibid., p. 30.

9. Ibid., p. 33.

10. Katz, *Irony of Early School Reform,* p. 47.

11. The relation went the other way as well. Horace Mann helped push through the legislative bills supporting and assisting railroad construction. Ibid., p. 35.

12. Ibid., pp. 49–50.

13. Ibid., p. 85.

14. It is possible to take a Schumpeterian view of schooling's failure to solve the social crisis in the cities: perhaps it was obstacles already present in the towns before the advent of large scale industrialization which could be blamed. On the basis of this analysis, the reformers attempted to create a new city, Lawrence, Massachusetts, which would avoid the problems of European industrial towns. A school system was part of this dream. Yet even the best possible schools "failed to maintain prosperity, social harmony, and morality" (Katz, *Irony of Early School Reform,* p. 97). Lawrence was subject to the same economic fluctuations as any other industrial town, and these fluctuations caused the same immorality and poverty as elsewhere. The reformers could not overcome the harsh realities of capitalist development; they could only foster an uneven economic growth.

15. William B. Whiting, a Massachusetts manufacturer, quoted in ibid., p. 88.

16. Ibid., p. 132.

17. Ibid., p. 139.

18. Ibid., p. 58.

19. Ibid., p. 53. This was the argument the reformers used against the academies having a monopoly on high school education.

20. Katz, *Class, Bureaucracy, and Schools,* p. 37.

21. Ibid., p. 39.

22. David Tyack, "Centralization of Control in City Schools at the Turn of the Century," in *The Organizational Society,* ed. Jerry Israel (Chicago: Quadrangle Books, 1971).

23. For a reinterpretation of the Progressive era in American politics, see Gabriel Kolko, *The Triumph of Conservatism* (Glencoe, Ill.: Free Press, 1963).

24. Katz, *Class, Bureaucracy, and Schools*, pp. 108–9.

25. Ibid., p. 109.

26. Ibid., p. 116.

27. "Equally interesting, especially after 1900, were changes in the actual content of the subjects themselves. The influences of commercialism and industrialism appeared throughout the curriculum. Commercial and business arithmetic, for example, began to receive extensive attention in the mathematics curriculum" (R. Freeman Butts and Lawrence Cremin, *A History of Education in American Culture* [New York: Henry Holt, 1953], p. 441).

28. David Cohen and Marvin Lazerson, "Education and the Corporate Order," *Socialist Revolution*, no. 8 (March/April 1972): 47–72.

29. Ibid., p. 51.

30. Stephan Michelson, "The Political Economy of Public School Finance," in *Schooling in a Corporate Society*, ed. Martin Carnoy (New York: David McKay, 1972).

31. Boston school superintendent (1908) quoted in ibid., p. 69.

32. Ibid., p. 68.

33. The parallel to the present-day measurement of educational success in nonindustrialized countries should be obvious. See Philip Coombs, *The World Educational Crisis* (New York: Oxford University Press, 1968).

34. "The classic statement for the comprehensive high school was the Cardinal Principles of Secondary Education issued by a special committee of the National Education Association in 1918. . . . The report proposed that 'differentiation should be in the broad sense of the term vocational . . . such as agricultural, business clerical, industrial, fine-arts, and household arts curriculums.' It supported the idea of a junior high school but limited its functions to exploration of vocations and prevocational guidance. This meant that a systematic and organized differentiation of students would not take place in the junior high school but would be postponed to senior high school. The junior high was defined as a period of exploration while the senior high was one of training. . . . The comprehensive high school also allowed for what the committee called the two components of democracy, specialization and unification. . . . The specialized and differentiated curriculum of the school was to train the individual to perform some task that would be good for the society. . . . Unification was that part of the ideal of democracy that brought people together and gave them 'common ideas, common ideals, and common modes of thought, feeling, and action that made for cooperation, social cohesion, and social solidarity'" (Joel Spring, "Education and the Corporate State," *Socialist Revolution*, no. 8 [March/April 1972]: 84–85).

35. Cohen and Lazerson, "Education and the Social Order," pp. 54–55.

36. Clarence Karier, "Testing for Order and Control in the Corporate Liberal State" (University of Illinois, 1972), p. 25. Mimeographed.

37. Heber Hinds Ryan and Philipine Crecelius, *Ability Grouping in the Junior High School* (New York: Harcourt Brace, 1927), quoted in Paul Lauter and Florence Howe, "How the School System Is Rigged for Failure," *New York Review of Books*, 18 June 1970, p. 16.

38. Hobson v. Hansen, Civil Action, no. 82-66. *Federal Supplement*, V. 269.

39. Karier, "Testing for Order and Control," p. 26. This is Karier's summary of the Court decision.

40. Cremin, quoted in Michelson, "Public School Finance," p. 150.

41. Cohen and Lazerson, "Education and the Social Order," p. 52.

42. Ibid., p. 54.

43. Joel Spring, "Education and the Corporate State," *Socialist Revolution*, no. 8 (March/April 1972): 76.

44. Samuel Bowles and Herbert Gintis, "IQ in the U.S. Class Structure," *Social Policy*, January/February 1973.

45. Karier, "Testing for Order and Control," pp. 13–14.

46. Ibid., p. 16.

47. Cohen and Lazerson, "Education and the Social Order," p. 59.

48. Ibid., p. 60; and John Dewey, *Democracy and Education* (New York: Macmillan, 1961).

49. Cohen and Lazerson, "Education and the Social Order," p. 61.

50. Raymond Callahan, *Education and the Cult of Efficiency* (Chicago: University of Chicago Press, 1962) and G. S. Counts, *The Social Composition of Boards of Education: Schools and Society in Chicago* (Chicago: University of Chicago Press, 1927).

51. Spring, "Education and the Corporate State," p. 85.

52. Henry M. Levin, *An Economic Analysis of Education Vouchers* (Papers in the Economic and Politics of Education, Stanford University School of Education, 1972). Mimeographed.

53. This example comes from the latest revision (1960) of the Stanford-Binet Intelligence Test as illustrated in Karier, "Testing for Order and Control," p. 18.

54. See Martin Carnoy, "Is Compensatory Education Possible?" in *Schooling in a Corporate Society*, ed. Martin Carnoy (New York: David McKay, 1972); also, Christopher Jencks, *Inequality* (New York: Basic Books, 1972).

55. Simon Kuznets extrapolated this argument to postulate that

capitalist development produced a tendency toward more equal income distribution. For a discussion of his argument and others related to income distribution, see Martin Bronfenbrenner, *Income Distribution Theory* (Chicago: Aldine, 1971), pp. 67–75.

56. In 1939, the average level of schooling in the labor force was 8.8 years while in 1965, it was 11.16 years. Variance dropped from 3.7 to 3.4.

57. Gabriel Kolko, *Wealth and Power in America* (New York: Praeger, 1965), p. 13.

58. Barry Chiswick and Jacob Mincer, "Time Series Changes in Personal Income Inequality in the United States," *Journal of Political Economy* 80, no. 3, pt. 2 (May/June, 1972): S56.

59. These mean years of schooling for sons are calculated from a table showing the probability of completing different levels of schooling given father's education. I took the mean of the less than eight years of schooling category as six years, which biases downward the mean years of schooling taken by younger age groups relative to older, since this open-ended category probably had a lot more sons with no schooling in it in the 1920s than in the 1950s Thus, in general, we tend to underestimate the average number of years of schooling in the lowest age categories of sons relative to the highest age categories, especially for those with fathers who had less than eight or eight-to-eleven years of school.

60. Bureau of the Census.

61. For a discussion of life choices versus death choices, see Erich Fromm, *The Revolution of Hope* (New York: Harper & Row, 1970).

62. Charles Silberman, *Crisis in the Classroom* (New York: Random House, 1970), pp. 284–97.

63. Karier, "Testing for Order and Control," p. 33.

EDUCATION AS INTERNAL COLONIALISM

6

THE EDUCATION OF BLACK AMERICANS IN THE UNITED STATES, 1865–1930

It is the whole of American society
that excludes, martyrizes, and kills
the black man. The good will
paraded by the North only
pointlessly confuses the issue . . .
*the black American is oppressed by the
whole of American society.*

—Albert Memmi

In chapter 5 we saw how capitalists and educators imposed public schooling and its centralized control on the white working (immigrant) class of the industrial North, primarily to maintain social stability in the disruptive conditions of growing American towns. Although there were positive effects from expanding schooling—for example, it may have contributed to higher economic output—workers' children were incorporated into *particular* (low) levels of the societal structure. Differential schooling rationalized the unequal distribution of product which industrialization produced. The colonization of working-class whites through the schools was therefore the process of indirectly defining and controlling the hierarchical structure so as to maximize economic gains for the dominant capitalist class. The formal education system legitimized that structure.

Other groups of Americans, however, were colonized directly, and their situation corresponded much more closely to the "traditional" colonizer-colonized relationship of an occupied people.[1] Native American Indians, Spanish Americans, and Afro-Americans all resided in North America as long or longer than the English farmers of the Eastern seaboard. The first two of these groups—particularly the Indians—had claims on *land,* one of the important bases of both precapitalist and capitalist wealth in America. Throughout the period of territorial expansion, European settlers degraded the Indian into an assigned state of savagery in order to delegitimize his right to stay on the land. As a savage, or subhuman, the Indian did not have any more claim on the vast hunting grounds than an animal might have. If he resisted white settlement, he was hunted down to be captured or killed. White attitudes toward Indians, therefore, emanated mainly from the demand for more land and the exploitation of that land in the capitalist production process.

Blacks were to labor what Indians were to land. In precapitalist times, Africans were brought to the United States forcibly to work as slave labor on sugar, cotton, and tobacco plantations, and although capitalist philosophy specifically spoke out against slavery, the practice continued in the United States well into the capitalist period (southern plantations were an integral part of the capitalist system). Like Indians, blacks were denigrated by whites to rationalize the gross exploitation of something they possessed—in this case, labor power. Just as Indians were *given* the minimum necessities of life by whites if they accepted white rule over their land, so blacks were treated with paternalistic "affection" by the slave-owning class if they accepted their complete subjugation.

Even though capitalist "humanitarian" values ultimately prevailed in the issue of slavery, the treatment of Indians, blacks, and other nonwhite groups did not improve with the expansion of capitalism. The demand for land grew, causing increased hardship for Indians. Blacks moved from slavery to sharecropping; instead of belonging to the landowner, they belonged to the merchant. Even with emancipation, their political rights were short-lived and their economic rights severely limited. Ultimately, once European immigration was ended, they were permitted to fill the need for a class of manual workers in the industrial and service sectors. But that step "up" the economic ladder was also full of pain—this time into permanently segregated, poor and politically powerless urban ghettos.

The economic imperatives that led whites to define the Indian as a savage and the black as capable only of simple manual labor, delimited the schooling provided for each group. If Indians were savages, they had to be Christianized, to be shown the white man's morality. If blacks were manual workers, they were to be given the limited skills necessary to perform their unskilled work function. Thus, capitalist needs defined people's roles in industrializing America. Indians stood in the way of the railroads (before that, in the way of plantations) and therefore had to be made the enemy. Blacks were needed as agricultural labor, and then as unskilled urban labor. These functions, after the Civil War largely defined by white northern industrialists, fixed the Indian and the black at the lowest rungs in the economic and human hierarchy.

In this chapter, we review the black situation in America *after* emerging from slavery, and the role that education played in that situation. As in other chapters, we concentrate on the changing economic role of the colonized and its effect on the education blacks got or did not get.

Black education in the United States after the Civil War depended on the social and economic utility that education was believed to have for the class of *white* persons in control of southern political and economic structures. When this control was in the hands of the "radical" northern humanitarians, blacks received an education designed to liberate them from a slave society and bring them into a modern industrial "meritocracy," in which their race would not be a factor in the social role they played. Even before the short period of Reconstruction was over, however, the new economic function of the black as a tenant farmer was taking place. When political control of this economy went back to the planters, education for both blacks and whites stagnated: it was considered an unnecessary evil in a system where workers were tied to the land. As power in the South shifted to independent white farmers, blacks became even worse off in the ensuing struggle between whites over educational funds. In the most recent stages of this struggle, which began over seventy years ago, white industrialists saw the blacks as a stable, docile industrial labor force which could be exploited more efficiently than whites and could also be an instrument for exploiting white workers. In this new role, blacks were trained to do primarily manual and skilled-manual work.

Only in the first phase of this period—Reconstruction—did blacks have anything to say about the kind of schooling they got or the kind of function they wanted to take in the planning of their education. Once northern capitalists gave the administration of the South back to the planters as part of the great compromise which made Rutherford Hayes President in 1877, blacks were gradually pushed back into a status that was only legally different from slavery. Those who were accepted as spokesmen by the white dominant classes were accepted precisely because they told these whites what they wanted to hear and, as black leaders, were willing to undertake projects that legitimized the subjugated status whites conferred on them.

We conclude that the role assigned to blacks after the Civil War was tied to northern capitalists as well as to southern planters. While northern capitalism has been associated with humanitarian treatment of the black—and it must be conceded that a humanitarian element was present in philanthropic efforts during Reconstruction and around the turn of the century—humanitarianism was always secondary to capitalists' economic needs. This economic need revolved first around exploiting southern resources, and later around exploiting southern markets and using southern labor, including blacks, to hold down wages in the North. Northern solutions to the black problem in the South were therefore conditioned by the imperatives of northern capitalism. Rather than liberating blacks from oppression by southern whites, northern liberals eventually changed the conditions of that oppression from a rural to an urban servitude.

The Economic Condition of Blacks in America

Before 1860, most blacks lived in the South and were slaves.[2] Since slavery was predominantly a rural institution, blacks were tied to plantation agriculture in a region that depended for manufactured goods on England and the North.

> City life proved to be clearly hostile to slavery. It corroded the master's authority, diminished his control, and blurred the line between freedom and bondage. Slavery was declining rapidly in vitality and in numbers in all the cities during the last forty years of its existence. While slaves made up 20 percent or more of the ten major slaveholding cities in 1820, they accounted for less than 10 percent by 1860. By that time they composed less than 2 percent of the total slave population.[3]

The emancipation of the slaves therefore created a large *rural* labor force, whose experience was almost totally agricultural. The Civil War left the South economically ruined. The Freedmen's Bureau, set up by the government to foster the blacks' economic and political position during Reconstruction, pushed at first for a wage-hire system to replace slavery. But this was doomed to failure: since a large portion of the planters' prewar capital was in slaves, emancipation left him only with land, unable to raise working capital for meeting payrolls while the crops matured. With the Bureau's approval, crops such as cotton were financed through sharecropping: the laborer agreed with the land-owner to work a crop through the course of the year, with the wages of the laborer paid out of the sale of the crop. Since the ex-slaves and poor whites who took up this sharecropping did not have any resources of their own, the landowner had to advance the tools, food, and clothing to keep the cropper and his family going until the crop was sold. But the planter had no capital, so he had to rely on the merchant to advance him the goods for his laborers. This system resulted in enormous exploitation of the laborer, who was forced to pay double and triple the market price for the goods advanced him, and often had nothing left over even in a good crop year.[4] Furthermore, the development of sharecropping created a profound social change in the life of blacks, since it removed family units from the communal quarters around the plantation house to isolated cabins on isolated tracts of land.[5]

Thus, the blacks' economic position changed little as a result of the war. They were no longer slaves, but the land-tenure system under which they worked had hardly changed. Most freedmen now worked the plantation as sharecroppers, bound to the land through the exploitation of the merchants. This exploitative system stretched from the local country merchants to a banking system which charged higher interest than in the North. The South's banks were, in turn, controlled by northern capital.[6]

> The Civil War was not fought by the Northern ruling class to free the slaves, as many mistakenly believe. It was fought to check the ambitions of the Southern slave-owning oligarchy which wanted to escape from what was essentially a colonial relation to Northern capital. The abolition of slavery was a by-product of the struggle, not its purpose, and Northern capitalism had no intention, despite the interlude of Reconstruction, of liberating the Negro in any meaningful sense. Having subdued the Southern planters, it was glad to have them resume their role of exploiters of black labor whom it could in turn exploit.[7]

Prior to World War I, then, blacks in the United States were predominantly a southern peasantry, working land that they usually did not own, disrupted from the communal setting of the plantation, and still at the bottom of an economic chain which extended to northern capitalists.

Very gradually, blacks began to play a more direct role in the industrial sector. During the movement to organize labor, blacks were used as scabs to break strikes and as an alternative source of cheap labor to depress white wages. Northern trade unions in those industries such as coal and steel which had branches in the South, could not enforce their wage demands as long as southern branches could supply national needs. Alabama industry, for example, used blacks to weaken white unions and keep wages low—the black worker initially filled unskilled positions which whites found undesirable:

> *The manifest result of the presence of the Negro labor here is that we have a more intelligent and orderly white laboring population than otherwise might be anticipated.* The Negro of Birmingham fills the industrial position which elsewhere in great manufacturing towns is filled by a low class of whites. The Negro here is satisfied and contented; the low whites elsewhere are dissatisfied and turbulent.[8]

But even though 40 percent of Birmingham's population was black in 1900, and even though blacks did move out of the South in substantial numbers around 1880, as late as 1910 the census showed 80 percent of the Negro population was still in the former Confederate states and that 90 percent of them lived in rural areas.[9] The big change in this pattern came during the First World War, when labor shortages in the North brought on by a war-caused halt in immigration forced northern capitalists to turn toward internal sources of cheap labor.

In the course of the nineteenth century, the demand for labor generated by the rapidly expanding economy had been filled by successive waves of immigration. World War I ended this system. European immigration was sharply reduced during the war, and the demand for labor increased as U.S. industry was called upon to supply the needs of the Allies and their prewar markets. At the same time, mechanization in agriculture and more intensive methods of cultivation reduced the need for increased farm labor with increased agricultural output. Thus, with the war, all the conditions for mass internal migration were fulfilled.

> The United States, having always relied on immigration from abroad, now discovered, quite suddenly as such things go, that it could get along by tapping its own surplus rural manpower just as Europe had been doing since the beginnings of the industrial revolution.[10]

This meant the urbanization of black people in America. Between 1910 and 1960, blacks changed from a southern rural peasantry into a substantial segment of the northern and southern urban working class (see table 14). The shift of blacks into northern factories during World War I created conflict with white workers as soon as unemployment increased after the war. Blacks were not unionized, and they continued to be used as scabs to break strikes. White workers saw—correctly—that blacks were their competition, especially in unskilled jobs. The blacks remained at the lowest skill categories of urban workers throughout the migration period. Of course, moving from country to city improved the black standard of living, but *urban* black males did not improve their occupational status and income position relative to urban white males except during World War II. It is noteworthy that black unemployment as a percentage of white rose from 112 in 1940 to 225 in the early 1960s.[11]

Table 14

Emigration of Negroes from the Eleven Former Confederate States to Northern and Western States, 1870–1960 (in thousands)

Decade	Number
1870s	47
1880s	59
1890s	242
1900s	216
1910s	480
1920s	769
1930s	381
1940s	1,260
1950s	1,170

Source: Paul Baran and Paul Sweezy, *Monopoly Capital* (New York: Monthly Review, 1966), p. 257.

Political Power, Racism, and the Black Condition

In many ways, the most powerful "education" Blacks have undergone in this country has taken place quite outside schools and quite contrary to the democratic rhetoric of the main line—i.e. white educational institutions. It has been a powerful socialization in what it means to be powerless. In various times and places it has meant walking to school in the red clay beside the road while white children rode by in a yellow bus; learning intricate rules of racial etiquette whose violation might mean death; gaining knowledge and skills useless in the job market that blocked people with dark skins; living under a system of law and order in which no Black has a voice.[12]

As long as blacks' status was fixed by slavery, there was little need for segregation. Slavery itself defined the blacks' place in society and assured their subordination and exploitation by whites. The fact that blacks were introduced into America as slaves (as part of a white Christian supremacy mercantile imperialism) established white-black relations until the present day. Although, as we saw in chapter 3, there was a period in nineteenth-century European-African relations where white superiority was reduced by missionary and capitalist ideals, the existence of large numbers of blacks *within* the United States living in a subordinate position appears to have solidified a deep-seated culture of racism.

In the South, three main groups interacted: (1) the blacks, largely rural slaves living on plantations in the lowlands, and interacting primarily with rich whites; (2) the planters, who controlled the wealth (slaves, land, railroads) of the agricultural society and the limited functions of the state governments; and (3) the upland, or poor, whites, who were yeomen farmers.

Clear class antagonism existed between poor whites and the planters: the small independent farmers resented the wealth and power of the lowland slave owners, and the slave owners considered the upland whites uncivilized. This antagonism was so profound that upland whites generally voted against secession in the state conventions of 1861, and many fought for the federal government in the Civil War.[13] At the same time, the poor whites and the blacks disliked each other: the whites blamed slaves for the lower prices of lowland cotton; thus, slaves (blacks) were seen as the poor whites' economic competitors in the agricultural labor market. Blacks, in turn, disdained the poor whites through the slave-planter relationship. The plantation owners, to colonized blacks, were the highest form of white society, but poor whites were typified by planters—and therefore by slaves—as "white trash."

Nevertheless, during Reconstruction, blacks and poor whites joined to bring the Republican party (northern capital) to power in the South, and, for a period, they had real political influence as swing groups necessary to both parties if they were to win state and local offices. These offices served during Reconstruction to profit one side or the other in a series of railroad feuds. Some railroad interests aligned with the Democrats and others with the Republicans. All statewide elections were very close,[14] but the Republicans and Democrats differed only when it came to black suffrage; otherwise their economic programs were basically the same. Poor whites were initially attracted to Republicans because of the promise of free land, but when this did not materialize, they became susceptible to Democratic campaigning.

In the early 1870s, after the passage of the Fifteenth Amendment (sponsored by Republicans) giving the blacks the right to vote, the planter-dominated Democrats began to appeal to poor whites by exploiting their long-standing feelings toward blacks.

> The Republican Party . . . is composed of the great body of Negroes, and of a large mass of the poor whites in the western or mountain, districts. But these small white farmers dislike the Negro, whom they know little about, and are easily alarmed at the thought of social equality with them. The Democratic politicians very naturally worked upon their fears on this point, and this they found their best argument put into their hands by those Republican leaders in the North who insisted upon this measure [the Civil Rights bill].[15]

Thus, the prewar dominant class regained power in the South within ten years of the war that destroyed their economic base. They did so by appealing to prewar prejudices, thus strengthening those prejudices and deflecting the class antagonisms between poor whites and planters toward the blacks. With the planters back in power, factions of northern capital came to terms with them, and the

Republican party collapsed. The compromise of the 1870s—the withdrawal of federal troops and the turning over of the administration of southern states to the archaic aristocracy—was a "tacit recognition that the renewed colonial status of the South had been accepted by both sides, with the Southern oligarchy exploiting the Negro and in turn paying tribute to Northern capital for the privilege of doing so." [16]

Once in power, the Black Belt oligarchs passed new state constitutions which set representation based on total population, both white and black. By controlling the black vote, they ensured the defeat of candidates who represented the poor white areas, even though in many southern states, like Alabama, economic power gradually shifted to the "white counties." [17] Conservatives padded returns from the Black Belt counties with black votes that may or may not have been real. Although the blacks had not been disenfranchised, their votes were under the control of the ex-slave owners. Unlike in the days of Reconstruction, when federal troops and the Freedmen's Bureau worked for blacks, during post-Reconstruction, blacks involuntarily served to keep the conservatives in power.

Education soon became an important issue in the struggle *between* whites. Conservatives opposed local taxation, since this would reduce their control over state revenues. But without local taxes, poor whites could not raise education levels in the white counties; the state legislatures (and hence state funds) were controlled by the conservatives. Discontent because of agrarian economic depression led to a split in the white vote beginning in the 1880s, and by the end of the decade, dissident whites in the South joined with northern Populists in a general movement of labor and farmers against big capitalism. Although this was a white movement, the Saint Louis convention of the Farmer and Labor Alliance in 1889 took a strong stand on black political and economic rights.[18]

The conservatives destroyed Populism in the South on two counts: first, they continued to rig elections through delivery of huge votes from the Black Belt counties, thus making it difficult for southern Populist candidates to win. Second, faced with the threat of disruption of Black Belt control, the "Conservatives raised the issue of race supremacy again, stating that the Populist program as adopted in St. Louis was 'subversive to white supremacy.' " [19]

> As a radical movement of the yeoman white farmers . . . it failed precisely for the same reason that the agrarian radicals who cooperated with the Negroes during Reconstruction had failed—an inability to make economic issues paramount to the race issue.[20]

Populism in the South, therefore, initially followed a racial policy consistent with its egalitarian principles, but this policy, and then southern Populism itself collapsed under the pressure of white-supremacy tactics. Many disappointed Populists made blacks the scapegoat of their frustration.

> Turning from a hopelessly stronger foe to a helplessly weaker one, they convinced themselves that the Negro was an author rather than a fellow victim of their defeat. This mood offered a stimulus rather than a check to racism.[21]

This stimulus resulted in black disenfranchisement in the former Confederate states, and the enactment of segregation, of Jim Crow laws throughout the South. Between 1890 and 1901, Constitutional Conventions were held in the southern states to disenfranchise black people: poll taxes, literacy requirements, and "grandfather clauses" which allowed anyone to register whose father or grandfather was eligible to vote in 1867, all were used to keep the blacks from voting.

> In part this was presented as a guarantee that in the future neither of the white factions would violate the white man's peace by rallying the Negro support against the other. In part disenfranchisement was also presented as a progressive reform, the sure means of purging Southern elections of the corruption that disgraced them.[22]

But it would have been impossible to pass such legislation at the state level without northern compliance. The fact that the Supreme Court had upheld infringement of black civil rights in a series of cases between 1873 and the early 1890s, gave the signal to southerners that northern liberals had no power over them. A less direct, but more important factor in the southern mood, was the climate of Social Darwinism in which the progressive movement flourished, and U.S. imperialism at the end of the century. Racism justified the colonization of Cuba and the Philippines, and southerners realized that northerners who had pushed for a colonial war against Filipinos in the name of white supremacy could not very well criticize the South's treatment of the Negro.[23] In fact, none of these justifications was even necessary, since northern capitalists, liberal and conservative, conciliated southern whites throughout this period of disenfranchisement in order to gain southern support for measures that would strengthen corporate control over the economy and put an end to the Populist movement. Northern capitalist interest in combating Populism led to cooperation with southern conservatives, even when their tactics (white supremacy) may have offended some northern sensibilities.

Jim Crow, after all, had its origins in the North. By 1830, slavery was virtually abolished in the North, and the northern free black had obvious advantages over the southern slave. But blacks in the North were segregated systematically from whites on all means of transportation, in theaters and lecture halls, in churches, and often in schools, prisons, hospitals, and cemeteries. Only 6 percent of northern blacks lived in the five states—Massachusetts, New Hampshire, Vermont, Maine, and Rhode Island—that by 1860 permitted them to vote.[24] Before the Civil War, Abraham Lincoln himself made clear in 1858 that "I am not nor ever have been in favor of bringing about in any way the social and political equality of the white and black races . . . that I am not nor ever have been in favor of making voters or jurors of negroes, nor of qualifying them to hold office, nor to intermarry with white people, and I will say in addition to this that there is a physical difference between the black and white races which I believe will for ever forbid the two races living together on terms of social and political equality." [25]

The South did not adopt Jim Crow laws until the turn of the century, then usually after already disenfranchising blacks. The laws seem paradoxical in that for more than thirty years between the abolition of slavery and the passing of such laws, the social control of black labor had been left to sharecropping and other forms of peonage. There is evidence that the races had mixed fairly freely in the post-Reconstruction South, even though there was racial antagonism, lynchings, and other forms of brutality against blacks.[26] But Jim Crow laws in the South, as in the North, were legislated primarily in cities. Thus, segregation laws did not come to the South until the turn of the century because it was not until then that the South began to urbanize and industrialize significantly. Jim Crow was the result of industrial working conditions and urban living conditions; it was the natural extension of white supremacy in the close conditions of industrial urban life. Formal segregation was also necessary to keeping wages low in the factories. As discussed above, white workers were given status and kept orderly by placing black workers in conditions that stressed white superiority. Jim Crow served this function. In South Carolina, for example, textile workers of different races were "prohibited from working in the same room, or using the same entrances, pay windows, exits, doorways, stairways or windows at the same time, or the same lavatories, toilets, drinking water, buckets, pails, cups, dippers, or glasses at any time." [27] Rural segregation followed urban a number of years later.[28]

Jim Crow laws did not assign blacks a fixed and subordinate status in society, but rather tried to push them constantly farther down—to colorize them increasingly as work and pay opportunities opened up in industry and blacks came to towns and cities. The South adopted northern methods of subordinating blacks because northern economic structures began to appear in the South. The disruption of industrial urban life required social controls which—in the context of a racist society—took the form of extreme segregation. Northern liberals tolerated and even abetted these measures because they found their relationship to the southern elite more important than the condition of blacks. It was *that relationship* which was crucial to the exploitation of southern agricultural and mineral wealth, not social equality of blacks and whites. Furthermore, as we showed in chapter 5, northern liberals in the first two decades of the century were developing their own system of classifying people through the schools. At the same time that southern progressives were expounding the necessity of Jim Crow, northern educators were developing new concepts of equality of opportunity.

Thus, blacks found themselves at the bottom of a colonizing hierarchy. For the top of the hierarchy to maintain control over lower class whites, blacks were degraded and assigned an inferior status to all whites. Throughout this period and the urban racial violence that followed World War I, it was the dominant class that used white supremacy and segregation to keep white workers and white farmers as well as blacks in their place.

Black Education

It is in the context of blacks' changing economic position and of an increasing racism that we can now assess the role of the school system in maintaining black subordination. For all intents and purposes, formal schooling began for southern blacks during Reconstruction, although attitudes derived from the slave period have affected such schooling until the present day.[29]

> The peculiar circumstances surrounding the social control of the Negro population lent themselves to rationalizing the protective measures taken by the white population on the ground that Negroes were incapable of being educated in a formal sense and the institution of chattel slavery formed the best training ground for the limited capacities of the race. As the institution of chattel slavery dictated the type of education, or training, given to Negroes in ante-bellum days, it left an indelible stamp upon the attitudes which were to be social forces in determining the reaction of the whites to the education of Negroes in the future, after the institution itself had been abolished.[30]

Reconstruction Education was the badge of freedom to many ex-slaves, and they clamored for schooling. During the early days of Reconstruction, most schools for blacks were built by the Freedmen's Bureau and staffed by mission societies. On this base, and with the increased political power given blacks by the right to vote and federal occupation of the South, legislation was passed in which the states would provide for schooling (there was no state responsibility for schooling before the war). In this period, black children of school age *in the population* got the same expenditures on education per child as did whites even though there were fewer black than white children as a percentage of the child population *actually in school*. Thus, those black children *who attended school* had higher cost schooling per pupil than poor whites. Black students often had white teachers, and these were paid equally with white teachers in black schools. Soon, however, white teachers were replaced with blacks in the public schools, both because of an increased race consciousness, the poor quality of the white teachers, and the fact that black teachers would work for lower pay.

Conservatives at first accepted the equal opportunity afforded by the distribution of expenditures, largely because they believed that public schools were for the pauper class and therefore fitting for blacks, as they were for poor whites. This attitude also explains why states such as South Carolina and Louisiana even legislated racially mixed schools.[31] But white missionaries had a different view of the school. They represented radical reconstruction elements in the North and saw the schools as a place where blacks would become truly equal with whites in the South. The missionaries taught blacks to be proud of their race and to be conscious of class divisions in the region.

> Men and women, many of them heirs of the abolitionist tradition, went South with missionary zeal to help slaves achieve full freedom. Bringing the Gospel and secular knowledge, they believed in the capacity of their Black students.[32]

When blacks got the right to vote, mission bodies changed from primarily religious instruction in the schools to the creation of political awareness. The textbooks used in the missionary schools during Reconstruction were standard northern textbooks: *The Freedmen's Book*, for example, was widely used as a reader. It contained stories about such blacks as Ignatius Sancho, Toussaint L'Ouverture, and John Brown who had attained distinction, plus accounts of black revolts, and abolitionist writings. The book also had a speech by Congressman

"Pig Iron" Kelley who represented Pennsylvania coal and steel
interests active in Alabama, a speech which exorted Freedmen to
believe in racial equality through the economic imperative. These
teachings were "a curious mixture of political opportunism and high
idealism, a working together of Northern, capitalist-sponsored political
organizations such as the Union League, and the Northern religious,
philanthropic bodies." [33]

Reconstruction was a revolutionary period in the South, particularly
in education. Although it was short, it produced some black colleges,
primarily for teacher training, and these colleges in turn produced a
high percentage of black scholars in America. [34] But Reconstruction
education depended on the support of the North for radical social and
economic change in the South. Unfortunately for blacks, northern
capitalists were much more interested in exploiting southern resources
than in promoting black liberation. When the conservatives reestablished political power in the South, northern capital decided to come to
terms with them instead of trying to maintain direct control over
southern economies. Yet even if northern capitalists *had* maintained
direct control over the South, it is doubtful that the kind of teaching
that went on in Reconstruction schools would have been continued.
Those teachings were designed to liberate blacks from the attitudes of
slavery, but they were also geared to get blacks to act as a political
force against southern conservatives in a period when northern
capitalists were using black votes to maintain control over the southern
political structure. If the conservatives had collapsed as a political
force, it is improbable that the missionaries would have turned to
teaching blacks to struggle against industrialists and railroad interests.

Redemption   As the conservatives did regain political control in the
1870s, they moved steadily to cut down on black schooling. Since
education sponsored by missionaries was the outgrowth of an
industrial society and industrial interests struggling against conservative whites, schooling for blacks was seen by conservatives as
threatening the plantation system. Ten years after Reconstruction
began, funds for public education from the states—while still
apportioned on the basis of equal amounts for white and black

school-age children—were being drained off for other uses.[35] This maneuver affected white children as well as black children. By 1880, in comparison with 1871, the length of the school term dropped 20 percent in the South, while the outlays for schools fell 40 percent.[36]

Thus, after northern capitalists had compromised with southern conservatives in the "redemption" of 1877, southern education retreated to the limited role that public formal schooling plays in plantation societies. Schools were completely segregated. The average school term in the South in 1900 was less than one hundred days, about one-half that of New England. But even for such a short term, only about one-third of the school-age population was in school.[37] Annual expenditures per child in school in 1900 were $9.70 in Virginia and $4.34 in North Carolina, for example, while Massachusetts spent $37.76 per pupil.[38]

According to Tyack, southern education reflected the region's poor tax base, its thinly spread and rural population, and its high ratio of children to adults.[39] Education in the South was undoubtedly in part the result of the relative poverty of the region. But, as Medoff shows,[40] expenditures per school-age population in the South were also a function of the political power of the planter class:

> For the most part the southern planter class was not moved by the capitalist spirit, but rather sought to maintain the ante-bellum social relations of a slave society. The southern landowners turned to new forms of tenancy, credit relations, and laws to achieve its ends. Capitalist production, which was in theory based on the ideals of freedom, mobility, and democracy, and the social relations of slavery, were seen to be incompatible.[41]

The planter class did not invest in agricultural machinery or in industry (until much later); rather, they farmed inefficiently because their primary objective was not productive efficiency but to preserve the prewar social structure. As a result, large-scale cotton production shifted to Texas and Oklahoma, and even the "white counties" of the Piedmont increased their production more rapidly than the Black Belt. Mass schooling was dysfunctional for the planters, and from

Redemption (1877) until the rise of southern Populism in the 1890s, they kept state expenditures on education low and blocked efforts by the white counties to legislate local taxes. Educational expenditures per capita were kept low for *both* poor whites and blacks.[42]

W. E. B. DuBois charged that "enforced ignorance" was "one of the inevitable expedients for fastening serfdom on the country Negro." [43] Indeed, with the advent of the sharecropping system, earlier arguments for the education of blacks lost their meaning. Schooling for blacks during Reconstruction was based on the theory that they would be part of a new social order in which white and black would be equal and socially stratified without respect to race. But under tenant farming, an educated labor force, which understood interest rates and simple accounting methods, would be a liability to the system rather than an asset.

> The result was that the Negro tenant again figured in the agricultural scheme as he had before the war as a slave. He was a labor item, engaged in crude processes which required no special intellectual training; and, indeed, it was thought he would be unfitted for his role by the educational process. . . . If the Negro was to have a place only as a peon on a cotton farm, there was a danger that "education would spoil a good plow hand," and that it would make the Negro "get beyond himself," i.e., beyond his status as fixed by the economic system.[44]

The Populist Movement   Since the planters were holding the line on school expenditures while school enrollment was rising, expenditures per child actually fell between the 1870s and 1890 in some states. In Alabama, for example, expenditures per child *enrolled* were $3.85 in 1875 and in 1890, $2.29.[45] It was against this policy that poor whites began to revolt through the Populist movement. The Populists made efforts to enlist the aid of the blacks by promising in their platforms to uphold black suffrage and to aid in "the attainment of a high civilization and citizenship." [46] But the Populists could never overcome the advantage possessed by Black Belt Democrats in their control of the ficticious black vote. Furthermore, during the Populist conflict, black leadership sold out against their people's interest.

> In part, the Negro Democrats were financed by the growing industrial concerns in the industrial section of Northern Alabama, working hand-in-glove with the Black Belt Democrats against the Populist revolt . . . the vote for the Constitutional Convention pledged to disenfranchise Negroes was successful because of the huge vote for the proposal registered in certain counties of the Black Belt. Leading Negro Democrats worked vigorously for the calling of the Convention.[47]

Populist agitation was successful in putting pressure on the planters for increased political power for poor whites. We have mentioned that conservatives emasculated the Populist movement in the South by diverting it into a white supremacy stand originated by the conservatives and carried to its logically extreme forms by Populist elements themselves. In the case of schooling, which formed an important part of the Populist demands, this resulted in state laws which shifted the apportionment of funds for schooling from the state to local town officials.

Giving up the principle of "equal benefit" for all children, funds were apportioned on the basis of what town trustees felt was "just and equitable." [48] Other states followed the lead of the U.S. Congress in the District of Columbia in allotting tax money to black schools only in proportion to receipts from black taxpayers. "Certification" laws were developed which enabled the states to pay less to black teachers than to whites, and class sizes were made larger to accommodate the large numbers of black children seeking schooling.[49] The U.S. Supreme Court implicitly upheld these actions in *Plessy* v. *Ferguson* (1895).[50]

Poor whites got more funds for schooling, therefore, by competing for these funds with the one class of people below them in the social structure—the blacks. Not surprisingly, it was the *whites in the Black Belt* who gained the most from these arrangements. Once they could be assured that funds for schooling going to Black Belt counties would not end up in black schools, they legislated more funds for education, still on the basis of the *total number of children* in each county. The results were obvious: white counties did better, but whites in Black Belt counties did best of all.

Bond presents data for the Black Belt county of Wilcox, Alabama, which show that in 1876–77 to 1890, blacks and whites both received approximately equal expenditures on teachers' salaries per school-age child, around $0.90 to $1.20 per white child, and $0.80 to $1.00 per black child. In 1890–91, with the passage of "equal benefit" legislation, this changed drastically. By 1907–8, expenditures per white child were almost $12 per white child and less than $0.40 per black child. In 1929–30, white children received about $32 per child, and blacks, less than $1.[51]

Expenditures on all children in 1889–90, which can be taken as approximately equal to what white children were receiving in the white counties, were $1 per child, in 1907–8, slightly less than $3 per child; and in 1929–30, about $6.50. In other southern states, the figures confirm this pattern. In 1900, blacks in South Carolina, who comprised 61 percent of the population, received about 21 to 23 percent of the school fund, or one-sixth as much per child as whites; in Georgia, the average black child received at most one-fourth as much as the average white child, and in Virginia, about one-third as much. But these figures hide the fact that whites in Black Belt counties did much better than whites in the all white counties. While the Piedmont white child in Alabama, for example, got 7.5 times as much in school funds in 1907 as black children, the average Black Belt white child got 30 times as much. These ratios held into the 1930s.

A three-level system of education evolved: black children were dependent on white demands for more schooling, and as the demands of poor whites for more schooling increased, the average expenditures on blacks also rose, but evidently not as rapidly as the average. Black children, however, no longer received the same funds per child as white children, since they were not seen fit to get the same education as whites. At the next level, poor whites were also limited in school funds by state legislatures, still controlled—even after black disenfranchisement—to a large extent by the conservatives. But the Piedmont whites got the full amount per child allocated to each county in the state. The highest expenditures per child went to white children in the Black Belt counties, who were receiving not only the standard allotment per child in the state, but a large share of the money allocated to black children in their county.

With black disenfranchisement, black children ceased to exist so far as educational campaigns were concerned: all emphasis was laid on the education of white children. In the sections that follow, we show how northern philanthropies and the blacks' own leaders cooperated in black subjugation, and how northern capitalists brought blacks into the industrial structure and defined the type of economic role and education they were to have.

The Philanthropies and Education in the South   Northern philanthropies such as the Peabody Fund gave money to southern schools as early as 1868. Although the amount given for black education by the fund was limited, it did provide a series of grants which helped Booker T. Washington build up Tuskegee Institute.[52] Compared to the efforts of missionary societies at this same time, however, the influence of the Peabody Fund on the public education of blacks was "fragmentary." [53]

The period of great influence on southern education by northern philanthropies was deferred to the end of the century, when the South was already disenfranchising blacks and instituting Jim Crow. The policies of these philanthropies was tied to the Southern Education Board, whose members were interwoven with all the leading endowed philanthropic boards active in southern education.[54] The Board was composed of "moderate" northern capitalists, who were sensitive to the delicate racial and sectional issues, and progressive professional southern educators, who saw mass education as the key to regional progress.[55] The Board had no funds to distribute; its function was—through a propaganda campaign—to increase the demand for education in the South and the willingness for people to pay for that increase.

> The regional approach was at the center of the Board's plan of action. A single pervasive institution, the public school, was the lever by which it hoped to move the region, to solve all of the other complex problems arising from Southern poverty, ignorance, and racial tension. To translate into more recent terms, the Board viewed the South as an underdeveloped region, for which its task was to furnish technical assistance and a little money if the South would supply the educational enthusiasm and local leadership.[56]

The southern education movement took the form of a series of train trips through the South of influential northern philanthropists financed by Robert Ogden, manager of John Wanamaker's New York department store. In meetings with southern educational leaders, the Board quickly succumbed to the ideals of white supremacy; it was persuaded to subsidize a region-wide public school campaign, leaving the control of expenditures for schools to southern whites.

The position taken toward white supremacy by these northern capitalists, who may have been genuinely concerned about the social and economic constraints placed on blacks by southern whites, was completely consistent with their views of white racial and ethnic superiority as practiced in the North. As we showed in the previous chapter, this was a time of centralization of power in school bureaucracy, and the disavowal of the older ideal of the egalitarian social order. Education in the North was structured on the basis of class, a structure that corresponded to the increased specialization of labor in industry.

The main concern of the philanthropists was that southerners—including blacks—were uneducated and that the South was economically underdeveloped, not that blacks were segregated or that they were considered inferior. In the North, after all, educational segregation was practiced through large urban school bureaucracies which assigned black teachers to black schools in highly segregated cities. Northern capitalists were interested in southern economic development— achieved by the training of a large skilled labor force—an economic development in which progressive industrialists from both the North and South could participate. They were *already opposed* to class or racial *equality* before they headed South.

> [Railroad president and Southern Education Board member] William H. Baldwin's hard-boiled philanthropy assumed that the Negro "will willingly fill the more menial positions and do the heavy work, at less wages," leaving to whites, "the more expert labor." Baldwin's advice to the Negro was quite specific: "Avoid social questions; leave politics alone; continue to be patient; live moral lives; live simply; learn to work . . . know that it is a crime for any teacher, white or black, to educate the negro for positions which are not open to him." [57]

The result of the Board's education crusade, which covered every southern state except Mississippi with massive state campaigns by 1909, was to begin the creation of adequate common schools in the South *for whites*. In eleven southern states where the Board was active, annual expenditures for schools increased by $18 million between 1900 and 1909. During the years from 1900 to 1912 educational expenditure increased 180 percent in the southern seaboard, more rapidly than the true valuation of all property. Enrollments and attendance, expenditures per pupil, and the school term all increased rapidly.[58] High schools (predominantly rural) for whites also multiplied: between 1901 and 1916, the number of secondary students went from 16,000 to 64,000, with a ratio of 29 white students to one black. But this expansion took place at a time when black schools could be excluded from receiving their share of the increase. Thus, the impact of the Board's efforts was to drive blacks down farther relative to whites.[59]

> The philanthropists assumed that Southern sensitivity would permit discussion of racial issues only by Southerners. But they might as well have risked their timid millions and the added capital of good will so painstakingly accumulated by intersectional conciliation in bold entrepreneurship on the Negro's behalf, in ventures their Southern colleagues could not risk. They decided instead to intensify their original efforts for general popular education. Such action had much to be said for it, but as far as Negro education was concerned it was simply evasion. The real dilemma of the public school campaign was that white educational sentiment, as it grew, increased the temptation to take the Negro's share of school funds. Educational campaigners were tempted to promise taxpayers a fiscal saving through racial discrimination. The philanthropists, seeking allies against the demagogues who exploited lower-class prejudices, actually joined forces with the upper-class conservatives who quietly administered school discrimination.[60]

While the Board campaigned for mass education in the South and thereby increased the gap between white and black schools, some philanthropies donated funds directly to black education, but in ways consistent with southern sensibilities and their own view of the black

filling menial work positions. *Industrial education* was the solution to
the black education problem: it was a solution acceptable to northern
industrialists who wanted a well-trained, docile, cheap, unskilled and
semiskilled labor force for industrial development, acceptable to
southern whites, who did not want blacks reading books, and
acceptable to certain black leaders such as Booker T. Washington, who
saw in industrial education a type of schooling whites would support
and which would give blacks better jobs.

Hampton and Tuskegee Institutes became the models for this kind
of training, and it is significant that not only were they indirectly
founded by northern capitalists, they were subsequently heavily
supported by them. Washington himself was very sensitive to the fact
that whites preferred blacks to get manual training, and found in
J. L. M. Curry, the general agent of the Peabody Fund and a member of
the southern aristocracy, support for the kind of education Washington
proposed for blacks.

Industrial education, which represented the acquiescence by blacks
to subordinate status, was consistent with Washington's political
position regarding relations between blacks and whites. In 1895, at a
time when blacks were being disenfranchised and the North was
looking for a rationale to accept southern racism, Washington
provided it in his famous Atlanta speech: "The wisest among my race
understand that the agitation of questions of social equality is the
extremest folly, and that progress in the enjoyment of all the privileges
that will come to us must be the result of severe and constant struggle
rather than of artificial forcing." [61] He described the blacks as the
"most patient, faithful, law-abiding, and unresentful people the world
has seen," who could be depended upon to "buy your surplus land,
make blossom the waste places in your fields, and run your factories."
The Negro would continue to labor "without strikes or labor
troubles." [62]

W. E. B. DuBois was the foremost critic of the Hampton-Tuskegee
model. He argued that it legitimized the subordination of blacks in the
industrial system just as blacks had been subordinated through
sharecropping in post-Civil War southern agriculture.

Besides pointing out that outmoded vocations such as blacksmithing
were taught, he blamed Booker T. Washington for putting blacks into

the hands of the industrial North: "It (the vocational school) set its face towards the employer and the capitalist and the man of wealth. It looked upon the worker as one to be adapted to the demands of those who conducted industry" (W.E.B. DuBois, "Education and Work," *Journal of Negro Education* 1, no. 1 [April 1932]: 65). DuBois was also critical of the fact that Tuskegee, given its curriculum, neglected teaching about labor unions and labor movements. For this reason the black man had no conception of any democracy in industry. This contributed to his disenfranchisement and helped to build a caste system.[63]

Since Washington's views were consistent with the whole movement toward vocational education for the "less qualified," and with the potential for cheap docile labor which northern capitalists saw in the South, he attracted funds from northern philanthropics. Only part of the appeal for industrial education, however, was racial: manual training for lower classes had been pushed by industrialists and educators in the last three decades of the nineteenth century, and with the opening of the twentieth century, "the roots of vocational education, starting in urban schools, had been transplanted to rural areas, where they found favorable soil in agricultural communities. . . . These ideas . . . constituted one of the predominant patterns of the period. 'The school system should be aimed primarily to fit the student for actual life rather than for a university,' announced President Theodore Roosevelt." [64]

To the consternation of many college-educated blacks and some northern white liberals, the philanthropies, including the largest and most independent—Rockefeller's General Education Board—followed this theory to the letter, apparently deciding that the blacks' actual life warranted industrial training, while whites were to get academic education. Of course, Booker T. Washington and Hollis B. Frisell of the Hampton Institute were instrumental in legitimizing this view. Black academic colleges got almost nothing from any northern philanthropy, while white private colleges and black industrial institutes were well supported.[65]

Industrial education was also consistent with the economic change occurring in the South and the potential for further change envisioned by northern capitalists and southern progressives. Black labor was very important in the mines and foundries of Alabama and was used to break strikes in the North. Black *skilled* workers offered corporations in the South a way to avoid the labor troubles taking place in northern industrial centers. In 1906, the Tennessee Coal and Iron Company began to build up complete industrial and housing units, fitted with hospitals, welfare centers, and schools. These were intended to regularize black labor turnover; their object was not philanthropic, but "to make money for its [TCI] stockholders." [66]

In 1907, U.S. Steel Corporation purchased TCI and employed blacks as skilled workers and supervisors. U.S. Steel filled these positions with black workers as part of its continued struggle with northern union efforts to raise wages.

> These corporations, then, unaffected by any philanthropic considerations, were interested in labor from the standpoint of profits returnable from their investment. The use of Negro labor in Alabama industry was strictly in accord with the economic advantages to be derived in national and international competition.[67]

After TCI's takeover and the subsequent move to upgrade black workers, the biggest problem was the poor educational facilities for blacks in Birmingham. TCI made an agreement with Jefferson County officials whereby the company got the state appropriation for teachers' salaries for black schools while TCI would build and equip schoolhouses in the vicinity of its plants and mines.

On the plus side, the schools were among the best for blacks in the South, producing the highest achievement scores of any black schools in the region.[68] However, TCI policy was clearly racist and geared to keep wages down. By regularizing black labor, the company was able to keep white labor under control: the wages of laborers in the Alabama steel industry remained at about 60 percent of those in Chicago and Pittsburgh, and there were no strikes.[69] Furthermore, the company policy did nothing to spread high schooling for blacks even in Alabama. If anything, it reinforced the notion that blacks should only get high school education when this was connected directly to some type of jobs which required it. In 1930, over 50 percent of all blacks enrolled in the tenth through twelfth grades of public high schools in Alabama were in the Industrial High School of Birmingham.[70]

Black Schooling in the North   Blacks began coming North in large numbers during World War I. As noted, they formed part of the internal migration from rural to urban areas that continued unabated for the next half century. They also filled the lowest rungs of the industrial labor force, and were used by industrialists to threaten white workers organizing unions.

Jim Crow existed in northern cities, if not legally, through residential segregation, high rents, lack of accesses to services, and eventually, through the gerrymandering of school boundaries and de facto segregated schools.[71] Worst of all, these migrating blacks were condemned to low-level jobs, no matter how much schooling or training they got. The highest-status occupation for blacks was as teachers in black schools and colleges; it was impossible to make it in the white man's world itself.

> It is not necessary to create a devil theory to explain the anomaly that for Blacks the schools did not serve, on the whole, the traditional function of creating avenues of opportunity. Educators were probably no more racist, and perhaps less, than other citizens. They wished a "harmonious" and "efficient" system and were equipped neither by training nor inclination to challenge the discrimination that permeated almost all institutions.[72]

While educators may not have been *more* racist than the society around them, some of the leading northern educators relegated blacks to the bottom of the vocational ladder at a time when vocational criteria determined the amount and the kind of schooling children received (see chapter 5). White children were classified by vocational testing and guidance in junior high school to find whether they entered the academic, business, or vocational track of comprehensive high schools. It is significant that blacks were hardly mentioned in the early writings of experts in vocational counseling.[73] But blacks were deemed below the white classification scheme and were therefore segregated into low-cost urban primary and high schools. Elwood Cubberley wrote that segregated schools might be a good thing for "over-aged, defective, delinquent . . . or . . . negro" children.[74]

Some Reflections on the Analysis

Many critiques of black education in America have focused on it in terms of *segregated schools*. But segregation in schools is only colonizing if it is part of an overall effort to subordinate a particular part of the population. Upper class whites are also segregated into high-cost private schools, but rather than being subordinated by segregation, it allows them to build class mores and solidarity which strengthen their self-esteem and prepare them for leadership roles in the society. Similarly, segregated schools during Reconstruction allowed blacks to begin to overcome centuries of slavery by building black consciousness.

As Newby and Tyack have pointed out,[75] blacks themselves fluctuated between wanting school integration and school segretation, depending on which they believed *would give them more access to economic and political power*.

> . . . a demand for "integration" often has reflected a profound distrust of a white power structure that persistently refused to grant equal schools when they were separate; only if there were white children in classrooms as hostages would equality become real and Black patrons be recognized as citizens, not subjects, of the educational-political system. Thus the same persons who pressed for integration could consistently seek community control if that strategy could accomplish the goal of achieving power through schooling. Much of Black educational history seems not so much an evolving linear narrative as a sociology of oppression in which debates over means recur within a common context of victimization.[76]

Integration in the United States, where it occurred, meant integration on white conditions, and this, in turn, put the black at the bottom of the hierarchical occupational and income scale. Under those conditions, it is not surprising that many blacks formed separatist movements or wanted community control of public schools which would get the same apportionment of public funds per child as white schools. All these things are reactions on the part of blacks to their colonial status within the white system. As soon as that colonial status is removed, integration will occur, just as it will occur for working-class whites. Our analysis argues that it is the economic and social hierarchy that separates whites from blacks and lower classes from higher classes. Segregated schools are a manifestation of that hierarchy, and integrating schools will do little in itself to change the status of blacks in a racist U.S. society.

Reich, using white/black wage data, indicates that racism is profitable for capitalists, and therefore rational in terms of maximizing the returns to capital.[77] We argue in this chapter that northern capitalists were instrumental in exploiting black people through segregation, and in using them to keep wages for white workers low as well. Reconstruction was an interlude in which these capitalists were able to make important inroads into what was left of the South's resources. Eastern interests took over many of the railroads and built more; financiers such as Jay Cooke entered into the rich iron and coal deposits of Alabama. It was not possible for them to take complete political control, and so they accepted southern administration of the South, and hence, southern definition of the black role. Even where northern industry determined black conditions, however, blacks remained at the bottom of the occupational scale. It was only that, to work in industry, blacks required greater skill than in agriculture. Nevertheless, as we have shown, blacks remained segregated, poor, and in southern company towns, the wards of paternalistic white industrialists.

The colonization of black people in America had important ramifications for the colonization of people of color elsewhere. Perhaps the best period for understanding U.S. relations with the Third World today was in the beginning of this century, as northern philanthropies began trying to develop the South. Their objectives were clear: they saw in the South vast untapped human and physical resources which, if properly developed, could raise the welfare of the region and also could provide markets for products and cheap skilled labor for industrial production. Of course, these are now exactly the objectives of the United States assistance policy in the world's underdeveloped regions.

In studying the role of the philanthropies, we are helped by the fact that the southern groups involved are clearly identified by class and skin color. Thus, the northern capitalist members of the Southern Education Board dealt directly only with "progressive" elements of the southern aristocracy (read Third World national bourgeoisie)—those elements in the elite who shared their view of the region's industrial development. The Board would decide for blacks—and southern poor whites, for that matter—what the nature of the region's development would be, and what kind of educational system would suit that development. Only such people as Booker T. Washington, who had already established himself as standing for the kind of role the capitalists wanted the black to play in the South, were consulted by the Board in their campaigns.

> There had to be a working compromise between the "best North" and the "best South," a Get Together Club like that which was solving New York City's most baffling social problems. The "best North," in Ogden's scale of values, was composed of men like himself, conservative business and professional people; the "best South" included educators and a remnant of upper-class paternalists, "a minority powerful to restrain if not always powerful to accomplish." And if there were objections to "social equality," it was not necessary for Negroes to attend the meeting. After all, were prostitutes consulted when New York City's vice problem was being solved by members of the chamber of commerce? [78]

The connection of northern capitalists with educational policy in Third World countries did not have to wait for the era of mass assistance after World War II. The Phelps-Stokes Fund under the direction of a white man, Thomas Jesse Jones, formed close relationships in the early 1900s with British missionaries and officials who were developing their educational policy in the African colonies. In the

1920s (see chapter 3), Jones went to Africa for the British Colonial Office commissioned to do a study of education in Africa. He produced the Phelps-Stokes Commission reports, which called for educational adaptation—vocational education on the Hampton and Tuskegee model, primarily for rural trades. Jones made explicit that he thought that this model would serve to control unrest in the colonies better than academic schooling.

> The transplant of the idea to Africa had the same political, social, and economic implications that it had in the United States. It was Thomas Jesse Jones who suggested to the British that the unrest of India could be avoided in Africa by adopting the concept of "educational adaptation." Jones described the problems of India as "too many who were prepared to write and talk" and too few who were prepared to "till the soil and engage in the great and numerous mechanical operations." [79]

In the next chapter, we show how the concept of development and the philanthropic model that emerged out of its experience in the South combined with the missionary experience in China of this same period to produce "philanthropic" activity in the Third World. The parallels between this new wave of philanthropy and the subjugation of blacks in their transition from an agricultural to urban society are striking.

Notes

1. Albert Memmi, *Dominated Man* (New York: Orion Press, 1968).
2. According to Woodward, there were a few hundred thousand free Negroes living in the United States at this time, primarily in cities. C. Vann Woodward, *The Strange Career of Jim Crow* (New York: Oxford University Press, 1966), p. 13.
3. Ibid., p. 17.
4. Horace M. Bond, *Social and Economic Influences on the Public Education of Negroes in Alabama, 1865–1930* (Washington, D.C.: Associated Publishers, 1939), p. 120.

5. Ibid., p. 36. Sharecropping led to the decline of the large plantations and the rise of agriculture in the uplands of the South. These uplands were farmed largely by "poor white" yeoman farmers who had not been able to compete with the slave plantations before the war.

6. Ibid., p. 121.

7. Paul Baran and Paul Sweezy, *Monopoly Capital* (New York: Monthly Review, 1966), p. 252. Bond, *Public Education of Negroes,* documents the role played by northern iron and coal interests in Alabama during Reconstruction. The Republican party was organized by Eastern capitalists, and Congressmen like William ("Pig Iron") Kelley from Pennsylvania pushed to get Alabama readmitted to the Union with a Republican government, which would be favorable to the exploitation of her iron and coal fields by eastern capitalists. With the failure of the Republican party to gain control in the state, those capitalists—who had used the blacks as the mainstay of their voting base—compromised with the southern oligarchy, allowing them to hold power in return for acceptance of their prewar colonial status.

8. John W. Dubose, *The Mineral Wealth of Alabama*, quoted in Bond, *Public Education of Negroes*, p. 145. Italics Bond's.

9. Baran and Sweezy, *Monopoly Capital*, p. 253.

10. Ibid., p. 255.

11. Ibid., p. 261. However, black females have improved their relative income position, particularly in the 1960s.

12. Robert Newby and David Tyack, "Victims Without 'Crimes': Some Historical Perspectives on Black Education," in *Journal of Negro Education* (Fall 1971): 192–206.

13. Bond, *Public Education of Negroes*, pp. 6–7. Bond writes of Alabama, but the split was just as evident in other states. For example, the upland whites of West Virginia seceded from Virginia and were admitted into the Union as a separate state in 1863.

14. Ibid., chap. 5.

15. Nordhoff, *The Cotton States in 1874–75*, quoted in Bond, *Public Education of Negroes*, p. 69.

16. Baran and Sweezy, *Monopoly Capital*, p. 252.

17. Sharecropping and poor soil management led to the decline of the southern seaboard Black Belt relative to yeoman agriculture in the white counties. Bond, *Public Education of Negroes*, p. 131.

18. Ibid., p. 131.

19. Ibid., p. 131.

20. Ibid., p. 132.

21. Louis Harlan, *Separate and Unequal* (Chapel Hill: University of North Carolina Press, 1958), p. 42.

22. Woodward, *Strange Career of Jim Crow*, p. 83.

23. Harlan, *Separate and Unequal*, p. 43; and Woodward, *Strange Career of Jim Crow*, p. 73.

24. Woodward, *Strange Career of Jim Crow*, p. 20.

25. Ibid., p. 21.

26. Ibid., pp. 15–26.

27. Ibid., p. 98.

28. Ibid., p. 101.

29. Up to 1832, slaves received limited religious training, including learning how to read and write, besides the vocational skills some slaves learned on the plantations. But in that year, the Nat Turner Insurrection, led by a freedman, spread panic of slave rebellion in the South. By 1832, all southern states had passed antislave education laws. They could not learn to read and write, and could attend church services only under supervision. Laws were also passed banning freedmen from living and working in the South. See Bond, *Public Education of Negroes*, pp. 18–19, and Carter Woodson, *The Education of the Negro Prior to 1861* (Washington, D.C.: Associated Publishers, 1915).

30. Bond, *Public Education of Negroes*, pp. 20–21.

31. Newby and Tyack, "Victims Without 'Crimes,'" p. 194.

32. Ibid., p. 194.

33. Bond, *Public Education of Negroes*, p. 117.

34. Newby and Tyack, "Victims Without 'Crimes,'" p. 195.

35. Bond, *Public Education of Negroes*, p. 99. "During Speed's administration (Alabama, 1873–74), by his own admission, the public schools were barely operative" (p. 99).

36. David Tyack, *Turning Points in American Educational History* (Waltham, Mass.: Blaisdell Publishing, 1967), p. 268.

37. Harlan, *Separate and Unequal*, p. 9.

38. Ibid., p. 10.

39. Tyack, *Turning Points*, p. 267.

40. James Medoff, "Education and the Agrarian Order, 1880–1910" (Harvard University, Department of Economics, January 1972). Mimeographed.

41. Ibid., p. 9.

42. Bond, *Public Education of Negroes*, p. 162.

43. W. E. B. DuBois, "The Economic Revolution," in DuBois and B. T. Washington, *The Negro in the South* (Philadelphia, 1907), p. 102.

44. Bond, *Public Education of Negroes*, p. 142.

45. Ibid., p. 137.

46. Ibid., p. 141.

47. Ibid., p. 141.

48. Ibid., p. 160.

49. Tyack, *Turning Points*, pp. 268–69.

50. Harlan, *Separate and Unequal*, p. 12.

51. Bond, *Public Education of Negroes*, table 6, p. 162. The number of black children in the county was three to five times as great as the number of whites in this period.

52. The original grant for Tuskegee came from the Alabama state legislature as the result of a campaign promise by a white politician to the blacks of Macon County.

53. Bond, *Public Education of Negroes*, p. 263.

54. Harlan, *Separate and Unequal*, p. 85.

55. Most of the southern members were state college presidents. Thus, the Board's advice on policy came from progressive elements of southern conservatives.

56. Ibid., p. 79.

57. Ibid., pp. 77–78.

58. Ibid., pp. 248–49.

59. The Wilcox County data reported by Bond show teachers' salaries of $0.37 per black child to $12 per white child in 1907–8; by 1912–13, expenditures on white children had risen to almost $16 per white child in the county and fallen to $0.30 for blacks.

60. Harlan, *Separate and Unequal*, pp. 95–96.

61. Bond, *Public Education of Negroes*, p. 207.

62. Ibid., p. 208.

63. Patti McGill Peterson, "Colonialism and Education: The Case of the Afro-American," *Comparative Education Review* 15, no. 2 (June 1971): 151.

64. Raymond B. Fosdick, *Adventure in Giving* (New York: Harper & Row, 1962), pp. 86–87.

65. Harlan, *Separate and Unequal*, p. 94.

66. Bond, *Public Education of Negroes*, p. 240.

67. Ibid., p. 144.

68. Newby and Tyack, "Victims Without 'Crimes,'" p. 196.

69. Bond, *Public Education of Negroes*, p. 243.

70. Ibid., p. 258.

71. In 1919, however, the Commission on Race Relations, studying racial violence in Chicago, could still find that the school was one of the few places in the society where the races could get to know each other (Tyack, *Turning Points*, p. 273).

72. Newby and Tyack, "Victims Without 'Crimes,' " p. 200.

73. Ibid., p. 200.

74. Cubberley, *State and County Educational Reorganization*, quoted in ibid., p. 197.

75. Newby and Tyack, "Victims Without 'Crimes,' " p. 193.

76. Ibid., p. 193.

77. Michael Reich, "The Economics of Racism," in *Schooling in a Corporate Society*, ed. Martin Carnoy (New York: David McKay, 1972).

78. Harlan, *Separate and Unequal*, pp. 78–79.

79. Peterson, "Colonialism and Education," p. 157.

7

EDUCATION AND THE IDEOLOGY OF EFFICIENCY

UNITED STATES NEO-COLONIALISM SINCE 1945

World War I marked the beginning of the end of the British Empire and of both direct and free-trade colonialism. The war stimulated tariff-protected, import-substitution industrialization in India and, to some extent, in the large countries of Latin America. The United States increased her percentage of trade with the Third World, especially Latin America, and began to replace Britain as the main trading partner and foreign investor of Latin America and Asia. Britain's decline was marked by the return to protection in 1932, and by 1946 (Bretton Woods) it was the United States who became the main advocate of world free trade.[1]

The crisis in the world capitalist system in the 1930s seriously strained the bases for trade arrangements between the primary-goods producers and the industrialized economies. From 1929 to 1933, markets for primary exports collapsed, and with that collapse, the foreign exchange for importing consumption goods disappeared. Occupied Africa and Asia suffered less than the more developed Latin American countries (Argentina, Chile, Brazil, and Mexico) partly because a smaller fraction of the population in subsistence-agriculture countries was in the monetary sector. Because the drop in demand for imports was greatest in the United States, countries such as Chile, Peru, and Central America, which had a high fraction of their trade with the United States, lost practically all their export earnings between 1929 and 1933.

The crisis changed the United States as well. The singular dedication to private enterpirse as the basis for economic expansion was abandoned in 1932, and new system of capitalism, which had been taking shape since the turn of the century,[2] and was based on state intervention and support, became the dominant form. World War II turned the United States into a controlled economy in which government and private capital worked together. Postwar, U.S. foreign policy was built on an ideology of state-supported private enterprise.[3]

Japanese conquest disrupted colonial rule in Asia, setting in motion nationalist wars of independence and revolutions in China, Indochina, Indonesia, and Malaya. India and the Philippines both had independent governments two years after the war. The war played a different role in Latin America: because of its strategic importance militarily and as a source of raw materials, the United States successfully tied Latin American economies into the U.S. war production effort. While many nascent industries had difficulties during the war because of supply shortages, war-oriented production flourished.[4]

The war not only destroyed some colonial relations and helped build others, but it changed the nature of the imperial struggle which had been going on since the end of the nineteenth century. Western European nations—previously protagonists in the conflict between expanding capitalist forces—were physically and economically destroyed by the war. The Soviet Union and the United States emerged as the new world powers. The struggle shifted to a conflict between U.S. state- (and military-) supported large private multinational corporations and the bureaucracy of the Soviet Union.[5]

With its tremendous economic base, the United States became the main standard bearer for capitalism around the world, and moved to break up the British and French empires by supporting anticolonial independence movements in their colonies. Where these independence movements were communist, however, the United States used military and paramilitary assistance to set up and support U.S.-oriented governments independent of the former colonial rulers.[6]

The capitalist structure that the United States pushes for is much more "enlightened" than the colonial or neocolonial relation Britain and France had with nonindustrial nations. While the British and French sought direct commercial advantages, the United States looked for long-term stability of independent, "capitalist-oriented" state bureaucracies that would promote economic growth. Stability and order through democratic governments would create long-term advantages for U.S. private enterprise without the moral and pecuniary cost of administering foreign colonies. Also in contrast to British and French imperial policies, the United States does not see itself as maintaining an empire. The U.S. corporate self-image is one of helping other countries help themselves: since the United States is the world's most successful example of national economic growth (despite occasional setbacks)—these corporations argue—the best strategy for other countries to increase material output is to imitate the United States model. The ideal future in this model is a U.S.-type consumption goods economy with high levels of material consumption per capita.[7]

But like Britain before 1914, the power of the United States after World War II makes it pervade every economy and every culture. Nations that attempt to break away from the U.S.-dominated economic system feel this power most directly.[8] U.S. corporations and foreign aid try "peacefully" to promote the kind of development they think best for the world's peoples, but keeping the empire functioning requires increasing covert and overt military intervention. A large part of foreign "aid" is for the military, for Central Intelligence Agency operations (hidden in other government expenditures), or for police training and equipment.[9]

Foreign Aid

This mixture of humanitarianism and profit motives, which stimulated northern intervention in southern education for a half century after the Civil War, also led to the granting of U.S. assistance for economic and social development to foreign countries almost a century later. There was a general feeling that the United States—a rich country—should devote some of its resources, both private and public, to helping poor people achieve higher standards of living.

But, more important, economic growth was and continues to be viewed by U.S. business operating abroad as the key to the expansion of their profits and to political "stability." At the end of the nineteenth century, the threat to this stability was the Populist revolt, a movement that attacked big business and the ties between large corporations and public functionaries. Northern philanthropies and their allies, progressive southern aristocrats, placated the Populist white yeoman class at the expense of the blacks. In Europe at the end of World War II, the threat came from communists in France, Italy, and Greece, who intended—at least in the eyes of U.S. policy makers—to ally those countries with the Soviet Union against U.S. "interests."

However, from the 1950s to the present, guerrilla movements have disrupted and, in some cases, overthrown, U.S.-supported governments favorable to the free operation of U.S. companies in their countries. In the South, in Europe, and in low-income countries around the world, economic growth was supposed to cut off the support for such movements by eliminating poverty and social injustice. With increases in consumption per capita, support for capitalist institutions (such as private property, free enterprise, free trade, and equal treatment for foreign investment) was also supposed to increase.

As the most powerful capitalist nation after the war, the United States attempted to construct a new international system that would give the United States access to the resources it needed to increase its own consumption, and provide the markets and investment opportunities for U.S. private companies operating abroad. This system depends, in each "independent" country, on a political situation which allows U.S. capital to move freely. Under ideal conditions, economic growth, democratic elections, and the free-enterprise system coexist, producing a replica of U.S. development on a small scale.

The U.S. government feels strongly enough about maintaining this system that it has sent its troops abroad continuously since 1945 to intervene in a variety of small and large conflicts. Almost 100,000 Americans have died fighting in Asia in the last twenty-five years, a figure equal to about 40 percent of U.S. losses in World War II. In addition to direct intervention, the bulk of U.S. foreign assistance has been for military equipment, military training, and police training in any country that faces even the smallest threat of internal political conflict.

Alongside the massive U.S. military presence, the stability-maintenance role of foreign aid for economic development has probably been small. Nevertheless, it is part of an effort to promote capitalist development without resorting to military confrontation. Assistance has not been particularly large, nor is there evidence that it even contributes to long-run economic growth, but it is large enough to be used as an effective tool of leverage on low-income countries' economic and social policies.[10]

The United States uses assistance for education now, as the British and French used assistance in the nineteenth century (and in the present), to expand that education which is complementary to keeping order in the "empire" and which subsidizes the expansion of capitalist enterprise, particularly (for U.S. assistance) American-based multinational corporations and financial institutions.[11] With U.S. hegemony, expansion and reforms of formal schooling become means of promoting *U.S.* concepts of an "efficient" and "democratic" society.[12]

With U.S. help, low-income countries concentrate on making their economies and societies more "modern": together with U.S. assistance agencies, they define "development" in terms of management and industrial country resources (including technology). Management is, in turn, defined in terms of the allocation of these scarce resources to competing ends. Since one of the principal aims of U.S. development policy is to preserve or improve capitalist structures in the Third World—institutional structures which fit into an international system of trade and investment—the efficiency solution to development implies that sustained growth and progress would follow from making imperfect capitalist systems work better, and by making more resources (including technique) available. Completely excluded from this analysis is the possibility that the domestic and international economic and social structure championed by the United States and other capitalist societies is itself responsible for the lack of resources or for the observed "inefficiencies" in the economic and educational systems.

The Origins of U.S. Education Policy in the Third World

Assistance for education by the Agency for International Development (AID), the World Bank, and other donor agencies, including private foundations and missionary societies,[13] is ostensibly designed to promote economic growth, but the *context* of educational grants, as well as the technical advice which accompanies them, puts certain conditions on the development process.[14] The aim is to build institutions that complement a capitalist organization of production—an economic organization that channels a high percentage of the increment of output into the hands of a relatively few people and that accepts and even requires foreign investment—and a polity which serves this type of hierarchical structure and U.S. military interests.

The use of education to achieve both this goal and the humanitarian purposes of foreign assistance bears a close resemblance to earlier efforts in the South. Indeed, the origins of U.S. educational policy in the Third World today can be traced to missionary work in the South and abroad and to the policies and methods of philanthropies around the turn of the century.

Like today's development assistance programs, the efforts of the Southern Education Board, Rockefeller's General Education Board, and others working in the South were a mixture of humanitarianism and the promotion of an economic development that was consistent with the needs of the capitalists who staffed the boards. Education was viewed as a key variable in terms of both the philanthropies' humanitarian and economic-growth goals. Throughout the nineteenth century, progressive industrialists felt that schooling prepared people for participation in the good life provided by capitalist society.

Theoretically, giving poor people schooling led to jobs, income, and social stability. At the same time, of course, a schooled labor force and higher incomes in the South would increase both the markets for northern industrial goods and investment opportunities.

But, as we have seen, the growth of schooling successfully stimulated by the philanthropies hardly reached the poor—particularly the black poor. This was due to the structure of the philanthropies themselves: the boards of directors determining their policies included progressive southerners from the planter class, who advised the boards in terms of their class interests. At the turn of the century, this meant placating white Populists at the *expense* of the blacks, in order for the old aristocracy to keep control of state funds. The significance of this advice was that it was acceptable to the northerners who controlled the boards, despite its clear implications for black education. Northern capitalists chose to deal with the class in the South that they felt culturally and economically closest to, and chose to follow a strategy which obviously had little short-run benefits for the poorest and most oppressed group in southern society—all this to maintain political stability in the region and an economic growth favorable to northern capital and to its southern intermediaries.

Fifty years later, the United States is following the same strategy in parcelling out its foreign assistance, private and public. The group whose advice and cooperation is most favored in foreign countries is the progressive bourgeoisie—as in the South, usually born of the landowning aristocracy. It is this bourgeoisie that is most attuned to the development process the United States wishes other countries to follow. Again, as in the South, the domestic group is usually more conservative than the U.S. businessmen or government bureaucrats coming to assist in development: when humanitarian concerns emerge in assistance discussions, the United States is usually advised by its intermediaries to go slowly in order to avoid ever-present local conflicts.

Thus, the pattern of growth which emerges from U.S. support of local bourgeoisies is distributed extremely inequitably and is often accompanied by cruel dictatorships. While the conditions extant in each society are the direct responsibility of those who control the society, U.S. agencies *choose* to deal with those particular intermediaries rather than representatives of the oppressed, especially those representatives who argue that foreign private investment and U.S. development strategy and goals are inconsistent with the well-being of their people.

Parallel to this background of the overall strategy of economic development through education, the detailed strategy of international education draws its origins from missionary efforts in China, Japan, and the Near East.

> The institutions that were formed were American, built with American money, staffed with American teachers, using American programs, methods, and standards. Only the students were foreign, and the best of these were selected for further training in the United States. It was this early flow of selected foreign students to selected American colleges, usually Presbyterian, Baptist, or Methodist, that set a pattern which still dominates much of our thinking about foreign students.[15]

The American missions of the late nineteenth and early twentieth centuries operated in the same context as their sister British missions of the same time.[16] The United States expanded its borders on the basis of Indian conquests and the Mexican War. Manifest Destiny was openly condescending and imperialistic, and by the 1890s was heightened by "objective" theories of white racial supremacy.[17]

The Yale University missions in Hunan Province, China, were typical of the American institutions Bowles describes. Hunan became known to a wide audience in the United States when an American railroad company got a concession to build a railroad from Hankow to Canton across the entire length of Hunan. William Parsons, the chief engineer of a survey team sent to Hunan by the railroad, saw great commercial potential in the province, especially in the coal deposits there. He recommended:

> First, the Chinese should be encouraged to attend occidental colleges. Secondly, schools could be established in Hunan which would "sweep away the incrustations that hamper progress." And finally, colleges in the United States should train students in the Chinese language and mercantile customs. Such a system would "give us a hold over foreign trade in China which present methods could never do."[18]

Armed with the spirit to convert Chinese from their "trite maxims and hoary traditions," and to help open Hunan to Western influence and control, young Elis joined the scramble into Hunan. They founded a school, Yali, in Changsha. The curriculum was taught largely in English and concentrated on weaning the students from Chinese to Anglo-Saxon culture. Yali's graduates found jobs with Christian missionaries or in business houses engaged in foreign trade. With the leadership of Sun Yat-sen, himself educated in Hawaii, Western-educated Chinese such as those from Yali organized a reform society that drew most of its recruits from mission schools. They attempted to turn China toward European values and institutions.

American missions had this strong influence wherever they were established. They educated the pro-Western political leaders and professional classes. Important in forming the system of higher education, they continued their existence even in the face of nationalism. "In the extreme instance of Communist China, the very virulence of the official anti-Western expression is continued tribute to the effectiveness of the American influence established there through education." [19]

American missionaries carried the heritage of Reconstruction in challenging the established order through their schools. In 1865, the U.S. North was intent on breaking up the political and economic power of the southern landowners who had tried to secede from the Union. By the 1890s, U.S. expansion had reached the Philippines and the Caribbean and missionaries operated consistently with the need to form groups allied to American capitalism. As in Reconstruction, the main result of missionary activity was the creation of an elite who provided leadership for the next generation. The difference between the South and foreign operations, however, was the lack of political and economic support for blacks in the South after 1877, contrasted with the continued and close relations with missionary-trained elites in Asia and the Near East. The difference between the failure of black power in the South and the success of local U.S.-supported bourgeoisies in the Philippines and the Near East reflects the importance of backing schooling with economic and political power to overcome control by the landed aristocracy. Schooling alone was never enough to achieve social mobility.

During World War II, the U.S. international education effort was necessarily concentrated in the Western Hemisphere. At the same time, the urgency of the war combined with the general move toward government expansion to herald a new era in foreign aid. The public sector drew not only on the experience of the philanthropies but also on its personnel. Under the directorship of Nelson Rockefeller, the Office of Inter-American Affairs was charged with formulating and executing "programs in the commercial and economic fields which, by the effective use of governmental and private facilities, will further the commercial well-being of the Western Hemisphere . . . and which, by effective use of governmental and private facilities, in such fields as the arts and sciences, education and travel, the radio, the press, and the cinema, will further the national defense and strengthen the bonds between the nations of the Western Hemisphere." [20]

The Office was an outgrowth of the Rio Charter, which was designed to counteract German influence in Latin America. Under the threat of various Latin American countries remaining neutral or pro-German, the United States moved to ensure that it would control resources in the Western Hemisphere. Although most of the effort of the Office was in coordinating production of war material and its transportation, it was also involved in influencing the long-run development of the region. At the First Conference of Commissions of Inter-American Development in May 1944, recommendations were made for government and business in the development of hemisphere resources. The conference was told that "with the strength and vitality of private initiative behind its work, (the conference) can provide a bold and vigorous leadership in directing plans, thoughts, and hopes to the almost unlimited opportunities and possibilities for economic progress in the years of peace to come." [21] The conference made a set of recommendations which supported equal treatment of foreign and domestic investments in the hemisphere, the encouragement of private enterprise in developing hemisphere resources, mutual aid for petro leum exploitation and development of hydroelectricity, the affirmation of free trade, through the reduction of trade barriers and preferences, and inflation controls.[22]

Education was promoted by the Office in the missionary tradition of language training for U.S. representatives who were to serve in Latin America, support of students from Latin America coming to study in the United States and of U.S. students going to Latin America, assignment of English teachers and establishment of English teacher-training courses in Latin America, and aid to U.S.-sponsored schools (privately funded institutions) and national schools in Latin America. The Office recognized that "one of the most effective methods of developing mutual understanding and desire for cooperation is through a wide interchange of scholars, students, and teachers." [23]

The wartime organization of assistance formed the basis for later U.S. aid programs. Educational assistance, under its conception as a complement to the expansion of trade and development in the U.S. model, was used primarily to train elites in the United States and to promote international studies in U.S. universities. Schooling was seen as a means of influencing national elites to lead a U.S.-inspired and financially supported economic and political development process.

Until the late 1950s, the World Bank (IBRD) and the Agency for International Development (AID) were the major aid donors (both Western-industrial-country controlled), and they concentrated on building roads, hydroelectric plants, irrigation projects, and the like. These "infrastructure" expenditures were designed to stimulate the growth of private investment in industry and to improve access to raw materials, especially for export. The infrastructure role of education was confined to building an elite supportive of U.S.-style development. But in the late 1950s, these aid donors, joined by U.S. foundations, decided to assist schooling as an investment in skilled labor. Schooling was rediscovered to be a social investment which created a modern labor force with modern "attitudes" toward technological and social change. Policy had come full circle back to philanthropic strategy at the turn of the century.

Yet, why the return to large-scale educational assistance in the 1960s? First, many underdeveloped countries were having problems paying for educational expansion themselves. With pressure from the

unschooled for more primary schooling and pressure from industrialists for more technicians and skilled labor, many countries found
that they could not meet both demands. Second, foreign investors—
who were increasingly shifting into manufacturing in underdeveloped
countries—were especially influential in pushing for expanded technical higher education to supply their labor needs. Third, U.S. foreign
policy makers were gradually convinced by U.S. academics that
investment in schooling was a necessary input into economic growth.[24]
All these reasons added up to spending more on schooling for
economic growth and the political stability necessary for continued
capitalist development. Support for U.S. orientation continued through
increased numbers of foreign students in the United States and
increased involvement of U.S. universities abroad, while the assistance
to lower levels of schooling was a response to new demands.[25]

The Pattern of U.S.-Promoted Capitalist Development

Educational assistance is based not only on the desire to increase
profits for American investors and on some concept of U.S. national
security but also on the humanitarian qua capitalist ideal of stimulating
individual improvement for the poor. Nevertheless, we have stressed
the contradiction between these two goals: Assistance is given through
intermediaries who maximize their own gains with the granted funds.
More important, the structure of capitalist development is apparently
such as to minimize the possibility for the poor of improving their
position relative to the rich. Thus, the humanitarian ideal of bringing
the poor out of their oppression is not achieved by foreign assistance,
just as it was not achieved in the South by philanthropies. To the
contrary, the emphasis on capitalist development, on bourgeois control
of the economy, and on making the inequitable structure more
efficient, as opposed to radical change of the structure itself, may keep
the poor in their place longer than had the United States not
intervened.

The now-industrialized capitalist countries were able, often with
considerable upheaval, to make the transition from feudalism to
capitalism, or, in the case of the mercantile white-settlement colonies,

from plantation economies to autarkic industrialization. Under capitalism, they have managed to sustain increase in economic output over a long period of time; there is little question that the capitalist organization of production can produce increases in output and, over the long term, increases of consumption in the mass of the population.

But capitalist growth has also been characterized by unchanged or increasingly unequal income distribution, and unchanged (high) or increasing unemployment. Furthermore, the likelihood of certain groups getting low earnings and high unemployment is passed down from generation to generation. As an example of this pattern, income distribution in the United States became more unequal between 1910 and 1929, equalized approximately to the 1910 level between 1929 and 1944, and has remained approximately unchanged between 1945 and 1970, perhaps improving somewhat at the end of this period.[26] The Gini coefficient of income distribution in the United States, however, is one of the lowest in the world, so it could be argued that the distribution of income in 1910 was already more equal than the minimum level of political acceptability.[27] Furthermore, despite recovery from the depression, post-World War II unemployment averaged 5.6 percent in nonwar years.[28] Magdoff and Sweezy argue that the unemployed plus those employed in defense production or directly in the military has been approximately constant since 1938.[29] In other words, they claim that the United States solved the critical unemployment problem of the 1930s by preparing for war. The rate of unemployment in the United States has not fallen below 5 percent except in periods of rapidly expanding defense spending.

But income inequality and unemployment are relatively small in the United States compared to lower-income capitalist societies. For example, there is evidence that Mexico, which is pointed to as a paradigm of successful capitalist growth in Latin America (an average increase in gross national product per capita of 2.7 percent between 1950 and 1968), has a steadily more unequal income distribution since 1950 (see table 15). Although unemployment data are only approximate, the Banco Nacional de Mexico estimates that unemployment and underemployment in 1969 was about 40 percent.[30] Similarly, Brazilian income distribution apparently became more unequal between 1960 and 1970 (see table 15). The Brazilian economy expanded rapidly in the last three years of that period, but unemployment has remained high.

Table 15

Income Distribution in the United States, Brazil, and Mexico, 1950–70 (Gini coefficients)

Year	U.S. Family Income	U.S. Individual Income[a]	Year	Mexico Individual	Year	Brazil Individual
1950	.375	—	1950	.50	1960	.52 (1)
1955	.366	—	1958	.53		.50 (2)
1960	.369	.338	1963	.55	1970	.64 (1)
1965	.360	.341	1968	.58		.57 (2)
1970	.353	.356				

[a] Wages and salaries only.

Sources: U.S. family and individual income: Peter Henle, "Exploring the Distribution of Earned Income," *Monthly Labor Review* 95, no. 2 (December 1972): 16–27. Henle points out that the primary reason that the distribution of family income becomes more equal while individual incomes are tending toward inequality is probably that a higher number of families in 1970 than in 1960 or in 1950 have two or more members working. Also, federal transfer payments are more extensive. Thus, an individual who may show up as a low-income earner may belong to a family which is middle income.

Mexico: 1950–63: David Barkin, "Acceso a la educación superior y beneficios que reporta en Mexico," *Revista del Centro de Estudios Educativos*, 1, no. 3 (1971): 47–74. 1968: David Barkin, "Mexico's Albatross: the U.S. Economy" (Paper presented to University of Texas Conference on Mexico-U.S. Economic Relations, April 1973).

Brazil: (1) Albert Fishlow, "Brazilian Size Distribution of Income" (University of California at Berkeley, 1972). Mimeographed. (2) Carlos Langoni, "Distribução da renda e desenvolvimento econômico do Brazil," *Estudos Econômicos* (São Paulo) 2, no. 5 (1972).

Indeed, despite an average growth rate of about 2.2 percent per capita in Latin America between 1950 and 1968, unemployment increased from 5.6 to 11.1 percent of the labor force between 1950 and 1965, and the participation rate of the population in the labor force fell from 34.8 to 34.6 percent (see table 16).

The general employment situation in Latin America as a whole is one of disequilibrium between the population in the mass and the economic

Table 16

Population, Labor Force, and Employment in Latin America, 1950–65

	1950	1955	1960	1965
Total population (thousands)	151,116	173,104	199,307	229,691
Rate of participation (% of total population)	34.8	34.8	34.7	34.6
Labor force (thousands)	52,664	60,240	69,160	79,473
Persons employed (thousands)	49,739	56,077	62,866	70,651
Persons unemployed (thousands)	2,925	4,163	6,294	8,822
Rate of unemployment (% of labor force)	5.6	6.9	9.1	11.1

Source: Secretariat of the Organization of American States, General Secretariat, *Employment and Growth in the Strategy of Latin American Development: Implications for the Seventies,* Seventh Annual Meeting of the Inter-American Economic and Social Council (CIES), Panama, September 1971, p. 2.

structures of the hemisphere. The quickening growth of population in the region, its rapid urbanization, and the high growth rate of the labor force are part of a complex socioeconomic situation that may be summarily described as an employment crisis, manifested partly by a relatively high rate of open employment—particularly in urban areas—but also by extensive underemployment and a low rate of participation.[31]

In Asia and Africa, the situation is probably even worse.:

. . . the previous industrial development plans of the ECAFE countries have not made any sizeable impact on the over-all employment situation, and that the employment opportunities have lagged far behind the growth in the labour force. In some countries, like India, Pakistan and Ceylon, the backlog of unemployed and under-employed at the end of the plan period appeared to be far larger than at the beginning of the plan period—indicating that the new employment opportunities have not kept pace with the growth in the labour force. Such data as are readily available do suggest that the situation on the employment front is assuming quite serious proportions. In the Republic of Korea, despite all efforts at industrialization, the number of unemployed and underemployed persons has increased in 1963 to 703,000 and 2,220,000 respectively. Notwithstanding the rapid development of manufacturing industries, the total number of unemployed persons in the Philippines is estimated to have increased from 540,000 in 1959 to 577,000 in 1960, 618,000 in 1961 and 662,000 in 1962. In India, the backlog of unemployed which was estimated to be around 5 million at the beginning of the Second Plan period has been estimated to have increased to 9 million during the beginning of Third Plan period and is expected to be of the order of 9–10 million at the beginning of the Fourth Plan period. In other countries like Indonesia, Burma or the Republic of Viet Nam where the development plans remained practically inoperative either due to economic and political instability or serious shortage of external and internal resources, the impact of development planning on employment was even less significant.[32]

Capitalist development is therefore almost universally marked by a generally positive increase in per capita income, by an income distribution that is unchanged or becoming more unequal, and by a high and even increasing unemployment rate in the low-income countries.[33]

The Role of Schooling in the U.S. Development Model

Formal schooling is part and parcel of the characteristics of capitalist growth. In the U.S. capitalist development model, the state is to provide the infrastructure investment for the expansion of the private sector. A skilled labor force is an important part of the infrastructure. But the social and economic structure supported by U.S. technology and investment clearly favors the mechanization of agriculture and industry, pushing people out of these jobs into urban services. Since the aim of the model is to accumulate capital for accumulation's sake—to produce goods for exchange value rather than use value—full employment is not a primary objective of the economy. Since schooling reinforces the hierarchy of occupational roles, anyone with schooling attempts to flee the countryside to seek his or her fortune in the city, even though poverty in the city may be as bad as on the farm. Furthermore, schooling selects people on the basis of academic performance and location (access to schooling), which are, in turn, related to social class. Thus, the school system, as we have argued throughout this study, tends to maintain an unchanged income distribution and hierarchical structure.

As the number of primary school graduates increases, the unemployment rate among those graduates also increases, especially among the young who are just getting out of school. Therefore, the income sacrificed by a primary graduate who goes on to secondary school decreases. In many African countries, for example, it is almost impossible for a primary school graduate fourteen or fifteen years old to get a job. The alternative to attending secondary school is "leisure." Since the alternative to attending secondary school becomes economically less attractive as it gets harder to find work with only primary education, the economic incentive to attend secondary school rises. The pressure on the government to provide secondary school grows as the alternatives to school attendance disappear. Later in time, as secondary school expands, employment opportunities for secondary school graduates become scarcer and less prestigious. Secondary school graduates find the university a more viable alternative and put pressure on government to expand that level of schooling. Although the figures in table 16 do not show it, we can deduce that the average education of unemployed in Latin America (and Asia and Africa too) is increasing over time.

As the educational system expands in the face of unemployment, people compete for a limited increase in jobs by taking increased amounts of schooling, since schooling is the allocator of occupational roles. Not only does the average level of schooling in the employed labor force increase, but the average schooling of the unemployed also grows. Unemployment is generally higher among the young and among those with less schooling, and highest among the youth with little schooling. Among those who are salaried (not owners of physical capital), getting more schooling is usually an important determinant of how much a person in a given age group earns.[34]

The pressures for increased schooling do not come only from the uneducated or less-than-average-educated masses. The production of sophisticated consumption goods and services requires skilled workers. An ordered, "modern" capitalist society requires socialized participants at all levels of the social structure. Each level has its expected behavior patterns. Thus, industrialists and "progressive" politicians, aided by the United States and other industrial countries, help expand the educational system. There are opponents to expansion as well. Professionals often try to protect their favored position by arguing against academic secondary and university enrollment increases. Conservative landowners see the growth of the public educational system as providing an enlarged power base for the bourgeoisie, which is a direct threat to their own power. All these forces clash on the school system, which reflects the greater issues of economic and political power in the society. In the postwar period, the industrialists —foreign and domestic—the masses, and the politicians favoring the U.S. development model are winning this struggle and expanding schooling substantially.

Income Distribution and Schooling   Who gets this schooling? If it were allocated randomly, every child would have an equal chance to get the best jobs and highest salaries (provided that schooling remained an important determinant of income) and an equal chance of being unemployed. But in capitalist economies (and in many postrevolutionary state capitalist economies as well), schooling goes to those children whose parents are wealthy, have high education, or high social status. The school system is ostensibly a meritocracy—grades, not parental background, determine who goes to the higher levels—yet factors outside the school are so important in influencing children's school performance, aspiration, and motivation that social class is still the most important variable in predicting *how far* a person gets in school. This is no accident. The school system is structured, through its tests, reward system, and required behavior patterns, to allow

children of an urban bourgeoisie to do well, and to filter out children
of the poor, who are not socialized to function in the highest echelons
of a capitalist economy and bourgeois culture.[35] The school system is
therefore a mechanism to maintain class structure in a capitalist
society. It provides a legitimate institution, accepted by all classes in
the society (on the belief that it *is* genuinely meritocratic), for passing
social position from generation to generation.[36]

   The dilemma for the ruling class is how to provide more schooling
while maintaining its advantaged position. Usually this problem is
solved by creating a "dual" school system, for example, a private
system alongside a much poorer public system, especially at lower
schooling levels. In many countries children from wealthy families
attend private schools at the primary and secondary level, and then a
public, subsidized university which selects most of its entrants from
private schools. A vocational track parallel to an academic track serves
the same purpose. The lower-social-class children, because of their
poorer grades, end up in the vocational track, thus being guaranteed an
occupation as a factory worker or technician. Wealthier children enter
the academic track, which gives them access to white-collar roles or to
a university and the professions. The most important elements of these
parallel systems is to preserve levels of education that are higher than
the average levels of schooling for children of the higher social classes.
As the average level of education eventually climbs into the secondary
cycle, differences among schools appear even at higher levels: there are
"prestige" universities with the "best" students and run-of-the-mill
universities, while degrees from foreign universities rank higher than
local degrees—all this to select people for the top jobs in the status
hierarchy.

   The average level of schooling increases, but the schooling of
children from high-income families is always much higher than that of
children from low-income families. Everyone gets more schooling, but
the social structure is preserved. The high-paying, high-status jobs go,
on the average, to people whose parents also had high income and
status. As the number of these jobs increases, people from lower
socioeconomic backgrounds also get high incomes, *but they represent a*

small percentage of their social class, while almost all those from high-income families are assured high-status positions.[37]

The implications of such an educational system for income distribution are obvious. Even though the variation in the years of schooling individuals get may grow smaller as the average number of years of schooling increases—and there is some evidence that it eventually does[38]—access to various positions in the social structure is preserved through the school system. The poor remain relatively poor and the rich remain rich. If income distribution improved over time, this maintained social structure might be acceptable, since the *relative* differences between the poor and the rich would be steadily reduced. But there is no evidence that income distribution is automatically improved in capitalist development. In fact, in the postwar period, the distribution of U.S. individual and family income has remained essentially unchanged, and Mexican and Brazilian income distributions have become more unequal, despite large increases in the average level of schooling in all three countries (see table 15). Available data show a positive but weak relation between a society's distribution of years of schooling and its income distribution, and a possible negative connection between changes in the average schooling level and the equality of income distribution.[39]

The Neocolonialism of "Efficiency" Solutions to Development

The U.S. model of development, stressing higher consumption for all through increased national product per capita, has not worked for most people living in underdeveloped countries (in 1960, the bottom 40 percent of Brazilian income recipients earned only 12.5 percent of total income; in 1963, the bottom 40 percent of Mexicans earned 10.5 percent of total income, and in 1959, the bottom 40 percent of U.S. income recipients earned 15 percent of total income). The lowest-income 50 percent of the population in nonindustrialized countries is not participating in whatever growth occurs. They are left relatively and even absolutely worse off by capitalist development.[40]

> In most Third World countries, the population grows, and so does the middle class. Income, consumption, and the well-being of the middle

class are all growing while the gap between this class and the mass of people widens. Even where per capita consumption is rising, the majority of men have less food now than in 1945, less actual care in sickness, less meaningful work, less protection. This is partly a consequence of polarized consumption and partly caused by the breakdown of traditional family and culture. More people suffer from hunger, pain, and exposure in 1969 than they did at the end of World War II, not only numerically, but also as a percentage of the world population.[41]

The essence of the U.S. solution to development problems such as unemployment, inequitable income distribution, and low growth rates lies in increasing the resources available for growth through foreign private and public investment and in improving the efficiency of the economic and social system. Improved efficiency depends on overcoming traditional elements in the social structure, and by improving the management of schools, factories, communications, and so forth.

This solution assumes that the problems of distribution and unemployment can be overcome by increasing the *quantity* of economic product per capita: that is, the poor will be better off absolutely and perhaps relatively if there are more consumption goods available, and if the growth rate is high, and the labor market and the schools can be made to work efficiently, unemployment will disappear. The solution further assumes that when institutions such as schools do not seem to be working efficiently, both the institutions and society are *irrational.* We argue that the first assumption is incorrect: experience in low-income countries—even those rapidly increasing their economic output—shows an increase in consumption for only part of the population. This part (generally called the middle class) participates in capitalist growth, but the poor do not. Neither is unemployment reduced by increasing economic output (the best example is probably Puerto Rico, where unemployment remained at 12–15 percent between 1940 and 1960 despite a 4 percent per capita growth rate and an emigration to the U.S. mainland of much of the increase in rural adult population) nor by increasing the average amount of schooling in the labor force.

The solutions to full employment and the equitable distribution of goods and work cannot be found in an educational system that reproduces inequality. Yet, it is difficult to imagine a society which relies on a capitalist hierarchy for the production and distribution of goods and services to have anything but such an educational system. The more education is relied on to allocate roles in such a society, the more hierarchical it will have to be, and the more responsible it will be for screening these children with bourgeois attitudes and skills from those without. All this is almost obvious.

But the alternative of radically restructuring the economy and society and changing the way goods are produced and distributed is not an "allowable" or even desirable alternative from the standpoint of those who would maintain U.S.-dependent capitalist economies in the nonindustrialized countries. So the United States, the international agencies, and the domestic elites who depend on foreign investment and aid, respond to the dilemma of educated unemployed and unequal income distribution by expanding schooling even more, at the same time attempting to reform the system so that it produces its output of students more "efficiently" and fits students more closely into occupational roles. As a result of expanded education, however, even if it is being produced at lower cost per pupil at each level, more is spent on education than before.[42] It simply takes more formal education to get the same job. Behind this strategy is the hope that increasing the average level of schooling will increase economic growth enough to overcome the problems of income distribution. The idea is to make the consumption of the poor high enough in absolute terms that they will be satisfied with it even if it represents a very small share of total income.

To solve the unemployment problem, "major" changes in school curriculum are proposed to make the school-labor market intersection more efficient. Agricultural, vocational, and technical education, as well as "nonformal" education, such as agricultural extension services and special training institutes, will "fit" people better to their "possitilities" than academic instruction that has no specific job orientation. In some countries, for example, Colombia and Venezuela, this vocational orientation is combined with the "experimental" comprehensive high schools and the expansion of primary education from six years to eight or nine years. But these were exactly the reforms undertaken in the United States when manufacturing became more complex and the schools had to prepare a more highly structured labor force (see chapter 5), and it is exactly the solution for black education supported by northern capitalists (see chapter 6). Vocational training is an effective way of preparing this skilled labor force while maintaining an unchanged social structure. Vocational education prepares people specifically for being factory workers—hopefully docile workers, as was planned for blacks in the South. It is impossible to go anywhere else in the occupational hierarchy.

Therefore, vocational training is secondary schooling for the urban poor, for those who cannot make it in the academic track, and for whom *those who run the economic and social system deem it appropriate and desirable to take vocational training.* This training defines the type of work they will do. For some, it means access to a well-paying factory job, but for most, it only paves the way to the marginal service sector (small garages, repair shops, and so forth). Children of the wealthy or the urban middle class do not take vocational education: their appropriate training is public or private academic education leading to the university. Thus, the concept of equal opportunity developed in the United States as the poor began to move into secondary schools is now being transferred to the nonindustrialized countries' educational systems for much the same reasons, and with predictable results.

Even if we disregard the distributional outcome of the vocational training emphasis, we conclude that this proposed solution to the unemployment problem incorrectly assumes that the problem is on the supply side; that there is a "mismatch" between skills provided by the schools and the available jobs in the market. There is also the assumption that schools can convince people to want certain kinds of jobs by training them for those jobs. This was Buxton's assumption in 1838, and it has changed little since then. Both assumptions are not supported empirically, and show little understanding of labor markets. First, education does not create demand for skills except for those of teachers.[43] But teacher training is a special case, since it is still high-status training, especially for women. Unemployment of school leavers is high in underdeveloped countries because, at the going wage and the technology used by capitalists, there are fewer jobs than people available and capable to do them.

> . . . curriculum reform will not alter the current situation, since the causes of underutilization of manpower have very little to do with what is taught in the schools. Moreover, lower level schooling can nowhere prepare individuals for specific occupations. Indeed, the attempt to do so would vastly increase educational costs and, if anything, reduce the existing flexibility of the system. To my mind, there are more viable strategies that can be pursued, and these hinge on examining what goes on outside the schools rather than what goes on inside them.[44]

Second, motivations of students depend on perceptions of subsequent opportunities. These perceptions, in turn, are derived from the realities of the socioeconomic environment. British attempts to impose agricultural occupations on Africans through formal schooling during the mid-nineteenth century and colonial rule were only partially successful. Africans saw the highest rewards in European-type work, not in agriculture. Today, the nationalist bourgeoisie is the highest class in capitalist countries. The kind of schooling their children take is the most desirable and most aspired to by other social classes.[45]

> Those who criticize the "irrational" nature of African demand for "academic" as opposed to "vocational" education fail to recognize that the strength of academic education has lain precisely in the fact that it is preeminantly a *vocational* education providing access to those occupations with the most prestige and, most important, the highest pay.[46]

Vocational education alongside academic may solve the basic capitalist development dilemma of increasing economic production while maintaining the social structure (particular capitalists' control of production), but such a combination cannot reduce unemployment, equalize income distribution, or provide equal access to jobs for different social groups. Quite to the contrary, its primary purpose is to divide labor before it enters the job market into clearly identifiable work classes.

The viability of an "efficiency" solution—such as vocational education—to educational problems depends on the assumption that schools are indeed being mismanaged. There is some element of mismanagement in every organization, but it is just as reasonable to assume that schools and the labor market and other elements of the capitalist economic structure are being managed very well, but are meeting objectives that U.S. businessmen and assistance agencies choose to ignore.

In the case of education, it is usually assumed by U.S. and other industrialized country experts[47] that schools are primarily places to develop vocational (cognitive) skills that fit in with a societal objective of maximizing economic growth. But that is not the only and probably not the main function of schools. Schools transfer culture and values and they channel children into various roles. They help maintain social order. The common school is the institution that developed within capitalist economic and social structures to prepare individuals for assuming various roles in those structures.[48]

The close tie between nonindustrialized (or industrializing) and industrialized economies—a partnership in development—proposed by assistance donors in itself poses an important contradiction.[49] It is argued that this partnership will result in higher growth through additional resources being made available for investment and by the increased importation of better management for more efficient use of resources. This assumes again that a more intimate relationship between the "developed" and the "underdeveloped" countries will solve development problems by eliminating irrational elements in "traditionally oriented" societies.

Yet, it seems much more persuasive to assume that any economy already tied through trade and investment to the industrial countries is also going to have an employment structure and technology that is tied into the international system. This, in turn, has a significant effect on the labor market and educational system. What are viewed by U.S. economists as inefficiencies in labor markets and educational structures due to their not being sufficiently "modern," we argue are rather the result of imported capitalist forms distorted to fit the condition of nonindustrialized economies and, in large part, to meet the needs of the domestic bourgeoisie and industrial country corporations. Even closer ties to high-income countries *may* mean higher economic output in the short run, but also means greater distortions to bend the local economy into the industrial country mold, and the maintance of control over local resources by foreign capital.

Nonindustrial countries attempt to produce approximately the same set of consumption goods as the industrial countries now consume, using the same technology and organization of production as in the high-consumption economies. This pattern of production is promoted on the assumption that today's low-income economies can replicate, in temporally compressed form, the historical development process of already industrialized countries.[50]

If a society is developing under the concept of producing high-income-country consumption goods, only a small number of people in the economy will be active in producing or consuming these goods. Educational expenditures will be concentrated in urban areas to train these relatively few people to function in the technologically advanced sector and to produce sophisticated consumer goods, especially consumer durables. Imported technology and organization of production apparently make it more *profitable* and *socially preferable* to produce goods which higher income groups can consume.

Such development diverts economic surplus away from the peasants to industry, services, and plantation agriculture. The rural poor are drawn from the land, seeking better conditions in urban areas. Since the "modern" sector in the nonindustrialized economies employs only a limited percentage of the labor force, capitalist development is, as we have pointed out, almost universally marked by significant and even increasing unemployment in the nonindustrial countries (see table 16).

What does this policy of building closer links to high-income capitalist countries with stress on better management rather than structural change imply for the people of nonindustrialized countries? The rich countries choose to blame development problems on mismanagement, not on the existing *capitalist* relations in the low-income society nor on the existing ties between the industrialized and nonindustrialized economies. Donor agencies make clear that the present international system should be strengthened—that dependency should be increased—and they carefully omit any mention of radically changing the wealth and power structure within nonindustrialized societies and between industrialized and nonindustrialized societies as a prelude to economic development.

Not surprisingly, then, the "efficiency" analysis excludes the possibility that educational systems and labor markets are *well managed* within the limitations of a system that only maximizes the productive potential of a small percentage of the population. *The exclusion of this possibility consciously detracts from social structural issues which question the international system of trade, investment, and aid, and the role that nonindustrialized countries play in that system.*

This is analogous to the stress put on IQ by U.S. educators: they argue that the socioeconomic system objectively selects people for higher-status occupations and income on the basis of "intelligence" or school performance. Bowles and Gintis show, however, that adult IQ differences are a much less satisfactory explanation for economic success than are social class or years of schooling. Furthermore,

> . . . while one's economic status tends to strongly resemble that of one's parents, only a minor portion of this association can be attributed to social class differences in childhood IQ, and a virtually negligible proportion to social class differences in genetic endowments—even accepting the Jensen estimates of heritability. Thus, a perfect equalization of IQ's across social classes would reduce the intergenerational transmission of economic status by a negligible amount.[51]

The accent on objective tests—on "ability" differences among pupils as a key to economic success—has been used to legitimize social-class-based economic and social hierarches. It has been used to argue that becoming a blue-collar worker is not based on the family's working-class status but on the working-class child's lower "ability" as defined by the school.

Similarly, the distortions and inequities of school systems and the labor market are blamed on "inefficiencies" and "mismanagement," or the lack of "ability" to run the system properly. We argue here that the most advanced management techniques—including suggestions of systematic cost-effectiveness and cost-benefit analysis and program budgeting—will solve neither the educated unemployment problem nor the pressure of the population for more schooling than the society can "afford." These problems are due primarily to the nature of the capitalist world's "social structure," not to differences in "ability" between peoples of nonindustrialized and industrialized countries. Just as ability testing has been used to legitimize the class structure of industrialized capitalist societies by putting the onus of blame on individuals for their failure to do well on such tests, so the "efficiency" criteria for school systems and labor markets are used to *legitimize the international class structure* by putting the onus of blame on the inability of nonindustrialized peoples to manage their own institutions efficiently or to mobilize adequate resources for economic growth.

We can go further in our analogy and analyze the effect of the "efficiency" movement in the United States before and during World War I. Chapter 5 showed that one of the most important results of the alliance between educational reformers and businessmen—an alliance that stemmed from the common vision that the two groups held of societal progress and their common class values—was an emphasis on school efficiency. Efficiency was interpreted by schools as the effectiveness with which they prepared children for future work. Since schooling was conceived as preparation for work, schoolmen turned to factory efficiency studies and models to organize the schools.[52]

Scientific management in industry differentiated production further and schools followed suit by differentiating courses. This led to a new concept of equal opportunity. This new concept, developed to resolve the conflict between equality and efficiency, was the "opportunity for all to receive such education as will fit them *equally well* for their particular life work."[53] Thus, as the differentiation of schooling spread, the notion of equal school achievement for equal ability emerged.

Once this system of "equal opportunity" was implemented, its success could be measured by the number of pupils who were kept in school, and how well the schools trained people for available jobs. The incorporation of vocational training into the high schools alongside academic and business courses during and after World War I was the triumph of the comprehensive high school.

We mention, this reform again because it so closely parallels developed country solutions to educational development problems. With the types of efficiency reforms recommended by developed-country agencies—reforms almost identical to those in the United States fifty years ago—the social structure will be *maintained,* and students from poorer families are highly likely to continue to form the lowest rungs in the social hierarchy. Furthermore, if we consider that with AID, World Bank, or foundation financing, schools in the nonindustrialized countries will continue to be hooked into industrial country norms of "excellence"—particularly through the close ties between industrial/nonindustrial economies—graduates of the highest levels of education in the nonindustrial countries will still have less access to resources and less chance for economic success than university graduates in the metropole centers. The social structure *among* nations will also be maintained with developed country-promoted efficiency reforms.

As an important side effect, the multinational corporations and other foreign investors use foreign, vocationally trained labor to compete—as a docile labor force—with U.S. workers, keeping U.S. wages from rising as rapidly as they might without the expansion of schooling abroad. This is completely analogous to the training of black workers in the South in order to fight labor in the North. Although there is little data available on the role of U.S. companies abroad in training skilled labor, it seems that the role of the World Bank in secondary schooling and in vocational training—all in the name of making growth rates abroad more rapid—fits well into the pattern of multinationals moving their production abroad wherever pools of skilled workers are found. In most cases, managers are imported from the United States or Europe, so local workers never learn the necessary skills to run the firm by themselves. This international division of labor was created by the industrial countries themselves, and is part of their ideological thrust into the Third World.

Notes

1. See Bruce Nissen, "The World Bank, A Political Institution," *Pacific Research and World Empire Telegram* 2, no. 6 (September–October 1971).

2. See Gabriel Kolko, *The Triumph of Conservatism* (Glencoe, Ill.: Free Press, 1963).

3. Harry Magdoff, *The Age of Imperialism* (New York: Monthly Review, 1969), p. 45.

4. A Memorandum written in 1944 makes clear the effect of the war on Latin American industry: "Development of production in the other Americas, as in the United States, almost entirely has been for war or essential civilian purposes since Pearl Harbor. The growth of new industries and improvement of transportation which were going on in Latin America prior to Pearl Harbor in large measure were slowed or postponed as it became more difficult, if not impossible, to obtain many types of equipment and industrial materials when United States capacity was diverted to war production. Nevertheless, there has gone forward in various lines substantial development for war needs. This includes the extension of air transport, the building of strategic highways, improvement of health and sanitation services and the expansion of essential civilian industry in neighboring countries" (John C. McClintock, "Inter-American Cooperation in Economic Development," Inter-American Affairs Office, 1944).

5. By the late 1950s and early 1960s, with the postwar redevelopment of Europe and Japan, a substruggle for world markets began again among the capitalist countries.

6. The most famous cases of this type of action are the Congo (now Zaire), Vietnam, and Guyana.

7. W. W. Rostow, *The Stages of Economic Growth* (New York: Cambridge University Press, 1970).

8. For an account of U.S. direct intervention in other countries, see Richard Barnet, *Intervention and Revolution* (New York: World Publishing, 1968).

9. Magdoff, *Age of Imperialism*. We discussed the nature of postwar imperialism in chapter 2. For a description of police training expenditures in Latin America, see North American Congress in Latin America (NACLA), "U.S. Police Assistance Programs in Latin America," *Newsletter*, May–June 1970.

10. See, for example, Teresa Hayter, *Aid as Imperialism* (London:Penguin, 1971).

11. Magdoff, *Age of Imperialism*, p. 44. On the link between multinational corporations and U.S. foreign aid, see Steve Weissman, "Foreign Aid: Who Needs It?" *Pacific Research and World Empire Telegram* 3, no. 4 (June 1972).

12. For the reader who doubts that some U.S. policy makers still see educational assistance as a means to keep underdeveloped countries from going "communist," see William Y. Elliot, ed., *Education and Training in the Developing Countries* (New York: Praeger, 1966).

"In retrospect, it is clear that our first efforts were too much shaped by expecting miracles from reliance on 'economism' where they should first have been directed toward bolstering groups who could rule these countries and rule them effectively, developing the bases for later constitutionalism, while keeping them from falling into the Communist trap. In other words, our first effort should have been, and can still be, one of education: real education that trains those political leaders and their civil servants and technicians and supporters who can keep their country on the road to stable freedom" (William Elliot, "The Road to Self-Help," in ibid., p. 5).

13. AID, the World Bank (IBRD), U.S. nonprofit foundations such as Ford and Rockefeller, and the governments of Great Britain and France are now by far the largest donors of educational assistance. AID gave an average of $85 million annually in the late 1960s; IBRD, about $50 million annually, and the Ford Foundation, about $40 million. UNESCO, an agency usually identified with educational assistance, has more limited funds and mainly provides technical aid. Its influence is important, but it has much less leverage on host country policies than do the major donors of financial aid.

14. Hayter, *Aid as Imperialism*.

15. Frank Bowles, "American Responsibilities in International Education," *The Educational Record* 45, no. 1, (Winter 1964): 19–20. Bowles was education program director of the Ford Foundation.

16. See J. F. Ajayi, *Christian Missions in Nigeria, 1841–1891* (Evanston: Northwestern University Press, 1965).

17. Jerry Beardsley, "When God and Man Left Yale" (School of Education, Stanford University, December 1971), pp. 13–15. Mimeographed.

18. Ibid., p. 17.

19. Bowles, "American Responsibilities," p. 20.

20. Office of the Coordinator of Inter-American Affairs, "Summary of Activities," 11 January 1943, p. 1.

21. Cordell Hull, quoted in McClintock, "Inter-American Cooperation," p. 4.

22. Ibid., pp. 4–5.

23. Office of the Coordinator of Inter-American Affairs, "Summary," p. 8.

24. See, for example, Theodore W. Schultz, "Investment in Human Capital," *American Economic Review* 51 (March 1961).

25. The North American Congress on Latin America (NACLA) stresses the second of these demands—corporate needs:

"Aside from this general indirect subsidy, specific foreign aid programs and other government agencies socialize the direct and indirect operating costs of the corporations, transferring those costs to the public sector, by:

"(1) setting up programs and institutions—within and outside universities—to train managerial personnel, skilled labor and other manpower needed by local branch plants of the multinational corporations. . . .

"(2) subsidizing university and non-university research projects, both in Latin America and the United States, directed chiefly toward specialized technological and scientific problems of the corporations. . . .

"Most important, foreign aid facilitates long-range corporate planning and minimizes the risks of long-range overseas investment by . . . further stabilizing the local investment climate through such measures as :

". . . structural and curriculum reforms in the Latin American universities, designed to change prevailing (leftist) political orientations, under the guise of 'depoliticizing,' 'professionalizing' the universities. Thus, foreign corporations are assured of well-trained, upwardly mobile and ideologically compatible elites and technicians who hope to use foreign interests to advance their own careers, and who do not see their interests as inherently conflicting with those of foreign investors" (NACLA, *Yanqui Dollar* [New York: NACLA, 1971], pp. 45–46, 48–49).

26. For the period 1910–59 see Gabriel Kolko, *Wealth and Power in America* (New York: Praeger, 1962), Chapter 1. For the period 1944–63 and a different measure of income inequality (Gini coefficients), see T. P. Schultz, "Secular Trends and Cyclical Behavior of Income Distribution in the United States, 1944–65." In *Six Papers on the Size Distribution of Wealth and Income,* ed. Lee Soltow (New York: Columbia University Press, 1969). For the decade of the 1960s, see Peter Henle, "Exploring the Distribution of Earned Income," *Monthly Labor Review* 95, no. 2 (December 1972): 16–27.

27. For example, the Gini coefficient of income distribution (the Gini coefficient is the ratio of the area above the Lorenz curve of income distribution to the triangle of perfect income equality—a Gini coefficient of zero represents perfect equality, while a Gini equal to 1.0 is perfect inequality)

in the United States in 1965 was about 0.35 as compared to 0.45 in West Germany (1964), 0.37 in Norway (1963), and 0.32 in England (1966). See R. Hollister, "The Relation Between Education and the Distribution of Income: Some Forays" (University of Wisconsin, 1970). Mimeographed.

28. We consider 1951–53 and 1965–68 as war years.

29. Harry Magdoff and Paul Sweezy, "Economic Stagnation and the Stagnation of Economics," *Monthly Review* 22, no. 2 (April 1971): 1–11.

30. Banco Nacional de Mexico, Annual Report, 1970.

31. Secretariat of the Organization of American States, General Secretariat, *Employment and Growth in the Strategy of Latin American Development: Implications for the Seventies* (Seventh Annual Meeting of the Inter-American Economic and Social Council [CIES], Panama, September 10–20, 1971, p. 1.

32. M. Mehta, "Industrialization and Employment with Special Reference to Countries of ECAFE Region," Bangkok, Asian Institute for Economic Development and Planning, 1968, pp. 24–25. For African data on unemployment of graduates, see Archibald Callaway, "School Leavers in Nigeria," *West Africa* (March 25, April 1, April 8, and April 15, 1961), pp. 325, 353, 371–72, and 409, respectively.

33. Unemployment is really an *invention* of capitalism. In traditional economies, all members of the community are employed. If there is less work, all members share the decreased work in some fashion. In socialist societies there is also full employment, by definition. Wages may be low and occupational hierarchies still present, but there is work for everyone. In capitalist society the jobs available are determined by the amount of physical capital and land in the economy, and the wages of labor. But even if wages are low, employers may find that capital intensive techniques of production result in lower costs than substituting labor for capital. Employers may also prefer capital to labor because capital doesn't strike or get sick.

Postwar development is characterized by importation of foreign techniques of production which are more capital intensive than local wage rates would deem efficient in the short run, but which in the long run may pay off to the capitalist because of economies of scale and wage-rate legislation.

34. For a review of some of the earlier literature on this issue, see Mark Blaug, *An Introduction to the Economics of Education* (London: Penguin Press, 1970), chap. 1. For a later piece, see Zvi Griliches and William Mason, "Education, Income, and Ability," *Journal of Political Economy* 80, pt. 2 (May/June 1972): S74–S103.

35. See Herb Gintis, "Education and the Characteristics of Worker Productivity," *American Economic Review* 61 (May 1971): 266–79; and Robert

Dreeben, *On What Is Learned in School* (Reading, Mass: Addison-Wesley, 1968).

36. Samuel Bowles, "Unequal Education and the Reproduction of the Social Division of Labor," in *Schooling in a Corporate Society*, ed. Martin Carnoy (New York: David McKay, 1972).

37. We assume that the high earnings positions in a society can be identified with university education (the highest income is, however, associated with physical capital ownership). In the United States, less than 25% of those white males 25–34 years old in 1962 with *fathers* who had less than completed high school had attended college, while about 80% attended college of those white males whose fathers had some college. This, of course, does not distinguish between the kind of colleges attended, nor the number of years attended, both of which would favor the higher class children. See Martin Carnoy, "Notes on the Macrotheory of Education and Politics: A Political Economy Approach" (Stanford University, School of Education, 1973). Mimeographed. See also table 13, above.

In other countries, the case is even clearer. In Kenya, for example, income of family is the single most important factor determining who goes on to secondary schools. In a sample of Kenyan primary students, Mwaniki could not find any low-family-income students in high-cost primary schools. Dinguri Mwaniki, "Education and Socioeconomic Development in Kenya: A Study of the Distribution of Resources for Education" (Ph.D. dissertation, Stanford University, School of Education, 1973).

In Puerto Rico in 1960, about 55% of those admitted to the main (Rio Piedras) campus of the University of Puerto Rico came from families where the father was professional/higher-white-collar, retail proprietor, or farm-owner-manager. Approximately 14% had lower white-collar-worker fathers, while only about 25% came from manual-worker families and 1% from farm-labor families. Leila Sussman, "Democratization and Class Segregation in Puerto Rican Schooling: The U.S. Model Transplanted," in *Education and Development*, ed. Thomas La Belle (UCLA Latin American Center, 1972). Again, this does not include success rates in college, which are much higher for the higher class groups.

38. See Hollister, "Education and Distribution of Income."

39. D. Barkin, "Acceso a la educación superior y beneficios que reporta en Mexico," *Revista del Centro de Estudios Educativos* (Mexico) 1, no. 3 (1971): 47–74: A. Fishlow, "Brazilian Size Distribution of Income," University of California, Berkeley, 1972 (mimeographed); and Barry Chiswick and Jacob Mincer, "Time Series Changes in Personal Income Inequality in the United

States from 1939, with Projections to 1985," *Journal of Political Economy* 80, no. 3, pt. 2 (May/June 1972): S34–S66.

40. Barkin, "Acesso a la educción."

41. Ivan Illich, *The Celebration of Awareness* (Garden City, N.Y.: Doubleday, 1970) p. 165.

42. As the average level of education increases, there is usually an increased proportion of pupils in secondary and higher education, which is much more costly than primary. In addition, all costs of education are rising. See Philip Coombs, *The World Educational Crisis* (New York: Oxford University Press, 1968), pp. 48–54.

43. Indeed, in many underdeveloped countries, teachers form a substantial fraction of university graduates. A rapidly expanding educational sector is usually the most important employer of university and higher secondary school graduates. H. Thias and M. Carnoy, *Cost-Benefit Analysis in Education: A Case Study of Kenya* (Washington, IBRD and Johns Hopkins, 1972), chapter 5.

44. Philip Foster, in Lewis Brownstein, *Education and Development in Rural Kenya* (New York: Praeger, 1972), pp. x–xi.

45. When a whole society devotes itself to self-sufficient agriculture, such as Tanzania, Cuba, or China, and working in rural areas is glorified rather than deprecated, then the value of agricultural training increases. But this requires a change in the social structure which places elite cadres in rural situations. People's status consciousness does not necessarily change, but the status structure does. In that case, rural vocational education may replace academic training as the most prestigious course to follow.

46. Philip Foster, "The Vocational School Fallacy in Development Planning," in *Education and Economic Development*, ed. A. Anderson and M. J. Bowman (Chicago: Aldine, 1965), pp. 145–46.

47. See Coombs, *World Educational Crisis*, for a prime example of this type of analysis.

48. See Michael Katz, *Class, Bureaucracy, and Schools* (New York: Praeger, 1971), and *The Irony of Early School Reform* (Boston: Beacon Press, 1970).

49. See Coombs, *World Educational Crisis*, chap. 6, and *Partners in Development* (Report of the Pearson Commission).

50. In reality, it is extremely difficult for societies today to duplicate the process of change which took place in the industrial countries in another historical period. Those countries grew as a result of a dominance of world

trade through their technological advancement and military power, in addition to their well-developed internal markets.

51. S. Bowles and H. Gintis, "IQ in the U.S. Class Structure," *Social Policy* (January/February 1973): 7.

52. Joel Spring, "Education and the Corporate State," *Socialist Revolution* 2, no. 2 (March/April 1972): 80–81.

53. See chapter 5, note 31.

8

WHAT IS TO BE DONE?

Our understanding of history influences the way we try to achieve social change. Western historians and social scientists have accustomed us to a particular interpretation of history: it is *ideas* that mold the actions of men and women.[1] Educational history is written with philosophers as the driving force behind educational change. The study of that change is, therefore, the study of changes in *ideas* about education and of the *individuals* who came up with these ideas.

This interpretation has important implications for social action: it tells us that in order to change institutions, or even the social order, all we have to do is produce "good" ideas. Thus, the individual has the power to appeal to a rational social order with rational thought and affect change. In the case of educational history, the interpretation goes even further: it implies that schooling as a producer of creativity is a causal factor—the starting point—for economic and social change, and that therefore the educational philosopher is instrumental in those changes.

342

The present study rejects this view of history. We argue that even though changes in educational philosophy had influence on educational reform, in practice the philosophies that were most influential were those consistent with economic and social changes taking place at the same time. We argue that the way society organizes formal schooling is a function of the economic and social hierarchy and cannot be separated from it. We contend that the schools function to reinforce the social relations in production, and that no school reform can be separated from the effect it will have on the hierarchical relations in the society.

This approach would judge the schools not in terms of themselves but in terms of society's economic and social institutions and the way each social group fits into these institutions. For example, many educators have observed that inner-city schools are prisonlike and oppressive, and teach black and other poor children in ways which have little to do with their reality and are irrelevant to their interests. We argue that any analysis that treats these as *school system problems alone* is incorrect. The inner-city school is a manifestation of black people's role in the advanced capitalist, racist U.S. economy. Even if the economy were not racist, the lowest social classes would attend schools which are different in operation and purpose than those for middle- and upper-class children.[2] The *why* of school structure, therefore, depends on a description of the economic and social relations among individuals. The success of educational reforms, in turn, depend on the relation of those reforms to change in the economic and social structures.

Thus, the analysis of the larger system of economic and social organization is crucial to understanding the schools. But what is the analysis of that system? Orthodox economic theory is based on an individualistic view of society, in which societal *structures* are analyzed from the standpoint of their *efficiency* in maximizing *individual* welfare. The analysis derives its description of societal change from marginal changes in the "average" individual's condition.

From this it is an easy step to understanding why educational expansion has been associated so categorically with societal improvement. First, as we observed in chapter 1, orthodox economic theory

assumes that capitalist economic organization, particularly the productive hierarchy based on property ownership, is an optimum
relationship among individuals. The social relations of production
reach an optimum when a society becomes highly capitalistic. Mass
schooling as a means of organizing the ignorant and uncivilized to
support the capitalist system by accepting their low-status roles in it, is,
in *that* analysis, a positive function of schooling.

Second, we observe that individuals who go to school have higher
incomes and occupational status than those who do not. Orthodox
analysis concludes that expanding schooling increases individual
welfare and thus makes the society better-off. Since the neoclassicists
assume that all individuals have an "equal" chance to have high or low
schooling and incomes in a capitalist economy—income is based on
ability rather than status at birth—the issues of *who* gets income and
schooling, the issue of social class, and of who makes decisions in the
society are, by definition, irrelevant. In practice, of course, the
neoclassical economics and its sociological and political science
counterparts are biased toward European bourgeois values and tastes,
and assumes that it is *that culture* and the propertied class who should
define and control world social change. Again, based on that belief, the
expansion of schooling oriented toward European bourgeois values and
norms denotes societal progress.

Our analysis of the economic system rejects these assumptions. We
reject the notion that even idealized capitalist relations in production
are socially optimal. We do not assume that in capitalist economies
everyone has an equal chance to take schooling or to work at various
occupations, nor that everyone has political power even in a
"democracy." Instead, we assume that capitalism destroys the feudal
class structure and replaces it with new social classes. These classes are
based on acquired property ownership and the production of goods
rather than inherited title, land, and the serfs to work the land. We
argue that formal schooling is an important component of the
capitalist system, primarily as an *allocator* of social roles, and only
secondarily as a transmitter of cognitive knowledge. We identify a
ruling class in capitalist societies, just as capitalist economists and
philosophers found it simple to identify the ruling class in feudal

societies. The most economically and politically powerful in capitalist societies are those who own the most capital, plus those, as in feudal societies, who control the military and the state apparatus. Like any other group in a position of power, the ruling class attempts to perpetuate its control of the economy from generation to generation. Since schooling is defined by the ruling class as a source of status, they attempt to control the structure of schooling and to ensure that it allows their children to reach its highest levels. But just as important, schooling legitimizes the myth of capitalist "meritocracy." Since schooling is a visible allocator of social roles, success in school becomes one way to reach higher social status (ownership of real property is the other). Success or failure in school is made an *individual responsibility:* if a child does not do well, it is his or her *individual* fault, not the obvious fact that the opportunity of one social class to succeed is actually less than another. This individualization of responsibility diffuses class identity and interclass hostility. Like the family and church in feudal society, the school in capitalist societies reinforces acceptance of differential roles in the economy and society as a "just" and "correct" way of organizing human relations.

Becoming a blue-collar worker—the society argues—is not based on one's family's working-class status but on lower "ability" as defined by the school. It is not class origins that bring an individual to where he is in the social structure, but his own inability to do well in school. But parents' social class is a much better explainer than IQ of both the occupational status of a person and his or her income.[3] The relationship is particularly strong if we include race as part of social class. Thus, even if we equalize IQ among different class groups graduating from high school, this will not equalize incomes of occupation among graduates. IQ—or cognitive ability—is not the key outcome of schooling in determining future social role. The most obvious confirmation of this statement is the case of women. Women get approximately the same scores on high school aptitude tests as men; yet, women with the same amount of schooling and the same cognitive ability get into much lower status occupations than men on the average and receive much lower incomes. Similarly, equalizing test scores for lower-class white or black students to those of higher-class students will not equalize the behavior patterns—the noncognitive preparation—of those different groups of students. Nor will it change the perceptions that poor students have of society's view of them, nor will it change the desired occupations of people who feel incapable of achieving high status and income.

The class structure of capitalist economic institutions is, therefore, reflected in a class system of education—a point ignored by orthodox economists and capitalist educational philosophers because, for them, capitalism provides equal opportunity for all, if it can only be made to work properly. The class system of education provides a vehicle for one class to "civilize" others and to ensure that society remains orderly and safe and that the ruling class stays at the top of the social ladder and retains political power.

If we accept this alternative analysis of the economic and political structure and the role schooling plays in it, we must reject the hypothesis that formal schooling in a capitalist economy can develop everyone to his or her full potential as well as the hypothesis that expanding schooling in and of itself increases social welfare. Instead, like the capitalist organization of production, schooling is an institution that maximizes the welfare of a small group and leaves everyone else in a less-than-optimal position; one of the most important functions of schooling is to convince individuals that their economic and social position is the best they can do.

Thus, we reach the conclusion that, for a relatively small group, capitalism and schooling serve individual needs and allow a wide range of choice in the type of work and life the individual pursues. Those in this small group feel a genuine sense of self-fulfillment and accomplishment, they like the kind of work they do, and they have the security of social position and accumulated wealth. But for the large majority, schooling in a hierarchical society is required to *limit* individual choice by *defining* well-specified and uncreative roles in the social and economic hierarchy. Schooling defines people's potential for them on the basis of the hierarchy's needs, not their own. Schooling for a hierarchical structure is therefore a colonizing device which sometimes changes the *kind* of choices people have, but still serves to limit control over their own lives.

What Does the Historical Analysis Tell Us about Schooling?

Most of this study focuses on historical examples. We want to show that changes in the nature of schooling were the result of significant changes in economic structures, *and* that these changes did not originate from the masses, but from a relatively small ruling group *in response to its own needs*. School-system reforms, including expansion, were instituted when the elite with economic and political power found such reform consistent not only with a hierarchical view of societal organization, but a hierarchy that kept them at the top. Even when reforms were a response to an implied threat of social disorder, they were applied in a way that left the operation of the school system and its benefits in the hands of the ruling group. Under certain conditions, the ruling group was domestic and independent; under others, it was foreign; and under yet other conditions, it was dependent on foreign ruling groups for its wealth and position of power. In the latter case, the domestic elite mediated local conflicts and instituted local school reforms based on its economic and social relations with industrialized countries.

Schooling expanded most rapidly when the ruling class invested in industries, such as in the United States and southern Brazil. Industrialization increased the need both for a differentiated labor force and for social control. Schooling served both these objectives: it produced the noncognitive skills necessary to function in the new structure of production (responsiveness to increased economic rewards, punctuality, a proper mixture of self-discipline, docility, and initiative corresponding to occupational level in the hierarchy) and it legitimized the capitalist class structure. In both the United States and southern Brazil (and after World War I, in India as well), schooling expanded to meet the needs of industrialists. Its form and content was reformed to be based on people's function in a capitalist hierarchy. But Brazilian schooling is only recently being reformed in the same way as U.S. schools were fifty years ago. Since the Brazilian economy, including her industrialization, took place within a dependency relation with the United States and Europe, it was constrained by that relationship. Likewise, the school system reflected the needs of a limited industrialization and the continued power of the plantation owners and the church in the dependent economy.

In summary, the historical evidence shows that schooling expanded in the context of imperial and colonial relations between and within what are now national states. In the mercantile period of imperialism, schooling was largely limited to consumption by children of the well-to-do merchants and some nobility. Universities provided the few professionals, philosophers, and religious thinkers required by precapitalist societies. Since the European precapitalist social structure was organized mostly on the basis of family position and landownership, and almost everyone lived in cohesive villages, institutions like the church were adequate for social control. Training was achieved by apprenticeships. But even in the mercantile period, schooling was used by the church and state to provide moral guidance to the unruly poor in the metropole urban centers, and to try to convert natives in the colonies to Western values and norms. As the Indian, Brazilian, and Peruvian cases illustrate, formal schooling was used to pacify natives, either directly as in the Jesuit *reducciones*, or indirectly, by providing special education for native elites which would make them intermediaries between the colonizers and the indigenous masses. In both cases, the purpose of this pacification was to allow the colonizers to exploit the colonized by conducting trade on grounds favorable to the colonizer, by extracting direct taxes from the indigenous population, or by getting cheap (often slave) labor to work mines and plantations.

With the rise of capitalism in Europe and then the United States, schooling became an important socializing and training institution, and an allocator of social roles. It gradually replaced the church and community as the most important nonfamily institution for legitimizing the perpetuation of the social structure from generation to generation, and transmitting the rules and regulations of the social contract. As capitalism spread, primarily through English merchants and the English Navy, Western schooling was used to bring people into extensions of the British economy, usually at low levels of what had become a worldwide capitalist hierarchy.

One of the main purposes of this study is to show how schooling expanded differently under different conditions of imperialism. We find that under *direct* colonialism, or the occupation of one country by another, industrialization was thwarted to prevent competition with the colonizer economy. Schooling was primarily for "civilizing" and governing the conquered people. Thus, it was limited to a relatively small percentage of natives.

Where economic exploitation was *indirect,* through a European intermediary group, metropole controls over domestic economic policy were not as tight. In eventually trying to develop in the European model, local elites often imported European educational reforms and even began investing in manufacturing, which stimulated the rise of domestic capitalism and therefore the expansion of schooling. Those nations, like the United States, which became economically independent of the European metropole, industrialized to a much greater extent than any export-dependent, free trading partner of Britain. But even though in both the United States and Britain, schooling expanded more rapidly than in the dependent, free trade colonies, or the directly controlled parts of the British Empire, schooling in the industrialized economies was used to colonize working people within the country to fit into roles needed by the industrialists, and into a hierarchy which they dominated.

The Case Studies

As England exercised her industrial power, mercantile imperialism was gradually replaced by capitalist, or free-trade imperialism. Yet, even with the advent of capitalism in Britain, she retained her mercantile colony in India, destroying whatever industry that precapitalist economy had, and treated India as a plantation extension of Britain's own economy. It was capitalist, not mercantile, imperialism that made India into a plantation economy so that it could not compete with British manufacturing. Schooling was reformed to develop an Indian bureaucracy. This bureaucracy was the intermediary between the mass of Indians and the British administrators. The schools were available for only a small percentage of young Indians, and those who went on to secondary schools and universities were turned into loyal British subjects, speaking English and learning to conduct themselves in a manner befitting a British civil servant. British economic and administrative policy at this time demonstrated clearly that the Lancashire textile producers were in the colonial driver's seat and were not at all interested in *Indian* development. Even British colonial administrators, who were somewhat more sympathetic to raising tariffs for increased local revenues, wanted to expand schooling primarily for increased *social control,* especially after the Indian Mutiny of 1857. When education finally did expand after the First World War, the expansion was defined by pro-Western educators, British and Indian, and was designed to develop larger numbers of anglicized Indians.

With industrialization, Britain also began to explore Africa. In our analysis of West African education, we show how the early missionaries essentially *failed* to bring capitalism to Africa through schooling. The period between 1800 and 1870 in Africa was an experiment with the capitalistic ideal: to the British bourgeoisie, capitalism was so inherently logical and perfect that it was only necessary to introduce it into another culture to have it accepted. They believed that both Britain and the other economy would profit from this relationship. But Britain had difficulty ending the slave trade, which it had been so active in promoting only a few years before, and the "legitimate" trade did not flourish. Many African groups were hostile to the European trader and missionary.

When the British annexed Cape Colony (Gold Coast) and Lagos (Nigeria), the experiment was over. Competition between France and Britain promoted almost total European occupation of West Africa by 1904. After that occupation was complete, education in British areas expanded on much the same basis as in India: Primary schooling was decentralized, on the philosophy that schooling was largely an individual choice in plantation economies, needed primarily to maintain social control while inducing a certain amount of social change. Secondary schooling was limited in Africa to a few higher schools in urban areas, designed to produce a bureaucratic subelite. As in India, it was this subelite that generated the nationalist bourgeoisie.

In both British and French colonies in Africa economic change and therefore educational reform were directly controlled by European administrators and legislators. Native groups were one of many constituencies whose views on education were taken into account. But native groups had little power until they began to form a direct threat to European interests. Furthermore, colonization was successful enough that urban natives, most in contact with the European, eventually took European values and styles as their ideal. Although Europeans had difficulty imposing European capitalism in Africa because of African resistance, once this resistance collapsed under European military power, schooling and other institutions were very successful in helping Africans want to emulate Europeans, including turning African economies into appendages of industrial countries.

In Latin America, free-trade imperialism was much more successful for Britain, because a Europeanized elite, some of it eager to adopt capitalist philosophy, already existed *before* British merchants moved in. Latin American countries emerged from the mercantile relations with Spain and Portugal as plantation economies that could trade only with their colonizer metropole; they traded *that* dependency for free-trade dependency under Britain and the United States. The ruling group in Latin America became free-trade middlemen—plantation owners and merchants. Schooling hardly changed in this transition, since, in fact, the economic and social structure did not change. Indigenous populations and slaves were the plantation and mining labor force before and after independence.

The existence of a European elite served the industrial countries well in Latin America, but by working through it, Britain and the United States gave away direct control over Latin American economic conditions. For all intent and purposes, maintaining direct control was not an important factor in the British–Latin American or U.S.–Latin American trade, since domestic Latin American ruling elites were not about to pull out of the international system. *But they did have choices of how to maximize their well-being which were not available to Africans and Indians.* These local elites looked to Europe for models, so it was not unnatural that when faced by internal struggles and changes in economic structures, they should rely on expanding formal schooling for social order and control.

Brazil's period of educational expansion began with the triumph of an elite group committed to protectionist industrialization within the export-trade/foreign-investment dependency framework. In this same period, millions of immigrants came to Brazil, first to work in agriculture, then migrating to the cities. Schooling was used in part to incorporate (civilize) immigrant groups into the Brazilian economic structure and in part to train an industrial work force.

In Peru, schooling expanded without industrialization, almost purely as a mechanism of social control in a period of potential conflict which would have been disastrous for the ruling class. Peru's elite looked to schooling to incorporate indigenous population into the lowest level of the occupational structure and to preserve the dependent capitalist system.

In both Brazil and Peru, the ruling class expanded public primary education while keeping secondary and higher education reserved for a limited number of higher-social-class children. Both were economies dominated before 1940 by plantation raw-material production, despite some industrialization in Brazil beginning at the end of the nineteenth century. Even the expansion of public primary schooling was therefore limited. In the plantation sector, schooling was avoided by the ruling class in favor of more direct methods of control. It was primarily in the cities and towns, undergoing important structural changes, and particularly in industrializing areas, that schooling was provided by the public sector.

The local ruling elite not only looked to schooling as a European solution to problems of domestic conflict, but also as a way of making their countries safe and attractive for foreign investment. A century ago, the Peruvian bourgeoisie reasoned that if they civilized the Peruvian Indian, their "modernized" country would bring Europeans to invest and develop Peru's resources. We do not have such strong evidence that this was the attitude in Brazil, but educational expansion and foreign investment in manufacturing went hand in hand—enough so as to make us believe that the Brazilian bourgeoisie was also interested in attracting foreign capital partly through educational expansion, although the main purpose of more education in Brazil was apparently industrialization.

The Latin American elite wanted to provide the conditions whereby *its* income would increase. They envisioned that with the expansion of investment (domestic and foreign), the economic surplus would increase and they would profit. Public education became a mechanism to achieve this end. Simultaneously, the educational system was so structured that the social classes remained intact. Schooling control was centralized even at the primary level (although financing was partly decentralized), and was completely copied after European curriculum and organization. This was not a result of the *failure* by the domestic ruling class to develop an internal market or an indigenously oriented culture. Rather they were *successful* at maximizing their income, wealth, and power through *maintaining* a dependency relation with Europe and imposing an educational system which was designed to *limit* access to the export surplus. Developing internal markets and relying on domestic investment as an alternative policy would have required rapid and undesirable changes in the social and economic structures.

The northern United States already had an internal market at the end of the eighteenth century. Industrialization in the early nineteenth century soon led to a societal crisis: the dissolution of the family/village unit and Irish immigration into urban areas of the Northeast threatened uncontrollable crime and a breakdown of social order. The new industries also needed labor socialized to work in the factory system. Early school reform in Massachusetts and then other northern states attempted to meet these needs by centralizing control over schools in the hands of professional educators who shared the interest of urban merchants and manufacturers in the industrialization of America. The revisionist interpretation of American public education which we summarize in our analysis shows that schooling was used to *control* social change in a way that maintained the social-class structure. The schools were supposed to make orderly and decent people out of the poor, and prepare the more able of them for skilled factory work. Although the early reformers such as Horace Mann probably believed that everybody had an equal chance to succeed in school, in practice the schools guaranteed differential access by using grades and entrance examinations to determine who got into higher levels. Lower-class children—even those who attended primary school—were highly underrepresented in public high schools.

When the high schools expanded later in the century because of the increased output of the primary schools and the increased complexity of industry, new reforms were needed to prepare a more highly differentiated labor force. The second set of U.S. school reforms developed tracking and counseling systems within the comprehensive high school based on future career roles. The concept of equal opportunity implicit in the earlier reforms was forsaken by the second reform in favor of equal opportunity for everybody of *equal ability.* Student ability and vocational aptitude testing at every level became an integral part of schooling. Not surprisingly, schooling reformed in this way maintained the class structure, since, on the average, children from lower-social-class families had vocational "aptitudes" highly related to those of their parents.

At the same time, non-Caucasian minorities in the United States did not even get the ambiguous benefit of being fit into the expanding economy. Our analysis makes clear why this was so: industrialists' labor needs were being met out of immigrant labor until the end of World War I. All but a few liberals considered blacks, Chicanos, and Native American Indians unsuitable and undesirable for incorporation. It is true that there were special schools for both blacks and Indians even at the college level. But these were limited to relatively few of their race and were *trade schools,* which taught them how to be skilled at tasks occupied by whites with much less (or no) schooling. There was no way more than a few token members of each of these groups could participate in the white-dominated society. Those who did participate usually became intermediaries who wittingly or unwittingly served to oppress their own people. Internal colonialism in the United States was/is analogous to the direct colonialism in India, and, later, in Africa and Asia. The majority whites (in India, the minority) had *direct* control over the lives and aspirations of minority groups, through military power and economic domination. More successfully even than the British in India and Africa, and as successfully as the French in Africa, U.S. educators were able to impose low-level vocational education on U.S. minority groups.

Only when the European migration was halted out of fear of imported anarchism and communism did significant members of these minorities begin getting into the lowest rungs of the urban occupational structure. They became the newest wave of "immigrants" into urban areas, and were schooled to fit that role. But, unlike previous waves, they were faced by racial, in addition to class discrimination. Not only did they get the worst jobs, but they also got lower pay than whites doing the same work. Nevertheless, like previous immigrant groups, they in general believed that through schooling they would be assimilated and, as individuals and a group, would succeed in the white man's world.

Thus, our historical analysis shows that there is a class bias in the educational system, a bias derived from the class structure in the economy. The educational system reflects the relation between different social classes, and changes and reforms in a particular school system reflect the changes being effected or desired by the group in power. The fact that the ruling class controls the schools does not lead necessarily or even logically to benefits for those whom they dominate. The analysis shows that in India, West Africa, Brazil, Peru, and the United States, under very different conditions, schooling attempted to keep under control social situations which could have turned radically against the interests of the ruling domestic and/or foreign bourgeoisie.

When it was useful for the ruling class to reform the school system, it did so, but always with its own interests in mind. Foremost in these interests was the rationalization by the schools of the perpetuation of a hierarchy in which the group in power remained at the pinnacle of the hierarchy, and in which the least powerful and/or least threatening groups remained at the bottom. The composition of enrollment in schools, the grading system, the selection process for higher levels of schooling, all guaranteed that the "right" people would succeed in a system based on "merit" and "equal opportunity."

Since schooling was and is organized to maximize gains to the ruling class, we conclude that even *within* the capitalist system, the organization of schooling by dominated groups would have been different from the organization provided by the ruling class. But the mass of people were and are colonized by other societal institutions, such as the work place, and by the very structure of knowledge. Therefore, the changes they demanded in schooling were limited and distorted by the greater reality. Both conclusions are illustrated by our case studies. In the United States, Catholic immigrants transmitted different values and norms in their own schools from those in the centralized public schools run by city business interests. Yet, immigrants wanted to move up in the structures run by these same interests, so Catholic schools deviated largely in cultural ideas and ethnic identity, not in questioning the role of the worker in a capitalist economy. Nevertheless, even this cultural identity poses a threat to the ruling class, who see in ethnic heterogeneity the possibility of diverse values and independent interpretations of what the societal structure should be. Similarly, Africans exerted some influence over what schools taught in the relatively decentralized school systems of British Africa. Their demands on schooling were toward more academic subjects, however, better suited to making them like their European colonizers.

Current Educational Change in Light of the Historical Analysis

School Reform   Our historical interpretation argues that reforms initiated by a capitalist ruling group—even as a response to their perception of mass "needs"—primarily served the capitalists themselves. In today's world, education has taken an even more important role in government policy than it did in the past. Can the past tell us anything about the prospects of educational reform today?

There are two kinds of ruling-class educational reforms: those the ruling group initiates to change society in ways that will benefit it; and those reforms developed by the elite in response to demands by other groups. It is important to differentiate these reforms because they represent two different kinds of action. In the first, the ruling class has a vision of society which it attempts to achieve in part through schooling. The British attempted to "change" Africans into "civilized" traders, so that West Africa would become profitable for British merchants looking for new markets and so that slave trading would end. The British defined the African's new roles, just as the European slave trade helped define his role in the three hundred years between

1500 and 1800. Schooling was one of the tools by which the British hoped to convert Africans into the new mold. Similarly, the Peruvian government wanted through schooling to assimilate Indians into the lowest levels of a "new" Peruvian society, one that would appear civilized to Europe and attract foreign investment. The early U.S. reform, begun in Massachusetts by Horace Mann, was also designed to incorporate the masses (artisans, small farmers, and immigrants) into a new economic structure controlled by the Massachusetts bourgeoisie through professional educators. In every case, then, educational reforms initiated by a ruling class, either domestic or foreign, attempted to use schooling for its own ends, on the assumption that however it wanted to organize society was good for everyone.

In the Massachusetts case, we have strong evidence that the top-down reforms were resisted by the working class on the very rational grounds that they would be beneficial primarily to the rich, not to working people. In the other reforms we examined, we do not have such evidence, but we show that the reformed school systems were highly class structured—even more than in the U.S North—and permitted very little class mobility. Indeed, the Indian, African, and Latin American economies were such that there were relatively few positions available for educated people. Until recently, the solution to this problem in most dependent situations was to restrict higher levels of schooling to children of the bourgeoisie and a small middle class.

But as schooling expanded and became clearly identified as a means for *some* poor children to achieve higher status, demands for school reform began coming from nonruling groups.

After World War I in Latin America and even earlier in India, the middle class (small merchants and lower level bureaucrats) began demanding access to higher education. Because the middle class had some economic and political power and did not need radical change in the economic system to achieve its goals, it managed to open universities to middle-class children. The important point here is that the middle class was successful because it was small and its incorporation did not require altering the hierarchical capitalist system, especially as that system required more levels of hierarchy. This particular change was possible for the ruling class to grant because fulfilling it did not change the basic relationships in production, nor did it diminish ruling class power.

In the United States, the situation was more complicated because control of schools had originally been vested in local communities, fairly democratically operated, and there was a heritage of local control which the reformers had to break in order to impose centrally dictated curriculum and teacher accreditation. Thus, demands for more and better schooling in the United States were intertwined with the issue of centralized vs. local control. In Latin America, local control was dominated by the conservative church and landed interests, and in parts of Brazil, by particular immigrant groups. Again, the issue of school expansion and reform was often involved with wresting control of schools from local interests, but in that case, local control of school was in the hands of another elite group, not the masses.

Today, we have both kinds of ruling-class reforms taking place. In chapter 7, we described U.S.-initiated educational reforms in the nonindustrialized countries. These reforms are an attempt by progressive elements in the U.S. corporate structure and state bureaucracy to control social change in the world. The reforms may also be a response to a crisis in world capitalism caused by nationalist revolutionary movements, movements that feed on poverty and oppression in the capitalist nonindustrialized countries. Thus, it is imperative for the United States and other industrial-country governments to promote development abroad, although they are constrained to work within the capitalist economic framework. They reason that expanded schooling on the U.S. model will serve the purposes of the ruling class.

The United States is presently exporting reforms *which were carried out domestically before 1920*. For example, the *comprehensive high school*—a main feature of U.S. nineteenth-century high school expansion—is being exported to Latin America. As we argued in chapter 5, the expansion of high schools on that model was designed to maintain the class structure behind a façade of democracy and equal opportunity. Children of all classes attended the same public high school, participating in the same sports teams and in some of the same extracurricular activities, but academically, attending different courses based on their "vocational aptitudes." Testing and vocational guidance are also being exported, on the same rationale given for similar reforms in the United States around 1915: industries need differential labor for their complex operations, so the schools must select children more systematically according to their abilities and the needs of the economic system. All these reforms are designed to maintain social control and social structures while expanding schooling.

It would be unreasonable to assume that the United States at this point in history, still controlled by large, hierarchical corporations and their military allies in the state bureaucracy, would be willing to export any reforms that do radically change the economic structures of other capitalist countries dependent on the United States itself. The U.S. government and the international institutions are primarily interested in making such structures more *efficient* and more effective producers of material output, but within *capitalist institutions,* or at least institutions which are amenable to capitalist penetration and control.

Governments that accept the reforms, or do the initiating of reforms themselves with U.S. technical assistance, are in much the same position as the Peruvian government one hundred years ago. The fortunes of the national bourgeoisie in a dependent country are tied to the acceptability of their exports and investment markets in the international capitalist system. They want to "modernize" their country in order to attract foreign investment. With World Bank, AID, and foundation help, they launch on this project. An important part of modernization is a literate population, a skilled labor force, and *domestic stability.* More schooling is supposed to promote all three. But again, we cannot expect national bourgeoisies to give up power and wealth to the masses *voluntarily.* Thus, the national bourgeoisies undertake—together with the U.S. government and the corporate-controlled international financial institutions and foundations—reforms that increase their wealth and solidify the power of metropolis corporations *and* the national bourgeoisies. These reforms are supposed to create favorable conditions for foreign and domestic *private* investment on the grounds that *only* by increasing such investment is economic growth possible (within a capitalist system).

United States and international institution-initiated reforms *appear* to be a response to mass demands, since the masses in nonindustrialized countries want more schooling in the hope of avoiding poverty. But the reforms respond in terms which promote the development and maintenance of U.S.-type capitalist economic structures. These are hierarchical and do not mobilize the poor for the development effort or result in mass participation. Instead, capitalist production in the dependent setting does not solve the unemployment problem and excludes the poor from sharing in the economy's higher output. If the schooling reforms imported from the United States are regarded as contributing to the perpetuation of an inequitable economic and social hierarchy, then they should be opposed.

This may seem a harsh treatment of U.S.-initiated reforms, but our analysis leads to the conclusion that the U.S. government at this point in history is attempting to export educational reforms which will help maintain control of nonindustrial country economic and political institutions by elites friendly to foreign investment and capitalist hierarchies. The only changes these reforms will promote will tend to diffuse conflict, not by alleviating oppressive conditions, but by legitimizing those conditions through "ability" tests and vocational guidance. Whether such attempts at diffusion will succeed in a *dependent* economy is another matter. Just because they contributed to maintaining the social structure in the United States does not mean that in countries with a smaller capital base, industry will be able to absorb the output of the schools on anything like the scale it did in the United States.

Although some reforms *do* originate in nonruling-class groups, there should be no illusion about them: the ruling class will translate the reforms into a product acceptable to themselves. For example, blacks want community control of schools. They may get control at the community level, but do not gain power over the school board which sets standards and allocates local funds, nor over the state legislature which allocates state aid to education.

Rural areas in nonindustrialized countries want more primary schools. They get a school, but it only goes to the third grade. Even if it goes to the sixth grade, primary school graduates from rural areas cannot find jobs that meet their aspirations.

Furthermore, mass demands arise from the colonized condition, so they are distorted to fit into the way the hierarchy has defined these groups' role for them. But in the colonized context, the demands are legitimate. At the same time, the contradictions raised by the struggle to achieve reforms could be an important step in the decolonization process. Thus, despite the fact that the top of the hierarchy shapes the nature of any reform gained by the masses, those who already understand that a complete restructuring of society is necessary for development should not oppose reform simply because it is not radical or reconstructive in itself. Any reform should be analyzed in terms of the contribution it makes to eroding the hierarchy and putting control of institutions in the hands of the people who use them.

To put the difference between ruling-class-initiated and mass-initiated reforms another way: our analysis makes clear to us the fundamental necessity to change the economic and social structure before the system of public schooling can be changed. Ruling-class-initiated reforms in a capitalist country public school system will always be applied in a way that will reinforce capitalist hierarchies. In turn, those at the top of the hierarchy will always *try* to coopt mass-initiated reforms in a way that will protect their position. But in the very act of cooptation they will have to contend with a threat from the masses, thus giving at least some legitimacy to the demands of the masses. In supporting such demands, those who are less colonized and more aware (*concientizados,* in Freire's terminology) can help the process of reform be a step to liberation.

Yet, it is not easy to distinguish between the two types of reforms. For one thing, those who head the hierarchy usually argue that *all* reforms are a response to public demands. Earlier histories of education described every educational change in terms of its response to mass pressure, even, as we learn now from Michael Katz and others, in cases where no pressure existed. This is part of the hierarchy's colonization of knowledge. By trying to convince people that whatever the hierarchy judges to be good is good for everyone—indeed, a response to their very own needs—they diffuse the real conflicts that exist between the interests of the mass of citizens and the interests of the hierarchy itself.

We therefore have to look carefully at the content and origins of programs initiated by the government, the foundations, or other private groups. What is the reason for the reform? What is its function? Can it become the basis of a process of decolonization or is it likely to make schooling a more efficient colonizer?

Consider, for example, the decentralization of big-city school systems in the United States. It is not obvious where this reform most recently originated, but it is likely to lead to more control by each local community over its high schools and community colleges. In a colonized context, that may turn out to be a "bad" idea, since it implies segregated schools and segregated control. It may also lead to more oppressive schools in particularly conservative subdistricts of the city. But at the same time, decentralization forces each subdistrict to struggle directly with the problems of schooling and face the reality of the kind of education its children are getting. At least in *some* subdistricts, this will lead to struggles that have the possibility of partially liberating the schools, and beginning to socialize children in very different ways from the way the larger district would have continued to do.

It is also sometimes difficult to determine who represents the top of the hierarchy. The university is a particularly ambiguous innovator. Whom does the university represent? Educational ideas and reforms originating in the university are usually colonizing, since they are derived from knowledge whose task is gathering and digesting information for control. But the universities are occasionally also a source of knowledge which seeks to decolonize—reconstructive histories of education are part of this type of knowledge. The university is therefore an innovation source which represents the needs of those who would use education for control; yet, at the same time, this source of innovation is itself the object of struggle, and produces some ideas useful for decolonizing the schools. Even so, it is not likely that U.S. universities will become centers of decolonization and reconstruction as long as they view their role as extensions of the rest of the educational system. They should be subject to exactly the same analysis as the primary and high schools.[4]

Why Schooling?

Why bother with schooling at all? Doesn't the analysis of this study really say that school system reform is not a source of radical change in the economic and social system; that to change the economic and social structure requires projects concerned directly with contradictions in that structure? The study does say this, but it is not necessary to make the dichotomy between the schools and economic hierarchies, since *both are part and parcel of the same system.*

As an example of this position, we can distinguish between three analyses of schooling and income distribution: The first, which we can call the "corporate-liberal" view, argues that schooling is a significant factor explaining individual income and occupation. In order to equalize incomes, it is necessary to equalize competencies, since it is the distribution of competencies which determines the distribution of positions in the hierarchy. Liberal policies therefore center on the issue of "equal opportunity" in access to schooling and schooling quality.

The second analysis, proposed by Christopher Jencks,[5] argues that schooling is *not* a significant factor explaining individual income and only a somewhat significant factor in explaining individual occupational status. Jencks infers from some empirical results that we should not look to schooling for improvement of income distribution and rejects the corporate-liberal notion that the distribution of rewards in the hierarchy is the result of the distribution of competencies. Instead, it is the result of political-economic forces which maintain or change the distribution of income and wealth, irrespective of the distribution of competence. Jencks argues that if we want to equalize the distribution of income, we must take political action to equalize income distribution. But this implies that while we take measures to equalize incomes, we don't have to concern ourselves with schooling, since schooling has little to do with income.

Our position is that schooling *is* a significant factor in explaining individual income,[6] but that as long as the hierarchical structure remains unchanged, *schooling will not be used to equalize incomes.* Schooling structure and distribution reflect the hierarchical social structure and organization of production. The distribution of schooling can be improved, as it has been in the last thirty years, but the payoff to schooling changes in a way that makes lower levels of schooling worth less over time relative to higher levels. Thus, the number of people who received secondary schooling increased markedly in the United States between 1939 and 1969, but the payoff to that level actually fell.[7] So just as the poor begin to get higher levels of schooling, the relative value in the labor market of those levels falls. Even when the society invests more in schooling for the poor, therefore, the labor market values that schooling less than before the poor were getting it. So income distribution does not improve in a capitalist society as the average level of schooling increases or as the distribution of schooling becomes more equal.

Nevertheless, we think it is a mistake to imply, like Jencks, that we should ignore schooling in restructuring society. If we begin to change income distribution through political action, we must also change the distribution of schooling, and especially its hierarchical structure and the way it transmits knowledge, or else we will not change one of the important factors contributing to the old structure of income. Not only that, but there are many people now in the school system willing to work toward changing the hierarchical structure of the society. Their point of contact with the system is the school. People can work outside the schools for change—political action for a more equitable income distribution and changes in relations in production—and at the same time support similar reforms initiated inside the schools.

What Should a New Educational System Be Like?

In this study we have stressed that schools help maintain a hierarchical structure, and help ensure that the same class of people end up at the top of the hierarchy in each generation, and the same class at the bottom. We contend that schools are able to legitimize grossly unequal access to goods and services in a capitalist society by colonizing children and their families to believe in the brand of "meritocracy" implemented by the schools: the school system ostensibly grades individuals not according to family background, but according to cognitive ability. Yet, as we have argued, cognitive ability is highly correlated with an individual's social class, and both social class and the amount of schooling an individual gets are better explainers of future income than cognitive ability. On these grounds, Bowles and Gintis argue that it is the noncognitive, or behavioral, skills associated with social class, and differentially reinforced by different kinds of schools and among students in the same school, which are the most important things learned by pupils for future roles in society.[8]

But even if upper-class pupils are rewarded for being aggressive and original, while lower-class children are rewarded for being passive or "civilized," all children are in some sense colonized by the schools because of the understanding of the society the school teaches them. This colonizing knowledge *is*, however, more detrimental to the lower classes than to the upper. The colonizing values which emerge from such knowledge

> develop, buttress, and rationalize the social organization of domination and the pyramidal structure. Operationally such values may be seen as the few over the many, white over third world, property and goods over people, man as conqueror of nature, fabricating it (and the people who live with nature) into goods and property which then dominates other people, men over women, continuous growth over regeneration and seeding.[9]

Knowledge itself emanates from the hierarchy. In a pyramidal, capitalist hierarchy, *learning* in public schools is organized to maintain that hierarchical structure. Children do not learn about their environment from the perspective of their own reality, but from the white, wealthy view. Thus, poverty, drug addiction, and crime are an individual failing rather than the result of an inequitable and racist economy; technological progress is defined as sending a man to the moon rather than organizing a community medical clinic; and children are taught to compete for the limited number of "top" positions in the society rather than working together to improve their collective condition. Thus, all children in school learn to evaluate society on grounds favorable to the rich and powerful. Children are taught that those in power are necessarily the best judges of good and bad, and are generally right because they have access to more information than the rest of the electorate. In other words, the schools, universities, and such other institutions as the media produce and interpret knowledge that colonizes: the abstract reality developed by this knowledge is made more *legitimate* than people's day-to-day experiences.

The new education must overturn these two elements of the old system. First, such education has a different economic and social system in mind. The alternative to the present schools is not the "open classroom" as Silberman has suggested,[10] or methods of teaching or curricula which present colonizing knowledge more efficiently. Those reforms are designed to *improve legitimization* of a pyramidal social structure and hierarchical relations in production. The new education should instead be designed to create or reinforce a *nonhierarchical* society, in which property will not have rights over people, and in which, ideally, no person will have the right of domination over another. This would not be an "egalitarian" society in the sense that everyone is the same: people would have different work, but that work would not give them authority over the lives of others. Work would be done *for each other,* out of common agreement and understanding. This simple ideal implies profound changes in the economic system (much more than simply redistributing income), including laws regarding ownership, and changes in the social structure, access to knowledge, and the nature of learning. Obviously, education would have to play a key role in developing such a society, for any transformation requires changing people's understanding of the social contract and the meaning of work, responsibility, and political participation.

The transmission of knowledge in a nonhierarchical society would be very different from the teaching-learning structure of today's school. Rather than abstracting from reality in order to set knowledge apart from the context in which it is transmitted, teaching and learning will deal with the reality of teachers and students. Paulo Freire's reading method is an example of learning in the context of reality. Freire used words that had strong political content: his claim was that reading could be taught more effectively if the words learned had important meaning to the learners. At the same time, reading becomes the affirmation of an individual's condition, and the path to awareness and action.[11]

The Washington, D.C., minischool is another example of an attempt to decolonize knowledge: in that school, the focus of the learning process was the children's institutional reality.[12] Learning was organized around visits to museums, television studios, and other interpreters of knowledge. The children were urged to question the structure of these institutions and to organize alternative structures for presenting the same type of material. The school, like Freire's reading method, was consciously political: its purpose was to demystify that which is really subjective, and to have children discover that institutional organization and purpose is not derived from "natural order" but from people's minds.

There are a lot of these "free" schools in the United States, largely in higher-income areas, but also in the inner-city ghettos.[13] They represent an attempt to decolonize children within the context of a hierarchical society, just as the Freire method is an attempt to *concientizar* (make politically aware) children and adults who are colonized and oppressed. Although their approaches vary, most free schools have in common the goal of changing social relations in production, and of demystifying institutions so that children as people can begin controlling them and using those institutions for purposes that suit them, not a small group of colonizers. Thus, to be a free school means being political and moving children out of capitalist, hierarchical structures.[14] The free schools and the Freire method also share a belief in people; that men and women are basically *epimethean*—that they love people more than products, love the earth in which they can meet one another, and collaborate in work to "enhance their ability to tend and care and wait upon the other." [15]

But the schools and decolonizing teaching methods we observe in capitalist countries are schools observed in a transition period. They must put much more stress on "defense" –self-protection against colonized knowledge—than would schools in a society that had already been reconstructed. In that sense, Illich's concept of deschooling society may be misleading. A reconstructed society may emerge after a long period of violent revolution, or may be built democratically. Once that society is achieved—*a society in continuous liberation*—education organized in schools may indeed be an inherently colonizing institution. But *in the transition toward the reconstructed society,* "free" schools or "liberation" schools may be the strongest element in decolonizing people in the society and breaking down its hierarchical structures. Both Illich and his critics do not seem to recognize that only a society already in the process of liberation can decide whether to have schools or not.

Nowhere is this clearer than in the nonindustrialized countries and among the poor in the industrialized countries. The strongest reality for people in both cases is the need to increase consumption. True, this is the result of a colonized condition: *desired* consumption even for the poor usually goes far beyond basic human necessities. But schooling is viewed (correctly) by the poor as the only chance—even if it is a small chance—of making it into the middle levels of the hierarchy. Furthermore, nonindustrialized societies as a whole legitimately want to increase their average consumption levels of food, medical services, and education itself. They view schooling as a means to prepare the trained personnel to accomplish this. Again, schooling does not *have to be* hierarchical, and, in fact, it may be necessary to undo behavior patterns learned in hierarchical family structures, at the same time helping children to learn basic cognitive skills, how to interact with their peers, and a critical awareness of their reality.

On the other hand, the use of higher levels of schooling to form elites is inconsistent with a nonhierarchical society, and also is inconsistent with the production of goods to fill mass needs.[16] Most such goods can be produced efficiently with labor trained on the job, using techniques developed by workers themselves. Where filling basic needs is concerned, most higher-level education is a luxury consumption good even in an industrial society.

In the final analysis, reforms and alternatives produce certain results, and these results are good for some groups in society and probably not for others. We argue that alternatives should be judged primarily on whether they increase the capability of a group or individual to make judgments about the way society is organized and about their own lives *in terms of their particular reality*. This kind of "schooling" requires systematic access to much more information than is currently available in schools, and a much wider range of interpretation of societal problems. Furthermore, such schooling would not build a consensual polity but would increase the possibility of polarization and conflict in the society, thus weakening the control of the old dominant class over economic wealth and the ideological framework for decision making.

As we have pointed out, freedom of movement and individualized instruction in the classroom is not the issue here. The issue is political and economic. How do we change a society that colonizes people to accept dominated roles, roles defined by a powerful, self-perpetuating group? One possibility is through alternative schools, but if these schools are to be a true alternative, they must face the issue of who runs the society and why. Teachers and students must also face their own reality in the school, and the function of that institution in perpetuating inequities.

Notes

1. This interpretation of history has been influenced by Idealism: Idealism asserts that external circumstances can be overcome by pure acts of will. It does not recognize the reality of external objects and that these objects can only be overcome by direct interaction with them. Thus, an Idealist history of early U.S. reform stresses the power of Horace Mann's ideas and discusses him as an agent of change rather than understanding the reform as a struggle between different groups interested in controlling the "objective" factors of production.

2. This statement would probably not hold true if families with low incomes and occupational roles in one generation were different from those in the next generation. In that case, the concept of social class would be meaningless, since low income and occupation would be a temporary situation rather than a permanent condition. It is evident, however, that income and status positions do persist from generation to generation, so that we can speak of different social classes even in supposedly classless countries like the United States.

3. Samuel Bowles and Herb Gintis, "IQ in the U.S. Class Structure," *Social Policy* (January/February 1973).

4. See Marcus Raskin, *Being and Doing* (New York: Random House, 1971), pp. 361–68.

5. Christopher Jencks et al., *Inequality* (New York: Basic Books, 1972).

6. Jenck's empirical analysis leaves out a number of important explainers of income, principally age, region, and number of weeks worked. While schooling does not explain a high *fraction* of income variance, it contributes significantly and positively to individual income.

7. The rate of return to private expenditures on high school—the payoff to schooling is measured as the increase in average income over lifetime associated with higher average schooling—fell drastically for white and nonwhite males and for white females in the period 1939–69. Only nonwhite females had approximately the same private rate of return to high school investment in 1969 as in 1939, but their rate was already low in 1939 (10%). The rate for white males fell from 49% in 1939 to 23% in 1949 to 15% in 1959 and then rose to 19% in 1969. The rate to nonwhite males fell from 27 to 15 to 13 and then rose to 16. The rate for white females fell from 25 to 20 to 15, rising to 19. The private rate of return to expenditures on college also fell in this period, but not by as much. For example, the rate to white males dropped from 21 to 15%, and for nonwhite males, from 15 to 14%. See Martin Carnoy and Dieter Marenbach, "The Return to Schooling in the United States, 1939–1969" (Stanford University School of Education, 1973). Mimeographed.

8. Bowles and Gintis, "IQ in the U.S. Class Structure."

9. Marcus Raskin, "Notes on Reconstructive Knowledge: Its Nature, Ethics and Teaching It" (Institute of Policy Studies, 10 November 1972). Mimeographed.

10. Charles Silberman, *Crisis in the Classroom* (New York: Random House, 1970).

11. Paulo Freire, *Pedagogy of the Oppressed* (New York: Herder and Herder, 1971).

12. Philip Brenner, "Political Knowledge and Experience in Elementary Education," in *Schooling in a Corporate Society,* ed. Martin Carnoy (New York: David McKay, 1972).

13. See Directory of the New Schools Exchange, Santa Barbara, California, and Bonnie Barrett Stretch, "The Rise of the 'Free School,' " in Carnoy, *Schooling in a Corporate Society.*

14. Jonathan Kozol, *Free Schools* (Boston: Houghton Mifflin, 1972).

15. Ivan Illich, *Deschooling Society* (New York: Harper & Row, 1971).

16. See, for example, Jim Hightower, *Hard Tomatoes, Hard Times* (Washington, D.C.: Agribusiness Accountability Project, 1972) for an analysis of the role of U.S. university agricultural research in producing labor-saving technology for large agricultural producers.

INDEX